Presented To:

_____

From:

_____

Date:

_____

The Ultimate Guide *to*
Understanding
the Dreams You Dream

BOOKS BY IRA L. MILLIGAN

The Scorpion Within
Rightly Dividing the Word

AVAILABLE FROM DESTINY IMAGE PUBLISHERS

The Ultimate Guide *to*
Understanding
the Dreams You Dream

Biblical Keys
for Hearing God's Voice
in the Night

IRA MILLIGAN

DESTINY IMAGE® PUBLISHERS, INC.

P.O. Box 310, Shippensburg, PA 17257-0310

"Promoting Inspired Lives."

This book and all other Destiny Image, Revival Press, MercyPlace, Fresh Bread, Destiny Image Fiction, and Treasure House books are available at Christian bookstores and distributors worldwide.

For a U.S. bookstore nearest you, call 1-800-722-6774.

For more information on foreign distributors, call 717-532-3040.

Reach us on the Internet: www.destinyimage.com.

ISBN 13 TP: 978-0-7684-4107-9

ISBN 13 Ebook: 978-0-7684-8859-3

For Worldwide Distribution, Printed in the U.S.A.

1 2 3 4 5 6 7 8 / 16 15 14 13 12

Dedication

This book is dedicated to my brother, Alvin, who first provoked my interest in writing. Some revelations in this book were given directly to him by his loving, heavenly Father and passed on to me in one of our many discussions about the Word of God.

Acknowledgments

I wish to express my heartfelt thanks to those precious saints of God who have supported my wife and me with their prayers and substance, allowing us to give ourselves wholly to prayer and to the ministry of the Word. Without them, this book would not exist. I am eternally grateful for them. I'm especially indebted to Vicki Camp and Jimmy Skinner for their help in proofreading the manuscript. I would also like to thank all of the dreamers who sent their dreams and gave me permission to use them. Their contributions have greatly enriched this book.

Author's Note

All references to Greek or Hebrew word definitions, with the exception of proper names, are from *Strong's Exhaustive Concordance,* James Strong, LL.D S.T.D. Thomas Nelson Publishers, 1990. The meanings of biblical names are taken from *A Dictionary of Scripture Proper Names* by J.B. Jackson, Loizeaux Brothers, 1909. Common names are taken from *The Name Book* by Dorothea Austin, Bethany House Publishers, 1982. Bold print, italics, and capital letters are used throughout for clarity of expression and for emphasis. They are sometimes used in the quotation of Scriptures for the same reasons. Comments within brackets are inserted by the author into many Scriptures to clarify and explain use in relation to the symbols under which they are listed.

Contents

PART II

KEY WORD DICTIONARY OF DREAM SYMBOLS WITH SCRIPTURAL ILLUSTRATIONS

Preface

The first publication of *Understanding the Dreams You Dream* was barely complete when I began receiving requests for more detailed information on the subject. From these requests, *The Ultimate Guide to Understanding the Dreams You Dream* was compiled and now published. It is not surprising that the first edition received such a response; almost everyone who obtains even a little knowledge of this subject immediately desires more. My own intense hunger for an understanding of dream interpretation was awakened when the Lord answered one of my Bible study questions with a dream. After that first experience came an earnest study of God's Word concerning dreams, and from that came a better understanding of how to interpret them. (An account of that first dream and its interpretation can be found in the Introduction.)

From the beginning, I have approached dream interpretation from a biblical standpoint, so I have used both the Bible and my experience as a Christian and minister in the writing of this book. Therefore, at the onset, I would like to clearly state that *every dream is not from God.*

The Scriptures declare, *"For a dream cometh through the multitude of business; and a fool's voice is known by multitude of words"* (Eccles. 5:3). In this verse, a fool's voice is equated to an idle dream; and as we know, God's voice is certainly not that of a fool. Also, there are other Scriptures that speak of dreams in a negative context. This is why I feel that a word of caution is necessary when advising people to pay attention to their dreams.

As humans, we tend to err to extremes. We tend to believe either that dreams are just so much nonsense, coming from eating too much, or that all dreams are important and that every symbol has a meaning. Ecclesiastes 5:1-7 is a caution against just such extremes, both in word and in dreams. My personal experience has been that most dreams are indeed meaningful and helpful, although not all.

Having said that, I must also quickly add that I have found that *most* dreams *are* from God. As such, they are an accurate reflection of our individual situations. But they are symbolic. Because dreams are symbolic, they appear meaningless. If, in an attempt to understand them individuals try to consult one or more of the books available on this subject today, they will often be left mystified.

The primary obstacle most dreamers must overcome to be able to understand their dreams is symbolism. To solve this problem, most authors instruct their readers to meditate on their dreams, which is good advice, yet it is simply not adequate. These authors usually provide the reader with some examples of what their own dreams have meant to them, but even though personal examples are both interesting and informative, they are quite limited in their application.

It is certainly true that through meditation much can be understood about our dreams; but I have found that when most Christians are told to meditate on their dreams, they do not have the foggiest notion of where to begin. Consequently, I have approached this problem three different ways: 1) specific, detailed directions on how and upon what to meditate; 2) personal examples of dreams from my own experience; and 3) a practical dictionary of symbol definitions.

It has been my experience that it is better to give students a place to begin meditating rather than to simply tell them to meditate—hence the symbol dictionary. I have found that a symbol dictionary enables most Christians to begin discerning God's voice immediately.

Additionally, I have attempted to present in this book both normal and the not-so-normal dream situations. To apply only one type of dream interpretation to all dreams is to be as inflexible as restricting each symbol to only one possible definition. For instance, because all dreams are not parables, an attempt to apply parabolic interpretation to a dream that is not a parable is an exercise in futility.

As with the first edition, my primary purpose for writing this book is to guide you safely through the complex world of dreams. There are several good books that explain why our Western society has tra-ditionally ignored or rejected the information contained in dreams. I have not, therefore, attempted to cover the history of dreams. (For background study, I recommend *Dreams: Wisdom Within* by Herman Riffel, Destiny Image Publishers, 1990.) However, in contrast, there has been little published on the subject of how to interpret dreams from a Christian perspective. Consequently, I have written solely to satisfy this need. It is my prayer that this book will add to your understanding and enjoyment of God's most common method of communication.

Introduction

Dreams remain one of the most controversial subjects in the Church today. Some people simply say, "I never dream." Others emphatically state, "I never pay attention to dreams. They're nonsense. They come from eating too much pizza." Yet others seem to obtain valuable insight from meditating upon their dreams. They claim dreams are a dependable source of guidance and information for their lives. Which group is right? Should we pay attention to dreams or simply ignore them as just so much junk mail?

The Bible gives us a direct answer to this question: *"And it shall come to pass in the last days, saith God, I will pour out of My Spirit upon all flesh: and...your old men shall dream dreams"* (Acts 2:17). That's God's promise—and by the way, one does not have to be an old man to dream. Young men and women dream, too! God is talking about our "old man," as in our carnal nature.

At the present time, He is indiscriminately pouring out His Spirit upon young and old alike. He uses dreams to encourage His children and direct them in their walk with Him, and He uses them to warn sinners to repent. The Scriptures contain numerous dreams; if they were removed, a large portion of the Bible would be missing. Without them, a large measure of God's guidance for the Church is also missing— including personal instructions for every individual.

Everyone has the ability to dream, so no one should be without God's personal guidance. God has used dreams to communicate with His people from the beginning. He doesn't change, so He has not changed, and will not change the way He speaks to us. Although dreams are only one of the many ways that He speaks, they are certainly a legitimate source of divine information and knowledge.

Dreams are elusive. Everyone has them, but they're like the morning fog; they quickly evaporate. If we do not make a deliberate effort to capture them, they simply vanish. By the time we get our morning coffee, they're usually forgotten. Very few are vivid enough to automatically burn themselves into our consciousness.

For those who don't seem to dream at all, my advice is to ask God for dreams and then to pay close attention each morning for His answer. I met one man who claimed he didn't dream; but after asking for dreams, he received *ten* in just three weeks. In the Bible, James said we receive not because we ask not, and Paul admonished us to seek God's gifts (see James 4:2; 1 Cor. 14:1).

Dreams are indeed a gift from God. They are one of His ways of imparting a word of wisdom and a word of knowledge to us (see 1 Cor. 12:8). In addition to wisdom and knowledge, some dreams are prophetic—inspired by and received directly from the spirit of prophecy. These messages should be considered as "thus saith the Lord."

We should no more ignore our dreams than our mail. Certainly all of our mail is not valuable, but wouldn't it be foolish to throw it all out unopened just because in the past some of it proved to be junk mail?

Sometimes, dream interpretation can be heavy stuff, so I've written this book in a conversational style interlaced with a little humor to lighten it up a bit. I have also covered the basic rules for proper dream interpretation and included a comprehensive symbol dictionary.

This ultimate guide teaches the *language* of dreams. It reveals much more than just what symbols mean; it also explains why they mean what they mean. I trust that God will be glorified and the reader blessed by the information contained herein. Thanks be to God for His unspeakable gift!

PART I

Dreams:
God's Primary Means of
Communication

God's Communication

*For God speaketh once, yea twice, yet man perceiveth it not. In a
dream, in a vision of the night, when deep sleep falleth upon men,
in slumberings upon the bed; then He openeth the ears of men,
and sealeth their instruction. ...Lo, all these things worketh God
oftentimes with man* (Job 33:14-16,29).

In this Scripture passage in Job, Elihu states that God gives us
sealed instructions in the form of dreams. Because these messages are
sealed (within parables), we seldom recognize them as being from God.
Treating dreams like junk mail, we often throw away the very answers
we ask for when we pray for counsel and guidance.

We often hear someone say, "I had a weird dream this morning!"
Paul said that God chose the foolish things of the world to confound
the wise (see 1 Cor. 1:27). Although many dreams are foolish or sense-
less to the world, they are precious to those who understand "the hidden wisdom" from above (see 1 Cor. 2:7).

The way God communicated with people most frequently in the
Bible was through dreams. The dreams recorded in the Bible often
seem ridiculous, yet their interpretations are quite sensible. For example, Pharaoh dreamed of seven cows that ate seven other cows. Then
he dreamed of seven ears of corn that ate seven other ears of corn! The
interpretation of these two strange dreams saved Egypt from starvation
(see Gen. 41:15-48).

The Bible reveals that in the past God spoke through dreams to saints and sinners alike—warning them, directing them, and helping them. He still does. By carefully studying the Bible to find out how God spoke to people in the past, we can learn His method of talking to us now.

How often does God communicate with us in dreams? Job 33:29 reveals that God gives us instructions "oftentimes," and Job even says that God visits us every morning! The postman arrives often and early:

What is man, that Thou shouldest magnify him? and that Thou shouldest set thine heart upon him? And that Thou shouldest visit him every morning, and try him every moment? (Job 7:17-18)

Although night visions, which are discussed later, are easily recognizable as being from God, dreams are not. Acts 2:17 states that it is our "old man" that dreams dreams; therefore, they are normally given in parable form. For this reason, they must be interpreted if we are to understand what God is saying:

And it shall come to pass in the last days, saith God, I will pour out of My Spirit upon all flesh: and your sons and your daughters shall prophesy, and your young men shall see visions, and your old men shall dream dreams (Acts 2:17).

Interpreting Your Dreams

If there be a messenger with him, an interpreter [of his dreams], *one among a thousand, to shew unto man his uprightness: then he is gracious unto him, and saith, Deliver him from going down to the pit: I have found a ransom* (Job 33:23-24).

Although much has been written about dreams, the enormous volume of information concerning dream interpretation found in the Scriptures has been all but ignored! The Bible is filled with dreams and their interpretations. It gives detailed instructions that tell and show us how to interpret them.

The Scriptures were written by the same God who talks to us in dreams. His language has not changed. Our dreams, like those described in the Bible, use word pictures or symbols to convey their concealed messages. Therefore, we can study the way symbols are used in Scripture as a guide to the way they are used in our dreams.

Those who attempt to interpret the Scriptures sometimes do so without leaving them in context. When they do this, they often assign meanings to them that the author never intended. Likewise, if the interpretation of a dream is to be accurate, the dream must be left in its setting. The dream and its symbols must be interpreted in light of the life circumstances of the person to whom it is given.

A Snap Shot

A dream is like a snapshot, which captures one brief moment out of a lifetime. It cannot be understood fully without knowing something about the life of the person it concerns.

Therefore, it is not enough to know the meaning of symbols alone. Nevertheless, without an understanding of symbols, we are greatly limited in our ability to navigate through the complex world of dreams.

Even when we are familiar with the background of the person a dream concerns, we should use caution when we apply a symbol's meaning. *Hasty dream interpretations should be avoided.* Even Daniel mulled over Nebuchadnezzar's dream for an hour before he ventured an interpretation, and he knew the king's lifestyle well (see Dan. 4:18-19).

One of the best ways to keep from either simply forgetting about a dream or jumping to conclusions concerning its meaning is to start a dream journal. Taking the time to write down a dream usually causes one to remember it in greater detail. It also provides a permanent record for reference.

By recording a dream and what it appears to mean, we can check back later to see if we were correct in our understanding of its meaning. This also appears to be the safest and quickest way to learn to interpret dreams correctly. Sometimes one dream by itself does not provide enough keys to know for certain what God is trying to say. But by comparing several successive dreams, we often find a progressive message unveiled before us. Remember that Job said, *"God speaketh once, yea twice..."* (Job 33:14). God is faithful to speak to us again and again if we are really trying to hear what He has to say.

Jesus said to be careful of both what you hear and how you hear it (see Mark 4:24; Luke 8:18). When we listen carefully to what God is saying morning after morning, we are assured of more to come, because He said, *"...unto you that hear shall more be given"* (Mark 4:24). Of course, the flip side of that is, *"...he that hath not, from him shall be taken even that which he hath"* (Mark 4:25).

When recording your dreams, be sure to include each dream's date, your location—home, vacation, etc.—the feelings that you experienced while dreaming, as well as anything important that is going on in your life at the time of the dream. By recording the background information, when you refer back to it later, you will still be able to place it into its proper setting.

Dream or Night Vision?

There is a difference between a dream and a night vision. A night vision requires little or no interpretation. In addition to the actual vision seen, a night vision usually has a voice speaking that gives the primary meaning and message of the vision. For example:

> *And a vision appeared to Paul in the night; There stood a man of Macedonia, and prayed him, saying, Come over into Macedonia, and help us. And after he had seen the vision, immediately we endeavored to go into Macedonia, assuredly gathering that the Lord had called us for to preach the gospel unto them* (Acts 16:9-10).

In contrast, a dream seldom lends itself to self-interpretation. *The most common type of dream contains more than one scene; a progressive message unfolds as the dreamer is carried along, either as an observer or as a participant.* Other dreams may contain two or three scenes that all speak a different message, but this is less common. Also, the scene changes in a dream sometimes give different viewpoints of the same subject or express the same idea in different ways rather than reveal a progressive message.

The First Scene

In a dream with more than one scene, *the first scene usually gives the setting.* Like the backdrop of a play, it sets the stage so that the sealed message it contains can be understood. For example, in the following Scripture, people walking on one another is mentioned before Christ's teaching is given:

> *In the mean time, when there were gathered together an innumerable multitude of people, insomuch that **they trod one upon another,** He began to say unto His disciples first of all, Beware ye of the leaven of the Pharisees, which is hypocrisy. For there is nothing covered, that shall not be revealed; neither hid, that shall not be known* (Luke 12:1-2).

This stage-setting gives us a parable of the Pharisees' hypocrisy. They trod on the people, oppressing them for their own purposes. They required others to conform to strict laws while they excused themselves from obeying them. Observing this setting makes us aware of emphasis and implications in Christ's words that we would otherwise miss.

In the same way, God usually reveals the subject of His message in the first scene of our dreams. Then, once the subject has been established, the subsequent scenes enlarge upon the plot and carry it forward. This progression can be seen in Daniel's interpretation of Nebuchadnezzar's dream in Daniel 4:20-27:

The tree that thou sawest, which grew, and was strong, whose height reached unto the heaven, and the sight thereof to all the earth; whose leaves were fair, and the fruit thereof much, and in it was meat for all; under which the beasts of the field dwelt, and upon whose branches the fowls of the heaven had their habitation: It is thou, O king, that art grown and become strong: for thy greatness is grown, and reacheth unto heaven, and thy dominion to the end of the earth. And whereas the king saw a watcher and an holy one coming down from heaven, and saying, Hew the tree down, and destroy it; yet leave the stump of the roots thereof in the earth, even with a band of iron and brass, in the tender grass of the field; and let it be wet with the dew of heaven, and let his portion be with the beasts of the field, till seven times pass over him;

This is the interpretation, O king, and this is the decree of the most High, which is come upon my lord the king: That they shall drive thee from men, and thy dwelling shall be with the beasts of the field, and they shall make thee to eat grass as oxen, and they shall wet thee with the dew of heaven, and seven times shall pass over thee, till thou know that the most High ruleth in the kingdom of men, and giveth it to whomsoever He will. And whereas they commanded to leave the stump of the tree roots; thy kingdom shall be sure unto thee, after that thou shalt have known that the heavens do rule. Wherefore, O king, let my counsel be acceptable unto thee, and break off thy sins by righteousness, and thine iniquities by shewing mercy to the poor; if it may be a lengthening of thy tranquility.

Notice that this dream has two scenes. The first scene establishes that the dream is about the growth and prosperity of King Nebuchadnezzar and his kingdom. The second scene reveals God's displeasure with the king's prideful conduct and foretells of certain chastisement to come.

Because dreams can cover several different subjects and areas of our lives, it is important to correctly discern the subject matter to which the dream refers if we are to utilize the message properly. If we don't do this, we may easily apply a dream to the wrong area of our lives, or even incorrectly apply it to another person when God is really speaking to us about ourselves.

This is especially true when a dream contains people we can identify. Friends and family members are often used as symbols. Sometimes they represent us, sometimes they represent another friend or family member, and sometimes they simply represent themselves. Only careful attention to all the scenes and symbols used in a dream will keep us from making this type of misapplication.

Application Aids Interpretation

Without proper application, correct interpretation is difficult, if not impossible. To determine what a dream is about and apply the message correctly, first ask yourself these two questions: *"Who* does this dream refer to?" and *"What* is it really about?" Then, examine the action in the dream to determine the message. In other words, what is the dream's setting? What are the people saying and doing?

To answer the first question, always examine yourself to see if the dream can apply directly to you. A dream is usually both for and about the one who dreams it. Because we do not know our own hearts, God uses dreams to reveal the deep, dark secrets of our hearts to us. The problem is, we really don't want to know the secrets of our hearts! So, God often has to use other people to represent different aspects of ourselves. These people may be strangers, family, friends, or just acquaintances. There may be just one person, or there may be several, they may be dead or alive, former friends or distant relatives. But their words and actions will reveal hidden virtues, faults, or sins about us that we are simply ignoring or have completely justified.

When answering the second question (what the dream is about), remember that God's ultimate desire is that we should walk in righteousness. As the preceding dream about Nebuchadnezzar shows, many of our dreams are about our personal conduct or holiness. Another area of our lives that God often communicates with us about in dreams is our livelihood. As John wrote in Third John 2, God desires above all things that we may prosper and be in health, even as our souls prosper. Therefore, God speaks to us concerning our relationship with Him, our jobs, our health, and our relationships with others.

For example, I once dreamed that I was having a blood test. I could see my blood as though I was looking through the microscope along with the laboratory technician. My blood had large, irregular, red cells with the word *meat* written on them. When I awoke, I knew that God was warning me that my cholesterol level was getting too high from eating too much meat.

Another significant dream was one that my wife had. We had a small service business, and unbeknown to us, our service manager decided to go into business for himself at our expense. My wife dreamed that he was in my office wearing a face mask like the one worn by the Lone Ranger, and he was stealing papers. She told me the dream, and when I went to the office and checked, I discovered that a card file containing all our customers' names and addresses was missing. Acting on the information in the dream, I immediately went to his house and recovered them. In doing so, I saved our business from considerable loss.

Although some dreams actually reveal the future—such as the dreams God gave Joseph and Pharaoh in Genesis— our dreams usually relate to our immediate situations. Most of our dreams address things that are relevant to our lives at the time we have the dream.

It is not uncommon for God to give a pastor or traveling minister a sermon topic or message in a dream. He may also show the pastor a problem in the church that needs to be dealt with. Although the subject matter of dreams is almost endless, that which concerns us concerns God; He is faithful to communicate with us when we diligently seek Him for His guidance.

Once we know the particular subject God is talking about and who He is referring to, proper dream interpretation is usually not difficult. But if these two things are not determined correctly, any interpretation we may venture will be misguided or incorrect.

Checking the Source

On the other hand, not every dream we have is from God. How can we tell the difference? When we learn to communicate with God by speaking to Him in prayer and hearing His reply, we soon learn that everything we hear is not His voice. Instead, God simply inserts a thought into our thoughts, often answering our questions when we are not even thinking about what we have asked.

Sometimes we receive God's thoughts in dreams the same way. We may be idly dreaming a rambling, almost incoherent dream, and God will insert a clear, meaningful message into it. Trying to remember our rambling dream is not practical, often not possible, and certainly not necessary. The portion containing God's message will be remembered if we faithfully try to do so. Sometimes we have no choice but to simply forget the rest:

> *But the Comforter, which is the Holy Ghost, whom the Father will send in My name, He shall teach you all things, and bring all things to your remembrance, whatsoever I have said unto you* (John 14:26).

As a general rule, if after substituting the symbols in a dream with the key words or thoughts they symbolize, you still find no recognizable message, then the dream is probably just junk mail, proceeding from somewhere in the confused or troubled regions of the soul. It is not from God. It should still be recorded, however, for later examination in relation to other subsequent dreams may reveal that its meaning was simply not apparent at the time it was received.

This is not to say that unless a dream is directly from God that it is not useful. Our dreams reveal the secrets of our hearts—even when we really don't want to know them. The Bible says that it is our spirits that truly know us, not our conscious minds (see 1 Cor. 2:11). Although there are times when our spirits will cry out for help to us in the night, these messages can be understood using the same method and keys used with other dreams.

Since some of our dreams are not from God, we should exercise reasonable caution when we apply them. We should observe the same basic precautions with dreams that we apply to other sources of personal guidance. Information and instructions obtained from dreams should be confirmed in other ways before we act upon them.

For instance, a strong obsession for something may cause one to dream of obtaining it (see Jer. 29:8). This happened to me once when I was attempting to sell a business that I owned. It had become a real burden to me, and I was anxious to sell it. One night I dreamed that a man came and paid me in cash the exact amount that I was asking! He never came, and it's good that he didn't. I finally realized there were other ways besides selling it to unload some of the burden. Later, it became a real blessing to me.

God's timing is another factor that must be taken into consideration when we are working out His will in our lives. Sometimes He tells us what He will do for us, but we have to wait for Him to do it. Joseph is a good example of this. He was 17 years of age when he had the two prophetic dreams recorded in the Bible. However, he was 30 years of age before they came to pass (see Gen. 37:2,5; 41:46). The Bible states, *"Until the time that his word came: the word of the Lord tried him"* (Ps. 105:19).

Although 13 years may be longer than most of us want to wait before our dreams are fulfilled, sometimes we really don't have a choice. If we try to rush things by taking them into our own hands, we usually wind up with an Ishmael in our lives (see Gen. 21:11). It is much wiser to obtain confirmation from other sources before we take action based on directions received in dreams: *"...In the mouth of two or three witnesses shall every word be established"* (2 Cor. 13:1).

Conversely, sometimes a dream simply confirms instructions that one has already received from a different source. God's dealing with Gideon is a good example of this:

> *And it came to pass the same night, that the Lord said unto him* [Gideon], *Arise, get thee down unto the host; for I have delivered it into thine hand. But if thou fear to go down, go thou with Phurah thy servant down to the host: And thou shalt hear what they say; and afterward shall thine hands be strengthened to go down unto the host. Then went he down with Phurah his servant unto the outside of the armed men that were in the host. And the Midianites and the Amalekites and all the children of the east lay along in the valley like grasshoppers for multitude; and their camels were without number, as the sand by the sea side for multitude.*

> *And when Gideon was come, behold, there was a man that told a dream unto his fellow, and said, Behold, I dreamed a dream, and, lo, a cake of barley bread tumbled into the host of Midian, and came unto a tent, and smote it that it fell, and overturned it, that the tent lay along. And his fellow answered and said, This is nothing else save the sword of Gideon the son of Joash, a man of Israel: for into his hand hath God delivered Midian, and all the host. And it was so, when Gideon heard the telling of the dream, and the interpretation thereof, that he worshipped, and returned*

into the host of Israel, and said, Arise; for the Lord hath delivered into your hand the host of Midian (Judges 7:9-15).

The power of this type of confirmation is seen in Gideon's reaction to this dream. An angel had visited him and commissioned him to deliver Israel. Then he supernaturally confirmed the commission. After the angel's visitation, God responded to Gideon's prayer and manipulated the dew both on the ground and on a fleece that Gideon placed out for additional confirmation. But it wasn't until Gideon heard his victory declared in a dream that he was bold enough to act upon God's command and go to war (see Judg. 6:11-22,36-40).

There is one obvious way of checking a dream to see if it is from God. *God's messages are always consistent with His written Word.* A dream may seem like a fable or even include wrong or sinful actions, but when properly interpreted, the message it contains will always be in accordance with the righteous principles of the Bible. Like some of the stories in the Bible, the dream content may appear very negative, yet contain beautiful, positive truth. A dream from God will never instruct us to do something evil. Like the Word itself, a dream from God will equip us to walk in truth and righteousness:

> *All scripture is given by inspiration of God, and* [every dream that is from God] *is profitable for doctrine, for reproof, for correction, for instruction in righteousness: that the man of God may be perfect, thoroughly furnished unto all good works* (2 Timothy 3:16-17).

R- and X-Rated Dreams

Understanding sexually explicit and violent dreams is especially helpful for enabling us to walk in righteousness. Dreaming of an illicit, intimate sexual encounter often reveals the need of deliverance from a spirit of lust (see Matt. 10:8). Although adultery and fornication are works of the flesh, it is abnormal to have sexually explicit dreams unless one is influenced by an unclean spirit. Such a spirit often makes it's presence known by taking advantage of a person's unconscious state (sleep) to act out it's desires in that person's dreams (see 2 Cor. 11:4).

Likewise, a terrifying dream of being stabbed or killed often reveals the presence of a spirit of fear from which one needs deliverance (see 2 Tim. 1:7; Heb. 2:14-15). I have personally known of Christians who were literally tormented by bad dreams until they were delivered through prayer. The very word used to describe such a dream, *nightmare*, means a dream given by a monster or demon.

Dreaming of personally hurting or killing someone can alert us to the presence of a spirit of jealousy or hate lurking somewhere beneath our consciousness (see Prov. 6:34; 1 John 3:15). Our unconscious rage or desire for revenge will be revealed by the violent behavior in the dream. James tells us that emotions like these come straight from the devil:

> *But if ye have bitter envying and strife in your hearts, glory not, and lie not against the truth* [deceiving yourself]. *This wisdom descendeth not from above, but is earthly, sensual, devilish* (James 3:14-15).

In R- and X-rated dreams, sometimes the individual symbols do not reveal anything specific within themselves; rather the feelings of lust, rage, hatred, or overwhelming fear give us the information we need to understand the significance of the dream. I stress *sometimes,* because there is another type of nightmare that everyone should be aware of, and in these dreams, the symbols are important. These terrifying dreams come straight from God! Job complained about having this type of dream in Job 7:13-14:

> *When I say, My bed shall comfort me, my couch shall ease my complaints; then thou scarest me with dreams, and terrifiest me through visions.*

In these dreams, the symbols are significant, but concentrating on them can sometimes cause one to overlook the main point. Like the man who "couldn't see the forest for the trees," focusing on the symbols in this type of dream may add confusion instead of bringing clarification. The best way to illustrate this is with an actual dream I encountered several years ago. (I provide this account with the full permission of the dreamer. Some details have been left out due to space limitations.) Instead of trying to identify the symbols and interpret them, first pay attention to the action of the dream.

This dreamer started her letter by saying,

Ordinarily, I don't have nightmares, the kind where you wake up in the middle of the night frozen with fear as if it really was happening, but I did the other night...If this was something from the Lord to minister a message to me, I don't know how to pray concerning this....

I dreamed I was standing in my bedroom by a window ironing when a blonde-haired woman (seemingly a neighbor, but I didn't know her) came in for help. She wanted to use our phone to call for help. After dialing she said, "I keep trying to call out on your line, but I keep getting a busy signal." I told her we didn't have our phone hooked up yet. She said she was trying to get away from someone. About that time, I looked out the window and saw the man that she was running from coming toward the house...When I saw him coming, I could tell that he was angry. (At this point, the woman disappeared from the dream.) The man got in through the back door....

The man grabbed me by the arm at knife point and began to drag me out the front door to a neighbor's house...The man was dragging me up the steps with him and was banging on their front door. They hesitated, but finally opened the door... at this time I broke free and began to run. The angry man cursed at me and swore he would kill me. I ran back to my house through the front door. I realized I had to get help so I jumped out the back door, and I began running down a black-topped highway. I saw houses and lights ahead....

Finally, after having a hard time deciding what house to go to for help, I ran up to a trailer house with a car parked in the driveway. As I ran up the steps, I saw that the door was a double glass sliding door. I saw a man standing at a desk talking on the phone. He motioned for me to come in. I went in and told him that I needed help, that a man was after me. I walked into an adjoining room to wait for him to get through with his telephone conversation, but I overheard him laugh and say to the other party, "Man, this is your lucky day—the woman that escaped from you just came up here for help!" I ran out the back door, trying again to figure out where to go and ask for help...[after another episode similar to those above, the woman ended the account of her dream with]...I was so scared! I woke up frozen in a state of fear.

When I received the letter telling of this dream, I contacted the woman and told her the dream seemed to be saying that she was under a perpetual curse. (Regardless of where she ran, every time she escaped, the evil man was able to find her and put her back in danger.) This action speaks of a permanent curse. The Scripture I gave her to read was Amos 5:19: *"As if a man did flee from a lion, and a bear met him; or went into the house, and leaned his hand on the wall, and a serpent bit him."* The primary symbol of her dream was the *back door.* A back door usually means the past. I told her that the dream appeared to be telling her that her present distress was coming directly from her past. Later, through counseling, she discovered that the curse came from an earlier period in her life when she had participated in the occult. When she asked God's forgiveness and renounced her involvement with the occult, her entire life changed dramatically.

In this dream, the evil man's actions revealed her problem. The back door revealed the source of both her problem and the answer to it. The man came *in* through the back door, and each time she escaped she ran *out* the back door to find help! Like Job, who said, *"For thou writest bitter things against me, and makest me to possess the iniquities of my youth"* (Job 13:26), it was not until she dealt with her past that she was set free. Although there are several more significant symbols in this dream, like the telephone that is not hooked up (ineffective prayer) and the trailer house (temporary refuge), they add nothing to the initial interpretation of the dream. Once she repented and was set free from the curse, her prayer life blossomed and her financial situation turned around beautifully. As Jesus said, once she knew the truth, the truth made her free (see John 8:32).

Emotions in Dreams

As we have seen, our emotions—as they are felt while we are dreaming—are significant. The emotional response to the message after we wake up can be misleading. For example, if we dream of a person's death and in the dream we are at peace, or even rejoicing, it does not follow that God is saying that person will die. In fact, if the person is lost, dreaming of his death may foretell of his repentance and consequential salvation. Although such a dream would trouble us upon waking, the key to understanding what a dream is saying is always found in the emotions we feel *while* we are dreaming.

Colors Are Important

Come now, and let us reason together, saith the Lord: though your sins be as scarlet, they shall be as white as snow; though they be red like crimson, they shall be as wool (Isaiah 1:18).

Although most of our dreams are in black and white, sometimes certain colored objects appear in them. *Colors are symbolic, supplying additional information about the objects that are colored.* For example, if you previously owned a blue car of a certain model and you dream of owning and driving that same car, God is probably talking to you about your past. The blue car represents an earlier period of your life—although not necessarily the exact time when you owned the car.

On the other hand, if you dream you are driving a blue car that is yours, but in real life you have never owned such a car, then the color has a different meaning. In the first example, the color blue simply identified the car as something that is part of your past. In the second example, the color blue is referring to the spiritual aspects of your present life or ministry (see BLUE and AUTOMOBILE in the Key Word Dictionary).

Literal or Symbolic?

Another common problem in solving the riddles offered to us by dreams is that of discerning when a dream is symbolic (a parable) and when it is literal. *As a general rule, if a dream can be taken literally, it should be.* If there is something in a dream that is not literal, however, then the entire dream should be interpreted as if the objects, and sometimes even the people it contains, are symbols.

For instance, in the previous example concerning the two blue cars, neither dream can be taken literally. In the first example, you no longer own the car. Therefore, you cannot be driving it as your own. In the second example, you have never owned such a car, so again the dream must be symbolic.

However, if you dream you are driving the car you really own, to the job you presently have, and that you are involved in an accident on the street on which you actually work, then you should pray for God to prevent this from happening to you and drive carefully!

There will normally be a key—a clue—something in each dream that will reveal whether it is literal or symbolic. As a rule, if there is an object or person in a dream that cannot be taken literally, then the entire dream should be viewed as symbolic or as a parable. However, if everything in a dream is as it actually is in real life, the dream is usually literal.

For instance, I once dreamed that my brother called me and asked if I was interested in renting a house that his employer had for rent. I said that I was, and in the dream I went and examined the house. It was a light-colored brick. Inside, the floor was littered with trash. I noticed that quite a lot of money was scattered among the trash.

After I awoke, I was still meditating on the dream when my phone rang. It was my brother calling. He asked me the same question he had asked in the dream, "Are you interested in renting a different house?" I replied, "Yes, I've been praying for a better place." When I actually saw the house, it was identical to the one in the dream, trash and all. I rented it, and in addition to the money that was scattered on the floor, the landlord gave us half the first month's rent for cleaning it. (Two biblical examples of literal dreams are found in Genesis 20:3-7 and First Kings 3:5-15.)

Changeable or Unchangeable?

Regardless of whether a dream is literal or a parable, there are several Scripture examples that show us that, when necessary, we can change the outcome from that in the dream. The situation a dream reveals or foretells can usually be changed through prayer:

> *Thus hath the Lord God shewed unto me; and, behold, He formed grasshoppers in the beginning of the shooting up of the latter growth; and, lo, it was the latter growth after the king's mowings. And it came to pass, that when they had made an end of eating the grass of the land* [in the dream or vision], *then I said, O Lord God, forgive, I beseech Thee: by whom shall Jacob arise? for he is small.*

> *The Lord repented for this: It shall not be, saith the Lord. Thus hath the Lord God shewed unto me: and, behold, the Lord God called to contend by fire, and it devoured the great deep, and did eat up a part. Then said I, O Lord God, cease, I beseech Thee: by whom shall Jacob arise? for he is small. The Lord repented for this: This also shall not be, saith the Lord God* (Amos 7:1-6).

One can see from the example quoted from Amos 7 that Amos' intercession changed God's mind concerning destroying the nation of Israel. Like the prophecy given by Jonah against Nineveh, dreams often warn of impending trouble or danger. These warnings are given so that we can pray and, when necessary, repent. *Prayer changes things!*

Repetitious Dreams

Sometimes as we meditate on a dream we realize that we have dreamed the same thing before. The second dream may not always use the same objects or people, yet the same hidden message is apparent. An example of this is found in the two dreams of Pharaoh mentioned in the preceding chapter. In the first dream, seven cows ate seven other cows. In the second, seven ears of corn ate seven other ears of corn. The two dreams use different symbols, yet obviously contain the same message.

Joseph declared that the repetition of the message meant it was established of God. In other words, it would certainly happen! From this we can see that repetitious dreams are especially important.

> *And Joseph said unto Pharaoh, The dream of Pharaoh is one: God hath shewed Pharaoh what he is about to do. ...And for that the dream was doubled unto Pharaoh twice; it is because the thing is established by God, and God will shortly bring it to pass* (Genesis 41:25,32).

Shortly before going into full-time ministry, I had two dreams: In the first, I was driving a school bus across a river, and the bridge I was on suddenly came to an end! As I sailed off the end, I was gripped with fear. As I fell, I found myself hoping that the water wasn't too deep so that maybe I could drive out.

A few months later, I dreamt that I was teaching a class about prophetic ministry. After the session was over, I was driving across the top of a very high building when I suddenly drove off the edge! As I fearfully plunged downward I thought, *I have a parachute to keep from me from falling too hard.*

The fulfillment came about three months later. I was suddenly thrust into full-time ministry and had to completely trust God for my income. Although I was fearful at first, I soon realized that God was well able to supply my needs, even without a regular salary.

Understanding Symbolic Dreams (Parables)

All these things spake Jesus unto the multitude in parables; and without a parable spake He not unto them (Matthew 13:34).

Jesus gave an example for understanding symbols in the parable of the sower. Because most dreams are parables, the method He used to decipher this parable is also the proper way to unravel the mystery of dreams. Because Jesus said that the parable of the sower explains the way to interpret all parables, I have quoted it in its entirety:

Hearken; Behold, there went out a sower to sow: and it came to pass, as he sowed, some fell by the way side, and the fowls of the air came and devoured it up. And some fell on stony ground, where it had not much earth; and immediately it sprang up, because it had no depth of earth: But when the sun was up, it was scorched; and because it had no root, it withered away. And some fell among thorns, and the thorns grew up, and choked it, and it yielded no fruit. And other fell on good ground, and did yield fruit that sprang up and increased; and brought forth, some thirty, and some sixty, and some an hundred.

*And he said unto them, He that hath ears to hear, let him hear. And when he was alone, they that were about him with the twelve asked of him the parable. And he said unto them, Unto you it is given to know the mystery of the kingdom of God: but unto them that are without, all these things are done in parables: That seeing they may see, and not perceive; and hearing they may hear, and not understand; lest at any time they should be converted, and their sins should be forgiven them. **And he said unto them, Know ye not this parable? and how then will ye know all parables?** (Mark 4:3-13)*

By comparing the thoughts obtained from the Key Word Dictionary with Jesus' interpretation, you can see that He simply replaced each symbol in the parable with its respective meaning. Usually one word, or the thought contained in that word, was sufficient to give them the understanding He wanted them to have. I have inserted some additional symbol meanings into the text to help clarify the parable.

The sower [preacher] *soweth* [preaches] *the word* [seed]. *And these are they by the way side* [path of willful unrighteousness], *where the word is sown; but when they have heard, Satan* [the fowls] *cometh immediately, and taketh away the word that was sown in their hearts. And these are they likewise which are sown on stony ground* [hard hearts]; *who, when they have heard the word, immediately receive it with gladness* [the joy of salvation]; *and have no root* [conviction or steadfastness] *in themselves, and so endure but for a time: afterward, when affliction* [trouble] *or persecution* [opposition, rejection, etc.] *ariseth for the word's sake, immediately they are offended.*

And these are they which are sown among thorns [debts, natural responsibilities, etc.]; *such as hear the word, and the cares of this world, and the deceitfulness of riches, and the lusts of other things entering in, choke the word* [hinder its fulfillment or performance], *and it becometh unfruitful.*

And these are they which are sown on good ground; such as hear the word, and receive it, and bring forth fruit, some thirtyfold, some sixty, and some an hundred (Mark 4:14-20).

To further expand this parable, let us use the keys obtained from the Numbers chapter in the Key Word Dictionary. When we do this, we can see that 30-fold means *conformed* (and therefore accepted), 60 means *image*, and 100 means *fullness* or, in this case, *full measure*. Therefore, we can paraphrase the last sentence of the above verse in this way:

And these are they which are sown on good ground; such as hear the word, and receive it, and bring forth fruit because they are conformed to His image and likeness. For this reason they are abundantly fruitful.

Compare this paraphrased interpretation to the following Scriptures:

*For whom He did foreknow, He also did predestinate **to be conformed to the image of His Son,** that He might be the firstborn among many brethren* (Romans 8:29).

*Till we all come in the unity of the faith, and of the knowledge of the Son of God, unto a perfect man, **unto the measure of the stature of the fullness of Christ*** (Ephesians 4:13).

If ye abide in Me, and My words abide in you, ye shall ask what ye will, and it shall be done unto you. **Herein is My Father glorified, that ye bear much fruit;** *so shall ye be My disciples* (John 15:7-8).

Another example of this method of dream interpretation is found in the Book of Daniel. The Bible states that Daniel had understanding in all dreams and visions (see Dan. 1:17). In Daniel 2:31-45 and in Daniel 4:10-27, we find that Daniel, who was an authority in dreams, used exactly the same method of interpretation just illustrated when he explained the meaning of Nebuchadnezzar's dreams. He simply replaced the symbols with the key words or thoughts that the symbols represented to decipher the messages contained in the dreams.

To illustrate this method, let's consider the symbols in the two repetitious dreams I referred to earlier—where I drove suddenly off both a bridge and a tall building. The school bus in the first dream referred to my teaching ministry. The bridge was my support. My income suddenly came to an end, and I was thrust into full-time ministry. The broken bridge and falling both refer to loss of support.

In the second dream, I was ministering and suddenly found myself falling off a building, but was supported by a parachute, which in turn is supported by air. Air represents the Spirit. Through this, God was saying that even though my weekly salary would suddenly come to an end, He would sustain me.

Positive or Negative, Good or Bad?

Symbols, like most words, can be used both positively and negatively. For instance, when we use the word *cool*, we may be referring to something good or bad. "The soup is cool" may mean that the soup is cool enough to eat or that it needs to be reheated. "This room certainly is cool" may mean that the heat needs to be turned up or that the temperature feels good to someone who has just come in from the summer heat. Additionally, to say that someone is *cool* may mean that the person is not friendly or that he or she needs a jacket. It may even indicate admiration because the person "has it all together."

Likewise, almost all symbols can have both positive (good) and negative (bad) meanings. The following Scripture example uses each of two metals, brass and iron, as a symbol with two different, though related, meanings.

For brass [the letter of the law] *I will bring gold* [wisdom], *and for iron* [bondage] *I will bring silver* [knowledge or redemption], *and for wood* [works of the flesh] *brass* [God's grace or truth], *and for stones* [accusations witnessing against you] *iron* [strength or justification]: *I will also make thy officers peace, and thine exactors righteousness* (Isaiah 60:17).

Initially, brass is used to symbolize the Law of Moses; then it is employed to symbolize God's Word of grace and truth. The bondage of the law is symbolized by iron, which then comes to represent the power of the Holy Spirit given to Christians who are justified through Christ.

In this next Scripture, notice how the symbol for people—trees—is used both positively and negatively, both in a good and a bad sense:

And all the trees [people] *of the field* [world] *shall know that I the Lord have brought down the high tree* [haughty person], *have exalted the low tree* [humble person], *have dried up the green tree* [carnal person], *and have made the dry tree* [repented person, dead with Christ] *to flourish...* (Ezekiel 17:24).

The most important thing to remember about interpreting symbols is *never be narrow-minded.* Symbols, like words, are very flexible. When we know the context of a dream and the circumstances of the dreamer's life, we can properly assign the right meanings. Without this knowledge, we can only guess.

For instance, it is possible for an *ant* in a dream to mean several different things. One meaning comes directly from the Bible; others come from our personal experiences. In the Key Word Dictionary, I have listed several possible meanings. These include the following: industrious; wise; diligent; prepare for the future; nuisance; stinging or angry words. The context of the dream must determine which meaning to use in your interpretation.

When one dreams of ants at a picnic, the context would obviously lean toward "nuisance" as the meaning of the symbol, even though it is their industrious nature that makes them such a nuisance! To dream of ants gathering food would relate directly to the key word definition of "industrious, diligent preparation for the future." Likewise, dreaming of being bit or stung by ants would fit the "stinging or angry words" definition.

Sometimes a symbol has a meaning to one person that would not fit another. The example of the blue car, which we used earlier, could only mean the past to someone who had previously owned such a car. Another example is a pet dog. A dog is usually a symbol for an unclean spirit or attitude, such as strife or contention. But dreaming about your own pet dog, which you love, would normally symbolize something good, something close to you that you cherish, not something bad.

When we are trying to determine the object and subject of a dream, we ask ourselves the questions, "*Who* does this dream refer to?" and "*What* is it really about?" Likewise, when we are trying to decipher a symbol, the first question we should ask is, "What does this symbol mean to *me?*" Like the pet dog previously mentioned, only the pet's owner would recognize its correct meaning when used as a symbol in his or her dream.

I encountered an interesting example of this once when I was helping a pastor interpret a dream. In this dream, two angels came to her house and told her not to worry about YWAM (Youth With A Mission), that every need they had would be met. Although she had previously told me that her church was having financial difficulty, I could not see how God supplying a mission organization's needs had anything to do with her situation. Then she said, "We jokingly say that YWAM means, Youth Without Any Money, because they have to do so much with so little." It was not until then that I realized that God was simply using her personal perception of YWAM (doing God's work without any money) to assure her that He would meet all her own needs.

God will use names that rhyme, puns, riddles, proverbs, almost anything imaginable to hide the truth from our "old man" when He speaks to us in the night. God, who created the heavens and the earth and all things therein, has boundless imagination. If we are going to keep up with Him, we must stretch ours. He used the stars to represent Abraham's dependents, the sun to characterize Himself, the moon to portray the Church, lambs to illustrate His little children, and wolves to describe their enemies! He can and will use almost anything to get His point across.

God will speak to a plumber using pipe wrenches, plugged-up drains, and fireplugs; but He will employ completely different symbols when He talks to a doctor or teacher. Yet, there are objects that are common to everyone, and God uses these to speak to each of us at one time or another. Many of these common symbols such as objects, actions, people, places, and so forth, are listed and expanded on in the Key Word Dictionary in Part II.

The Dreamer's Dilemma

Have you ever dreamed that you won the lottery, but after waking, you couldn't remember the winning numbers? Frustrating! Equally frustrating is dreaming of looking for a specific house or room number, and although you wake up remembering the number, you have no idea what it means.

Have you ever dreamed of getting on an elevator and going to the ninth floor? This may mean good things are ahead. But if you've dreamed of getting off on the tenth floor, it could be bad news! Although numbers are rather common in dreams, most books about dreams just ignore them. This one doesn't. Chapters 4 through 8 provide an in-depth study on numbers, while the remaining chapters focus on the meanings of colors, locations, animals, vehicles, metal, trades, and several other categories.

A Number of Ways to Interpret Symbols

Many dream symbols are relatively easy to interpret because they have a limited number of applications. For instance, an apple in a dream can represent *sin*, as when Eve ate of the forbidden fruit, or it can portray *appreciation*, as when a child gives an apple to a teacher. A sour apple may refer to a person with a *bad disposition*, and a big apple may even represent *New York City*, because it's well known as "The Big Apple."

Dreaming about a basket of apples may signify that one is *fruitful*, bringing forth the fruit of the Spirit; or the apples may refer to *wise counsel*, as in Proverbs 25:11, *"A word fitly spoken is like apples of gold in pictures of silver."* Dreaming of a rotten apple may mean that one is keeping bad company, as in, "One rotten apple spoils the whole barrel," or dreaming about stealing a bright red apple may refer to one's natural passion for forbidden fruit. But there's certainly a limit to the various possible meanings an apple can convey; however, this limitation does not apply to numbers, the subject we will first examine. Numbers are virtually unlimited in their applications. They can mean almost anything.

It is not uncommon for dreams to include numbers within their content. Numbers are the very highest form of symbolism; therefore, their meanings are seldom understood. The number *one* has the potential of meaning anything from one person to one city to one nation to one universe! It has an unlimited number of meanings, or at least as many as there are things in existence! Because there are endless meanings for every number, of necessity, everyone must use a common reference before numbers can be considered useful in dreams. God has provided just such a reference tool for us—the Bible.

But before discussing the actual meanings of individual numbers, we need to examine how symbols obtain their various meanings in the first place.

How Symbols Acquire Their Meanings

There are four primary ways that symbols acquire specific meanings. One, which is probably the most common way, is by the symbol's *inherent character*. Because a symbol's basic characteristics are the same the world over, this is sometimes referred to as a symbol's *universal* meaning. For instance, in the Bible, God used innocent lambs to represent His children and merciless wolves to describe their enemies. The descriptive nature, or character, of these two animals clearly illustrates what they're depicting. Another example is the inherent characteristics of a motorcyclist. Motorcyclists often symbolize pride and rebellion because of the attitude many of them exhibit. "Individuality" or even "loner" are other possible meanings because cycles are usually ridden alone. Besides the rider's attitude, two characteristics of the machine itself are speed and agility. Noise is another. When one dreams of a motorcycle, the dream's content usually indicates which meaning applies.

Another way a symbol may obtain a specific meaning is through a dreamer's *personal experience*. An object, animal, person, color, or location may mean something to one person that it would not mean to another. If you've ever ridden a motorcycle and had an accident, motorcycles may mean sudden calamity to you! Another, more probable example is your pet dog or cat—either one may denote something precious to you because of your love for it. In another case, someone unfamiliar with your childhood home or toys would not see them the same way you do. The Bible has an interesting precedent for personal experience influencing spiritual perception:

> *And out of the ground the Lord God formed every beast of the field, and every fowl of the air; and brought them unto Adam to see what he would call them: and whatsoever Adam called every living creature, that was the name thereof* (Genesis 2:19).

In other words, God speaks our language. Often the way we perceive something carries over into our dreams, even when our perception is less than perfect.

A third way symbols acquire meaning is through *society*. Our *culture* may influence our perception of certain symbols and give them special meaning. If someone says that a disgruntled employee has "gone postal," most Americans know exactly what that means. But say that to an assembly in East Africa, and your interpreter will peer at you sideways with a funny look on his face! Likewise, there are several sayings and parables in the Bible that people from Western societies find difficult to interpret. Occasionally, even colloquialisms are used in Scripture.

If we are unaware of a certain Jewish saying, we could get the wrong impression of Jesus when reading the following Scripture passage:

> *And* [Jesus] *said unto another, Follow Me. But he said, Lord, **suffer me first to go and bury my father**. Jesus said unto him, Let the dead bury their dead: but go thou and preach the kingdom of God* (Luke 9:59-60).

Although it sounds like Jesus was being incredibly hard, that is not the case. The man's father was still alive. When the man said, "Suffer me first to go and bury my father," he actually meant, "Wait until after my father dies and I get my inheritance, *then* I'll follow You." Jesus was directly addressing this man's covetousness. He challenged him to forsake his inheritance and take up his cross.

If you are trying to help someone interpret a dream and you're unaware of that person's cultural perception of a symbol used in it, there's no possible way that you can offer a correct interpretation. On the other hand, some symbols first acquire meaning in one culture and later become accepted all over the world. A prime example is a red cross. Although it has no inherent character of its own, it has come to mean *medical aid* to all nations.

And last—and by far the most important when dealing especially with numbers—a symbol acquires meaning by the way it is used in *Scripture*. By studying the various ways numbers and other objects are used in the Bible, we can see exactly what they mean in our dreams. For numbers, there's no other dependable source of information available. When a dream is from God, and many are, we can always depend upon the *"more sure word of prophecy"* (2 Pet. 1:19) to show us exactly what He means—because God does not change.

Bible Numerology 101

The Bible is the only legitimate source of knowledge for the symbolic meaning of numbers. Therefore, our discussion is based solely upon the Word of God. God uses numbers in dreams identically to the way He uses them in Scripture. Subsequently, there is a double blessing in learning about numbers; we can understand both our dreams *and* the Bible more fully. Once we have mastered the message of our dreams, many passages in the Bible suddenly take on a completely new meaning.

Beginning in the very first book of the Bible, Genesis, even a casual reader soon discovers that it is filled with numbers. God numbers almost everything, and when He counts, He seldom does it for the same reason we do. His numbers reveal more than just quantity! For instance, let's take a look at the number *seven* in Scripture.

Number Seven—Complete

Because *God completed all* His work and *finished* it on the seventh day of creation, we can reasonably deduct that *seven* means "complete" (see Gen. 2:1-2). In fact, most Bible scholars agree that it means "complete," "finished," or "all." And because God rested after He finished, it can also mean "rest." In the same way, the other six days of creation reveal the meanings of numbers *one* through *six*.

Number One—Beginning

Understandably, the very first number mentioned in Genesis is *one*, and God defines it at the same time He introduces it. *"In the beginning...[was] the first day"* (see Gen. 1:1-5). Thus we can see that the symbolic meaning for *one* is "beginning." Another meaning is "first," as we might say, "God is number one in my book!" By this we mean that He comes first; He's the best, most important, and so forth. One thing is for certain, God is number one in every sense of the word! Of course, in the natural use of the word, *one* can also mean "singular," as in "one God."

Number Two—Divide or Judge

Next, the Bible defines the number *two*. In the second day, God divided the waters that were under the firmament from the waters above the firmament (see Gen. 1:6-8). It doesn't take a rocket scientist to glean from this passage that *two* means "divide." At the final judgment, God will divide the sheep from the goats (see Matt. 25:32). So, by extension, *two* means "to judge," "to discern," or "to set apart." In the same way, since the Bible requires a minimum of two witnesses before judgment can be rendered, occasionally "witness" is an acceptable meaning (see Deut. 17:6). In the Bible, the concept of dividing and judging are so closely interwoven that you seldom see one without the other.

One of the clearest examples of this is found in First Kings. When Solomon was first crowned king and was at Gibeon offering sacrifices, he had a dream in which he asked God for wisdom to govern Israel properly. After he returned to Jerusalem, two harlots were brought before him for judgment. Both had delivered a child, but one had accidentally killed her own baby and was claiming the living baby as her own:

> And the king said, Bring me a sword....And the king said, **Divide** the living child in two, and give half to the one, and half to the other. Then spake the woman whose the living child was unto the king, for her bowels yearned upon her son, and she said, O my lord, give her the living child, and in no wise slay it. But the other said, Let it be neither mine nor thine, but **divide** it. Then the king answered and said, Give her the living child, and in no wise slay it: she is the mother thereof. And all Israel heard of the judgment which the king had **judged**; and they feared the king: for they saw that the wisdom of God was in him, to do **judgment** (1 Kings 3:24-28).

One other thought should be considered here. These women each accused the other—one justly, the other fraudulently. Likewise, in court, the alleged perpetrator of a crime is called, "the accused." Thus, by extension, "to be judgmental" or "to accuse" is another meaning for *two.*

Number Three—Conform

Although the meaning for the number *three* may not be as easily discerned by reading the Book of Genesis, additional study of the Scripture reveals the meaning of *three* as "conform." In the third day, God caused the dry land (Hebrew, "ashamed land") to appear by dividing the waters (see Gen. 1:9). The dry, ashamed land corresponds to our repentance and confession as we come out of sin into conformity to God's image. Paul said that we are *"predestin[ed] to be conformed to the image of His Son..."* (Rom. 8:29b), even as Christ Himself was conformed to the express *"image of the invisible God"* (Col. 1:15b). So we should be conformed in all three areas of our beings—spirit, soul, and body. A few more meanings that convey this same concept are "obey," "imitate," and "copy."

Number Four—Rule or Reign

The number *four* is a little easier to define. In the fourth day of creation, God made "two great lights"—the sun and moon (see Gen. 1:16). These were made specifically to "rule" the day and night. From this, we can deduct that *four* means "rule." Although the primary meaning of *four* is "rule" or "reign," by extension, its meaning may include the ruler's subjects. Thus, the symbolism of *four* may include certain aspects of the world, as in the four corners of the world, or the four winds of the earth (see Rev. 7:1).

One word used extensively in Scripture, which embodies both ruler and subject, can also be a meaning for *four*—"kingdom." Also, by implication, "dominion" or "dominance" are sometimes the symbolic thought contained in the number *four.*

Number Five—Serve

As with the number *three*, it's a little more difficult to discover the meaning of number *five* from the record of creation than it is for numbers *one, two,* and *four.* The fifth day was the first day that living creatures were made. All living things were made for God's pleasure, to serve Him, so *five* means "service" or "works." When God challenged Job, He asked him, *"Will the unicorn be willing to serve thee? ...or will he harrow the valleys after thee?"* (Job 39:9-10). Of course, the answer is no! He works for God and only God!

This leads to a unique understanding of why God tells us that if we don't pay our tithe, we must add a fifth part to it. If we withhold God's just due, we will go into bondage (debt), and the borrower *serves* the lender! (See Leveticus 27:31; Proverbs 22:7.) Hence, *five* means "serve." We all serve something (or someone); the question is what or who? Are we serving a good master or laboring for a bad one? Often the choice is ours.

While we're talking about serving, by implication, *five* can also refer to "law." The Jews tried to become righteous through their own works by obeying the Law. So, *five* also points to legalism or one who is legalistic. According to Paul, the Law brought bondage, so five can also symbolize various addictions like alcoholism and gambling. And as we previously mentioned, bondage may include debt. The Bible also identifies another type of bondage—fear (see Heb. 2:15).

Number Six—Image

The sixth day also unveils the Creator's meaning for the number of that day. On that day, God made humanity in His own *image* (see Gen. 1:27). Although *six* has often been called "the number of man," that definition unjustly limits it. The meaning of *six* includes more than just "humanity." For instance, *"Nebuchadnezzar the king made an image of gold, whose height was threescore [60] cubits, and the breadth thereof six cubits"* (Dan. 3:1a). As the 60-cubit high and 6-cubic wide idol in this verse shows, *six* can refer to something besides humans. Even though idols are images, they aren't necessarily made like humans who have been made after God's own image. Instead, they usually portray demons (see Dan. 3:1; 1 Cor. 10:19-20). But being images, the number *six* fits them well. Later, after we discuss *ten* and *one hundred*, we will explore the meaning of John's infamous 666 that we've heard so much about.

Just how useful understanding numbers can be is shown in a dream that a pastor recently related to me. He dreamed he was defending himself with what he thought was a .36-caliber pistol. But after he shot and wounded his opponent, he realized that his pistol wasn't a .36-caliber after all, but rather it was a .32-caliber. The meaning? This pastor thought he was conformed to Christ's image (36), but God was showing him that he had a judgmental attitude instead. There's quite a stretch between the two. The image Christ portrayed was love. Jesus said He didn't come to judge the world, but to save it.

So there you have it. Seven days—seven numbers explained, but what about *eight* and *nine*? Again, the Bible has the answers. But before we look for them, we need to examine another concept about symbols—the difference between direct and implied meanings.

Roots or Branches

There is a basic interpretation for each symbol. These basic interpretations are comparable to tree roots. In the same way that *roots* produce plants with *branches*, each root meaning branches out and produces additional meanings through implication. In other words, branch meanings are implied meanings. To further complicate things, sometimes roots branch out in several different directions. Also, in some cases, even the branches produce branches. *Two* is a prime example. First, the root meaning for *two* is "divide." By implication, *divide* means "to judge." But to judge properly, one must have at least two witnesses. Subsequently, one branch of *judge* is "witness." Thus, by extension, *two* also means "witness." In the same way, it may even include the verdict!

If we don't search deep enough and uncover the roots, we may mistake a branch for a root, which sooner or later will lead to misinterpretation. Then, when we encounter the actual root, we will be stumped for an answer (pun intended). If we don't search and find the root meaning, we *will* misinterpret some symbols. But once we understand roots, the implied meanings are relatively easy to see and understand. We find this principal in the common, but somewhat mistaken, meaning for the number *eight*.

Number Eight—Put Off

Genesis 17:12 probably reveals the correct meaning for *eight* better than any other verse in the Bible. In it God tells Abraham, *"He that is eight days old shall be circumcised among you...."* Paul explains the meaning of circumcision:

*In whom also ye are circumcised with the circumcision made without hands, in **putting off** the body of the sins of the flesh by the circumcision of Christ* (Colossians 2:11).

In other words, the symbolic meaning for *circumcision* and the meaning for number *eight* are the same. On the eighth day we are to "put off" our "old man" or "old self." Therefore, we see that the inference here is *put off*. Now, it's commonly believed that *eight* means "new beginnings," and indeed, when we put off our old self, we are born again and we start anew. But the correct root meaning for this number is "put off," and therefore, the implied meaning, "new beginning" won't always properly fit. When circumcising a baby on his eighth day, one can hardly say the baby is having a new beginning, but the covering of his flesh is certainly being put off just as God commanded. Later, when we study the teens, we will see even more clearly why understanding root meanings versus implied meanings is so important.

There are several other passages of Scripture that confirm that "put off" is the proper root for *eight*. One really good example is when Noah came out of the Ark on the mountains of Ararat. When the flood was over, the earth certainly had a new beginning, but Noah didn't land or exit on the eighth year or the eighth month or even the eighth day. Rather, *"the ark rested in the seventh month, on the seventeenth day of the month..."* (Gen. 8:4).

And then Noah emerged on the *"...six hundredth and first year, in the first month, the first day of the month..."* (Gen. 8:13). As we can see from the numbers used, God finished His work (the ark rested in the seventh month), and started anew (Noah emerged on the first year, first month, and first day). With God, all beginnings are new, and the number *one* covers them all!

Another Scripture to help us properly understand *eight* is Exodus 22:30. God told Moses to allow the newborn offspring of the sheep and oxen to stay with their respective mothers for seven days, but on the eighth day they were to be sacrificed unto Him. Of course, sacrificing their flesh symbolizes the circumcision of our flesh ("putting off" our old self). Another similar reference is when Moses reiterated their wilderness journey where God destroyed ("put off") the old generation from among their tribes:

And the space in which we came from Kadesh-barnea, until we were come over the brook Zered, was thirty and eight years; until all the generation of the men of war were wasted out from among the host... (Deuteronomy 2:14).

It wasn't until they were conformed to His will and the old generation (old self) was put off ("wasted out") in the wilderness that they were allowed to go in and possess their inheritance.

Number Nine—Fruit or Harvest

The number *nine* means "fruit" or "harvest," and its meaning is made all the more interesting because of the age of Noah's grandfather Methuselah. He lived longer than anyone else in the Bible: *"And all the days of Methuselah were nine hundred sixty and nine years: and he died"* (Gen. 5:27).

Some translators say that his name means, "when he is gone it [the flood] shall come." Others say it means, "they died." Either way, as Hosea said, many centuries later, *"Also, O Judah, [God] hath set an harvest for thee..."* (Hosea 6:11). Methuselah's age at death signaled the beginning of God's first harvest of judgment upon the earth. The number 969 reveals that the earth's harvest was ripe; the image and fruit was rotten and rejected. The first harvest was by water; the second will be by fire:

And another angel came out of the temple, crying with a loud voice to him that sat on the cloud, Thrust in thy sickle, and reap: for the time is come for thee to reap; for the harvest of the earth is ripe (Revelation 14:15).

Although in both of the aforementioned harvests the earth is cursed, *nine* can also signify blessings. In fact, understanding the symbolic meaning of *nine* gives new and added dimension to one of Jesus' most moving parables:

What man of you, having an hundred sheep, if he lose one of them, doth not leave the ninety and nine in the wilderness, and go after that which is lost, until he find it? ...likewise joy shall be in heaven over one sinner that repenteth, more than over ninety and nine just persons, which need no repentance (Luke 15:4,7).

It's easy to see that *"ninety and nine"* refers to God's harvest of souls. And then later, when Jesus healed the ten lepers, He asked: *"Were there not ten cleansed? but where are the nine?"* (Luke 17:17b) Jesus was asking, "Where is My harvest of thanksgiving?" The fruit of *all* their lips should have been giving thanks to His name! (See Hebrews 13:15.)

We have now covered the basics. *One* is "beginning"; *two* is "divide" or "judge"; *three* is "conform"; *four* is "rule" or "reign" (over a subject); *five* is "serve" or "work"; *six* is "image"; *seven* is "complete"; *eight* is "put off"; and *nine* is "fruit" or "harvest."

When Moses gave the Law to the Israelites, he advised them to be circumspect, that is, to look around at the complete picture. When interpreting dreams, we should follow Moses' advice and not be narrow-minded! Sometimes there are slight overlaps in meanings. As we continue our study, we'll learn that numbers like *seven* and *thousand* come close to meaning the same thing at times; likewise, *five* and *eighteen* will have the same meaning in some cases. We've learned how important understanding roots are. When we studied the numbers *two* and *eight*, we also discovered that a root may produce a branch—implied meaning. Whether we use the root or the branch always depends upon the application. Once we've mastered the root meanings, we can safely move on to the implications and additions that they allow.

There is another minor point that we need to consider before we move on to more advanced numbers. When interpreting any symbol, there is always the possibility that it's not used as a symbol at all, but rather it simply means what it says (or is). When Joseph interpreted Pharaoh's dreams about seven cows eating seven other cows, seven cows meant seven years rather than "complete," and earlier, when he interpreted the butler and baker's dreams, the three branches and baskets meant three days (see Gen. 41:26; 40:12,18). At other times, and quite often in Scripture, the meaning is dual and can correctly be seen in its natural application as well as with symbolic meaning. A prime example is, "God is one!" He is indeed singular; there is only one God. But also, He is number one—the first, the beginning, the best, the most important, and He certainly should be counted as number one by all.

CHAPTER 5

Multiplied Multiples

"Multiples, multiples in the valley of decision..." Oops!

That's supposed to be, *"Multitudes, multitudes in the valley of decision: for the day of the Lord is near in the valley of decision"* (Joel 3:14). But it's close, anyway. After all, there are a multitude of decisions to make when God starts using numbers in dreams. In fact, we're now getting into the *really* interesting numbers—numbers like *ten, twenty, thirty,* or even *hundreds* and *thousands.* And when God puts dollar signs in front of them, they get even more interesting! Have you ever dreamed that you won a sweepstake? It'll get your attention, that's for sure. We'll discuss just such a dream toward the end of this chapter.

Growing a Garden

Just as we studied the base numbers individually, we also need to examine the numbers that contain multiple digits one at a time. As we progressed from one digit to another in the last chapter, you may have guessed that the meaning of each number in some way relates to the one preceding or following it; if so, you were right—it does. Jesus taught that His Kingdom was a lot like growing a garden:

> *...The kingdom of God is as if a man should scatter seed on the ground, and should sleep by night and rise by day, and the seed should sprout and grow, he himself does not know how. For the earth yields crops by itself: first the blade, then the head, after that the full grain in the head. But when the grain ripens,*

immediately he puts in the sickle, because the harvest has come (Mark 4:26-29 NKJV).

One is like a seed. We start our garden with a seed, and through the growth process, we obtain the harvest.

There are nine numbered steps from planting to harvest. Count them as I name them off. A seed is singular, and of utmost importance. Our garden *begins* when the seed is planted in fertile soil. The seed then *divides* itself and sends a root downward, and a shoot upward. A leaf breaks though the surface and *conforms* itself in every way to its parent plant. It struggles to survive and *conquer* drought, heat, insects—and if it prevails, it goes to *work* producing blooms, buds, etc. to form other seed to *replicate* itself. After the fruit or seed forms, it *completely* ripens and, finally, the husk, shell, or peeling is *put off* and the *fruit is harvested*. Once harvested, the fruit is appraised for its quality and *weighed* or *measured* for its quantity.

Number Ten—Weighed in the Balances

Appraising and weighing the fruit is the tenth step, and it corresponds to the number *ten*. *Ten* means to "weigh" or "measure" for the specific purpose of *accepting* or *rejecting* that which is weighed. During this process, most Christians simply say they are being tried. In his letter to the church in Smyrna, John admonished:

> *Fear none of those things which thou shalt suffer: behold, the devil shall cast some of you into prison, that ye may be **tried**; and ye shall have tribulation **ten** days: be thou faithful unto death, and I will give thee a crown of life* (Revelation 2:10).

So we see that dreaming of getting off an elevator on the tenth floor may be a warning that we are about to enter into a trial.

As mentioned in the first chapter, when we dream of taking an elevator ride, getting off on the ninth floor is fine, but we really don't want to get off on the tenth! If we dream that, we need to start praying Jesus' model prayer: *"Our Father which art in heaven, hallowed be Thy name. Thy kingdom come. Thy will be done.... And lead us not into temptation, but deliver us..."* (Matt. 6:9b-10,13). On the other hand, if we dream of getting off on the ninth floor in our local court house, and the ninth floor happens to be where the judge's office is, then *nine* simply means *nine*; and the message of the dream is written on the office door!

Opposite Interpretations

Now that brings up another interesting point. If one is tried and passes the test, the outcome is good. But what if one fails? If either quality or quantity is lacking in the person who is being "weighed" or "measured," the results will be disappointing.

When interpreting symbols, it's important to recognize this concept: *Almost every symbol can be interpreted two different ways—either negatively or positively.* Therefore, it's possible for each ordinary symbol to have a dual meaning. However, numbers are unique. For instance, how can "beginning" be positive or negative? Positives and negatives are opposites. The opposite of beginning is ending. Ending up in Heaven is not a negative! As we continue our study, we'll see that God has provided opposites for the base numbers in a very special way. In fact, they're not always opposites; sometimes they're actually results. But for now, let's return to the subject of double digits.

Two Times Ten

When we take a base number (one through nine) and multiply it by ten, we are weighing or measuring it to determine whether to accept or reject it. For example, two times ten equals twenty. *Twenty* means to "divide" or "judge" something and in the process determine whether to "accept" or "reject" it. When God numbered Israel, He counted only those who were twenty years old and upward (see Num. 1:3). Unless God accepts you when He judges you, He will not count you as His own. From this example, it's not difficult to see that *twenty* can mean "holy" (separated unto God and accepted by Him). Or, it can mean "unholy" (weighed in the balances and found wanting!). As always, the surrounding context within the dream determines whether the interpretation is positive or negative.

John saw four and twenty elders seated around God's throne:

> *And round about the throne were four and twenty seats: and upon the seats I saw four and twenty elders sitting, clothed in white raiment; and they had on their heads crowns of gold* (Revelation 4:4).

Seats indicate positions of authority, and crowns refer to recognized authorities. Likewise, *four* means to "rule." *Twenty* means "holy" if one is accepted, which these obviously are, because they are wearing white raiment, which signifies righteousness. These men represent far more than just 24 elders. They stand for all of God's holy, righteous, ruling elders who are even now ministering around His throne. At the same time, John saw four beasts that represent the apostles, prophets, evangelists, and pastor-teachers—but that's another book.

Thirty

The next number, *thirty* (three times ten) means "acceptably conformed" or, if one is conformed to this world, "unacceptably conformed," but "conformed," nonetheless (see Rom. 12:2). The best example of God's use of this number is Jesus' age when He began His ministry—*thirty*. In the Old Testament, a Levite had to be thirty years old before he could become a priest or serve in the tabernacle. And to legitimately serve Christ, we must be conformed to His image (see Num. 4:3; Rom. 8:29).

Joseph is another minister who was thirty before he took office (see Gen. 41:46). Until then, *"the word of the Lord tried him"* (Ps. 105:19b). If he had failed God's tests and conformed to the wishes of Potiphar's wife, the story would have ended in an entirely different manner (see Gen. 39:7-8). David was another who was thirty before he was promoted: *"David was thirty years old when he began to reign, and he reigned forty years"* (2 Sam. 5:4). And while we're discussing David, notice the length of his reign—forty years.

Forty

Many of the Old Testament kings ruled forty years. Why? *Forty* means "acceptable" or "unacceptable rule," or rule that has been determined to be good or evil. *Four* means "rule," and four times ten equals acceptable or unacceptable dominion. God revealed the sovereignty of His rule in the days of Noah when He sent forty days of rain and destroyed the world. At another time, He gave Nineveh forty days to straighten up. Likewise, Jesus took dominion and ruled over both His flesh and the devil when He completed His forty-day fast.

Another example of forty depicting rule, or dominion, is revealed in the biblical story of Elisha (see 2 Kings 2:23-24). Elisha cursed a group of young people who were mocking him. Afterward, two she

bears came out of the woods and executed God's judgment by maul-
ing forty-two of them. The bears represent the curse, forty portrays
dominion, and two implies judgment.

Fifty

In Scripture, *fifty* usually relates to ministry, as *thirty* does, but with
a different view. Concerning the Levitical priesthood, Moses wrote:

> *From thirty years old and upward until fifty years old shalt thou*
> *number them; all that enter in to perform the service, to do the*
> *work in the tabernacle of the congregation* (Numbers 4:23).

Thirty indicates whether a minister's *character* is conformed to
Christ's, and *fifty* considers whether his *service* is. Notice the *five* and
fifty in the following Scripture about Solomon's work force: *"These*
were the chief of the officers that were over Solomon's work, five hundred
and fifty..." (1 Kings 9:23). Also, when Jesus went to feed the five
thousand, *"...He said to His disciples, Make them sit down by fifties in*
a company" (Luke 9:14). It's very important to get a passing grade on
God's report card. Our works are regularly checked and graded. Solomon said, *"For God shall bring every work into judgment, with every*
secret thing, whether it be good, or whether it be evil" (Eccles. 12:14).

Sixty

Now *sixty* is quite intriguing. It's different! Because *six* means "image," *sixty* is the measure of our *image*. Our flesh is created in the
image of God, and our spirit is created in His likeness. The nature of
our flesh is totally unacceptable, while our spirit is ready and willing to
serve God. Paul said, *"...in me* [that is, in my flesh] *dwelleth no good*
thing" (Rom. 7:18a). Also, *"the carnal mind is enmity against God: for*
it is not subject to the law of God, neither indeed can be" (Rom. 8:7).
For this reason, the number *sixty* is seldom used in a positive sense in
relation to humankind because it refers more to the outward image
than to the inward likeness. As a whole, humankind does not have an
acceptable image.

Very few people have earned enough of God's approval so that
He can use the number *sixty* in a positive way when referring to them.
Enoch was one of the few:

And all the days of Enoch were three hundred sixty and five years: and Enoch walked with God: and he was not; for God took him (Genesis 5:23-24).

(We will investigate the full meaning of Enoch's age later when we discuss hundreds.)

A pastor had this dream:

I was in high school, trying out for the basketball team. The coach gave me three blue bowls and told me to take the players outside and line them up. I put out the bowls and we walked *exactly* sixty yards away from them. The coach said, "Go," and we started running for a bowl. The ones who raced to the bowls first got to try out for the team.

The interesting thing about this dream is the emphasis placed upon the exact distance of "sixty yards," which indicates a conformed image (one yard is three feet). The finish line was three blue bowls, which depicts a conformed, heavenly vessel. In this dream, God was reminding this pastor that all his efforts were to be directed toward being conformed to the express image of Jesus Christ.

Seventy

Seventy means "completely accepted" (or "completely rejected," as the case may be). Jesus used this number when He taught about forgiveness:

Then came Peter to Him, and said, Lord, how oft shall my brother sin against me, and I forgive him? till seven times? Jesus saith unto him, I say not unto thee, Until seven times: but, Until seventy times seven (Matthew 18:21-22).

Peter's question conveys our carnal idea of forgiveness. *Seven* means "complete," and we think we have forgiven when we have completely released someone from his or her indebtedness to us. But Jesus teaches that we must go farther. It's not enough to just forgive them; we must also completely accept them! Our concept is, "I'll forgive you this time, but I'm not going to let you get close enough to harm me again." Admittedly, it's not very wise to be like Abner and die, *"as a fool dieth"* (2 Sam. 3:33b), but in essence, Jesus said, "If you want Me to accept you after I've forgiven you, you also have to accept them."

That's the *real* meaning of *seventy times seven* used here; the meaning is not the multiplied product of 490.

For those who may have a problem believing that Jesus' reply to Peter's question was a parable, consider Matthew 13:34, *"All these things spake Jesus unto the multitude in parables; and without a parable spake He not unto them."* When we treat symbols literally instead of as parables, which they truly are, we completely miss what God is trying to tell us.

As we said, *seventy* can be negative too. One example found in the Bible is where, *"seventy men of the ancients of the house of Israel"* (Ezek. 8:11) were burning incense to other gods, and God asked Ezekiel:

> *...Son of man, hast thou seen what the ancients of the house of Israel do in the dark, every man in the chambers of his imagery? for they say, The Lord seeth us not; the Lord hath forsaken the earth* (Ezekiel 8:12).

The context shows that God was completely rejecting Israel at that time because of their evil worship. Noah's father is another good example. His was the last generation before the flood: *"And all the days of Lamech were seven hundred seventy and seven years: and he died"* (Gen. 5:31). It sounds like God was saying, "That's all, folks"; doesn't it?

Eighty

Eighty is well known as the age of Moses when God sent him to Pharaoh to deliver Israel (see Exod. 7:7). Also, Caleb was *eighty-five* when he conquered Mount Hebron (see Josh. 14:10). Although their accomplishments at that age were impressive, the meaning of their age makes them even more impressive. These men had *acceptably put off the flesh* to the point that God could be glorified through them. On the other hand, *eighty* can also be used in a negative sense:

> *And Methuselah lived an hundred **eighty** and seven years, and begat Lamech: and Methuselah lived after he begat Lamech seven hundred **eighty** and two years, and begat sons and daughters.... And Lamech lived an hundred **eighty** and two years, and begat* [Noah] (Genesis 5:25-26,28).

Methuselah was Noah's grandfather, and Lamech was his dad. The ages of these two men epitomize their generations—rejected of God. Of their generations God said:

The earth also was corrupt before God, and the earth was filled with violence. And God looked upon the earth, and, behold, it was corrupt; for all flesh had corrupted his way upon the earth. And God said unto Noah, The end of all flesh is come before Me; for the earth is filled with violence through them; and, behold, I will destroy them with the earth (Genesis 6:11-13).

And He did just that!

Ninety

Ninety means "the fruit has been inspected." Probably the best known passage in the Old Testament using *ninety* is found in Genesis:

And when Abram was ninety years old and nine, the Lord appeared to Abram, and said unto him, I am the Almighty God; walk before Me, and be thou perfect....And I will make thee exceeding fruitful, and I will make nations of thee, and kings shall come out of thee (Genesis 17:1,6).

Appropriately enough, this visitation happened immediately before God fulfilled His promise to Abraham. Abraham was one hundred years old when Isaac was born. Of course, the fruit that God inspected and accepted was Abraham's faith, one of the nine fruits of the Spirit. And while we are on *ninety*, remember the "ninety and nine sheep" we discussed earlier when we were studying the number *nine*?

I say unto you, that likewise joy shall be in heaven over one sinner that repenteth, more than over ninety and nine just persons, which need no repentance (Luke 15:7).

Since they didn't need repentance, they were certainly accepted, wouldn't you say?

A "Winning" Dream

Now, let's look at an actual dream that contains numbers. In the beginning of this chapter, I asked whether you've ever dreamed that you won the sweepstakes. Well, I have, more than once. Regretfully, so far it has only been in my dreams. Here is one of those dreams:

The phone rang and my wife answered it. I could hear someone telling her that I had won $26,876. (When I awoke, I wasn't sure about the "76.") She asked whoever it was if he wanted to talk to me, and he said no, she was to just tell me that I had won.

Some background information might be helpful before attempting an interpretation. At this point in my life, I was doing a lot of self-examination and soul-searching and was questioning God concerning my "right standing" with Him. With this thought in mind, let's take a look at the dream. First, the indirect phone call (my wife answering and receiving the message instead of me) is God answering my questions through my dream. My wife represents my carnal mind, which receives the dream and passes the message on to my conscious mind as I awake. As I consciously pray and meditate upon the dream, I perceive the interpretation, which in turn edifies my spirit.

Second, winning something like a lottery or sweepstakes usually refers to being unexpectedly favored and blessed. Finally, the interpretation of the number 26,800 is: *Twenty-six thousand* means "the image has been judged as mature and acceptable." (How do I know that it's accepted? I won, remember?) *Eight hundred* means that the old self (carnal nature) has been fully put off. If the number *seventy-six* was the correct amount (I wasn't sure that I remembered the number correctly when I awoke), it confirms that the image was not only accepted, but was also complete (mature). So God was reassuring me during this time of self-doubt and self-examination that I was indeed *"...accepted in the beloved"* (Eph. 1:6).

The Fullness of Hundred

I'm sure you have noticed that I interpreted the number *eight hundred* as *"fully* put off." Like *ten*, *hundred* is also a unit of measure. It means "fullness." Now that we know the base numbers and the concept of measurement, it's easy to understand the meaning of the hundreds: fully begun (one hundred), fully judged (two hundred), fully conformed (three hundred), and so forth.

In Judges 7:2-7, God wouldn't allow Gideon to fight for Him until He had first reduced Gideon's army to three hundred men. Why? Gideon had to fully conform to God's plan before He would use him. With this concept in mind, look again at Enoch's age—three hundred sixty-five (see Gen. 5:23). *Three hundred* means that he was fully conformed. *Sixty* means that *what* he was conformed to was God's immaculate, though invisible, image (and God's image *is* acceptable!), and *five* refers to Enoch's service. So Enoch's age revealed that *God fully accepted Enoch's person and his works.* When God fully accepts the Church, He'll take us to Heaven too! The proper understanding of *hundred* would have saved many ministers a lot of embarrassment not too long ago. When the "prosperity move" was in its prime, the saints were promised that God would restore their offerings to them one hundred times over. One of the Scriptures used to persuade them to give was Mark 10:29-30:

> *And Jesus answered and said, Verily I say unto you, There is no man that hath left house, or brethren, or sisters, or father, or mother, or wife, or children, or lands, for My sake, and the gospel's, but he shall receive an* **hundredfold** *now in this time, houses, and brethren, and sisters, and mothers, and children, and lands, with persecutions; and in the world to come eternal life.*

The problem is, God will not fulfill a promise He didn't make. The Bible doesn't say God would *multiply* their return by one hundred. *Hundredfold* means "full return," not one hundred times as much. God is saying that if you give, leave, or lose something for His Kingdom's sake, in the long run you will not have lost anything because He will fully repay you. We receive back with the same measure we give, as Jesus said in Luke 6:38: *"Give, and it shall be given unto you... For with the same measure that ye mete withal it shall be measured to you again."* That Scripture doesn't actually mention an increase either; it says, "same measure." *Same* means "same," not more. When Isaac sowed and received a hundredfold return in Genesis 26:12, he received a *full* harvest. Even though there was a famine at the time, his crop wasn't affected. He reaped a full harvest because he sowed in obedience. Now a full harvest is certainly more than the seed planted, so notice that I'm *not* saying that God won't give you an increase; I'm just saying that *hundredfold* doesn't mean what some endorsers of the "prosperity move" said it meant.

To fully complete our abbreviated list for hundreds: *four hundred* implies full dominion; *five hundred* indicates full service; *six hundred* portrays a full image; *seven hundred* means completely full; *eight hundred* is fully put off; and *nine hundred* refers to a full harvest.

The Maturity of Thousand

Thousands are interpreted in the same way that hundreds are. *Thousand* is a unit of measurement like *ten* and *hundred* and refers to "maturity." So *one thousand* is "the beginning of maturity," and *two thousand* is "mature judgment." That's the reason Joshua told the people to stay two thousand cubits behind the priest when they went to cross the Jordan and enter Canaan. They were to use mature judgment in following their leaders (see Josh. 3:4). *Three thousand* refers to being "maturely conformed," as Paul mentions in Ephesians:

> *Till we all come in the unity of the faith, and of the knowledge of the Son of God, unto a perfect [mature] man, unto the measure of the stature of the fulness of Christ* (Ephesians 4:13).

Four thousand refers to "mature rule" and *five thousand* to "mature service." Using the same line of reasoning, *six thousand* is "a mature image," *seven thousand* is "simply mature," because one who is complete is mature. *Eight thousand* relates to "a mature attitude toward the cross," and *nine thousand* indicates "the fruit is ready for harvest."

Six Hundred Threescore and Six

Now, before we conclude this chapter, what about John's infamous 666 that we mentioned earlier? First, let's examine the passage in Revelation where John talks about 666:

> *And I beheld another beast coming up out of the earth; and he had two horns like a lamb, and he spake as a dragon....Here is wisdom. Let him that hath understanding count the number of the beast: for it is the number of a man; and his number is Six hundred threescore and six* (Revelation 13:11,18).

John identifies the beast as a man. Since we know that this is an evil man, we also know the symbolism used here is negative. Thus, the interpretation is simply this: *Six hundred* describes a *full* image, *sixty* means a *rejected* image, and *six* portrays an *image*, which John plainly declared is the image of man. So, in the same way that Christ was the express image of the invisible God, this beastly man will be the warped image of the invisible devil. He will *fully* reflect satan's *despicable image*.

Numbers to Live By

In the preceding chapter, we learned that *one thousand* through *nine thousand* reveals the measure of our maturity in many different areas of our lives. In the same manner, *ten thousand* through *nineteen thousand* measures things to determine their size, whether they are large or small. Even intangible things, like wisdom, might, or degree of difficulty can be measured. For instance, *ten thousand* can mean something very large, like an expansive business. It can also mean a very difficult trial—large insurmountable problems that simply won't go away, giant problems such as Israel faced when challenged by Goliath. Goliath was big trouble, but not too big for God. He defeated him through a little shepherd boy.

A Ten Thousand Dollar Dream

Understanding dreams can help defeat our Goliaths, too! I own a small boat, motor, and trailer. Once, when my outboard motor wasn't running right, I asked a mechanic how much he would charge to fix it. He said the repair would cost $55 an hour and would take about two hours. Besides needing the motor repaired, I was facing a lot of other problems too. Even my ministry wasn't going very well. About a week later, before I had the motor repaired, God began dealing with me about fasting, and during that time, I had this dream:

My outboard motor needed repair so I pulled my boat to a new marine dealer in town. Even though the dealer was closed, I left my boat in his driveway, which was rutted and rough. When I returned, I greeted the dealer and told him that I came to get my boat. I decided to ask him how much he would charge to repair it. I was thinking that he might be cheaper than the first mechanic who had already given me an estimate. But when I asked his price, he answered $10,000. I was aghast and informed him that the other dealer would fix it for only $110. (In my mind, I was figuring two hours at $55 an hour.) After consideration, the new dealer agreed to repair it for $85.

When I awoke, I realized that God was saying that my circumstances (my unhitched boat parked on a rough driveway) wasn't going to improve without repairs. The $10,000 was the insurmountable problems that I was facing at the time: debt, sickness, low income, stalled ministry, and so forth. The $110 was the trial I was in—the test I had to pass. Adding up the two hours at $55 each was counting the cost and making the decision to go ahead and pay the price (do the "work" of fasting) to fix the problems. Of course, the dealer represented the Lord, who was agreeing to repair the problems if I would work at putting off the flesh by going on an acceptable fast. (*Eighty* signified "putting off," and *five* indicated "work" or "fasting.") Thus, God confirmed what I was already feeling in my spirit— I needed to fast to overcome the enemy's opposition. (For an acceptable fast, see Isaiah chapter 58.)

Twenty Thousand

If *ten thousand* can mean a big trial, then couldn't *twenty thousand* mean something very, very holy or maybe a very big decision that has to be made? Consider these Scriptures:

*The chariots of God are **twenty thousand**, even thousands of angels: the Lord is among them, as in Sinai, **in the holy place*** (Psalm 68:17).

*Or what king, going to make war against another king, sitteth not down first, and **consulteth whether he be able** with ten thousand to meet him that cometh against him with **twenty thousand**?* (Luke 14:31)

Besides having to make a big decision, that king had better make a wise one, too! Can you also see a big trial coming in that Scripture?

Thirty Thousand

Now what about *thirty thousand?* See if you can determine something conformed, accepted, mature, and large in the following passage:

> *So Joshua arose, and all the people of war, to go up against Ai: and Joshua chose out thirty thousand mighty men of valour, and sent them away by night* (Joshua 8:3).

In case you had difficulty, *thirty* is "accepted and conformed." (*Chosen* shows acceptance, so *thirty* is "acceptably conformed.") *Thousand mighty men* implies "greatness" and *men of valour* refers to "maturity in battle." So Joshua accepted those who were (as Paul put it) *"strong in the Lord, and in the power of His might"* (Eph. 6:10b).

Forty Thousand

Forty thousand is quite similar, but the emphasis isn't just on a larger kingdom; instead, it emphasizes "wise rule." This fits the Scripture above where the king needed to make a wise decision about whether or not he should go to war. Words like *skillful* and *expert* are used in conjunction with this number. The following Scripture bears this out:

> *The sons...of valiant men, men able to bear buckler and sword, and to shoot with bow, and **skilful** in war, were **four and forty thousand** seven hundred and threescore, that went out to the war* (1 Chronicles 5:18).

The additional numbers also reveal that these warriors were completely conformed to an acceptable image. Likewise, the following use of *forty thousand* reveals an extraordinary ability to wage wise warfare: *"And of Asher, such as went forth to battle, expert in war, **forty thousand**"* (1 Chron. 12:36).

And while we're studying *forty thousand,* how about the controversial "hundred forty and four thousand" of Revelation 14:1-3?

Very few understand this Scripture:

> *And I looked, and, lo, a Lamb stood on the mount Sion, and with Him an hundred forty and four thousand, having His Father's name written in their foreheads. And I heard a voice from heaven, as the voice of many waters, and as the voice of a great*

thunder: and I heard the voice of harpers harping with their harps: and they sung as it were a new song before the throne, and before the four beasts, and the elders: and no man could learn that song but the hundred and forty and four thousand, which were redeemed from the earth (Revelation 14:1-3).

It's not the count, but the meaning of the number that tells the story. These people represent all the redeemed warriors of God's Kingdom—multitudes of them! These are the leaders, God's holy and righteous apostles and prophets, who rule with Him over His Kingdom.

Fifty Thousand

Let's review the basics in preparation for discussing *fifty thousand*. *Five* means "service" or "work," and *fifty* reveals that our works are tried (by fire), as Paul said in First Corinthians 3:13:

Every man's work shall be made manifest: for the day shall declare it, because it shall be revealed by fire; and the fire shall try every man's work of what sort it is.

As we've seen, *ten* and *thousand* are units of measure, *ten* meaning to "test" or "weigh," and *thousand* meaning "mature." But when a number is brought to the fifth place and becomes *ten thousand* or above, the thought of largeness is always involved in the interpretation. Comparing *fifty* to *fifty thousand* is like comparing a grocery cart to an eighteen-wheeler. So if *fifty* speaks of our daily testing and fiery trials, then *fifty thousand* is talking about a mighty big fire!

In fact, *fifty thousand* falls right in line with the other numbers we've studied. *Fifty* indicates the "quality of service," whether it's accepted or rejected, and *thousand* measures its quantity. So when God tried Israel's service, sometimes He rejected it with horrible consequences:

And [God] smote the men of Bethshemesh, because they had looked into the ark of the Lord, even He smote of the people fifty thousand and threescore and ten men: and the people lamented, because the Lord had smitten many of the people with a great slaughter (1 Samuel 6:19).

And sometimes Israel's service was excellent and thus graciously accepted by the Lord, as shown in this Scripture:

Of Zebulun, such as went forth to battle, expert in war, with all instruments of war, fifty thousand, which could keep rank: they were not of double heart (1 Chronicles 12:33).

Likewise, God's presence mightily testified of the righteous works of those who burned their idols in the New Testament. I find it interesting that fire was also used along with *fifty thousand* in this passage:

Many of them also which used curious arts brought their books together, and burned them before all men: and they counted the price of them, and found it fifty thousand pieces of silver. So mightily grew the word of God and prevailed (Acts 19:19-20).

Sixty Thousand

The meaning of *sixty thousand* agrees with what we've already learned about the reverse image of God. That is, our image just doesn't agree with God. I think it gives Him indigestion. There are only two passages in the entire Bible where *sixty thousand* is used. We only need to look at one of them to establish its meaning:

And it came to pass, that in the fifth year of king Rehoboam Shishak king of Egypt came up against Jerusalem, because they had transgressed against the Lord, with twelve hundred chariots, and **threescore** [sixty] **thousand** *horsemen.... And he took the fenced cities which pertained to Judah, and came to Jerusalem. Then came Shemaiah the prophet to Rehoboam, and to the princes of Judah, that were gathered together to Jerusalem because of Shishak, and said unto them, Thus saith the Lord, Ye have forsaken Me, and therefore have I also left you in the hand of Shishak* (2 Chronicles 12:2-5).

God was greatly displeased with His people at this time. Israel simply did not reflect His likeness.

Seventy Thousand

When King David committed the sin of pride by numbering Israel, God sent a plague and destroyed seventy thousand of David's subjects. David threw himself upon the mercy of the court, but God would not relent until His judgment was complete:

And David said unto Gad, I am in a great strait: let me fall now into the hand of the Lord; for very great are His mercies:

but let me not fall into the hand of man. So the Lord sent pestilence upon Israel: and there fell of Israel seventy thousand men. And God sent an angel unto Jerusalem to destroy it: and as he was destroying, the Lord beheld, and He repented him of the evil, and said to the angel that destroyed, It is enough, stay now thine hand... (1 Chronicles 21:13-15).

Although in this Scripture *seventy thousand* specifically relates to *complete* recompense for David's transgression, it can relate to anything where the measure is large and complete.

Eighty Thousand

The principle of thousands relating to largeness remains consistent throughout the Bible. In the following Scripture, *eighty thousand* refers to a failed attempt to bring an entire kingdom under one rule:

*And when Rehoboam came to Jerusalem, he assembled all the house of Judah with the tribe of Benjamin, one hundred and **eighty thousand** chosen men who were warriors, to fight against the house of Israel, **that he might restore the kingdom** to Rehoboam the son of Solomon* (1 Kings 12:21 NKJV).

It was a vain attempt to fully restore the whole kingdom to Rehoboam. It was vain because God was the one who cast off his rule:

Thus says the Lord: "You shall not go up nor fight against your brethren the children of Israel. Let every man return to his house, for this thing is from Me." Therefore they obeyed the word of the Lord, and turned back, according to the word of the Lord (1 Kings 12:24 NKJV).

Ninety Thousand

So far, we've been able to show scriptural examples for almost every number we've discussed, but regretfully, *ninety thousand* is not in the Bible. So we'll assume that the established pattern remains unchanged. If we follow the same train of thought that we've seen in the previous eight numbers, *ninety thousand* refers to a very large harvest, as will occur at the end of the world:

Be patient therefore, brethren, unto the coming of the Lord. Behold, the husbandman waiteth for the precious fruit of the earth, and hath long patience for it, until he receive the early and latter rain. Be ye also patient; stablish your hearts: for the coming of the Lord draweth nigh (James 5:7-8).

A Countless Multitude

I wonder if God decided not to number the harvest because it's *so* large! And if He had used *ninety thousand* in reference to it, some feebleminded person would have surely tried to restrict entrance into Heaven to just those few—simpletons discouraging the faith of the simple. In fact, there are some people who think that only one hundred forty-four thousand will make it. However, John saw so many in Heaven that no one could count them:

*After this I beheld, and, lo, **a great multitude, which no man could number**, of all nations, and kindreds, and people, and tongues, stood before the throne, and before the Lamb, clothed with white robes, and palms in their hands; and cried with a loud voice, saying, Salvation to our God which sitteth upon the throne, and unto the Lamb. And all the angels stood round about the throne, and about the elders and the four beasts, and fell before the throne on their faces, and worshipped God, saying, Amen: Blessing, and glory, and wisdom, and thanksgiving, and honour, and power, and might, be unto our God for ever and ever. Amen.*

And one of the elders answered, saying unto me, What are these which are arrayed in white robes? and whence came they? And I said unto him, Sir, thou knowest. And he said to me, These are they which came out of great tribulation, and have washed their robes, and made them white in the blood of the Lamb. Therefore are they before the throne of God, and serve Him day and night in His temple: and He that sitteth on the throne shall dwell among them. They shall hunger no more, neither thirst any more; neither shall the sun light on them, nor any heat. For the Lamb which is in the midst of the throne shall feed them, and shall lead them unto living fountains of waters: and God shall wipe away all tears from their eyes (Revelation 7:9-17).

This Scripture passage was just too beautiful to leave out a single word! I believe it reveals there will be a great number more than just 144,000 in Heaven, don't you?

Attractive Opposites

Occasionally, God uses repetition when He talks with us. Sometimes He uses it for emphasis and sometimes for other reasons. When Peter first began ministering, he ministered only to Jews. When it came time to start ministering to Gentiles, his religion got in his way. He was a Jew, and Jews didn't believe that Gentiles could be saved. But God had other ideas. So He spoke to Peter in a vision about his error. He sent him the same fax three times (see Acts 10:9-20). He wasn't just trying to emphasize His message; He was telling Peter to conform to what He was revealing to him.

On another occasion, God gave Pharaoh two dreams having the same meaning. Joseph interpreted the dreams, informing Pharaoh that the dreams were given in two forms because the matter would surely come to pass. The message of Pharaoh's dream contained good news and bad news. The good news? There's good times ahead. The bad news? They won't last! And besides that, God even revealed to Pharaoh when the market was going to crash (see Gen. 41:1-7,32-36)! God is no respecter of persons, and He doesn't change. He still warns those He loves about trouble ahead. Sometimes He uses numbers in the process.

To know what God is saying, we must understand His way of using numbers. I mentioned previously that He has a unique way of revealing *opposites* in numbers. *Eleven* through *nineteen* are simply opposite of *one* through *nine*.

Eleven—Last or End

One means "beginning"; *eleven* means "end" or "last." In one of Jesus' parables, He hired several laborers at the eleventh hour of the day. When it came to quitting time, He told His foreman to pay them *first*, because they were hired *last* (see Matt. 20:6).

Joseph was pretty sharp when it came to interpreting dreams, but not at first:

> *And he* [Joseph] *dreamed yet another dream, and told it his brethren, and said, Behold, I have dreamed a dream more; and, behold, the sun and the moon and the* **eleven** *stars made obeisance to me* (Genesis 37:9).

As mentioned before, sometimes a symbol has a double meaning. If he had understood more about numbers, Joseph probably would have guessed, or at least suspected, that his brethren wouldn't bow down to him until much later in life. In fact, he represented Jesus, and Jesus' brethren still haven't bowed to Him.

They won't until the eleventh hour, when they say, *"Blessed is He that cometh in the name of the Lord"* (Luke 13:35b). And again, God used *eleven* twice in Deuteronomy 1:2-3 to emphasize the fact that Israel's wilderness journeys were over:

> *(There are* **eleven** *days' journey from Horeb by the way of mount Seir unto Kadesh-barnea.) And it came to pass in the fortieth year, in the* **eleventh** *month, on the first day of the month, that Moses spake unto the children of Israel....Ye have dwelt long enough in this mount....go in and possess the land...* (Deuteronomy 1:2-3,6-8).

Twelve—Unity or Government

One and *eleven* are easy to see. But what about *two* and *twelve?* They're also opposites. Two means "divide"; *twelve* means "join." It's really that simple. But someone is sure to balk here and say, "No way—*twelve* means 'government!'" And it does, but only through implication. One of the primary purposes of government is to unify people. The root meaning of *twelve* is "join" or "unity," not "government." When interpreting the number *twelve*, "government" doesn't always fit. Good government produces unity, but unity doesn't always produce government.

Unity and *government* are closely related, but the difference between them when substituted for the number *twelve* can be readily seen in the following example. After Jesus fed the five thousand with bread and fish, His disciples, *"took up of the fragments that remained twelve baskets full"* (Matt. 14:20b). They gathered them up, uniting them after they were scattered—exactly what God is doing with His sheep. The purpose of church government is to unite the sheep, joining them to God through Christ. Without this understanding, the primary reason for using *twelve* as a symbol for government is lost.

Thirteen—Change or Rebellion

Compared to *two* and *twelve*, *three* and *thirteen* are easy! If *three* means "conformed," *thirteen* means to "change" and, by extension, "rebel." This is confirmed at the very first mention of *thirteen* in the Bible. There were five kings joined together and for *"twelve years they served Chedorlaomer, and in the thirteenth year they rebelled"* (Gen. 14:4; see also Gen. 14:1-3). It doesn't get any plainer than that! I believe that's the reason the United States of America began with thirteen colonies. We started in rebellion—or was it revolution? Anyway, I hope it doesn't end that way. Another good Scripture demonstrating the meaning of thirteen is Jeremiah 25:3:

> *From the **thirteenth** year of Josiah the son of Amon king of Judah, even unto this day, that is the three and twentieth year, the word of the Lord hath come unto me, and I have spoken unto you, rising early and speaking; but ye have not hearkened.*

If I can take the liberty to paraphrase here, Jeremiah's message says something like this: "From the time of your rebellion...even unto this day I have conformed—listened—to Him and judged you as rejected by Him, continually warning you, but you have not hearkened."

Fourteen—Double or Duplicate

By now you may be able to figure out *fourteen* through *nineteen*, but some of those numbers are rather difficult to interpret without an in-depth study. *Fourteen* is a good example of this difficulty; it means "double" or "duplicate." As we learned, *four* means "rule" or "reign," but it also includes the thought of the subjects who are ruled over—in other words, the whole kingdom. That makes it a little harder to identify its opposite. In fact, before we can explore the full meaning of *fourteen*, we must examine another concept concerning the teens, including *eleven*.

The Fruit of the Garden

You have read that the meanings for *eleven* through *nineteen* are opposite the base numbers, but it's not always quite that simple. Sometimes there's a little more to it than that. As we mentioned before, the interpretation of some of the teens is actually the result of applying the original numbers. Or the teen numbers can be compared to the *fruit* of a garden planted with the nine base numbers. Looking at *thirteen* and *three*, we see that rebellion and conformity are indeed opposites, but more than opposites, rebellion is the *result* of (forced) conformity.

God is the Alpha and the Omega, the beginning and the end. When He starts something, He finishes it. Therefore, if something has a beginning, it usually has an end. One produces the other. When we divide something, we often end up with two united wholes. For example, all the people in Heaven, and all the people in hell. When people are forced to conform, eventually they will rebel. When one man rules over another, the result is that he doubles or duplicates himself through his subject. An employer doubles her labor through an employee; a teacher replicates his knowledge in his students; a musician duplicates her skills in her protégé, and so forth. So a kingdom is the result of a king being duplicated in his subjects; his labor, his knowledge, his character—all are portrayed throughout his kingdom. That's the root meaning of *fourteen*, and that's the stated purpose of *the* King! King Jesus said, *"Verily, verily, I say unto you, He that believeth on Me, the works that I do shall he do also; and greater works than these shall he do..."* (John 14:12).

Before Elijah was taken up into Heaven, he asked his servant Elisha what he could do for him as a reward for his faithfulness. Elisha seized the opportunity and asked for a double portion of Elijah's anointing. During Elijah's ministry he performed seven recorded miracles. Although Elisha had been promised a double portion, he performed only thirteen miracles during his lifetime. But God is faithful. After Elisha died and was buried, some soldiers threw a dead man into his tomb. When the dead man touched Elisha's bones, he revived and arose from the dead. Therefore, Elisha was given his fourteenth miracle, completing his double portion as promised (see 2 Kings 13:21).

The following Scripture also reveals that *fourteen* is the doubling of *seven*:

And at that time Solomon held a feast, and all Israel with him...
*before the Lord our God, **seven days and seven days, even four-***
teen days (1 Kings 8:65).

And after satan destroyed Job's livestock, including seven thousand sheep, God restored his herd, giving him twice as much as he
had before:

And the Lord turned the captivity of Job, when he prayed for his
*friends: also the Lord gave Job **twice** [double] as much as he had*
*before....for he had **fourteen** thousand sheep...* (Job 42:10,12).

God commanded Moses to hold the Passover feast on the fourteenth day of the first month of the year (see Exod. 12:6). Why? Because Christ our Passover is sacrificed for us, and through Him we
become like Him (see 1 Cor. 5:7). Jesus said, *"...Every one that is per-*
fect shall be as his master" (Luke 6:40b). In other words, He duplicates
Himself in and through us. *"Herein is our love made perfect, that we*
may have boldness in the day of judgment: because as He is, so are we in
this world" (1 John 4:17).

Fifteen—Grace or Salvation

Fifteen isn't quite so complicated. It refers to "grace." For instance, God was gracious enough to raise Hezekiah from his deathbed
and extend his life fifteen extra years after he became sick. And as an
added gesture of His marvelous grace, He *saved* Jerusalem from being
attacked by the king of Assyria:

Go, and say to Hezekiah, Thus saith the Lord, the God of David
thy father, I have heard thy prayer, I have seen thy tears: behold, I
*will add unto thy days **fifteen** years. And I will deliver thee and*
this city out of the hand of the king of Assyria: and I will defend
this city (Isaiah 38:5-6; see also 2 Kings 20:6).

I might add that *grace* is more than "unmerited favor," as it is
so often defined. It's also God's divine ability reflected in people
(see 1 Pet. 4:10-11).

Sixteen—Free Spirit or Likeness

Sixteen isn't quite as straightforward as *fifteen*. What exactly is the
opposite of an image, anyway? Answer? *A free spirit, without bounds.*
Isn't that what your teenage son thinks he is? (Just kidding!)

The opposite of an image is whatever made the image in the first place. *Six* is like a mirror image. A mirror reverses the image it produces. God produced our flesh in His image. That means flesh is His opposite. (Boy, does that ever fit!) That's why it gives Him so much trouble! The image, our carnal self, cannot even obey Him (see Rom. 8:7). Once we understand that, we can see that the opposite of the image is the likeness of the One who produced it—God. And God is indeed a free Spirit. We might say that *six* often relates to the outward person, while *sixteen* relates more to the heart. Now that's not a steadfast rule, but it helps us better understand the relationship between the two. Another way of thinking about *sixteen* is simply "likeness." Remember, God made us in His image *and* likeness. They're not the same thing.

Seventeen—Incomplete or Immature

Tackling *seventeen* is easy compared to the last three. It simply means "incomplete" or "immature." The opposite of the meaning of *seven* ("complete") is "incomplete." The normal result of becoming a mature adult is to reproduce a baby who is immature, the opposite of the parent. Probably the best scriptural example showing the meaning of *seventeen* is Joseph. He was seventeen years old when he had his first dream about his brothers bowing down to him. In his immaturity, he didn't know that he shouldn't tell them! He learned quickly though; his brothers were good teachers (see Gen. 37:2-5). He was thirty-nine years old before his dreams came to pass. He was considerably more mature by then. And no, his age isn't listed in the Bible, but one can accurately compute it by the information given. You can also almost guess it by simply understanding the meaning of numbers!

Eighteen—Put On or Overcome

Eighteen is another easy one. It means "put on." Jesus used it in this way on two different occasions during His ministry. The first time referred to God's judgment falling upon some sinful people:

> *Or those **eighteen**, upon whom the tower in Siloam fell, and slew them, think ye that they were sinners above all men that dwelt in Jerusalem?* (Luke 13:4)

The second was concerning a woman whom satan had bound:

And, behold, there was a woman which had a spirit of infirmity ***eighteen*** *years, and was bowed together, and could in no wise lift up herself.* [After delivering and healing her, Jesus said,]... *Ought not this woman, being a daughter of Abraham, whom satan hath bound, lo, these* ***eighteen*** *years, be loosed from this bond on the sabbath day?* (Luke 13:11,16)

Nineteen—Lack or Ashamed

Nineteen is also simple, but needs a little more explanation. Because *nine* means "fruit" or "harvest," *nineteen* simply means "no fruit" or "no harvest." When there is a lack of fruitfulness, we call the land barren. In the Old Testament, when a woman was barren, she was ashamed. So by implication, *nineteen* can also mean "ashamed." Joab's army had defeated the army of Abner, but when the battle was over and Joab was able to gather his people together, he discovered that he had lost nineteen men and Asahel:

And Joab returned from following Abner: and when he had gathered all the people together, there ***lacked*** *of David's servants* ***nineteen*** *men and Asahel* (2 Samuel 2:30).

Joab may not have been ashamed, but he certainly couldn't have been proud of his accomplishments; he lost his brother Asahel in the battle.

In review, every symbol has a root meaning. Because we're talking about numbers, we can say that each symbol should be reduced to its common denominator—the root. Each root grows branches, and sometimes, even branches grow branches. But once we determine the root, we can easily follow the chain of deduction that leads to each branch, as you can see in the following summary, which includes the primary implied meaning along with each root: *Eleven* is "last" or "end"; *twelve* is "unity" or "government"; *thirteen* is "change" or "rebellion"; *fourteen* is "double" or "duplicate"; *fifteen* is "grace" or "salvation"; *sixteen* is "free spirit" or "likeness"; *seventeen* is "incomplete" or "immature"; *eighteen* is "put on" or "overcome"; and *nineteen* is "lack" or "ashamed." As you see, each extended branch is closely related to its root or source.

CHAPTER 8

Simple Solutions

Eleven Hundred

The meanings of other round numbers in the hundreds and thousands follow the same line of reasoning that we've uncovered in the preceding five chapters. If *eleven* is last, then *eleven hundred* has to be the last of the last. In fact, *eleven hundred* appears only three times in Scripture, and all three times it refers to the root of all evil—silver. The Greek phrase translated "love of money" in Paul's famous saying, *"The love of money is the root of all evil..."* is literally translated "fondness for silver" (1 Tim. 6:10).

Delilah betrayed Samson for eleven hundred pieces of silver (see Judg. 16:5). I'm sure her disloyalty earned her a place on the tail end of his list of favorites.

The other two references to eleven hundred pieces of silver are also found in Judges. The silver is rather tarnished here, too. It became a curse unto Israel because they used it to make a molten image:

> *And he [Micah] said to his mother, "The **eleven hundred** shekels of silver that were taken from you, and on which you put a curse, even saying it in my ears—here is the silver with me; I took it."... So when he had returned the **eleven hundred** shekels of silver to his mother, his mother said, "I had wholly dedicated the silver from my hand to the Lord for my son, to make a carved image and a molded image; now therefore, I will return it to you"* (Judges 17:2-3 NKJV).

After they cursed the silver and made an idol out of it, it's obvious that God put it last on His list, too. He doesn't seem to like idols very much.

Twelve Hundred

Twelve hundred is quite unique. Although *twelve* is mentioned 132 times in the Bible, *twelve hundred* occurs only once:

> And it came to pass, that in the fifth year of king Rehoboam Shishak king of Egypt came up against Jerusalem, because they had transgressed against the Lord, with **twelve hundred** chariots, and threescore thousand horsemen: and the people were without number that came with him out of Egypt; the Lubims, the Sukkiims, and the Ethiopians (2 Chronicles 12:2-3).

Twelve means "unity," and this multitude was certainly unified against Jerusalem. By the way, this Scripture is also a good example where the root meaning works well ("unity"), but the branch meaning ("government") just won't fit. There are a couple other numbers in this Scripture that are worth noticing—*five* and *sixty thousand*. This was a big operation against Jerusalem. God turned the bad and the ugly loose on them and left out the good altogether.

It looks like we've just run out of numbers. *Eleven hundred* is used three times; *twelve hundred* once; and *thirteen hundred* through *nineteen hundred* are not even in the Book. But if we stay on track, we can figure out what they all mean.

Thirteen Hundred

Thirteen means "rebellion," and *hundred* is "fullness," so *thirteen hundred* simply means "fullness of rebellion." This number brings to mind a revelation that God gave me many years ago. God is reluctant to destroy a person or nation until they have fully rebelled against Him. Once they do, they reach a point of no return, and He has no other recourse but to destroy them. That's the reason He commanded Israel to kill everyone in Canaan. Their cup of iniquity was so full that there was no room for redemption.

God actually waited four hundred years before sending Israel into the land. He told Abraham that his grandchildren would have to wait in Egypt for awhile; *"But in the fourth generation they shall come hither again: for the iniquity of the Amorites is not yet full"* (Gen. 15:16).

Fourteen Hundred Through Nineteen Hundred

Fourteen hundred covers "the whole kingdom"; *fifteen hundred* means "fullness of grace" or "radically saved"; *sixteen hundred* is "free as a bird"; *seventeen hundred* means "just a baby"; *eighteen hundred* is "pressed down and running over" (or "bankruptcy," whichever comes first); and *nineteen hundred* is "totally lacking in whatever counts." Now, what about the *thousands*? Let's take a look.

Eleven Thousand

In the same way that we were able to figure out the *hundreds*, we can discover the meaning of the *thousands*. Although *eleven thousand* is not in the Bible, *eleven* means "last" and *thousands* speak of "maturity" (completeness). The concept of largeness that we previously discovered is also retained in these numbers. Using this definition, *eleven thousand* should mean something like "the end of time." Maybe that is why God hasn't used it. We're not there yet.

Twelve Thousand

Twelve thousand is used thirteen times in Scripture and the very first Scripture reveals its meaning, *"So there were delivered out of the thousands of Israel, a thousand of every tribe, twelve thousand armed for war"* (Num. 31:5). Here we see beautiful unity, complete unity, every tribe perfectly represented and joined together for a common cause.

Another Scripture showing complete unity is this one: *"And so it was, that all that fell that day, both of men and women, were twelve thousand, even all the men of Ai"* (Josh. 8:25). It's obvious that they all died together, every one of them.

Thirteen Thousand

Thirteen thousand is not in the Bible either, but that's understandable; God already killed all of them because they fully rebelled back in *thirteen hundred.* (Just kidding!) *Thirteen thousand* simply means complete rebellion. Although the number isn't mentioned, one Scripture that shows how God feels about rebellion is Deuteronomy 21:18-21:

> *If a man have a stubborn and rebellious son, which will not obey the voice of his father, or the voice of his mother, and that, when*

*they have chastened him, will not hearken unto them: Then shall
his father and his mother lay hold on him, and bring him out
unto the elders of his city, and unto the gate of his place; and
they shall say unto the elders of his city, This our son is stubborn
and rebellious, he will not obey our voice; he is a glutton, and a
drunkard. And all the men of his city shall stone him with stones,
that he die: so shalt thou put evil away from among you; and all
Israel shall hear, and fear.*

Fourteen Thousand

As for *fourteen thousand,* the Scripture that captures the meaning
best of all is Job 42:12:

*So the Lord blessed the latter end of Job more than his beginning:
for he had **fourteen thousand** sheep, and six thousand camels,
and a thousand yoke of oxen, and a thousand she asses.*

Fourteen means "double," and in this Scripture, God is doubling
back to Job everything he lost (which was *everything*) during the horrible trial he endured. Job received full compensation. Before going on
to another Scripture that further illustrates God's use of *fourteen thousand,* let's examine a little background information about His penalty
for sin. First look at Isaiah 40:2:

*Speak ye comfortably to Jerusalem, and cry unto her, that her
warfare is accomplished, that her iniquity is pardoned: **for she
hath received of the Lord's hand double for all her sins.***

Also notice Jeremiah 16:18: *"And first I will recompense their iniquity and their sin double; because they have defiled my land...."* And
finally, Jeremiah 17:18: *"Let them be confounded that persecute me...
and destroy them with double destruction."*

Notice that in each case, just as God reimbursed Job double for his
righteousness, these people were recompensed double for their *iniquity.*
Now, with that thought in mind, let's look at another Scripture:

*But on the morrow all the congregation of the children of Israel
murmured against Moses and against Aaron, saying, Ye have
killed the people of the Lord. ...And Moses said unto Aaron...go
quickly unto the congregation, and make an atonement for them:*

*for there is wrath gone out from the Lord; the plague is begun. ... Now they that died in the plague were **fourteen thousand and seven hundred**, beside them that died about the matter of Korah* (Numbers 16:41,46,49).

They troubled Moses and Aaron, so God visited them with double trouble or, as Jeremiah said, *"double destruction."* Of course, *seven hundred* means that God's judgment was a full and complete "recompense of reward" for their sin (see 2 Thess. 1:6; Heb. 2:2-3).

Fifteen Thousand

Fifteen thousand is used only once in the Bible, and it refers to the last stronghold that Gideon defeated when by the grace of God he delivered Israel in the days of the judges. In this passage it signifies complete salvation:

*Now Zebah and Zalmunna were in Karkor, and their hosts with them, about **fifteen thousand men, all that were left of all the hosts of the children of the east**: for there fell an hundred and twenty thousand men that drew sword* (Judges 8:10).

Sixteen Thousand

The way God uses *sixteen thousand* in Numbers is ingenious:

*And all the gold of the offering that they offered up to the Lord, of the captains of thousands...was sixteen thousand seven hundred and fifty shekels. (For the men of war had taken spoil, **every man for himself**)* (Numbers 31:52-53).

Sixteen means "free spirit," and of course, *thousand* means "complete," so "completely free" is the picture or, as God puts it, "every man for himself." Now, is that neat or what?

Seventeen Thousand

Seventeen thousand is a contradiction of terms. *Seventeen* means "incomplete" or "immature," and *thousand* means "mature." Figure that one out! This number is used only once in the Bible, and there it emphasizes the *thousands* viewpoint and ignores *seventeen*. Curious? Look it up (see 1 Chron. 7:11).

Eighteen Thousand

Eighteen thousand is no problem. In Second Samuel 8:13, David fought against the Syrians, and as we say in the South, "He evermore put one on them!" *"And David gat him a name when he returned from smiting of the Syrians in the valley of salt, being eighteen thousand men."* This number was also used during one of Israel's many civil wars:

> *And Benjamin went forth against them...the second day, and destroyed down to the ground of the children of Israel again eighteen thousand men; all these drew the sword* (Judges 20:25).

Although the tribe of Benjamin eventually lost, before going down, the little tribe got in one last hit on Israel. The full implication of this civil strife isn't clear until you get to Judges 21:3, *"And said, O Lord God of Israel, why is this come to pass in Israel, that there should be to-day one tribe lacking in Israel?"* As a result of their fighting among themselves, Benjamin came within a hair's breath of being completely destroyed.

Nineteen Thousand

And now we come to the end. Last, but not least, that is. Although it's not mentioned in the Bible, *nineteen thousand* means "totally ashamed," "fully useless," "completely drained," "utterly barren," and so forth.

A Simple System

In summary, *eleven hundred* and *eleven thousand* are similar, as are *twelve hundred* and *twelve thousand*, all the way through *nineteen hundred* and *nineteen thousand*. There are minor differences, but they're mostly in quantity, not quality. As you can see, there are really only nine numbers to learn. Then, by learning to measure these base numbers by tens, hundreds, and thousands, you can achieve full understanding of the system. For the opposites, or results, you need only reverse the root meanings. And so, you can master the entire numerical system in short order. Simple, isn't it?

Coloring Within the Lines

Many dreams are in technicolor, but not all. Most dreamers are unaware that part of what they dream is in grayscale; they only notice certain things that are colored. Splashes of color give added meaning to our dreams and are every bit as significant as numbers. But searching out their meanings poses a slight problem. We learned the meaning of numbers directly from the Bible, but colors are a little different. Several important colors cannot be found in the Bible. The Bible is not exactly printed in grayscale, but it doesn't have pastels, either. In fact, it's a lot like our dreams; it only uses colors when they're needed to supply specific information. That gives us a clue. We can use the Bible to learn how God uses colors and then use the same reasoning to stay within the lines when interpreting colors of our own.

In Chapter 1, we discussed the four ways that symbols obtain meaning: inherent characteristics, personal experience, culture, and Scripture. When we studied numbers, we used Scripture as the sole basis for our definitions. These definitions came directly from creation and God's dealings with humanity. But in passing, we noted that culture also influences the meaning of certain symbols used in the Bible. So does inherent character. In fact, the primary characteristic of many symbols is a direct product of creation. A wolf devours lambs naturally, and lambs are defenseless by nature. Because inherent character is also used to determine the meaning of symbols in Scripture, we should consider it when searching for the meaning of colors, whether within or without Scripture.

Since there is no linear order to colors, when possible we will discuss them in the order suggested by the inherent characteristics given to them in creation. In the beginning, God started with darkness and then made light. We'll begin the same way. Darkness is the absence of light; black is the absence of color. So we'll ride in on a black horse right out of the pages of the Bible.

Black Is Lack

There are probably few passages of Scripture more controversial than the four horses of the apocalypse. One of those horses is black:

> *And when He had opened the third seal, I heard the third beast say, Come and see. And I beheld, and lo **a black horse;** and he that sat on him had a pair of balances in his hand. And I heard a voice in the midst of the four beasts say, A measure of wheat for a penny, and three measures of barley for a penny; and see thou hurt not the oil and the wine* (Revelation 6:5-6).

Although we want to avoid the aforementioned controversy, you should know that this passage refers directly to the terrible famine prophesied by Amos that occurred during the Dark Ages:

> *Behold, the days come, saith the Lord God, that I will send a famine in the land, not a famine of bread, nor a thirst for water, but of hearing the words of the Lord* (Amos 8:11).

The balances the rider was holding measured food, but not much of it. It was famine portions. A penny was a full day's wages, and a measure of wheat only one meal. During that spiritual famine, people worked all day for just one meal.

Because darkness is the absence of light, when light appears, darkness disappears. So the primary meaning of *black* is "lack." Ignorance is the lack of knowledge, so *black* may indicate "ignorance." In our culture, it's also the color used to recognize "death."

We wear it to funerals to signify our grief over losing a loved one. Death is the absence of life; subsequently, "death" is an extended meaning of *black*.

Black often means bad news, such as the report that Job received when satan destroyed his flocks and children (see Job 1:13-18). Job also used *black* to describe his condition when he was physically afflicted, *"My skin is black upon me, and my bones are burned with heat"* (Job 30:30).

Another way to envision the meaning of *black* is to think of the black darkness of night and what happens during that time, as we see in Proverbs 7:9-10:

In the twilight, in the evening, in the black and dark night. And, behold, there met him a woman with the attire of an harlot, and subtle of heart.

So *black* can mean "wickedness," "evil," "sin," "famine," "grief," "death," "ignorance,"—they're all ugly! However, almost all symbols have both positive and negative meanings. Therefore, black can also mean beautiful, *"I am **black**, but comely, O ye daughters of Jerusalem..."* (Song of Sol. 1:5). If that wasn't true, Ford and Chevrolet wouldn't make so many black cars.

In addition, the opposite of lack is substance, so *black* can also indicate "substance." In fact, it can mean the very opposite of drought and famine—abundance! An example? Read what happened when Elijah prayed for rain:

And it came to pass [as Elijah prayed] *at the seventh time, that he* [his servant] *said, Behold, there ariseth a little cloud out of the sea, like a man's hand. And he said, Go up, say unto Ahab, Prepare thy chariot, and get thee down, that the rain stop thee not. And it came to pass...that the heaven was **black** with clouds and wind, **and there was a great rain**...* (1 Kings 18:44-45).

Blue Is Spiritual

Next comes *blue*. It's very similar to *black* and also has a double meaning. First, *blue* is the color of the sky on a beautiful day, so it means "heavenly." In the beginning God created the blue heavens and the earth (see Gen. 1:1). Aaron wore a beautiful blue robe every time he went into God's presence, signifying that he was entering into the heavenly realms. *"And thou shalt make the* [priest's] *robe of the ephod all of blue"* (Exod. 28:31). Aaron's robe was part of *"the patterns of things in the heavens..."* (Heb. 9:23b).

The blue sky is composed of air, which symbolizes spirit, so *blue* can mean "spirit" or "spiritual." In fact, that is one of the most common usages that I've encountered. It also appears to be the root meaning, although these two, *heavenly* and *spiritual*, are often interchangeable, because that which is heavenly is spiritual. (Some spiritual things aren't heavenly, so the reverse isn't always true.) Jesus said that His words were spirit; therefore, another branch for *blue* is God's Word (see John 6:63). For example, a blue washcloth may refer to, *"the washing of water by the word"* (Eph. 5:26b) or spiritual cleansing.

Mentioning water, another part of God's marvelous creation is the deep blue sea. Anyone who has ever seen satellite pictures of the earth is struck by its beauty. The lofty, swirling clouds and the seas' awesome blue colors are spellbinding. In certain passages of Scripture, the sea represents either God or humanity, depending on the context, and the sea's color reinforces this symbolism. Isaiah declared, *"The earth shall be full of the knowledge of the Lord, as the waters cover the sea"* (Isa. 11:9b). But he also compared it to wicked and sinful men, *"But the wicked are like the troubled sea, when it cannot rest, whose waters cast up mire and dirt"* (Isa. 57:20). Then he used it as a symbol for the Gentile nations, *"...the abundance of the sea shall be converted unto thee, the forces of the Gentiles shall come unto thee"* (Isa. 60:5).

Returning to the subject of the sky, God's Spirit is *always* heavenly; human spirits are not. Neither are people always happy. When they're sad, we say they are "singing the blues." So instead of heavenly, *blue* may indicate that someone is down in the dumps. A very light shade of *blue* sometimes indicates the spirits of people, while any shade of *blue* can symbolize God's Spirit.

In another instance, after a friend of mine died, I once dreamed that I saw a picture of her. Her dress was an incredibly beautiful deep blue. As I watched, I saw her picture ascend out of sight. I awoke knowing that she was with God, eternal in Heaven.

In that dream, *blue* represented salvation. It can also mean healing. *"The blueness of a wound cleanseth away evil..."* (Prov. 20:30). But when one considers that *blue* often symbolizes God's Spirit and sometimes His Word, that's not too surprising. After all, *"He sent His word, and healed them,"* didn't He? (Ps. 107:20a). When painted objects are used as symbols, the paint's condition is also symbolic. Whether the paint is glossy or dull, off-color or the wrong color (pale horse, blue elephant, etc.) means one thing or another. So a light blue house with paint that is chipped and peeled may represent someone wounded or offended. It's not uncommon for a house to represent its owner, and in this instance, the decaying paint job may denote the need for spiritual repairs. Because *blue* is considered a "cool" color, it could even be saying that the person who lives there has grown cool toward others. These principles of paint condition, dark and light shades, and right or wrong color apply throughout the spectrum. A whole rainbow of colors exists with many different shades of meaning.

A Bow in the Cloud

Speaking of rainbows, the rainbow itself has a beautiful meaning. It denotes a covenant, an everlasting covenant:

> *I do set My bow in the cloud, and it shall be for a token of a covenant between Me and the earth.... And the bow shall be in the cloud; and I will look upon it, that I may remember the everlasting covenant between God and every living creature of all flesh that is upon the earth* (Genesis 9:13,16; see also Hebrews 13:20).

The full spectrum of God's love and wisdom is seen through the knowledge He gave Paul. Paul fans out love's many dimensions the way a prism spreads light's brilliant colors (see 1 Cor. 13). Also, he mentions the spectrum of God's wisdom in Ephesians:

> *His intent was that now, through the church, the manifold wisdom of God should be made known to the rulers and authorities in the heavenly realms* (Ephesians 3:10 NIV).

The Greek word translated *manifold* means "variegated," like the many colors of the rainbow. We'll take a peek through Paul's prism as we continue our colorful examination.

More Shades of Blue

Getting back to *blue*, since *blue* can represent God's Spirit, by extension it can also represent His love because God *is* love. And the fact that He's the God of peace, *blue* can symbolize "peaceful." Similarly, God is light, and as we've already discussed, *blue* symbolizes His Word because His Word is light. Then, there's always the traditional meaning—baby boys dressed in blue. With so many possible definitions to choose from, it's not hard to see that one should pay very close attention to the context in which *blue* is used before trying to decide exactly what it conveys.

Color Combinations

One more thought before we move on. Sometimes we dream of a combination of colors—*black and blue*, for instance. If someone takes a pounding, we may say, "He was beaten black and blue." It's a good way to describe a severe beating, and it can certainly mean that in a dream, too. *Black* signifies pain and suffering and *blue* a sorrowful spirit. As we continue, we'll see more combinations and find that *black* is more often than not the second color.

Green Equals Life

Although at this point we could go in several different directions, we will follow the order of creation. After God made the heavens and the earth, spoke light into existence, and divided the waters, He covered the earth with greenery.

> *And God said, Let the earth bring forth grass, the herb yielding seed, and the fruit tree yielding fruit after his kind, whose seed is in itself, upon the earth: and it was so* (Genesis 1:11).

The first plant mentioned here is grass. The world is covered with grass on every continent and every nation. Live grass is green, and the root meaning for *green* is "life." One can tell whether grass is alive or not by simply noticing if it is green. When it turns brown, it's dead.

Trees and most other plants are also green. Some plants stay green throughout the seasons; others lose their leaves in fall and wait for spring before being resurrected into new life. Herein lies a clue—*green* can denote resurrected life. Likewise, an evergreen tree may mean eternal life, because it never dies and stays green continuously; it appears to be everlasting.

In a negative sense, *green* can refer to the temporal state of humanity's flesh. Peter said, **"For all flesh is as grass, and all the glory of man as the flower of grass. The grass withereth, and the flower thereof falleth away"** (1 Pet. 1:24).

Jesus also used *green* to signify His flesh. When they were leading Him to Golgotha to crucify Him, He said, *"For if they do these things in a green tree, what shall be done in the dry?"* (Luke 23:31). So *green* and *grass* have much in common. The inherent characteristics of grass determine the symbolic meanings of both *grass* and *green*. The green color of grass indicates that it is alive. It multiplied and covered the whole earth, even as Adam was commanded to do. And when some grasses and other similar evergreen plants defy the seasons and refuse to die, they imitate eternity and give us a unique symbol for everlasting life.

Brown and Tan

As mentioned, when grass dies, it turns brown. In the same way that green grass indicates life in its different forms, its color in "death" reveals the root meaning for *brown*. In essence, *brown* is the opposite of *green*—death instead of life. When we live in the flesh, we are *green*. When we repent and die to sin, we turn *brown*. A repentant person is humble. Therefore, *brown* often denotes "humility" or one who is lowly. By extension, *brown* can also mean "common," "ordinary," or "poor," like a person carrying a sack lunch in a brown paper bag. *Tan* is simply a lighter shade of brown and denotes a similar meaning. In fact, *tan* is the color of desert sand and has the connotation of barrenness. Repentance is sometimes indicated by tan clothing or shoes.

Christmas Colors

There is another color closely associated with green—*red*. At first glance there seems to be no connection between the two, other than they are used together as decorations at Christmas time. However, the connection comes from the fact that *red* is conceived as a "warm" color and *green* often refers to "flesh."

Red denotes "passion." A passionate suitor buys red roses for his beloved. A matador waves a red cape before a charging bull. An angry person is said to be "seeing red." All these portray the concept of passion, and passion is one of the characteristics of flesh. Therein lies the connection. *Green* corresponds to flesh; subsequently *red* and *green* can indicate passionate flesh. Ever watch a child on Christmas morning?

Another common use for red is on stop signs and red lights. Interestingly enough, *green* signifies "go," while *red* means "stop." By extension, *red* can mean "danger," as in the bull charging the matador's cape above. And if the bull connects, the matador's blood may run red, giving us one more metaphor for *red*—*"blood."* Blood can mean so many things that we'll not even discuss the subject in this book, except to give its basic, root meaning—*"life."* So red's danger signal can even include loss of life. In fact, the red horse of Revelation 6:4 portrayed just that—persecution and martyrdom:

*And there went out another **horse that was red:** and power was given to him that sat thereon to take peace from the earth, and that they should kill one another: and there was given unto him a great sword.*

Danger Signals

Speaking of danger, watch out for *orange!* "Danger" may not be the primary meaning, but I've discovered that in many dreams, "danger" is a very common interpretation for *orange.* In fact, one of nature's primary warning colors is bright orange. South America has brilliant orange frogs that are so poisonous the natives use them as a source of poison for their hunting darts. Orange and black monarch butterflies are poisonous. And who wouldn't run from a tiger? Of course, not all orange creatures are dangerous. But every symbol has its opposite, doesn't it?

The root meaning for *orange* is "energy" or "power." Power is inherent in many orange things that God created. The earth's primary source of energy, the sun, was made on the fourth day and is rather orange in color. Closer at hand, fire is a chief source of power and it's usually orange. It can be dangerous, too. Fire is often associated with spiritual power. In Acts 1:8, Jesus told His disciples that they would receive power after the Holy Ghost came upon them, and in Acts 2:3-4, they did. Flames of fire were seen resting upon them when that happened. Those flames were probably orange.

One dream that particularly interested me was a dream where a woman and her family were attacked by fierce dragons. She discovered that her only effective defense was oranges! Even pieces of the oranges were sufficient to ward them off. The interpretation? If Golden Delicious apples can stand for wise counsel, as in Proverbs 25:11, *"A word fitly spoken is like apples of gold in pictures of silver,"* then couldn't a bag of oranges represent God's powerful promises, such as Psalm 91:13? *"Thou shalt tread upon the lion and adder: the young lion and the dragon shalt thou trample under feet."*

A Dangerous Combination

You may have noticed the color combination of the Monarch butterflies and tigers mentioned previously. Orange often spells trouble, but when combined with black, it's just plain bad news! Pay attention. It's nearly always a warning! On the other hand, it can spell bad news for the devil, too. The Holy Ghost baptism has really given him a hard time. I once dreamed about one of the old-time, Holy Ghost-filled preachers, and God compared him to a tiger in my dream. The orange and black stripes were plain to see. In another dream:

> I bought an antique sports car. I paid $350 for it. I was going to have it painted. I could see the colors in my mind's eye—bright fire orange with a black top! The paint job was expected to cost me $700. (I'm not sure that I've finished paying for it yet!)

A Clear-cut Combination

Now that we've returned to the subject of black color combinations, there is no doubt that *black and white* is the most common combination of all. And there's a very common meaning for it—"right and wrong." Have you ever heard someone say something like, "He won't compromise. With him, everything's either black or white"? *Legalistic* is another word for it, or *opinionated*. Of course, to that person, it's clear-cut; there are simply no gray areas. But we'll get to *gray* in a second. On the positive side, *black and white* can be saying, "Hey, can't you see? It's plain as day!"

Sometimes "salt and pepper" depicts integration—mixing it up. At other times, as when we speak of a black and white movie, we are simply referring to lack of color. And whether we're awake or dreaming, the word *color* can mean "flavor." So the *lack of color* can mean "mundane," "dull," "uninviting," "boring," and so forth, but dreams usually depict this with *gray* instead of *black and white*.

A "Gray" Area

Gray can mean "confusion," like being in a gray fog or without clear guidelines or boundaries. It's not unusual to hear someone say, "That's a gray area; I'm just not sure what to do there."

Smoke is *gray*, too, and "Where there's smoke, there's fire." So gray smoke can warn you of trouble brewing, or worse, let you know what just happened:

> *And he* [Abraham] *looked toward Sodom and Gomorrah, and toward all the land of the plain, and beheld, and, lo, the smoke of the country went up as the smoke of a furnace* (Genesis 19:28).

Just how gray is *gray?* The shade of gray depends on the amount of black and the amount of white mixed together. The more black, the darker the gray, and vice versa. So noticing whether something is simply a little off-white, or a darker shade of gray, can be informative when interpreting your dreams.

Pure White

As already discussed, the opposite of *gray* is clear-cut, distinct, without doubt or hesitation; it's either *black* or *white*. If it's *white*, it's "pure" and "righteous altogether"—or "pure evil"! In the Old Testament, God taught Moses how to determine if leprosy was cured or not:

> *And the priest shall look on the plague in the skin of the flesh: and when the hair in the plague is turned* **white**, *and the plague in sight be deeper than the skin of his flesh, it is a plague of leprosy: and the priest shall look on him, and pronounce him* **unclean** (Leviticus 13:3).

Some people have a way of "getting under your skin." When you're offended by them, you suffer from spiritual leprosy. It's contagious! And strangely enough, contrary to many Christians' belief that *white* means "right" ("righteousness," that is), in this Scripture, *white* portrays a plague and its uncleanness. But even Christians sometimes tell "little white lies," so they shouldn't be surprised that *white* has its opposite, too.

In fact, that brings up another use for *white* that I've encountered in dreams a little too often—"self-righteousness." Like a pregnant bride in a white wedding gown, we usually try to hide the truth about ourselves, sometimes even from our own selves. God reveals it to us in private dreams so that He won't have to humble us publicly.

White is mentioned in Genesis four times, and it's used negatively one out of the four: *"When the chief baker saw that the interpretation* [of another man's dream] *was good, he said unto Joseph, I also was in my dream, and, behold, I had three* **white** *baskets on my head"* (Gen. 40:16). But his white baskets meant bad news. Joseph correctly interpreted them to mean three days before the baker would be hanged by Pharaoh.

The Bible doesn't mention *white* in the record of creation, but there certainly were a large number of *white birds* created on the fifth day. The Holy Spirit is usually depicted as a *white dove*. On the other hand, a *white goose* can mean "pure stupidity"; as the saying goes, "He's like a goose;

he wakes up in a new world every day." And yet still, a *white swan* needs no explanation. Its natural beauty and gracefulness says it all.

None More Precious Than Gold

The only color actually found in the record of the original creation is gold. The river that watered the Garden of Eden had four branches: *"The name of the first is Pison* [meaning "increase" in Hebrew]...*where there is gold; and the gold of that land is good..."* (Gen. 2:11-12).

When the Bible says, *"the gold of that land is good,"* it implies there's gold of other lands that's not so good. *Gold* means "glory." From the beginning, God shows us that all "glory" is not good. Or as Jeremiah puts it, *"Thus saith the Lord, Let not the wise man glory in his wisdom, neither let the mighty man glory in his might, let not the rich man glory in his riches"* (Jer. 9:23). Why? Because God has decreed, *"That no flesh should glory in His presence.... [Instead] He that glorieth, let him glory in the Lord"* (1 Cor. 1:29,31). The gold of God's original creation is not only good, but it's God's! *"The silver is Mine, and the gold is Mine, saith the Lord of hosts"* (Hag. 2:8).

God doesn't really care for the natural gold; He doesn't need it. He made it for people. Just don't take His! It may be hazardous to your health:

> *And upon a set day Herod, arrayed in royal apparel, sat upon his throne, and made an oration unto them. And the people gave a shout, saying, It is the voice of a god, and not of a man. And immediately the angel of the Lord smote him, because he gave not God the glory: and he was eaten of worms, and gave up the ghost* (Acts 12:21-23).

Self-glorification is a snare, both for the fools who glorify themselves and for those who foolishly honor the fools. *"For if there should come into your assembly a man with gold rings...and you pay attention..."* (James 2:2-3 NKJV). Instead, we're supposed to, *"Mind not high things, but condescend to men of low estate. Be not wise in your own conceits"* (Rom. 12:16b), but *"...be clothed with humility..."* (1 Pet. 5:5).

Although the root meaning for *gold* is "glory," it has a lot of other meanings, too. One is "wealth," because of gold's great value, and by extension, "prosperity." When Moses brought Israel out of Egypt, they hadn't gone far before God called Moses up on the mountaintop to give him the Ten Commandments. While Moses was gone, Aaron took the Israelites' gold earrings and formed them into a golden calf to worship (see Exod. 32:2-8). He used their *earrings* to signify that he was telling them what they wanted to hear. We have some Aarons in our day, too.

Aaron also used *gold* earrings because *gold* meant wealth. He made them a golden *calf* because cattle signified prosperity. Cattle was their livelihood. When the herds increased, they had a "bull market." When bears ate the cattle, they lost their wealth, and the first "bear market" was born. Things haven't changed much in church *or* in the market, have they? Another meaning for *gold* is "rare," because God didn't create much of it. That's why it's so valuable. And one of the simplest and most often used extensions is "wisdom." We sometimes act like He didn't create much of that, either. In fact, when people are *"Professing themselves to be wise, they* [become] *fools"* (Rom. 1:22).

Actually, most rich people glory in their wisdom more than in their money. We've come to think that the two go together. It's not too unusual to hear the sarcastic remark, "If you're so smart, why aren't you rich?" So if I'm rich, I must be smart, right? On the other hand, dreaming of finding gold coins may mean that you really are getting smarter. God may use the symbol of *gold* to confirm that He's giving someone the spirit of wisdom and revelation.

There are several more symbolic meanings for *gold*. Even silence can be golden. But at the right time, so can words: *"A word fitly spoken is like apples of gold in pictures of silver"* (Prov. 25:11). Another common meaning for *gold* is "unchanging." Gold doesn't tarnish. It's one of the few things in nature that doesn't change. That is one of the reasons gold makes good idols. It even qualifies as a stand-in for God. He never changes. However, neither does the devil. He's always greedy. He's always trying to steal God's glory and make it his own because his own glory is *fools' gold*.

Gold is one of two things that either gets its name from its color or gives its color its name; I'm not sure which. In dreams, *gold* is *gold* regardless of whether you're talking about the color or the metal. If you dream something is *gold* in color, or something is made of *gold*, basically, it means the same thing. On the other hand, if something is gold-plated, it may not be as valuable as it first appears. If it's solid gold, it's as valuable as it can get—24 carat—genuine. "Glory," "wealth," and "prosperity"; treasures of "wisdom" and "knowledge"; "wise counsel" and "unchanging riches"; "beauty" and "value"—all are embodied in *gold*.

The Search for Silver

Silver is the other unique color/metal that gets its name from its color or gives its color its name. *Silver* means "knowledge." There are few things clearer in Scripture than the definition of *silver:*

> *Yea, if thou criest after* **knowledge,** *and liftest up thy voice for understanding; if thou seekest her as* **silver,** *and searchest for her as for hid treasures; then shalt thou understand the fear of the Lord,* **and find the knowledge of God** (Proverbs 2:3-5).

From this Scripture one can readily see that dreaming of finding silver coins, cups, bowls, and so forth, can represent receiving knowledge. With this thought in mind, the passage, *"A word fitly spoken is like apples of gold in pictures of silver"* (Prov. 25:11) becomes even more significant.

Silver and Gold

The *silver* background for the *golden* apples represents "adequate knowledge of the situation being addressed." Wisdom plus knowledge equals understanding. Both Proverbs and Paul placed these three sisters together:

> *That their hearts might be...knit together...unto all riches of the full assurance of understanding...of the mystery of God, and of the Father, and of Christ; in whom are hid all the treasures of wisdom and knowledge* (Colossians 2:2-3).

Notice Paul's use of the metaphors, *"riches...of understanding"* and *"treasures of wisdom and knowledge."* One's treasure makes one rich. Likewise, wisdom and knowledge combined gives us, "full assurance of understanding," which is faith! Now isn't that interesting?

Like *gold, silver* color and *silver* metal mean about the same thing. Unlike *gold, silver* tarnishes. This gives an added dimension to *silver* as a symbol. Some things need constant polishing, especially relationships! Combinations of *gold* and *silver* may be used to portray wisdom and knowledge as a team. Gold and silver tapestry and clothes are not uncommon in dreams. But clothes don't always mean what you might think. Sometimes people clothe themselves with spirits. Paul admonished the Roman church, *"But put ye on the Lord Jesus Christ"* (Rom. 13:14a). One can wear the devil, too, *"As he clothed himself with cursing like as with his garment, so let it come into his bowels like water...*" (Ps. 109:18). And as we mentioned before, we're supposed to be clothed with humility. In fables and sometimes in dreams, the spirit of death comes wearing a black, hooded cloak. In contrast to this, dreaming of someone wearing a beautiful gold and silver suit or robe may indicate that he or she is clothed with wisdom and knowledge.

Royal Purple

Royal robes are usually *purple*, embroidered in *gold*. The reason? The *purple* stands for the king's "royalty" and the *gold* trim his "glory." *Purple* also implies "virtue": *"He that ruleth over men must be just, ruling in the fear of God"* (2 Sam. 23:3b). That's the idea, but beware; Jezebel can wear purple, too.

Like virtue, in Bible days purple dye was valuable because it was comparatively rare. Paul encountered a virtuous woman on his second missionary journey:

> *And a certain woman named Lydia, a seller of purple, of the city of Thyatira, which worshiped God, heard us: whose heart the Lord opened, that she attended unto the things which were spoken of Paul* (Acts 16:14).

Blushing Brides and Hot Pink Shorts

Pink is another color closely associated with clothing. Little baby girls dressed in *pink* are the epitome of "sweetness" and "innocence." Another distinct meaning is "chaste" or "modest." And who hasn't heard of a blushing bride? In another sense, *pink* may indicate that "God has fulfilled one of His promises":

> *A new heart also will I give you, and a new spirit will I put within you: and I will take away the stony heart out of your flesh, and I will give you an* [pink] *heart of flesh* (Ezekiel 36:26).

The opposite of "chaste" and "modest" is "lascivious." For instance, a girl in hot-pink shorts may imply "passion" and "lust." Potiphar's wife was probably dressed that way when she tried to tempt Joseph.

The Hidden Meaning of Yellow

Last, we come to *yellow*. *Yellow* is an interesting color for several reasons. Like the others, it has several different, though related, meanings.

However, the root meaning isn't apparent at first. In fact, it's somewhat hidden.

Of the two times *yellow* is used in the Bible, one is in reference to the plague of leprosy and the other is Psalm 68:13: *"Though ye have lain among the pots, yet shall ye be as the wings of a dove covered with silver, and her feathers with yellow gold."*

Of course, the dove symbolizes the Holy Spirit. And that gives us the key we need to unlock the hidden meaning of *yellow*. The Holy Spirit is a gift—*yellow* means "gift!" I know the Church usually pictures the dove as white, but the Bible doesn't. It describes it as yellow and silver! (*Silver* fits perfectly, too. The *gift* is the Spirit of *Truth!*)

Yellow can also represent the opposite—the devil's evil gifts. God gives us the Comforter; the devil gives us the spirit of fear. A coward is declared to be "yellow," but why? How did *yellow* become associated with fear? The Bible says, *"For God hath not **given** us the spirit of fear; but of power, and of love, and of a sound mind"* (2 Tim. 1:7). If God has not *given* us the spirit of fear, then where does it come from?

Besides the Holy Spirit, *yellow* can be a symbol for God's other gifts too. One night I dreamed of a yellow rose garden smothered in weeds. I sensed the need for some workers to do the weeding. After I awoke and meditated on what it could mean, God gave me the interpretation. He showed me the church needed more marriage counselors. In this dream, God's gift of marriage was depicted as yellow roses. We usually think of red roses when we think of romance; but the dream's emphasis wasn't romance, but rather the *gift* of marriage. *"And Jesus answering said unto them, the children of this world marry, and are **given** in marriage"* (Luke 20:34). And as with every other gift that God gives, He expects us to keep the weeds out of it.

Although of a different type, another gift God has given us is the discerning of spirits (see 1 Cor. 12:10). Once, as I was preparing to teach a seminar for a church where I hadn't ministered before, I had this dream:

> I and a friend named Jim C. walked into a large, strange building. We were looking for snakes. Jim said that simply seeing them wasn't sufficient; we had to smell them. As we walked in, I saw two snakes on my left. I noticed that I couldn't smell them. Both snakes were white in color with light yellow heads. Then I saw two more. I counted four altogether. One snake stood out among the rest. This snake had a large nose like a parrot's beak

and it began crawling toward me. I sensed that it could crawl very fast. I asked Jim if it was a parrot beak snake, and he said no, it was a horn nosed snake. As we went further into the building, we saw a meat display case with what I thought were pork chops in it; except these chops were made from cotton mouth snakes instead of pork. Jim picked up one and held it up to show me that it was harmless and good to eat. Then I awoke.

In this dream, Jim C. represents Jesus. He's my friend and instructor throughout the dream, and his initials are a dead giveaway. We were looking for snakes, which represent demons. As the dream clearly revealed, we can't go by what we see (we walk by faith, not by sight); we must smell (discern) them instead. The first *two* snakes indicated the need to judge or discern; their yellow heads referred to a gift, which in this case, portrayed the gift of discerning of spirits. I had trouble smelling them, but Jim didn't.

Also, I didn't know what kind of snake the most prominent one was. I thought it was a parrot beak snake, which would be a spirit of deception. (Parrots mimic, and a mimic deceives others by pretending to be something that he's not.) Instead, this snake was a horn nosed snake! A horn represents authority, as does four. (There were four snakes in all.) In other words, God was showing me that the church I was preparing to minister in had a large, swift, witchcraft spirit operating in it.

Then He showed me that I was not to worry. I would not be harmed by the experience, but instead it would be good food for me. Although in the natural, a cotton mouth is very poisonous; when dealing with spiritual serpents, God promised, *"Nothing shall by any means hurt you"* (Luke 10:19b).

Even as God admonished Israel when they were about to enter Canaan, God used this dream to admonish me, *"Neither fear ye the people of the land; for they are bread* [food] *for us..."* (Num. 14:9b). Even before I went to this church, I knew what I would encounter when I got there, and I had the promise of victory. After I arrived, although it wasn't clear at first, before long I discerned the spirit which the dream warned me about.

Of course, *yellow* can also warn us of impending danger in the same way that yellow traffic lights caution us to slow down at intersections. And finally, a traditional use of *yellow* is the bright yellow ribbons people attach to their doors and tie to their gate posts to welcome home-comers. I'm not sure where this custom came from, but because it's part of our culture, it shouldn't be ignored when interpreting dreams.

Draw Out the Colors

Then there's lavender, mauve, beige, violet, and dozens more shades and colors that we simply don't have the space in this book to write about. However, if you dream of one, simply apply the same type of reasoning that I've used here. As you meditate, simply ask yourself, *Of what does this color remind me? What was I feeling when I dreamed about it?* Often, the answers will be clues. In every case, there's something within the dreamer's own consciousness or experience that will help solve the riddle. Like sweet water from a deep well, it has to be drawn out. *"Counsel in the heart of man is like deep water; but a man of understanding will draw it out"* (Prov. 20:5).

CHAPTER 10

Homing in on God's Will

Several years ago I worked as a serviceman for a major appliance company. During that time, I was responsible for an out-of-town service route. Once, I was sent on a service call to a small town in central Louisiana; my directions read, "14 miles from Dry Prong on Highway 167." Since that highway runs north and south through town, I could go either way. When I reached Dry Prong, I stopped and called the dispatcher who originally took the directions and asked for clarification. She said, "Try north." I did, and it was wrong. In fact, I had driven right past the customer's house on the way into town. Because of the indefinite directions, I drove a total of 56 unnecessary miles that morning before finally finding the correct house.

Vague, imprecise directions not only waste time and resources, they also can be quite frustrating! Trying to do the will of God when you're uncertain as to exactly what it is can be equally frustrating. In Ephesians 5:17 Paul said, *"Wherefore be ye not unwise, but understanding what the will of the Lord is."* We might think, *Yeah, Paul, that's easy for you to say....* Nevertheless, it's obvious that God expects us to know His will, and the only possible way that can happen is if He reveals it to us. So He does. But even though His directions are usually quite precise, they aren't always understood.

He is continually making His will known using several different methods. One of His favorite methods is dreams. In fact, directions are given in several different forms using many different symbols. Compass directions, right and left turns, and even front and back yards give clear directions once the symbolism contained within them is understood. In this chapter, we will identify directions as they are given in the Bible.

Timing Is Everything

Everyone who serves God for any length of time learns that timing is of critical importance when receiving directions. Like the sons of Issachar, we must learn to recognize the signs of the times. Those who know the times lead the race:

> *And of the children of Issachar, which were men that had understanding of the times, to know what Israel ought to do; the heads of them were two hundred; and all their brethren were at their commandment* (1 Chronicles 12:32).

When interpreting dreams, one of the first questions we should ask ourselves is this: "Is this dream referring to the past, present, or future?" To obtain the correct answer, first examine the dream's setting. Where did it take place? What objects or people took part in it? Often the most important key is in the first scene. If its setting is in the past, the dream is probably pointing backward in time. In other words, God is dealing with the dreamer about the past. Past events affect our present circumstances as sure as old spending habits affect our current bank accounts. Before God can change present conditions, sometimes He has to remind us of whatever brought those conditions into existence in the first place.

The Past

Since our past is behind us, dreaming of something behind us may indicate our past. Our back yards are another simple way of referring to yesterday. Trouble that comes in through the back door is nearly always coming from the past. Although these directions in time are simple, they're often overlooked.

Another purpose God may have for placing something behind us in a dream is to show that it's lurking there. It may indicate something that's hidden from our view. A back room that is closed up and unused may represent something we're unaware of, but more likely portrays something we're avoiding. Sometimes it's a repressed memory. Some things are just too painful to willfully remember. Therefore, God has to prompt us to bring them to mind so that He can deal with them properly. If God wants to point to our childhoods, He may put us in our childhood homes. When He wants to direct us even further back, into our distant past, He may place us in our grandparents' homes. Each place indicates a different period of time. In the case of the grandparents' house, it may even imply time before the dreamer was born.

The Future

Obviously, the opposite of past is future. When a dream refers to our future, we usually say it's prophetic. In the same way that our back yards can reflect our past, our front yards can predict future events. Sometimes these events are current, already in progress; sometimes they are distant, like the promises in Joseph's dreams.

The Bible also reveals another symbol used in dreams to point forward in time—the morning sun. Each day begins with the sun rising in the east; therefore, an eastward direction may indicate "beginning." Also, because God gave the Law before He gave grace, *east* can represent the Law. In fact, there are many Scriptures where this holds true.

In the Old Testament, the Hebrew word for *east* is literally "facing the rising sun," or "in front." Herein lies a clue. That which is before or in front of us is our future. So if God is speaking of time, an eastward direction may be future tense in the same way that our front yards represent that which is ahead of us.

The Present

Before we move westward, let's consider one more thought. Simple deduction says that if the back yard can mean our past and the front yard our future, then our livingrooms may indicate present circumstances. So we have past, present, and future all illustrated by simple, everyday symbols.

Interpreting the Rooms of Your House

While we're on the subject, let's consider other rooms of the house, including the upper and lower floors. First, our houses often represent ourselves. So the things we do within our houses correspond to the things we do within ourselves. We cook up things in the kitchen, which represents our hearts. Jesus said:

> *A good man out of the good treasure of the heart bringeth forth good things: and an evil man out of the evil treasure bringeth forth evil things* (Matthew 12:35).

Even more to the point, the Bible makes a direct comparison between an oven and our hearts: *"For they have made ready their heart like an oven…in the morning it burneth as a flaming fire"* (Hos. 7:6). In like manner, a refrigerator may indicate coldheartedness. Or because we store things in it, it may refer to something tucked away in our memory.

People also store things in the basement, where it's often dark and clammy. This room may portray those deep, dark thoughts we don't want to display in the living room, where everyone visits during the day. Likewise, the upper floor corresponds to those lofty thoughts, wonderful intentions, and high praises to God we entertain at other times. Like the 120 in the upper room, it's a good place to have a visitation from God (see Acts 1:13-14). On the other hand, it's not a good place to fall asleep: *"And there sat in a window a certain young man named Eutychus, being fallen into a deep sleep…fell down from the third loft, and was taken up dead"* (Acts 20:9). Even farther, above the upper floor is the attic, which often refers to one's mind or memory—including things put away and long forgotten.

After each day's work, we rest in our bedrooms. Likewise, Christians rest in the finished work of Christ at the end of their "days" here on earth. People clean themselves in private, using bathrooms, so a bathroom reflects prayer, such as confession and repentance, because that's the way we dispose of the uncleanness (sins) of the flesh. Along the same line of reasoning, the front porch is open to the public; it shows that which is revealed to all. When the dream's emphasis is inside versus outside the house, it may be depicting the concept of being included or excluded, or even saved or lost. Christians are inside while sinners are outside. Or as John put it:

> *Blessed are they that do His commandments, that they may have right to the tree of life, and may enter in through the gates into the city [house]. For **without** are dogs, and sorcerers, and whoremongers, and murderers, and idolaters, and whosoever loveth and maketh a lie* (Revelation 22:14-15).

On the other hand, it's better to be outside if there's evil in the house: *"It is better to dwell in the wilderness, than with a contentious and an angry woman"* (Prov. 21:19).

In many houses there are varied and sundry other rooms—guest rooms; sewing rooms; utility rooms; and in some homes, even trophy rooms. Any one of them can represent something important. Both the floor that the rooms are located on and each room's purpose are meaningful. Of course, where the room is located in the dream may not be where it is located in reality. While we're asleep, God can remodel the house to say whatever He wants it to say. Each symbol can teach us something about ourselves and others we live with. By paying close attention, we can "home" in on God's precise instructions for our lives (pun intended). Just how precise God can be is seen in the following dream had by a Christian lady with marital problems:

> A tornado hit our home without warning. I watched my husband hang onto the windowsill with all his might. I grabbed my children and ran into our deep closet and waited. After the storm was over, we went out and discovered our house had not been destroyed. All kinds of things had been knocked over, yet the house was in one piece.

This dream warned her of a potentially destructive problem coming against her family. At the same time, it showed her what to do when the storm came. It plainly instructed her to run into her prayer closet and wait upon God (pray!). It also contained a promise of victory—in the end, the home was left intact. In fact, not only was it intact, but in "peace."

Sometimes God may use different parts of the house's construction instead of specific rooms or appliances to give instructions. To illustrate, let's examine the foundations: *"If the foundations be destroyed, what can the righteous do?"* (Ps. 11:3) A cracked slab is serious, whether it's literal or spiritual. To prevent its destruction in the coming storms, Jesus admonished us to build our spiritual houses on the solid rock of His teachings:

> *Whosoever cometh to Me, and heareth My sayings, and doeth them, I will show you to whom he is like: he is like a man which built an house, and digged deep, and laid the foundation on a rock: and when the flood arose, the stream beat vehemently upon that house, and could not shake it: for it was founded upon a rock* (Luke 6:47-48).

Dreaming about the foundational issues of our lives can prevent disaster before problems appear and tear our houses apart. Although there are several things that might qualify as "foundational" in our personal lives, when dreaming about the Church, there are only two things specifically declared as foundational in Scripture. One is leadership:

*Now therefore ye are…of the household of God; and are built upon
the foundation of the apostles and prophets, Jesus Christ Himself
being the chief corner stone* (Ephesians 2:19-20).

The other is the seven foundation doctrines of the Church:

*Therefore leaving the principles of the doctrine of Christ, let us
go on unto perfection; not laying again the foundation of repentance from dead works, and of faith toward God, of the doctrine
of baptisms, and of laying on of hands, and of resurrection of the
dead, and of eternal judgment* (Hebrews 6:1-2).

This is God's blueprint for proper construction. Here, the seventh
doctrine (perfection) is named first, as it should be. The other six doctrines are listed in correct order for building the house of God.

Stairs are another part of the house that quite often appear in
dreams. They may suggest the need to "climb up higher" and take
a look in an upper room or even the attic. Steps may also suggest
a process, like the 12 steps of Alcoholics Anonymous. Windows are
another favorite hiding place. Windows can mean anything from revelation knowledge (because they allow light in) to a weakness of our
flesh because they provide an opening for the "thief" to get inside (see
Joel 2:9). An open window may refer to "a window of opportunity,"
or it may simply suggest the need to let in some fresh air. In the Bible,
a window even became a way of escape for Paul when he was being
persecuted: *"And through a window in a basket was I let down by the
wall, and escaped…"* (2 Cor. 11:33). Doors have a similar meaning. Of
course, Christ is *the* Door! (see John 10:9)

Last, our offices, whether within the house or in separate quarters,
may represent our positions or work. It can refer to our secular jobs or
spiritual ministries. Other items within the home are also meaningful:
the washing machine; the iron and ironing board; even the toaster and
the burned toast (but we won't go there!). As we've discussed, the
number, color, position, and use of each item teaches us something,
that is, if we have ears to hear what it has to say.

How Far Is East From West?

Let's move on toward the setting sun. Earlier, I mentioned that *east*
means "beginning," and by extension, it can mean the Law. Since the
opposite of the Law is grace, one meaning for *west* should be obvious.

God said, *"As far as the east is from the west, so far hath He removed our transgressions from us"* (Ps. 103:12). One might ask, "Just how far is east from west, anyway?" The answer? Let's take a look.

We were destroyed by the Law because it imputed sin unto us (see Rom. 5:13). And even the least sin is fatal: *"For whosoever shall keep the whole law, and yet offend in one point, he is guilty of all"* (James 2:10).

Now keep in mind that the Law was before grace, as the sun shines in the east before setting in the west. Jesus said, *"I am the light of the world..."* (John 8:12b). He is the spiritual light even as the sun is the natural light. At His birth, the Magi came, saying, *"Where is He that is born King of the Jews? for we have seen His star **in the east**"* (Matt. 2:2a). He had to arise from the east, because He had to be, *"made under the law, to redeem them that were under the law"* (Gal. 4:4b-5a). Then, in the same way the sun sets in the west at the end of the day, *"in the end of the world...[Jesus] appeared to put away sin by the sacrifice of Himself"* (Heb. 9:26b). So the sun rose under the Law and went down to provide grace. So, how far has He removed our sins from us? Just how far is east from west? As far as the Law is from grace!

Where the Wind Blows

Let's look at some scriptural shadows showing the effects of east and west winds (see Heb. 10:1). Keep in mind these shadows were designed to teach us the devastating effects of the Law. Our first shadow is one of Pharaoh's dreams depicting famine: *"And, behold, seven thin ears and **blasted with the east wind** sprung up...and...devoured the seven rank and full ears"* (Gen. 41:6-7a). The east wind blasted the crop, destroying it. The Law did exactly the same thing to the earth's harvest of souls.

Our second illustration includes one of the many times the Law-giver Himself cursed Egypt:

> *And Moses stretched forth his rod over the land of Egypt, and the Lord brought an east wind upon the land all that day, and all that night; and when it was morning, the east wind brought the locusts....and they did eat every herb...**and there remained not any green thing** in the trees, or in the herbs of the field, through all the land of Egypt* (Exodus 10:13,15).

It's not hard to see the picture here. The locusts devouring every green thing represents the flesh being destroyed by the Law. But afterward, look at what happened to the locusts:

> And the Lord turned a mighty strong **west** wind, which took away the locusts, and cast them into the Red sea; there remained not one locust in all the coasts of Egypt (Exodus 10:19).

Isn't that beautiful? The east wind that cursed the land with locusts represents the spirit of the Law. Paul said the Law is spiritual! But he also said, *"For the law of the Spirit of life in Christ Jesus hath made me free from the law of sin and death"* (Rom. 8:2). The "Spirit of life" destroyed the locusts. Even the parable of the *Red* Sea is superb. God's mighty west wind of grace has removed every destroying law and cast them into the sea of His blood! Not one curse remains! Hallelujah! And this picture was given to us even before Moses gave the Law. God's plan of redemption was finished even before the Law was put into motion.

Lightning From the East

I mentioned that in the Hebrew language, *east* means "facing the rising sun" or "in front." Therefore, it is similar in meaning to your front yard—that which is ahead of you. Something that's imminent may come from the east. A prime example is the Lord's return:

> For as the lightning cometh out of the east, and shineth even unto the west; so shall also the coming of the Son of man be (Matthew 24:27).

In the natural, lightning may shine from any direction on the compass. But the heavenly display of power we're waiting for only comes from the east. Expectancy is another synonym for this direction.

Go West

East means "beginning"; *west* means "end." Similar to *one* and *eleven*, isn't it? Jesus' death was at the end of the age, so by extension *west* can stand for "the cross." Revival comes by way of the cross; therefore, west can signify "revival":

> Ask ye of the Lord rain in the time of the latter rain; so the Lord shall make bright **clouds**, and give them **showers** of rain, to every one grass in the field (Zechariah 10:1).

Those revival showers come right out of the west. Jesus said, *"When ye see a **cloud** rise out of the west, straightway ye say, There cometh a **shower**; and so it is"* (Luke 12:54b).

The Right and Left Hand of God

Everyone knows that a compass needle points north—but not the biblical compass. The Hebrews looked toward the east to orient themselves. Facing east, north is on one's left hand and south is on one's right. These directions are quite significant in the following passage of Scripture:

> *When the Son of man shall come in His glory...then shall He sit upon the throne of His glory: and before Him shall be gathered all nations: and He shall separate them one from another, as a shepherd divideth His sheep from the goats: and He shall set the sheep on His **right hand**, but the goats on the **left**. Then shall the King say unto them on His **right hand**, Come, ye blessed of My Father, inherit the kingdom prepared for you from the foundation of the world.... Then shall He say also unto them on the **left hand**, Depart from Me, ye cursed, into everlasting fire...* (Matthew 25:31-34,41).

Those who are rejected are placed on His left (north) side. Those who are blessed are set on His right (south). Studying this Scripture, we can see that *right* can mean "accepted," and *left*, "rejected."

Peter said that Jesus is on the right hand of God: *"Who is gone into heaven, and is on the right hand of God; angels and authorities and powers being made subject unto Him"* (1 Pet. 3:22). Jesus is not only *on* God's right hand, He *is* God's right hand! He's the visible expression of the invisible God: *"Thy right hand, O Lord, is become glorious in power: Thy right hand, O Lord, hath dashed in pieces the enemy"* (Exod. 15:6). If Jesus is on God's right hand, who is on the left? Obviously, God is! God is a Spirit. Jesus is both supernatural God and natural man. God, the Spirit, is on the left, or north. Jesus, the man, is on the right, or south. *Left* corresponds to that which is *spiritual* and *right* corresponds to that which is *natural*. This is one of the most important directions given to us through the Word of God.

When someone dreams of making a right-hand turn, God is speaking of a natural change. When one makes a left-hand turn, the change is spiritual. The right turn may involve a job or career change or even speak of moving to a new location. The spiritual change may mean anything from salvation to a change in attitude. One of Jesus' "hard sayings" includes this important concept of *right* meaning "natural" and *left* meaning "spiritual." Jesus said:

> *But I say unto you, That whosoever looketh on a woman to lust after her hath committed adultery with her already in his heart. And if thy right eye offend thee, pluck it out, and cast it from thee: for it is profitable for thee that one of thy members should perish, and not that thy whole body should be cast into hell. And if thy right hand offend thee, cut if off, and cast it from thee: for it is profitable for thee that one of thy members should perish, and not that thy whole body should be cast into hell* (Matthew 5:28-30).

Have you ever wondered why He emphasized *"right* eye" and *"right* hand"? A man can lust with his left eye, and a left-handed man steals better with his left hand than with his right! *Right* signifies "natural." Jesus is saying, if you are consumed with natural lust, pluck it out. Getting rid of your right eye won't solve your problem if you still have your left one. But if you remove the lust, you are free. Likewise, getting rid of covetousness will solve the problem of stealing, while losing your right hand just won't do the job. God loves puns, and *right* direction may mean "right choice" or simply "correct." For instance, Jesus is on the right side of God.

Aren't you glad He's not on the *wrong* side? Another example: *On* the right may mean *in* the right. Besides puns, political views may also be included, as in "far right," "right wing," or "left wing." But I'd better keep going before I get "way out in left field."

Out of the North

Jesus is on the right side, and God is on the left or north. The predominate meaning for *north* is "above," in the sense that God is above all. This includes preeminence and sovereignty. God is the judge of all the earth, so a primary extension of *north* is judgment. God's judgment comes out of the north:

> *And the word of the Lord came unto me the second time, saying, What seest thou? And I said, I see a seething pot; and the face thereof is toward the north. Then the Lord said unto me, Out of*

the north an evil shall break forth upon all the inhabitants of the land (Jeremiah 1:13-14).

God rules from His throne, which reveals that His throne is on the north side. The devil's attempts to usurp God's throne requires him to ascend to the north:

> *For thou hast said in thine heart, I will **ascend** into heaven, I will **exalt** my throne above the stars of God: I will sit also upon the mount of the congregation, in the sides of the **north*** (Isaiah 14:13).

God is a spirit, so another branch of *north* is "spiritual." Therefore, "spiritual judgment" is also a legitimate expression for *north*. In the same way that we saw east and west winds can represent the spirits of the Law and grace, a north wind can represent spiritual judgment: *"The north wind driveth away rain: so doth an angry countenance a backbiting tongue"* (Prov. 25:23).

Down South

Conversely, a south wind brings in the natural blessings (or so it would seem). The captain who was given charge of taking Paul to Rome thought so, anyway: *"And when the **south wind** blew softly, supposing that they had obtained their purpose, loosing thence, they sailed close by Crete"* (Acts 27:13). But were they in for a surprise: *"But not long after there arose against it a tempestuous wind, called Euroclydon"* (Acts 27:14). Oh well, it was good while it lasted.

North means "above"; *south* means "beneath" or "down." We reflect this in our everyday sayings of "up north" and "down south." When the stock market crashes and businesses fail, we say the market's "gone south." Abraham went down south and got into *trouble: "And Abraham journeyed from thence toward the south country..."* (Gen. 20:1). Because south and right are synonymous, south can also mean *"natural."* Natural blessings are real, but short-lived. Paul said the things which are seen won't last:

> *While we look not at the things which are seen, but at the things which are not seen: for the things which are seen are temporal; but the things which are not seen are eternal* (2 Corinthians 4:18).

Abraham's brief problem came from pursuing what he could see with his natural eye instead of what God revealed to him through the spirit. *"For he* [Abraham] *looked for a city which hath foundations, whose builder and maker is God"* (Heb. 11:10). He may have been looking for a city, but he was looking in the wrong place. He not only got himself in "hot water," but he also caused trouble for the king. *"But God came to Abimelech in a dream by night, and said to him, Behold, thou art but a dead man, for the woman which thou hast taken; for she is a man's wife"* (Gen. 20:3). It didn't take Abraham long to correct his mistake; the king saw to that.

The Right and Left Way

Another meaning for *right* is "weakness." *Right* signifies "natural," and natural includes flesh. Jesus said the flesh is *weak! "Watch and pray, that ye enter not into temptation: the spirit indeed is willing, but **the flesh is weak"*** (Matt. 26:41). Because the human spirit is ready and willing to serve God, and *left* indicates "spirit," a further extension of *left* is "strength." When Solomon built the temple in Jerusalem, he erected two pillars in the porch. When he set up the right pillar, he *"called the name thereof Jachin,"* meaning "he will establish" in Hebrew. When he set up the *left*, he *"called the name thereof Boaz,"* meaning "in him is strength" in Hebrew (see 1 Kings 7:21).

Paul said, *"I can do all things through Christ which strengtheneth me"* (Phil. 4:13). God illustrated this in the Old Testament by using left-handed men to do superhuman feats:

> But when the children of Israel cried unto the Lord, the Lord raised them up a deliverer, Ehud...a Benjamite, **a man lefthanded**: and by him the children of Israel sent a present unto Eglon the king.... And Ehud said, I have **a message from God** unto thee.... And Ehud put forth his **left hand**, and took the dagger from his **right thigh**, and thrust it into his belly (Judges 3:15,20-21).

Ehud carried the dagger on his right thigh because it signified God's message of natural deliverance; however, he stabbed the king with his left hand because his left represented God's anointing. For most people, the left hand is their weak hand because the majority of people are right-handed. God's strength is made perfect in our weakness (left hand). The right hand represents the arm of flesh or human strength. As we've already pointed out, Jesus said, *"The spirit indeed is willing, but the flesh is weak"* (Matt. 26:41b). In other words, of themselves, people really don't have any strength.

Left can also represent the gifts of the Holy Spirit. To illustrate, let's take a look at some more left-handed Benjamites. First, their ancestor, Benjamin, was Joseph's younger brother. Joseph is a type of Christ. To illustrate: Joseph was his father's favorite son; his brethren turned against him; he was unjustly accused and imprisoned; and finally, he was exalted to Pharaoh's right hand. All of these situations (and more) parallel the life of Jesus. In the same way that Joseph pictures Jesus, Benjamin portrays the Church. Benjamin was found with Joseph's cup, and whoever had Joseph's cup was to become his servant (see Gen. 44:12,17). Likewise, we drink from Jesus' cup and become His servants (see Luke 22:20).

Jesus' servants are to be like their Master: *"The disciple is not above his master: but every one that is perfect shall be as his master"* (Luke 6:40). Jesus knew and accurately revealed the secrets of people's hearts, so we should have the same ability:

> *And the children of Benjamin were numbered.... Among all this people there were seven hundred chosen men **lefthanded;** every one could sling stones at an hair breadth, **and not miss*** (Judges 20:15-16).

We shouldn't "miss" either. We're supposed to be able to hit them right between the eyes:

> *But if all prophesy, and there come in one that believeth not, or one unlearned, he is convinced of all, he is judged of all: and thus are the secrets of his heart made manifest; and so falling down on his face he will worship God, and report that God is in you of a truth* (1 Corinthians 14:24-25).

Sounds like the modern church could use a report like that!

A Dream of Direction

Speaking of the modern church, following is a dream a lady recently had concerning it. Key words are in italics:

> In my dream I was on a porch of a rather large house on a hill overlooking a lake. When I glanced out toward the *western* horizon, toward the lake, I had a fleeting glimpse of a small tornado. It had *rainbow colors* emanating from it. I crouched on the *porch* (which was on the *west side* of the house) and covered my head, preparing for the wind. I don't recall feeling

or hearing the wind. The tornado passed by the house without hurting me or damaging any nearby property.

Next Scene: I was looking out over the lake and saw a large tornado heading toward the house. It was very close. The sky was gray, even though there was a little sunshine. I was calling to the people that were around to take cover, because this tornado was big and moving very fast. It was very windy. I don't recall what everyone else did, but I went *into the house* to take cover. The tornado passed close by the *north* side of the house, but again did no damage. As I looked through a *window*, I saw the tornado move toward the *north*, then up into the sky where it broke into many swirling, separate clouds. The clouds then dissipated, the sky quickly cleared, and the sun came out.

Even though the clouds cleared and the sun came out, I still sensed danger and that everyone needed to be warned. I called the operator to connect me to the police or fire department to sound the warning sirens. The operator was giving me the runaround and wouldn't connect me to the appropriate emergency personnel. I began urgently raising my voice, saying, "Don't you understand? People need to be warned! The danger isn't over yet!" Then I woke up.

First, the dreamer represents Christians who are watchful and alert to that which is coming upon the earth. Peter said, *"For the time is come that judgment must begin at the house of God: and if it first begin at us, what shall the end be of them that obey not the gospel of God?"* (1 Pet. 4:17).

This storm comes directly from God, out of the west. Although Christians are subject to His judgment, they're covered by their covenant with God through Jesus Christ. This is represented by the rainbow emanating from the small tornado of His approaching judgment. It's also revealed by the porch. In this context, being on a porch represents being exposed to something while being sheltered at the same time. So the dreamer is exposed to God's judgment, but isn't harmed because she is properly covered by her covenant with Him; neither does she feel the wind of His anger.

The second scene isn't quite as comforting. The sunshine represents God's blessings upon the earth at this present time. *"God be merciful unto us, and bless us; and cause His face to shine upon us"* (Ps. 67:1). It includes the prosperity, freedom, peace, and innumerable other blessings that He has beamed down upon us for so long. The very large, very close storm portrays the impending destruction that He's promised every nation that departs from His grace. *"The wicked shall be turned into hell, and all the nations that forget God"* (Ps. 9:17).

It moves on the north side and dissipates, but the danger lingers. God is clearly showing the world that His judgments are once again averted by His mercy. Even in the midst of wrath, He remembers mercy, but eventually, His judgments will surely come to pass:

> *For the vision is yet for an appointed time, but at the end it shall speak, and not lie: though it tarry, wait for it; because it will surely come...* (Habbakuk 2:3).

How much longer before "the big one" touches down? No one knows, but the imminent danger sensed by the dreamer tells us that it's very close. However, like those she tries to warn, few will believe what's coming upon the earth. Revival is our only hope. *"O Lord, I have heard Thy speech, and was afraid: O Lord, revive Thy work in the midst of the years, in the midst of the years make known; in wrath remember mercy"* (Hab. 3:2). Salvation is the only safe haven. Only those who run "into the house" will have shelter in the coming storm of His fierce judgment.

Also in this dream, the dreamer uses a form of the word *west* twice in the first scene and *north* twice in the second scene. The first scene is about grace, and the second about impending devastation. As she remembered it, she recorded it. That's important.

When recording directions as they appear in dreams, there is one very important concept that everyone should observe. *Don't assume anything.* For instance, if something is on your left hand, don't automatically assume that it's on the north side. In the first place, if you're facing any direction other than east, north is not on the left. Second, even if you are facing *east*, and *north* is on your left, *north* and *left* may be closely related, but they don't have the same root meaning. *Left* means "spiritual" and *north* means "above." Also, when you assume something, you wrongly add that assumption to what the dream actually says.

Look at the men who attempted to build the tower of Babel:

*And the whole earth was of one language, and of one speech. And it came to pass, **as they journeyed from the east**, that they found a plain in the land of Shinar....And they said, Go to, let us build us a city and a tower, whose top may reach unto heaven; and let us make us a name...* (Genesis 11:1-2,4).

As you continue reading, you'll discover that although they were traveling "from the east," they definitely weren't heading west! The cross was nowhere in sight. Instead, they were backsliding from God! In this case, *east* clearly represents "beginning." The Pharisees were coming from the *east* when Jesus confronted them about their selfish views on divorce:

He [Jesus] *saith unto them, Moses because of the hardness of your hearts suffered you to put away your wives: but **from the beginning it was not so*** (Matthew 19:8).

They had "journeyed from the east," by departing from the way marriage was in the beginning. Those who were attempting to build the tower of Babel were doing the same.

Three Views of the Cross

Let's summarize the Bible's unique compass: Hebrews orient themselves by facing the *eastern* sun, which symbolizes their adherence to the Law in their vain attempts to make a place for themselves with God. On their right hand, toward the *south*, lies their natural, temporal blessings. On their left, to the *north*, judgment impatiently awaits like a hungry vulture perched atop a barren tree. If they repent and turn fully around and face the *western* Son, they behold the end purpose of the Law, which they have struggled to obey (see 2 Cor. 3:13; Gal. 3:24). When they lay down their dead, religious works and take up the cross, they finally discover what it really means to be true children of Abraham.

The *northward* bound, unbelieving Gentiles glance at their compass to assure themselves that they are indeed racing toward the judgment bar of Almighty God. *"As it is appointed unto men once to die, but after this the judgment"* (Heb. 9:27). If, in their attempt to escape destruction, they turn *eastward*, to their *right* in self-righteousness, trusting in the arm of the flesh, they usually becomes beguiled and misguided by the map of religious tradition and formalism.

As they approach mid-life and find themselves in crisis, they may turn and *go south* toward the pleasures of this world. There, they shall surely perish. But, if they come to themselves and heed the gentle call of God's precious Spirit, they will make a spiritual turn to the left and find their place in the *western* setting Son. There, Christ *"ever lives to make intercession"* for them, and there, at the end of the day, they find rest from their own futile efforts at righteousness (see Heb. 7:25).

On the other hand, Christians orient themselves by facing *westward*, steadfastly looking to the cross of Jesus Christ as the power of their salvation (see 1 Cor. 1:18). Forgetting the *eastern* Law, which is forever behind them, *"and reaching forth unto those things which are before,* [they] *press toward the mark for the prize of the high calling of God in Christ Jesus"* (Phil. 3:13b-14). By faith, they earnestly search *"for a city which hath foundations, whose builder and maker is God"* (Heb. 11:10). They know that it's located somewhere to the *north*, on their right, because their guide book, the Holy Bible, declares that, *"Beautiful for situation, the joy of the whole earth, is mount Zion, on the sides of the north, the city of the great King"* (Ps. 48:2). They disdain to go *south*, which lies to their left, toward a world which has rejected its Savior. But they know that if they were to make a mistake and get lost, they need only turn and look toward the setting Son. There, their loving Savior always beckons the way back home.

From this simple, threefold picture, you can see that it's not the direction in which you look that determines the meaning of what you see. Rather it's your perspective, determined by where you're coming from. Your viewpoint is what's important. We each have the land before us. We each have to make our own choice:

> *And the Lord said unto Abram, after that Lot was separated from him, Lift up now thine eyes, and look **from the place where thou art** northward, and southward, and eastward, and westward: for all the land which thou seest, to thee will I give it, and to thy seed for ever* (Genesis 13:14-15).

All Creatures Great and Small

When God created the world's inhabitants, He first made the birds and fish and then progressed to land animals. All in all, Genesis lists five different types of creatures that He made. Although His animal creation included every creepy-crawly thing in existence, He mentions only a few by name. We'll keep our discussion down to a few, also.

It wasn't until the fifth day that God made living, moving creatures, and that gives us a clue as to what animals were made for: They were all created to serve Him. (Remember, *five* means "service.") This information also helps us to see how creatures are used as symbols. So let's take a look at the Genesis record:

> *And God said, Let the waters bring forth abundantly the moving creature that hath life, and fowl that may fly above the earth in the open firmament of heaven. And God created great whales, and every living creature that moveth, which the waters brought forth abundantly, after their kind, and every winged fowl after his kind: and God saw that it was good. And God blessed them, saying, Be fruitful, and multiply, and fill the waters in the seas, and let fowl multiply in the earth.*

> *And the evening and the morning were the fifth day. And God said, Let the earth bring forth the living creature after his kind, cattle, and creeping thing, and beast of the earth after his kind: and it was so. And God made the beast of the earth after his kind, and cattle after their kind, and every thing that creepeth upon the earth after his kind: and God saw that it was good.*

And God said, Let us make man in our image, after our likeness: and let them have dominion over the fish of the sea, and over the fowl of the air, and over the cattle, and over all the earth, and over every creeping thing that creepeth upon the earth. So God created man in his own image, in the image of God created he him; male and female created he them. And God blessed them, and God said unto them, Be fruitful, and multiply, and replenish the earth, and subdue it: and have dominion over the fish of the sea, and over the fowl of the air, and over every living thing that moveth upon the earth (Genesis 1:20-28).

The Fish of the Sea

The waters brought forth the fish and fowl. Water often depicts things that are spiritual, and because the fish and fowl were brought forth from water, their source reveals that they relate to spiritual things—especially things that relate to the soul. For instance, Jesus used *fish* as a type of "lost souls." He said to Peter and Andrew, *"Follow Me, and I will make you fishers of men"* (Matt. 4:19b). We know that most symbols have opposite meanings, so *fish* can also represent souls that are saved. After all, fish don't cease to be fish just because they've been caught! Now there are several different kinds of fish: big fish, little fish, cute fish, ugly fish, dangerous fish, schooling fish—the list goes on and on. So rather than trying to identify each particular fish and its symbolic meaning, we'll discuss different groups of fish and what they portray. However, let's first examine one fish specifically mentioned in the Bible.

A Naked Scavenger

Clearly identifiable from its description in the Bible is the catfish. Now I love to eat catfish, but under Moses Law, like many other delectable foods, they were forbidden: *"And whatsoever hath not fins and scales ye may not eat; it is unclean unto you"* (Deut. 14:10). Although catfish have fins, they don't have scales. Now why did God single them out like that?

The answer is that although most creatures are covered with something—scales, feathers, hair, or even clothes in the case of people—catfish are as naked as the day they were born (or hatched, I should say). Because catfish are uncovered, they were declared unclean under Moses' Law. This reveals that we are also unclean when uncovered.

Because most of us wear clothes, we consider ourselves to be covered. God thinks otherwise. When Adam and Eve made themselves aprons out of fig leaves, God said, "That just won't do!" (Well, not exactly, but close.) He made fur coats for them instead. Of course, something had to die before it would share its hide with Adam, so God killed it. That is the message. That's the central theme of the entire Bible. Jesus had to die to cover us with His blood; otherwise we would still be unclean in the sight of God.

Now there is one more characteristic of catfish that makes them forbidden under the Law. They are scavengers. They feed right off the bottom of the lake. God does not want us to eat from the offscouring of this world. He wants us to feast on the Bread of Life. So the catfish is a miniature picture of a sinner feeding on filth. Of course, if you dream that you catch one, it may represent a sinner saved by the grace of God. Hmm...then maybe the Gospel could be compared to the hook, line, and sinker that he swallowed, right? Or, maybe the net?

Every Creeping Thing

Catfish aren't the only fish forbidden by the Law. So are crawfish. Or, if you don't eat crawfish, what about shrimp or lobster? They're all in the same boat. Moses didn't call them by name, but they are all considered forbidden foods. Now, what did they do to deserve that? They just have too many feet, and besides that, they "creep" around:

And every creeping thing that creepeth upon the earth shall...not be eaten. ...or whatsoever hath more [than four] *feet among all creeping things that creep upon the earth, them ye shall not eat...* (Leviticus 11:41-42).

God just doesn't like creeps! For that matter, I'm not too fond of them either. Now, since the ordinances of the Law have been removed, all these things are acceptable table fare, but the message they were made to teach still applies.

Notice that all three of these crustaceans—crawfish, shrimp, and lobster—also feed off the bottom, like catfish. Besides the obvious picture that fact reveals, crawfish are also famous for "crawfishing" their way out of uncomfortable situations (like we all have a tendency to do at one time or another). And shrimp? Just like their name implies, they're just too small for the job. Now lobster, they're different. They belong on a king's table! They're much too expensive for poor people to eat. They're part of the lifestyle of the rich and famous. That may explain how they got on God's rejected list. Of course, they can represent His blessings too. After all, we are children of the King!

Clean or Unclean

There are quite a few more unclean creatures on God's list of "Thou shalt not eat...," but usually it's not difficult to see why He made each one. The individual characteristics of each one reflect some aspect of humanity. Creatures that Moses listed as unclean portray a host of evil things:

> *Now the works of the flesh are evident, which are: adultery, fornication, uncleanness, lewdness, idolatry, sorcery, hatred, contentions, jealousies, outbursts of wrath, selfish ambitions, dissensions, heresies, envy, murders, drunkenness, revelries, and the like; of which I tell you...that those who practice such things will not inherit the kingdom of God* (Galatians 5:19-21 NKJV).

> *Mortify therefore your members which are upon the earth...inordinate affection, evil concupiscence, and covetousness, which is idolatry.... ...also put off all these; anger, wrath, malice, blasphemy, filthy communication out of your mouth. Lie not one to another, seeing that ye have put off the old man with his deeds* (Colossians 3:5,8-9).

There are more, but that's enough for you to get the idea. God probably made a specific creature to represent each and every one of these unclean things. Or is it the other way around? I've seen several carnivorous souls that reminded me of piranhas. And who wouldn't recognize a loan shark? Or what about an octopus taking a pretty girl out on her first date?

And, as always, there's a flip side. God created many clean creatures, too. As long as a fish was covered and had fins, it was considered fine table fare. In dreams, *fish* not only represent souls, but they can also stand for the Holy Spirit:

> *If a son shall ask bread of any of you that is a father, will he give him a stone? or if he ask a **fish**, will he for a **fish** give him a serpent?...If ye then, being evil, know how to give good gifts unto your children: how much more shall your heavenly Father give the **Holy Spirit** to them that ask Him?* (Luke 11:11-13)

If *fish* can represent the Holy Spirit, common sense says they can also represent unholy spirits. In fact, it's usually unclean spirits that produce, *"the motions of sins, which...work in our members to bring forth fruit unto death"* (Rom. 7:5).

Besides souls, the Holy Spirit, and unclean spirits, *fish* can also manifest the hidden motives of the heart. Some *fish* are clever predators; they disguise themselves to deceive their unaware prey. God's fishermen must also be clever. *"...He that winneth souls is wise"* (Prov. 11:30). Soul fishing is always a waiting game. It doesn't pay to get impatient or lose hope. Asking the right questions when you're fishing for answers helps fill your creel too; it's like baiting your hook with just the right bait. And if you can stand one more pun, you *must* have the right *line* if you expect to catch anything.

A Bird's Eye View

Now let's ascend and get a bird's eye view of this picture. In the same way that God declared some fish were clean and others weren't, He also considered birds to be clean or unclean. When I first started preaching, I was guilty of the same mistake that most young preachers make—oversimplification. (That's a kind way of saying *narrow-mindedness.*) I used to teach that the Law only commanded us not to do things that we would naturally do. I didn't think God would forbid something that we weren't going to do anyway. But I was wrong.

Another Naked Scavenger

To illustrate my point, let me ask you a question. Have you ever been tempted to eat buzzard? Me neither! But they were forbidden as food under Moses' Law. Now it's not difficult to understand why God would say, *"Thou shalt not covet."* Likewise, everyone has been tempted to lie at one time or another. But why in the world would God command us not to put buzzard on the table? This is one of the clearest pictures in the Bible showing us that the Law is spiritual, rather than carnal. God wasn't giving Israel a set of dietary rules; He was teaching them to discern the difference between acceptable and unacceptable behavior. The lesson of the buzzard is exactly the same one as the catfish—both are uncovered and both are scavengers. Because buzzards are creatures of the air instead of water, they reflect people's spirits instead of their souls.

A buzzard is a perfect picture of a seemingly spiritual person who isn't under authority. Feathers cover their bodies, but nothing covers their heads:

> But I would have you know, that the head of every man is Christ; and the head of the woman is the man; and the head of Christ is God (1 Corinthians 11:3).

If you are in rebellion, you're unclean. If you're not under authority, you're a buzzard in God's sight, even if you can soar in the heavenly realms! Truly spiritual people aren't scavengers, either. They won't eat things like pride and prejudice, envy and jealousy, hatred and anger, because all those things are buzzard bait. They're roadkill.

Birds of the Night

There are several more forbidden birds on Moses' list. And just as you detest buzzards (or if you're from the city, vultures), you probably won't like these either! You'll find the complete list in Leviticus 11:13-19. For our purposes, we'll name only a few of them. The first one is the owl. Owls are birds of the night. Paul said, *"Ye are all the children of light, and the children of the day: we are **not of the night,** nor of darkness"* (1 Thess. 5:5).

Like catfish and buzzards, owls may stand for sinners or unclean spirits. On the other hand, an owl may represent one who is skillful in discerning of spirits because of its acute vision and hearing. These wonderful characteristics aid them in the night, making them expert hunters even in almost total darkness. I'm sure someone reading this book is going to think, *I thought **owls** meant wisdom!* Everyone has heard the saying, "He's a wise old owl." There are times when *owls* do mean "wisdom." Jesus said, *"The children of this world are in their generation wiser than the children of light"* (Luke 16:8b).

As with every symbol, an *owl* may represent either good or evil, which is determined by the dream's content, not by the fact that an owl is an owl. God didn't make any bad creatures; however, He did create some to represent evil. He said everything that He made was *"very good"* (see Gen. 1:31). Paul, in reference to clean and unclean things said, *"There is nothing unclean of itself..."* (Rom. 14:14b).

In fact, even a vulture can represent something good. Jesus used them to represent angels in a parable about the resurrection. *"For wheresoever the carcase is, there will the eagles* ["vultures" in the Greek] *be gathered together"* (Matt. 24:28). There are few dead carcasses that vultures can't find. As they circle overhead, their acute sense of smell enables them to locate the dead even when the carcass isn't visible from the sky. Jesus used their unique ability to assure us that not a single dead person would be overlooked in the resurrection.

Birds of Prey

Besides vultures and owls, eagles and fish hawks are also on Moses' list. Both of these predators feed on fish. God doesn't like competition. He said, *"All souls are mine"* (Ezek. 18:4a). He doesn't like sharing His "fish" with spiritual predators. One of the most vivid and memorable dreams I've ever had was about a hawk:

> I dreamed that I was looking out my window and saw a hawk alight in a tree. I was using a pair of binoculars, but at first, I couldn't get them to focus properly. Then, when they suddenly came into focus, I realized the hawk had a man's head! I watched him spread his wings and drop to the ground. As he landed, he became a well-dressed man. He was wearing a suit. He looked toward me and realized I was watching him. He knew that if he walked away, he would look suspicious, so he walked toward me instead. He came into the house, and at this point, I saw that he was carrying a shotgun. The gun was beautifully engraved and inlaid with gold.
>
> As he entered the house, I asked, "Hunting quail?" His reply was unintelligible so I repeated the question, but I knew that in reality he was "a hunter of the souls of men." He nodded affirmative to my question, and I asked him if I could examine his shotgun. I placed it to my shoulder and noticed that the action wasn't properly fitted to the stock. It looked impressive, but it wasn't very powerful. I also noticed that it was foreign made. I handed it back to him and told him that it needed repairs. I said, "You'd better take that gun to a good gunsmith; it's dangerous." Then I awoke.

Three years passed before I met this hawk. And just like the dream depicted, at first I didn't recognize him for what he really was. When I finally focused in on him, I realized that he was a sorcerer, although he had every appearance of being a "well-dressed" preacher. He was hunting souls, but he wasn't hunting them for God's glory; he was hunting them for his own. His speech was eloquent and his teachings were beautiful, but forged in a foreign land. His doctrines came straight from the pits of hell. His purpose was to draw away disciples after himself. He was indeed an evil hunter of the souls of people.

In addition to hawks, there are several more fish-eating birds forbidden under Moses' Law: cormorants, pelicans, and herons, to name a few. When used in a context like the dream above, they each portray the wrong spirit.

Earlier, I mentioned that eagles were also forbidden to eat. Yet God uses eagles as a type of the prophetic anointing. Compare, *"And by a prophet the Lord brought Israel out of Egypt, and by a prophet was he preserved"* (Hos. 12:13), with, *"Ye have seen what I did unto the Egyptians, and how I bare you on eagles' wings, and brought you unto Myself"* (Exod. 19:4). Here, God uses the eagle's unique characteristic of carrying her young on her back as a picture of His powerful deliverance of Israel from slavery in Egypt. He refers to it again in this Scripture:

> *As an eagle stirreth up her nest, fluttereth over her young, spreadeth abroad her wings, taketh them, beareth them on her wings: so the Lord alone did lead him, and there was no strange god with him* (Deuteronomy 32:11-12).

In this Scripture, He even compares the eagle to Himself. So, like the lowly, unclean catfish, the lofty, majestic eagle can represent both the clean and the unclean, depending upon its use in one's dream.

Another one of the eagle's characteristics is seen in Psalm 103:5: *"Who satisfieth thy mouth with good things; so that thy youth is renewed like the eagle's."* Here the reference is to the eagle's seasonal molting and renewing its plumage. No doubt that's what is meant in this next Scripture too:

> *But they that wait upon the Lord shall renew their strength; they shall mount up with wings as eagles; they shall run, and not be weary; and they shall walk, and not faint* (Isaiah 40:31).

Creatures of the Night

Birds have unique characteristics that enable them to be used in many different roles in dreams. In addition to being able to fly, they're very colorful, their habits and habitat are varied, they walk on two legs, and they are the only creatures with feathers. But they are not the only ones that fly. Bats fly too. Bats are different from birds in many respects, yet they are similar in that they have only two legs and can fly. Like owls, they are creatures of the night. They're also on Moses' list of forbidden foods.

One species is called vampire bats because they drink blood. This, along with all their other faults, makes them a perfect symbol for witchcraft, and that is usually what they signify. There are a few more things they can represent, like near blindness, giving rise to the expression, "Blind as a bat." Bats usually portray something negative. In fact, it's hard to imagine them being used any other way. But they have one redeeming trait—they invented radar (well almost, anyway). A bat uses sound as a type of radar to fly in complete darkness. This is comparable to discerning of spirits, one of the nine spiritual gifts given to the Church.

Multitude of Meanings

There are several more Scriptures where birds are used symbolically. In the following passage, evil is symbolized by a restless raven and rest and peace by a dove:

> *And he* [Noah] *sent forth a raven* [from the ark], *which went forth to and fro, until the waters were dried up from off the earth. Also he sent forth a dove.... But the dove found no rest for the sole of her foot, and she returned unto him into the ark.... And he stayed yet other seven days; and again he sent forth the dove out of the ark; and the dove came in to him in the evening; and, lo, in her mouth was an olive leaf plucked off: so Noah knew that the waters were abated from off the earth. And he stayed yet other seven days; and sent forth the dove; which returned not again unto him any more* (Genesis 8:7-12).

Thousands of years later Isaiah wrote, *"But the wicked are like the troubled sea, when it cannot rest"* (Isa. 57:20), and a thousand years after that, Jesus interpreted Noah's actions:

> *And into whatsoever house ye enter, first say, Peace be to this house. And if the son of peace be there, your peace shall rest upon it: if not, it shall turn to you again* (Luke 10:5-6).

Birds can also represent gossip and slander, as seen in the following Scripture:

Curse not the king, no not in thy thought; and curse not the rich in thy bedchamber: for a bird of the air shall carry the voice, and that which hath wings shall tell the matter (Ecclesiastes 10:20).

Why, the little tattletale! They can also represent the cause or spirit behind a curse: *"As the bird by wandering, as the swallow by flying, so the curse causeless shall not come"* (Prov. 26:2).

Beasts, Cattle, and Creeping Things

As the sixth day of creation dawned, God undertook another momentous task, the formation of land animals:

And God made the beast of the earth after his kind, and cattle after their kind, and every thing that creepeth upon the earth after his kind: and God saw that it was good (Genesis 1:25).

Notice there are three specific classifications mentioned here: *beast*, *cattle*, and *creeping things*. They are three important keys to understanding the symbolism hidden in animals.

An elder who was quite concerned about a distressing situation in his church was earnestly seeking God for help: He dreamed that a dangerous bear was approaching him. Suddenly a giant snake appeared between him and the bear. The snake killed and ate the bear, swallowing him whole in the process. Then the serpent turned toward the elder, becoming a huge gorilla in the process. The startled elder awoke in fear.

Earlier we introduced Elisha's bears that mauled 42 scornful kids and showed that they represented a curse. The Bible teaches that a serpent may also be a curse:

*And the Lord God said unto the serpent, Because thou hast done this, **thou art cursed** above all cattle, and above every beast of the field; upon thy belly shalt thou go, and dust shalt thou eat all the days of thy life* (Genesis 3:14).

In the elder's dream, one curse devoured another! That's exactly what the Gospel is all about! *"Christ hath redeemed us from the curse of the law, being made a curse for us: for it is written, Cursed is every one that hangeth on a tree"* (Gal. 3:13). After dying to atone for our sins, destroying the curse that we were under in the process, Jesus arose to walk in the power of an endless life. Thus He became the "stronger than he" of Luke 11:21-22:

> *When a strong man armed keepeth his palace, his goods are in peace: but when a stronger than he shall come upon him, and overcome him, he taketh from him all his amour wherein he trusted, and divideth his spoils.*

A gorilla is the "strong man" of the forest, even as Christ is the "strong man" of His creation. Through this dream, God was assuring the elder that He had indeed intervened on his behalf and, through the cross of Christ, had completely resolved his threatening problem.

This dream clearly illustrates two of the three classifications of land creatures mentioned. A *beast* is a creature that dominates. For example, *"A lion which is strongest among beasts, and turneth not away for any"* (Prov. 30:30). As one can see from this dream, these animals represent danger, power, strength, leadership, and other similar characteristics. The serpent is one of the *creepy creatures*. The Hebrew word translated *creep* actually means "to glide swiftly," like a serpent slithering through the grass. They are sneaky. This corresponds to everything from wisdom to witchcraft. In contrast, *cattle* are gregarious animals and represent the social aspect of humankind. They follow the leader.

The Beast of the Earth

The *beast* category includes the antichrist of John's vision:

> *And I stood upon the sand of the sea, and saw a **beast** rise up out of the sea, having seven heads and ten horns, and upon his horns ten crowns, and upon his heads the name of blasphemy* (Revelation 13:1).

On the other hand, the beast category also includes John's vision of Christ's ministers in the King's throne room:

> *And before the throne there was a sea of glass like unto crystal: and in the midst of the throne, and round about the throne, were four beasts full of eyes before and behind. And the first beast was like a lion, and the second beast like a calf, and the third beast had a face as a man, and the fourth beast was like a flying eagle* (Revelation 4:6-7).

The lion represents the apostles; the calf (or ox) portrays the evangelists; the man depicts the pastor-teachers; and as we have already seen, the eagle represents the prophets.

There are several animals named in the Bible that are beasts of burden. They all belong to the same category as cattle. Some are considered clean, and others unclean. Interestingly enough, the difference has nothing to do with whether they're tame and useful, or even whether they're good table fare, but instead it depends upon what they wear on their feet and how they eat! Moses' only concern was whether their hooves were solid or divided, and whether they chewed a cud or not:

> *Whatsoever parteth the hoof, and is clovenfooted, and cheweth the cud, among the beasts, that shall ye eat. Nevertheless these shall ye not eat of them that chew the cud, or of them that divide the hoof: as the camel, because he cheweth the cud, but divideth not the hoof; he is unclean unto you* (Leviticus 11:3-4).

The latter part of this Scripture is another one of those buzzard laws. I don't think I'd care for camel meat anyway, what about you? The writer of Hebrews said the Law had *"a shadow of good things to come, and not the very image of the things..."* (Heb. 10:1b). Paul compared the Law to a bronze mirror, which produces a somewhat dim and distorted reflection (see 1 Cor. 13:12).

The Law governing clean and unclean creatures contains many obscure pictures such as they describe. Let's take a closer look at some of these clouded images.

Dividing the Hoof and Chewing the Cud

Dividing the hoof relates to "rightly dividing the word" (see 2 Tim. 2:15); in the spirit, we walk with our words. Adam and Eve *"heard the voice of the Lord God walking in the garden."* (Gen. 3:8a). That's the reason God said you should have *"your feet shod with the preparation of the gospel of peace"* (Eph. 6:15). That's also the meaning of the strange custom described in Ruth:

> *Now this was the manner in former time in Israel concerning redeeming and concerning changing, for* **to confirm all things; a man plucked off his shoe, and gave it to his neighbour:** *and this was a testimony in Israel* (Ruth 4:7).

Giving another person one's shoe was the same as saying, "I give you my word."

Whether you dream of *hooves* or *shoes,* they mean the same thing— "words." And since we walk with words, by extension "walk" is another meaning for *feet* and *shoes.* Moses' Law reveals that those who try to use God's Word without correctly dividing it are considered unclean (in error) in the eyes of God. Dividing the Word is what we're doing right now. We're dividing the natural ordinances to obtain the spiritual meanings. In other words, we're separating the natural from the spiritual. And the way we're doing it is by chewing the cud.

That's what meditating upon the Word is all about. We have to "chew on it awhile" before we can grasp the underlying thought behind some of its hard sayings. Through meditation, we break them down until we comprehend their true meaning. Then, once we understand them, we can do what they instruct us to do, utilizing them to direct our lives. Otherwise, we're just swallowing the Word whole without benefiting from it.

Bulls and Oxen

Dreaming of an animal with hooves, divided or otherwise, doesn't necessarily mean the animal refers to words. There are several more characteristics that should be taken into consideration. For example, bulls often have horns and are known for aggression. *Horns* mean "power" and "authority," but not necessarily legitimate authority. Quite often a bull symbolizes "opposition" and "persecution." Another meaning is "idolatry," or by extension, it can stand for "false religion." When the stock market is involved, a bull refers to "prosperity." Occasionally, it means the same as when a person says, "That's just a bunch of bull."

On the flip side, when Paul was defending his apostleship to the Corinthians, he used *oxen* symbolically to represent God's ministers: *"For it is written in the law of Moses, Thou shalt not muzzle the mouth of the ox that treadeth out the corn..."* (1 Cor. 9:9), especially the evangelistic aspect of the ministry, *"...that he that ploweth should plow in hope; and that he that thresheth in hope should be partaker of his hope"* (1 Cor. 9:10). Why are oxen used to depict ministers? There are three specific reasons.

First, oxen are neutered animals. Evangelists are not supposed to gather for themselves, but for God. The Church is the King's harem, not the evangelist's nor the pastor's. Ministers are to be spiritual eunuchs in the house of their God. Second, oxen are used for sowing and reaping. As Paul mentioned in First Corinthians 9:10, the ox was the primary animal used for plowing and threshing. Third, oxen are used to depict ministers because increase in the Body of Christ is by their labors: *"Where no oxen are, the crib is clean: but much increase is by the strength of the ox"* (Prov. 14:4).

A Hog of Himself

Oxen have a divided hoof and chew the cud; therefore, they are clean. On the other hand, hogs have divided hoofs, but are considered unclean. Everyone knows that pork is one of Moses' forbidden foods. But like catfish, they taste mighty good! So why is pork declared unclean? Hogs don't chew the cud. We've already discussed the spiritual picture behind cud chewing and what it signifies, but there are a couple more reasons that hogs wouldn't have qualified anyway.

When pigs eat, they always make "hogs of themselves." Really, they are gluttons. They have to be. Unlike other land creatures that depend upon their fur for warmth, they must depend upon their fat. Although they do have some hair, it is completely insufficient to "cover" them. So they eat everything they can to provide a surplus layer of fat for protection.

They're just like unsaved rich people. Their covering is their surplus, not their God. They trust in their riches: *"Jesus...saith unto them, Children, how hard is it for **them that trust in riches** to enter into the kingdom of God"* (Mark 10:24b). Also, like catfish and vultures, hogs are scavengers. So we have three unclean creatures: swine on the land, catfish in the sea, and vultures in the air representing the unclean aspects of the human body, soul, and spirit.

A Horse of a Different Color

Another domesticated animal determined to be unclean under the Law is the horse. Moses declared them unclean because their hooves aren't divided, but that didn't keep Jesus from riding on one. He rode into Jerusalem on a donkey, but He'll be riding a warhorse when He returns for His next visit:

*And I saw heaven opened, and behold **a white horse;** and He that sat upon him was called Faithful and True, and in righteousness He doth judge and make war. His eyes were as a flame of fire, and on His head were many crowns....and His name is called The Word of God* (Revelation 19:11-13).

Horses have been used for work, war, and transportation for centuries. Two of these three categories usually determine how they're used in dreams. Although they were the primary means of transportation for centuries, they have been replaced in modern times with "horseless carriages"—automobiles. But in many parts of the world, they are still used as draft animals.

Also, as in the Scripture from Revelation 19, *horses* can still mean war. Their courage, speed, and stamina have made them invaluable war allies throughout history. As we learned when we discussed colors, there are four horses in the sixth chapter of Revelation. The first was white, the second red, the third black, and the fourth pale. Purity, persecution, famine, and death—each rider carried a message from God. There is one more factor that enters into the interpretation of their messages—*time*. Their messages were consecutive. Each horse represented a specific period of time.

I once dreamed of 13 evil women, riding 13 black horses in the middle of the night. When I awoke, I asked God what in the world that was all about, and He said, "Thirteen evil weeks." And indeed they were. I had exactly 13 weeks left on my job before we moved, and those 13 weeks gave new meaning to Jesus' words, *"Take therefore no thought for the morrow: for the morrow shall take thought for the things of itself. **Sufficient unto the day is the evil thereof"*** (Matt. 6:34).

After that, at another time, in another state, I dreamed of four horses. The first two were strong, beautiful, quarter horses. The third was like the first two, but as I passed by, he lifted up his heel, threatening to kick me. The fourth was a lean, mean, red horse that opposed me and tried to bite me as I attempted to pass by him. Because I had been introduced to the concept of time as it related to horses in my previous dream, I knew exactly what God was saying. He was giving me advanced insight into the next four weeks of ministry.

I called several ministers with whom I was working and explained the dream to them. I warned them that toward the end of the third week we would be threatened, and the fourth would be curtains. It came to pass just as the dream depicted. The first two and a half weeks were unusually productive; but toward the end of the third week, the devil raised his ugly head. By the beginning of the fourth, we were facing stiff opposition and by its end, total rejection. I left then; enough is enough!

Now, hold your horses. Don't think that I'm teaching that every horse you dream about means exactly one week in time; rather *one* of the meanings for a *horse* is "a specific period of time." That time period may be any length that God assigns to it, not just one week, as in my dreams. In fact, each rider of the four horses of Revelation rode for a different length of time. The white horse represented the Church's expansion and rapid growth for the first hundred years or so. The red horse ran longer, for the saints were persecuted sporadically until A.D. 325. The black horse had the most stamina of all, because he started his race about A.D. 325, and he didn't tire out for over a thousand years. It wasn't until about the time of Martin Luther that he was sent back to the barn. And, if the pale horse's two riders, death and hell, had stayed in the saddle much longer, it would have spelled curtains for the whole human race. They managed to destroy one-fourth of the world's population as it was. Their ride coincides with the era of the bubonic plague or the black death, as it was called (see Rev. 6:1-8).

Now war, work, and time, by themselves, aren't the only things to consider when you dream about horses. The common term, *horsepower,* involves work and time together. The two are inseparable. If God uses a horse to refer to your work, He usually has time in mind also. A similar and somewhat related meaning is seen in the word *horseflesh.* The emphasis here is "flesh," or "the works of the flesh," when the two are combined. So "war," "work," and "time," sometimes individually, sometimes entwined, are some of the things that *horses* convey in our dreams.

One more thought: the white horse of John's vision in Revelation 6:2 is a type of the Holy Spirit. And besides the Holy Spirit, a horse may symbolize our own spirits, as well. Like people, some horses are quite "spirited," while others are just worn-out old nags.

Countless Creature Characteristics

Under the Law, if a creature had more than four feet, wasn't covered with fur, feathers, or scales, and had solid hooves, it was unclean. Also, even if its hooves were divided, if it didn't chew the cud, it was still considered unclean. But these weren't the only criteria for judging uncleanness. Moses listed several more creatures as unclean without giving any specific reason. Usually, one can determine the reason by examining the inherent characteristics of the unclean animal. For example, we've seen several reasons that hogs are on God's unclean list, but there's one more reason.

Hogs don't have sweat glands. That's why they're always wallowing in the mud. They can't rid themselves of their body heat any other way. Dogs are similar, except dogs pant when they get hot. What's the picture here? Heat is passion. When people wallow in the filth of this world to relieve their passions ("body heat"), they are as unclean swine. When they rid themselves of their anger and frustrations through swearing and cursing, they pant like dogs and offend God with their sin:

> *But above all things, my brethren, swear not, neither by heaven, neither by the earth, neither by any other oath: but let your yea be yea; and your nay, nay; lest ye fall into condemnation* (James 5:12).

Of course, dogs will bite the hands that feed them, too. They often represent strife in dreams. Solomon said, *"He that passeth by, and meddleth with strife belonging not to him, is like one that taketh a dog by the ears"* (Prov. 26:17).

The Bible never speaks well of dogs, unless you commend them for eating Jezebel (see 1 Kings 21:23). But occasionally, they are used in a positive sense in our dreams. Many cultures consider a dog to be humanity's best friend, and guard dogs can even represent God's ministers who are faithfully watching for the welfare of the saints. They can also represent the not-so-faithful:

> *His watchmen are blind: they are all ignorant, they are all dumb dogs, they cannot bark; sleeping, lying down, loving to slumber* (Isaiah 56:10).

Cats are closely akin to dogs in that both are common house pets; however, they have a completely different meaning. Cats are fiercely independent. They have a mind of their own. They are associated with witchcraft in many fairy tales, and sometimes that's what they stand for in dreams. A cat can represent several other spirits, too. I was traveling with another minister several years ago when one night he dreamed that he was watering his cat. In the process, he almost drowned it. He said the cat looked pitiful. He woke up feeling sorry for it. When he asked me what I thought it meant, I simply asked him, "Do you ever feel sorry for yourself?"

His reply was, "All the time."

There are many other fish, birds, mammals, reptiles, insects, and spiders named in the Bible—far too many to discuss individually. One more that we should discuss, though, is the spider. *"The spider taketh hold with her hands, and is in kings' palaces"* (Prov. 30:28).

Those who have tried ridding their houses of spider webs have learned something about this little creature. *"He takes hold with his hands,"* meaning, they're very tenacious. They *never* give up. That's a very positive trait! But what they build with their hands is another story. I hate spider webs! Likewise, it would be hard to place a black widow spider into a positive setting. They're the epitome of evil.

Consider that:

Beavers are industrious

Elephants are powerful

Foxes are cunning

Wolves run in packs and devour innocent lambs

Lambs are defenseless

Vipers are deadly

Hogs are filthy

Sharks are ruthless

Mules are stubborn

Monkeys are mischievous

Fleas are insignificant

Flies are unclean

Sloths are lazy

Snails are slow

Moles are hidden

Turkeys are dumb

Swans are graceful

Cats are predators

Tigers are dangerous

Giraffes are exalted

Bears are grouchy

Deer are swift

Mice are timid

Rats carry plagues

Kangaroos jump

Birds sing

Goats butt

Skunks stink

Hornets sting

Moths corrupt

Rabbits increase

Roaches infest

Scorpions sting

Dogs bite...

the list goes on and on.

Almost every creature has some characteristic that sets it apart and speaks clearly to those who have ears to hear. All we have to do is learn to listen.

Various Vehicles

A popular television safety advertisement ends with a horrific car crash and advisedly says, "You can learn a lot from a dummy." No doubt that's true if you can find one that talks—especially after being decapitated in a crash! Actually, you may not learn much from a dummy, but one thing you *can* learn from is your dreams, especially when you learn what the cars, trucks, vans, trains, and buses that you dream about are saying. When your ship comes in, it's carrying a message too, that is, if you're not waiting over at the airport.

Vehicles constantly appear in our dreams. They symbolize different things, both to us and about us, in the same way that our personal automobiles reveal a lot about us. To illustrate, let's examine a few vehicles. Most people choose a vehicle that suits their own personal tastes, that is, as far as their pocketbooks will allow. The wealthy tycoons will choose an expensive sedan; the Don Juans, a sleek convertible; the exhibitionists, a sports car, or if they can't afford that, a jalopy with loud pipes. On the other hand, stay-at-home moms with several children want a van, and farmers need a pickup truck. In each case, the vehicle is more than transportation; it's an extension of its owner.

Therefore, if God wants to talk to us about our families, He simply puts us into a van or SUV and off we go. If He wants to talk about our church families, He loads in a couple of children from other families in the church along with ours. Or He may just let the pastor drive. Of course, if the pastor's wife is driving, that's another story!

If He wants to warn us about trouble ahead, He may drive us down a muddy road. Or if the problem involves contention, there's another way of depicting it—the common fender bender. A dream about an automobile wreck may warn you of an impending clash with one of your peers. The carnage caused by "road rage" that we hear so much about is a natural expression of a spiritual problem.

Through dreams, God can warn us about potential blowups—or blowouts, as the case may be—whether they happen in us or in one of our peers. Nahum may have been referring to something he saw in a dream when he prophesied of the high speed and hazardous transportation of our day: *"The chariots shall rage in the streets, they shall justle one against another in the broad ways: they shall seem like torches, they shall run like the lightnings"* (Nah. 2:4).

One young lady dreamed that she was driving her husband's car at night. When she had car trouble, she stopped and looked in the trunk to discover a dead man. She was horrified and ran and told her husband. He said, "Oh, don't worry; I'll take care of it." She realized that he was responsible for the presence of the dead man and had no intention of reporting it to the authorities. She became fearful that she was going to get into trouble because of her involvement and was indecisive as to what she should do. Then she woke up.

The interpretation? Her husband was a cocaine addict. God was dealing with her about her codependence. She had to decide if she should leave and thus bring him into accountability for the error of his ways or not.

Crashes in the Ministry

Besides talking to us about family and church matters and warning us about trouble ahead, God also uses vehicles when He wants to talk to us about our ministries. Teachers usually dream about school buses, prophets about airplanes. Of course, prophet-teachers may dream about both at one time or another.

When I was very young in ministry, the pastor of the church I attended began to fall away from God. During that time, I had a dream:

I was an aircraft mechanic at an airport. (In reality, I had earlier served as a jet mechanic in the U.S. Air Force.) I was working on a helicopter and realized that it had a defective part. When I attempted to explain the problem to the pilot (who was the pastor), he said, "Oh, that's not what's wrong; it's just a little overheated." I realized that he was just too lazy to care. I knew he was wrong, but because he was in charge, I conceded and decided not to say anything more. Then I woke up.

A few weeks later, I dreamed:

I was a passenger in a large airliner. I was conscious that there was very little food on board. I realized the plane was having engine trouble so I prayed and asked God if it was going to crash. He answered, "Yes, it will crash." I asked, "Will there be any survivors?" He said, "Eighteen will survive." After flying for a short time longer, the plane turned into a helicopter. Soon afterward, it turned into a blimp. Then the scene changed. Although I wasn't conscious of any crash, suddenly we were all in the ocean in chest-deep water. It was night, and there was no land in sight.

It wasn't long after I had these two dreams that things begin to "go sour" at church. Among other things, the pastor left with another man's wife. After the smoke cleared, the assistant pastor called a meeting to discuss the church's condition. Exactly eighteen "survivors" showed up for the meeting. I wasn't surprised, only disappointed. The defective condition and progressive changes in the airplane accurately depicted the deteriorating condition of the church during that time. The pastor was selfishly unconcerned, even though many people were hurt in the church's "crash."

In both of these dreams, the church was depicted as some type of airplane, and the pastor as the pilot. In the first dream, the helicopter represented the "hovering" condition of the church. Although the church had taken off with great power and speed not long before, at the time of the dream, it was hovering stationary in the air. (For about six months prior to this dream, the church had been having a phenomenal revival both in spirit and numerical growth, but the revival had begun to wane.) The pilot was warned that the defective part had to be repaired, or the helicopter would certainly crash.

In the second dream, again the church was represented by an airplane. This time it was a fully loaded airliner. (The church had about one hundred members at that time.) As it flew, it changed into a helicopter, but only hovered for a short time. Then it became a blimp, which although blimps have engines, they also can be moved by the winds. Likewise, this church began to be *"tossed to and fro, and carried about with every wind of doctrine"* (Eph. 4:14). I was warned and informed throughout this experience. Although I was not able to pre-vent the impending crash, I wasn't caught by surprise because God clearly showed me what was happening. I also received several dreams at that time showing me what to do, and what not to do, in regard to what was happening.

Years later, I experienced a similar dream, but this time it was about two ministers whom I knew and their individual downfalls:

A short, powerful, jet fighter was taking off. I saw the plane's tail had been modified. It had a clamp on it that wasn't sup-posed to be there. The pilot began to do low altitude stunts. At first, all went well; but then, he tightened the rolls (actually end-over-end cartwheels) and lost altitude. He hit the ground, bounced, and went straight up! At first, it looked like he had recovered, but then the jet blew up. Debris began to rain down. The fallout was going to be dangerous, especially if the engine was to fall on someone. A small nut hit me. I was dodging to stay out of the fallout. I went around the falling debris to avoid getting hit.

I saw the two pilots parachuting down and said, "Thank God they got out safe." I saw that someone on the ground was with the one who landed first. I waited for the second one to land. I told someone (an investigator?) that the pilot had been doing aerobatics at 1200 feet, and that he had failed to keep, or hold, a reference point; therefore, he crashed.

There is only one reference point that never changes—the Word of God. When this young minister lost sight of *the* reference that all things are judged by and began to trust in his own understanding, he lost control and crashed. Much later, the other pilot also came drifting down, long after the fallout from the first one had settled.

Transportation in the Bible

You may be wondering if anything like this is in the Bible. Although airplanes and automobiles were not yet invented when the Bible was written, horses, wagons, chariots, and even iron chariots were in daily use. Horses and ordinary chariots were used much as we use cars; and donkeys, mules, camels, and wagons were used like trucks. Iron chari-ots were the armored tanks of their day. There were no airplanes, but that didn't seem to bother God. When He wanted to take someone somewhere in a hurry, He just took him in His own private jet:

> *And when they were come up out of the water, the Spirit of the Lord caught away Philip, that the eunuch saw him no more.... But Philip was found at Azotus: and passing through he preached in all the cities, till he came to Caesarea* (Acts 8:39-40).

How's that for first-class travel? Faster than the Concord! Philip didn't have to wait around at the airport for his luggage, either.

Ships and boats were common in Bible days, too. In fact, Paul used *shipwreck* as a metaphor for the modern, Laodicean church's "greasy grace" doctrine: *"Holding faith, and a good conscience; which some having put away concerning faith have made shipwreck"* (1 Tim. 1:19). In our society, the metaphor more likely used is *train wreck* or *plane crash.*

James used the picture of a ship in a different way. He compared the ship's helm to a proud tongue:

> *Behold also the ships, which though they be so great, and are driven of fierce winds, yet are they turned about with a very small helm, whithersoever the governor listeth. Even so the **tongue** is a little member, and **boasteth** great things. Behold, how great a matter a little fire kindleth* (James 3:4-5).

It's not hard to turn a ship, but an unskilled skipper may capsize it if he tries turning it too fast. He also may run into rapids unless he knows how to steer clear of them.

The Travels of Jesus

As He so often did, Jesus gave us one of His living parables during His ministry at Lake Gennesaret:

> *And it came to pass, that, as the people pressed upon Him to hear the word of God, He stood by the lake of Gennesaret.... And He entered into one of the ships, which was Simon's, and prayed him that he would thrust out a little from the land. And He sat down, and taught the people out of the ship* (Luke 5:1,3).

After Peter received the Holy Spirit, Christ caused him to separate himself from "land" (carnal ways) and began to preach through him. Peter's ship represented Peter himself. Likewise, in the following

Scripture, the disciples' ship represents their lives being tossed by a storm. But when Jesus stepped into their situation, their problems were over:

> *And when even was now come, His disciples went down unto the sea, and entered into a ship, and went over the sea toward Capernaum. And it was now dark, and Jesus was not come to them. And the sea arose by reason of a great wind that blew. So when they had rowed about five and twenty or thirty furlongs, they see Jesus walking on the sea, and drawing nigh unto the ship: and they were afraid. But He saith unto them, It is I; be not afraid. Then they willingly received Him into the ship: and immediately the ship was at the land whither they went* (John 6:16-21).

One more beautiful, living, ship parable right from the pages of Scripture occurs after Jesus had finished teaching the people. He commanded Peter to push off from shore:

> *Now when He had left speaking, He said unto Simon, Launch out into the deep, and let down your nets for a draught. And Simon answering said unto Him, Master, we have toiled all the night, and have taken nothing: nevertheless at Thy word I will let down the net. And when they had this done, they enclosed a great multitude of fishes: and their net brake. And they beckoned unto their partners, which were in the other ship, that they should come and help them. And they came, and filled both the ships, so that they began to sink* (Luke 5:4-7).

Can't you just see the "catch" when revival comes? Instead of building a bigger church to hold the new converts, a church will invite their "partners" to come and receive the surplus into their churches. Hopefully, we'll soon reach that place of spiritual maturity and unselfishness before Jesus returns.

Other Types of Traffic

Other than camel caravans, there is nothing else similar to *trains* recorded in Scripture. However, they are rather common in dreams. They usually communicate one of two things: "something traditional," since trains run on tracks and cannot easily change directions, or "a continuous chain of events," since they are composed of a "chain" of cars. In fact, sometimes a simple *iron chain* can also mean "without interruption." When used as a pun, a *train* means "training," as in being taught.

In addition, *railroad tracks* can have a dual meaning. The most common is "tradition" or "habit" because they're always the same, but a more subtle meaning is "caution." One should stop, look, and listen before crossing tracks because of the obvious danger. On the positive side, *trains* can refer to "staying on track," as in Paul's admonition to the Thessalonians: *"Therefore, brethren, stand fast, and hold the traditions which ye have been taught, whether by word, or our epistle"* (2 Thess. 2:15).

Military vehicles, such as tanks, fighter jets, bombers, battleships, and navy destroyers, usually indicate spiritual warfare. Soldiers in uniform also fall into this category.

Large trucks, such as eighteen-wheelers, may represent "large churches" or simply indicate "large burdens" and "responsibilities." I once dreamed I was driving someone else's freight truck. Someone told me that in three years I would be given the title to it. At the time of the dream, I was assisting another minister, pastoring a small church. Three years later, I was called upon to be the senior pastor.

Pickup trucks usually refer to "individual works" and "personal ministries." They can depict one's "secular job" or "spiritual ministry." A pickup with a dead battery won't start. A truck with a flat tire won't roll. A minister without a fresh charge of God's Spirit won't do either. Sometimes we need to trade in our old pickup and get one with a more powerful engine. Of course, we'll have to pay the price, but that can't be helped.

Specialty vehicles have a lot to say, too. An *ambulance* comes to our "aid," but I'd just as soon not need one. A *school bus* takes us to school when we need to "learn something new." A *bulldozer* "overcomes everything in its path" and can "make a way where there is no way." A *farm tractor* "plows" and "plants," and a *combine* "harvests that which was sown." There's a message in each and every one of these if we're listening to what they have to say.

The King's Highway

If we dream of driving backward, looking over our shoulders, we're going by our past experiences instead of being led by the Spirit. If we drive backward by looking in the rearview mirrors, we are ministering by the letter of the Word instead of by the inspiration of the Spirit. Paul said that God *"hath made us able ministers of the new testament; not of the letter, but of the spirit: for the letter killeth, but the spirit giveth life"* (2 Cor. 3:6). We must drive forward, facing forward, to pass God's driver's exam.

An old gravel road often represents God's highway: *"Thus saith the Lord, Stand ye in the ways, and see, and ask for the old paths, where is the good way, and walk therein, and ye shall find rest for your souls. But they said, We will not walk therein"* (Jer. 6:16).

Why a gravel road? The *rocks* represent "God's Word." But even a *wooded path* through the forest can be His way too. *"Thy word is a lamp unto my feet, and a light unto my path"* (Ps. 119:105). And in rare cases, even the *freeway* can be the right way. But getting in the fast lane on the *expressway* is usually not His way:

> *Enter ye in at the strait gate: for wide is the gate, and broad is the way, that leadeth to destruction, and many there be which go in thereat* (Matthew 7:13).

Sometimes we are inconvenienced by having to take a *detour.* Other times we might find ourselves on a *dead-end street.* A *muddy road* indicates "fleshy desires" and "temptations." A *rocky road* speaks for itself. *Paved roads* are better, smoother, and usually mean that God has us on the right road to get us where He wants us to go, that is, if we heed the signs like we're supposed to. *Maps* help too, and there's no map more accurate than the Word of God.

Train stations, bus stations, and *airports* all mean the same— "waiting." And waiting is something that no one enjoys. Waiting to depart indicates waiting on God's timing before embarking on some venture that He has assigned you to. Waiting for someone's arrival may indicate you're anticipating a divine appointment (whether you are aware of it or not). Whether you're waiting or traveling down the King's highway, driving or riding as a passenger, it all has meaning. Whatever means of transportation you find yourself using, whatever circumstances you find yourself in, all situations speak volumes if you're listening. Come to think of it, you *can* learn a lot from a dummy.

CHAPTER 13

That's All, Folks!

Before closing, I want to cover several categories that don't contain enough items to each warrant a separate chapter, yet they're too important to ignore. They include the metals that we haven't already discussed. One verse of Scripture names almost every one of them: *"Only the gold, and the silver, the brass, the iron, the tin, and the lead"* (Num. 31:22).

Metals Other Than Silver and Gold

We've already discussed *gold* and *silver* in Chapter 9. Remember, *gold* is "glory" and "wisdom," and *silver* represents "knowledge," including intimate knowledge. Now we'll examine brass, iron, tin, and lead. Also, Ezra mentioned copper, and Paul referred to a coppersmith named Alexander.

It's easy to glean the meaning for *iron* from Scripture. It means "strength." Sometimes the Bible refers to an *"yoke of iron,"* of bondage (see Jer. 28:13); other times it compares iron to the strength of God's Spirit given to break heavy yokes off of its victims. Either way, "strength" is the primary meaning. Joshua told Israel they would, *"drive out the Canaanites, though they have **iron** chariots, and **though they be strong"*** (Josh. 17:18). He knew they could do all things through Christ who strengthened them (see Phil. 4:13).

Tin usually means "cheap," "weak," even "worthless." *"And I will turn my hand upon thee, and purely purge away thy dross, and take away all thy tin"* (Isa. 1:25). *Tin* is just not worth much, and *lead* is not much better. It's heavy, and it often represents "heavy burdens," grievous to be borne.

*And, behold, there was lifted up a talent of lead: and this is a
woman that sitteth in the midst of the ephah. And he said, This is
wickedness. And he cast it into the midst of the ephah; and he cast
the weight of lead upon the mouth thereof* (Zechariah 5:7-8).

Well, that's one way to get rid of witchcraft! Copper and brass are
related, because ancient brass is an alloy of copper and tin. In Bible
days, pure copper was considered as valuable as gold: *"Also twenty ba-
sins of gold…and two vessels of fine copper, precious as gold"* (Ezra 8:27).
Both *copper* and *brass,* in one way or another, represent "words"—
sometimes God's Word, sometimes people's words. Probably the most
famous occurrence of brass in Scripture is John's description of Jesus,
whom he witnessed while he was on the isle of Patmos:

*And in the midst of the seven candlesticks one like unto the Son of
man, clothed with a garment down to the foot, and girt about the
paps with a golden girdle. His head and His hairs were white like
wool, as white as snow; and His eyes were as a flame of fire; and
His feet like unto fine brass, as if they burned in a furnace; and
His voice as the sound of many waters* (Revelation 1:13-15).

In the natural, we walk with our feet. In the spirit, we walk with
our words. Jesus' feet being as fine brass depicts the pure Word of God:
*"The words of the Lord are pure words: as silver tried in a furnace of
earth, purified seven times"* (Ps. 12:6). Here His Word is declared to be
completely pure. In fact, it is purified the same way silver is purified—
by fire. *Fire* and *affliction* are synonymous: *"Behold, I have refined thee,
but not with silver; I have chosen thee in the furnace of affliction"* (Isa.
48:10). Jesus didn't just preach the Word; He *was and is* the Word. He
was purified in the furnace of affliction and came forth as fine brass.

God's Gold or People's Brass

As with most other symbols, the meaning for *brass* can be reversed,
too. *Brass* can mean the cheap, impure words of people. Several times in
Scripture we find hallowed, gold shields being replaced with brass ones.
That speaks volumes! It usually happened after God left and went some-
place where He felt more welcome. Without Him around, Israel was
easy pickings for their warlike neighbors. So they usually tried to bribe
their way out of bad situations by giving God's gold away. Then, the
place looked kind of empty, so they replaced it with brass. Anyway, gold
and brass look a lot alike if you keep the brass polished, so who cares?

*And it came to pass in the fifth year of king Rehoboam, that Shishak king of Egypt came up against Jerusalem...and he took away all the **shields of gold** which Solomon had made. And king Rehoboam made in their stead **brazen shields**, and committed them unto the hands of the chief of the guard...* (1 Kings 14:25-27).

This discussion may be a little more serious than first meets the eye. God's gold is God's glory. Our shield is God's glory, not His promises. His promises are conditional. We seldom live up to them. His glory is the reason He gives us grace and keeps the devil off our necks when we can't meet His conditions. Whenever we lose faith, or He gets disgusted enough to turn us over to our enemies, whichever comes first, we're in a heap of trouble. But thank God, it takes a lot to get Him disgusted. That's why our shield depends upon the measure of faith we're able to acquire. Let's take a look at a couple of Scriptures:

And the Lord said unto Moses, I have seen this people, and, behold, it is a stiffnecked people: now therefore let Me alone, that My wrath may wax hot against them, and that I may consume them: and I will make of thee a great nation. And Moses besought the Lord his God, and said, Lord, why doth Thy wrath wax hot against Thy people, which Thou hast brought forth out of the land of Egypt with great power, and with a mighty hand?

Wherefore should the Egyptians speak, and say, For mischief did He bring them out, to slay them in the mountains, and to consume them from the face of the earth? Turn from Thy fierce wrath, and repent of this evil against Thy people. Remember Abraham, Isaac, and Israel, Thy servants, to whom Thou swarest by Thine own self, and saidst unto them, I will multiply your seed as the stars of heaven, and all this land that I have spoken of will I give unto your seed, and they shall inherit it for ever. And the Lord repented of the evil which He thought to do unto His people (Exodus 32:9-14).

Take note that Moses pointed out that if God didn't do what He had promised, even though Israel failed to meet His conditions, He was going to lose face. The Egyptians simply wouldn't understand. They would only see that the Israelites' God had failed to perform what He had promised! Moses correctly saw that God would lose face, regardless of whose fault it was. So often it's that way, and God knows it. Therefore, His stated policy is: *"For Mine own sake, even for Mine own sake, will I do it: for how should My name be polluted? and I will not give My glory unto another"* (Isa. 48:11).

So when we replace His glory with ours, replacing gold with brass, sooner or later we fail. Brass shields just won't do. God will not defend your reputation. He'll only defend His! If you take His glory, you're on your own. So, *"Above all, taking the shield of faith, wherewith ye shall be able to quench all the fiery darts of the wicked"* (Eph. 6:16).

If you trust in your own righteousness, declaring to God how you've met all His conditions, which no person can truly meet, you've deceived yourself. You're holding up a brass shield against an enemy who cannot be defeated without God's intervention. Only one warrior has ever successfully bruised satan's head. And He'll do it again when we trust in Him: *"And the God of peace shall bruise satan under your feet shortly. The grace of our Lord Jesus Christ be with you"* (Rom. 16:20). Notice it's *"the God of peace"* who bruises satan, not the person God is using to accomplish it.

Why did we discuss all that? We are supposed to be discussing dream symbols, not theology! Oh, but we are. Take note of all that we've covered. *Fire* often depicts "trials" and "afflictions." *Brass* represents either "God's Word" or "our words." *Gold shields* portray "God's glory" and *brass shields,* "human substitutes." Above all, different metals can tell the whole story once we have the fundamental understanding of how they are used.

A Person's Name and Trade

Why do you think Paul went to the trouble of telling us that Alexander the troublemaker was a coppersmith? We can only guess, but we can make an educated guess. Let's examine that passage of Scripture:

> *Alexander the coppersmith did me much evil: the Lord reward him according to his works: of whom be thou ware also; for he hath greatly withstood our words.* ***At my first answer*** *no man stood with me, but all men forsook me: I pray God that it may not be laid to their charge* (2 Timothy 4:14-16).

Alexander was one of Paul's accusers; we can be almost certain of that. Otherwise, Paul wouldn't have been "answering" him. But Alexander wasn't just another Jew accusing Paul of preaching against Moses' Law. To begin with, the name *Alexander* is Greek, not Hebrew. Alexander was probably a philosopher. Why a philosopher? Because he was a coppersmith. Have you ever noticed how often God uses people's names to describe their character and their trade to tell us something about their ministries? (For instance, look at what Peter and John were doing when Jesus first called them—see Matthew 4:18,21.) *Alexander* means "man-defender," and he used copper to fabricate things. I believe Alexander had more flaws in his gnostic doctrines than dents in his pots and pans. Only someone who could fabricate doctrines deceitful enough to sway others away from the simple truth of the Gospel would prompt such a warning from Paul:

> *Beware lest any man spoil you through philosophy and vain deceit, after the tradition of men, after the rudiments of the world, and not after Christ* (Colossians 2:8).

It's only a theory. We won't know for sure one way or the other until we ask Paul in person, which may not be as long as some may think!

Power and Authority

Alexander the troublemaker brings us to another subject—people. People identify themselves in different ways, and often their identity gives special meaning to their appearances in dreams. For example, almost everyone has dreamed about *police*. These men and women are the epitome of authority. Sometimes their authority is used properly to protect us; sometimes, as in every profession, they abuse their authority and use it selfishly. Either way, "power" and "authority" are the primary meanings, and "protection" and "abuse" are branches of the same. Subsequently, police officers may be for or against us. They may represent God's angels or satan's demons. They can even represent themselves, if we actually know them in person.

When *soldiers* appear in dreams, they represent "force" and "power," similar to *police*. The might of the *armed forces* may represent the hosts of the "armies of the Lord," and a *general* may represent "Christ" Himself. A *foreign army* usually stands for "satan's forces."

Doctors are similar because they're also licensed authorities; however, their real authority comes from their "knowledge," not from government. They usually imply "healing" in one form or another. Sometimes a *good doctor* represents the "Great Physician." In the same way, *college professors* and *lawyers* are authorities by reason of their "knowledge."

Besides the ***power that comes through military might and physical strength*** and the influence that comes through knowledge, there are two other divisions of authority that can be closely related to one another: ***political power***, which is influence and authority obtained by *position*, and wealth. A rich man's power and influence is by reason of his vast *resources*. Often, power-hungry people are seldom satisfied with the limited power they have, so they attempt to broaden their influence into other areas as well. Wealthy people run for political office; lawyers become senators; and poor politicians use their influence to obtain wealth.

If God wants to talk to us about our strength or weakness, our power or lack thereof, He may use someone in one of these four divisions of authority to illustrate His message. There are four areas of spiritual authority and power that closely parallel these four natural divisions. It helps to understand the comparisons. ***Human military might*** is no match for God's mighty power; however, His power and might are often represented by humanity's machinery and weapons. Jesus said, *"But ye shall receive power, after that the Holy Ghost is come upon you"* (Acts 1:8a). The power promised here is the Greek word *dunamis*. It means "force." In fact, it's usually translated "miracle."

The ***power and influence obtained through education*** also has a spiritual parallel: *"A wise man is strong; yea, a man of knowledge increaseth strength"* (Prov. 24:5). The difference as to whether his strength is carnal or spiritual depends upon what type of knowledge he has. Paul said:

> ...*I count all things but loss for the excellency of the knowledge of Christ Jesus my Lord: for whom I have suffered the loss of all things, and do count them but dung, that I may win Christ.... That I may know Him, and the power of His resurrection...* (Philippians 3:8,10).

Godly spiritual power and authority obtained through knowledge can only come from personal, intimate knowledge of God. *Political power* is influence and authority obtained through position. The spiritual authority that parallels political authority is probably the most abused and misused power in the Church:

> *But Jesus called them unto Him, and said, Ye know that the princes of the Gentiles exercise dominion over them, and they that are great exercise authority upon them. But it shall not be*

*so among you: but whosoever will be great among you, let him be
your minister; and whosoever will be chief among you, let him be
your servant* (Matthew 20:25-27).

The full implication of this passage of Scripture is beyond the scope
of this book, but the correlation between politicians and pastors, elders, apostles, and so forth should be obvious enough for everyone to
see how God may use one to represent the other.

Governors and *presidents* usually represent "Christ," unless they're
crooked (in the dream, not in real life). The president's true character seldom enters into the picture—only his position. Otherwise, God
couldn't use any of them to represent Himself. Even "Honest Abe"
wasn't that pure.

The fourth division, **power obtained through wealth,** also has its
spiritual parallel. Solomon compared wealth to the knowledge of God
and concluded that the knowledge of God is far greater in value: *"For
wisdom is a defence, and money is a defence: but the excellency of knowledge is, that wisdom giveth life to them that have it"* (Eccles. 7:12).

Eternal life comes through unwavering faith in Jesus Christ alone.
You can't buy it. When we know Him (not just know about Him), we
have the *"riches of the full assurance of understanding..."* (Col. 2:2b).
Full assurance is faith. *Faith is the currency of the Kingdom of God.*
Abraham was prosperous because he was strong in faith; we should be
too (see Rom. 4:20).

When God wants to point out something in any one of these four
divisions of authority, He has an endless list of trades to choose from.
The natural and social power and authority wielded by police, doctors,
lawyers, politicians, business people, oil tycoons, and others closely
parallels the spiritual power of godly *people in the Kingdom of God:*
*"But when the multitudes saw it, they marvelled, and glorified God,
which had given such power unto men"* (Matt. 9:8).

God Uses All People

Besides authority, there are several other things that tradespeople
can depict. Telephone repair people, automobile mechanics, crooks,
thieves—there is no limit to the number of people that God can use
when He needs to talk to us. A telephone repair person may show up
to inform us that God is getting a busy signal every time He tries to

call, or a vehicle mechanic may tell us that we need a Holy Ghost oil change in our lives.

At other times, relationships tell the story. *Mothers* are our "source"; *fathers* are our "authority." *In-laws* are occasionally "out-laws," depending upon whether we have a good relationship with them or not. Sometimes, the word *law* is the clue we need to get the message. It was Moses' father-in-law who advised him how to set up elders to keep order in the camp (see Exod. 18:12-23). Elders should still enforce the ordinances established by each local church. On the other hand, if they act legalistically, they may attempt to enforce laws that the members aren't really obliged to keep.

The *pastor* may portray "Christ" in a dream, because the pastor represents Christ when speaking before the church. Subsequently, a *pastor's wife* may typify "the Church." Our *natural fathers* may represent our "heavenly Father," and our *natural mothers,* our "churches." A woman's *husband* may stand for "Christ" because, *"he* [or she] *that is joined unto the Lord is one spirit"* (1 Cor. 6:17), or he can portray "the devil," depending upon the character of the husband! An *ex-husband* may represent a Christian woman's "relationship with the world" before she "married" Christ.

Brothers and *sisters,* as well as *old friends* and *acquaintances,* often portray "ourselves." One of the neatest tricks that dreams play on us is to incorporate several different people in one dream and have everyone of them correspond to a different aspect of ourselves. It's very common to dream of three different people—one for the spirit, one for the soul, and one for the body—all in the same dream. Sounds like *me, myself,* and *I;* doesn't it? Evil sometimes comes in threes, too.

At times, *our children* represent "ourselves" and sometimes "themselves." They can even stand for those in our church, especially if there are church children with them in the dream. And last, but not least, *grandparents* usually depict "the past." Whether a person is dead or alive doesn't always enter into the picture. In God's eyes, they're all still alive. Actually, the dream usually refers to what we have inherited from them:

> *When I call to remembrance the unfeigned faith that is in thee, which dwelt first in thy grandmother Lois, and thy mother Eunice; and I am persuaded that in thee also* (2 Timothy 1:5).

It should be obvious that if we can inherit our grandmother's faith; we can also inherit her faults. If God wants to point out either of these, why wouldn't He just put her into our dreams? As we discussed in the chapter on directions, you may appear in her house, or you may dream of her dress or jewelry. Of course, this applies to grandpa's stuff, too.

Acts of God

Another group of related symbols that are very common in dreams are acts of God. Even though most good things that happen are also acts of God, I'm referring to the insurance companies' definition. They blame things like fire, storms, earthquakes, and volcanoes on Him. They reason that if the world self-destructs, it is His fault because He created it. They blame everything that destroys property and hurts people without their help on Him. It could be that they're right.

Fires, tornadoes, floods, and other natural disasters usually come in two different categories: good and bad. You might be wondering how a violent storm could be considered good, so let's take a quick look. Because God's power is so awesome, He often depicts His arrival as a storm. In fact, when He came down to Mount Sinai, He gave the Israelites a taste of all four—fire, storm, earthquake, and volcano:

> *And it came to pass on the third day in the morning, that there were thunders and lightnings, and a thick cloud upon the mount, and the voice of the trumpet exceeding loud; so that all the people that was in the camp trembled.... And mount Sinai was altogether on a smoke, because the Lord descended upon it in fire: and the smoke thereof ascended as the smoke of a furnace, and the whole mount quaked greatly* (Exodus 19:16,18).

Some people think that if a dream scares them, it's not from God. That's foolishness. When God sends His power, it usually scares the daylights out of our flesh, regardless of how spiritual we are. The Bible says God's arrival on Mount Sinai even scared Moses: *"And so terrible was the sight, that Moses said, I exceedingly fear and quake"* (Heb. 12:21). Thus, fear is not a proper yardstick to judge whether a dream is from God or not. If Noah had thought that way, he probably would have drowned:

> *By faith Noah, being warned of God of things not seen as yet,* **moved with fear,** *prepared an ark to the saving of his house; by*

the which he condemned the world, and became heir of the righteousness which is by faith (Hebrews 11:7).

Joel seemed to be referring to atomic power when he prophesied of the endtime outpouring of the Holy Spirit: *"And I will show wonders in the heavens and in the earth, blood, and fire, and pillars of smoke"* (Joel 2:30). Sounds like a pretty good description of an atomic bomb explosion, especially for someone who hasn't seen one.

Atomic explosions, fires, storms, earthquakes, volcanos, even *avalanches* may signify "a mighty move of God"—storms and earthquakes in particular. Storms bring rain and lightning, and *lightning* is a type of "power from Heaven." *Earthquakes* often signify "repentance." Our flesh is made of earth, so when we quake like Moses, we're repenting.

Volcanoes are also acts of God, but we can have our own little volcanic eruption without God's help. Sometimes when we explode in anger, we erupt like a miniature volcano. But according to James, *"The wrath of man worketh not the righteousness of God"* (James 1:20), so we can't blame our rage on God. On the other hand, if someone is mad at us, God may let us know about it by also portraying it as a fiery volcano.

Sometimes before earthquakes and volcanoes appear, they are preceded with earth tremors. Likewise, sometimes before we erupt, we are given some advance warnings, if we're listening. God can prevent "volcanoes" from erupting and keep "earthquakes" from tearing down everything we've built, *if* we're paying attention. Similarly, He can warn us when a tornado or hurricane is coming so that we can take preventive measures, whether the storm is literal or in the spiritual realm.

Raging fires may depict any number of things, including "revival," "destruction," or "passion." It pays to seek God for the specific meaning when we dream of potentially destructive "acts" like these. Paul used *burn* as a metaphor for inordinate lust:

*And likewise also the men, leaving the natural use of the woman, **burned in their lust** one toward another; men with men working that which is unseemly, and receiving in themselves that recompence of their error which was meet* (Romans 1:27).

One's *automobile* usually represents "one's life." Consequently, if your car is on fire, it may mean you're being consumed by passion. What kind of passion? God used fire to describe His own burning anger: *"For a fire is kindled in Mine anger, and shall burn unto the lowest hell, and shall consume the earth with her increase, and set on fire the foundations of the mountains"* (Deut. 32:22). "Anger," "hatred," and "lust" are all portrayed by *fire*. Fires, like most other symbols, can be positive too. Not all fire is destructive. In fact, some fire can be quite instructive!

> *And the angel of the Lord appeared unto [Moses] in a flame of fire out of the midst of a bush: and he looked, and, behold, the bush burned with fire, and the bush was not consumed....And when the Lord saw that he turned aside to see, God called unto him out of the midst of the bush, and said, Moses, Moses. And he said, Here am I* (Exodus 3:2,4).

When Moses turned aside to see what the fire was all about, the angel of the Lord spoke to him and set his heart ablaze. He fanned the passion back into flame that Moses once had for his brethren. Zeal for God's children is a good passion to have.

The Four Seasons

The four seasons are another group of symbols that frequently serve as messengers in dreams. *Spring* speaks of "revival" and "renewal." During this season, dead things suddenly spring into life. It is a time of refreshing after the long, dreary winter. It may foretell of a "new thing" that God is causing to "spring forth" in the land: *"Behold, I will do a new thing; now it shall spring forth; shall ye not know it? I will even make a way in the wilderness, and rivers in the desert"* (Isa. 43:19).

Summer, on the other hand, is a time of "toil" and "labor," *"He that gathereth in summer is a wise son: but he that sleepeth in harvest is a son that causeth shame"* (Prov. 10:5). It may also represent "trials" because of the intense heat and droughts that many parts of the country endure during this time.

Autumn is "colorful," "beautiful," and implies that "summer is over." Times are changing. Old things pass away to make room for new. Sometimes these changes are for the better; sometimes for the worse: *"The harvest is past, the summer is ended, and we are not saved"* (Jer. 8:20). Sometimes the changes refer to putting off our old traditions to make room for new ways to come as when a tree drops its leaves in preparation of forming new buds for spring.

The *winter* season usually implies "waiting." It is a time of "planning" and "preparation" for spring planting. Sometimes it portrays a period of "desolation" and "barrenness" in one's life. The coldness of winter may speak of "rejection" and "isolation." The four seasons are summed up in God's promise of their perpetuity:

> *While the earth remaineth, seedtime and harvest, and cold and heat, and summer and winter, and day and night shall not cease* (Genesis 8:22).

Rain and *snow* are closely associated with "the cycle of nature." A winter setting with a snow-covered hillside may reveal God's continual mercy upon the land. The *snow* represents "His righteous covering" and *winter* a period of patient "waiting upon God." A *soaking rain* may represent "His Spirit being poured out" upon a dry and thirsty land. It can also portray the misery of "being without shelter in a time of trouble." In the Bible, Isaiah used *clouds, rain,* and *snow* as metaphors for both "our thoughts" and "God's thoughts," as well as for "God's Word":

> *For My thoughts are not your thoughts, neither are your ways My ways, saith the Lord. For as the heavens are higher than the earth, so are My ways higher than your ways, and My thoughts than your thoughts. For as the **rain** cometh down, **and the snow from heaven,** and returneth not thither, but watereth the earth, and maketh it bring forth and bud, that it may give seed to the sower, and bread to the eater: so shall My word be that goeth forth out of My mouth: it shall not return unto Me void, but it shall accomplish that which I please, and it shall prosper in the thing whereto I sent it* (Isaiah 55:8-11).

The Lights of the Heavens

There's one more group of symbols that everyone should be familiar with: *the sun, the stars,* and *the moon.* If one doesn't understand the spiritual significance of these three symbols, many Scriptures remain a mystery. Likewise, when they appear in our dreams, their message remains a mystery, too. All three of these were made on the fourth day of creation. Earlier we saw that *four* means "rule." Let's take a closer look at what God made on the fourth day:

> *And God said, Let there be lights in the firmament of the heaven to divide the day from the night; and let them be for signs, and for seasons, and for days, and years: and let them be for lights in the firmament of the heaven to give light upon the earth: and it was so. And God made two great lights; the **greater light** to rule*

*the day, and the **lesser light** to rule the night: He made the **stars** also* (Genesis 1:14-16).

The greater light no doubt refers to the sun. It doesn't take much research to learn that God made *the sun* to represent "Himself": *"For the Lord God is a **sun** and shield..."* (Ps. 84:11). Notice God's pun in the following verse: *"But unto you that fear My name shall the **Sun** of righteousness arise with healing in His wings"* (Mal. 4:2a).

The *stars* are relatively easy to understand, too: *"And they that be wise shall shine as the brightness of the firmament; and they that turn many to righteousness as the stars for ever and ever"* (Dan. 12:3). In fact, both the *sun* and *stars,* plus *the moon,* were used in one of two dreams that got Joseph into so much trouble:

> *And he dreamed yet another dream, and told it his brethren, and said, Behold, I have dreamed a dream more; and, behold, the **sun** and the **moon** and the eleven **stars** made obeisance to me. And he told it to his father* [Jacob], *and to his brethren: and his father rebuked him, and said unto him, What is this dream that thou hast dreamed? Shall I and thy mother and thy brethren indeed come to bow down ourselves to thee to the earth?* (Genesis 37:9-10)

Jacob understood the symbolism of his son's dream all too well. He just didn't like what it meant. Jacob was Joseph's father, and he knew *the sun* represented "himself." God is our heavenly Father, and God said *the sun* represented "Him" and "His Son." So we see that *the sun* can represent "our father," either heavenly or earthly, and it can also represent "Christ." Jacob realized the *eleven stars* represented "Joseph's brothers," and Daniel said *stars* represent "Christ's witnesses." Either way, they represent "people."

Also, Jacob referred to *the moon* as "Joseph's mother." Joseph was a type of Jesus, and his mother represented "the Church." Jesus said, *"My mother and My brethren are these which hear the word of God, and do it"* (Luke 8:21b). Those who hear the Word and practice it are believers. Collectively, the believers are the Body of Christ, which is the Church.

Stars represent each of "God's children individually," and *the moon* represents "God's children collectively." *"And* [God] *hath raised us up together, and made us sit together in heavenly places in Christ Jesus"* (Eph. 2:6). The Church is the "lesser light" that God set in the heavens "to rule the night." We receive the light of the Son and reflect it to a world that lies in darkness. All sinners are in darkness: *"For they that sleep sleep in the night; and they that be drunken are drunken in the night"* (1 Thess. 5:7).

In summary, *the sun* represents "God"; *the stars* depict "the saints"; and *the moon* portrays "the Church." What is the significance of all this? To answer that, we'll first examine a very important endtime Scripture, and then we'll look at a prophetic dream that God gave me several years ago. When God promised that He would give us dreams, He also made a reference to the sun and moon:

> *And it shall come to pass **in the last days**, saith God, I will pour out of My Spirit upon all flesh: and your sons and your daughters shall prophesy, and your young men shall see visions, and your old men **shall dream dreams**.... The **sun** shall be turned into darkness, and the **moon** into blood, before that great and notable day of the Lord come* (Acts 2:17,20).

This Scripture has nothing to do with the natural sun or moon. The early Church suffered severe persecution. The latter Church will, too. The "lesser light" that God made "to rule the night" will be turned into blood. The "greater light" that He made "to rule the day" won't be giving much light at that time, either. To further clarify this analysis, take a close look at the following Scripture:

> *Moreover the light of the moon shall be as the light of the sun, and the light of the sun shall be sevenfold, as the light of seven days, in the day that the Lord bindeth up the breach of Hs people, and healeth the stroke of their wound* (Isaiah 30:26).

If the natural sun's light ever gets seven times brighter, it will also get seven times hotter. Talk about a barbecue! If that happens, we won't be here for Jesus to come back for. *Sevenfold* simply means a complete unfolding. Before Jesus returns, God is going to give the Church the full revelation of Himself. Therefore, the Church's light will be "as the light of the *Son*" (pun intended). At that time Jesus' promise will be fulfilled where He said, *"Verily, verily, I say unto you, He that believeth on Me, the works that I do shall he do also; and greater works than these shall he do; because I go unto My Father"* (John 14:12). Now let's take a look at my dream:

On December 6, 1985, I dreamed about the moon:

It was a bright, beautiful, full moon. It was being approached by a large mass of earthen material that was traveling through space. It was as though a planet had been crushed and the loose debris was going to collide with the moon. The crushed material was divided into two waves of tan-colored dirt. The total mass of the waves was so great that if both were to hit the moon at once, I knew the moon would be knocked completely out of orbit! Therefore, the mass was divided into two waves, the second larger than the first. I realized the moon would be greatly enlarged as a result of each impact. Then I awoke.

I wrote the interpretation in my dream journal. *The moon* is "the Church," which sits in heavenly places with Christ. The large mass of *earthen material* is people from every nation being drawn toward the Church. (The *tan* color shows that these people are dead in trespasses and sins.) The *two waves* are two approaching "revivals." If God saves everyone that He plans on saving all at one time, the Church will not be able to absorb the increase (it will be knocked out of orbit); therefore, He has divided the endtime harvest into two consecutive waves.

The second wave of revival is going to be larger than the first. Since I had this dream, the first wave of revival has already begun in many parts of the world.

The only symbol in this dream that we haven't discussed is the *dirt*. The Bible says our bodies are made of dust: *"And the Lord God formed man of the dust of the ground, and breathed into his nostrils the breath of life; and man became a living soul"* (Gen. 2:7). People are made of earth, so *earth* represents "people." You can see why I interpreted the *tan earth* as "sinners."

There are many more groups and divisions besides numbers, colors, animals, vehicles, metals, people, power, acts of God, the four seasons, and heavenly and earthly bodies to consider. These simply serve to illustrate the way a family of objects or actions are used to portray a complete picture. Each individual member adds to and complements the other members of its family. When you dream of something that belongs to a group not referred to in this book, simply meditate upon how it relates to the other members. By comparing it with its aunts and uncles, brothers and sisters, you can unearth "the rest of the story."

CHAPTER 14

Well, Almost All...

You didn't really think that a preacher would actually conclude on his first closing, did you? Well, then you're not disappointed! There are some important rules to follow when interpreting dreams.

Rules to Follow

The first rule: *Most dreams are messages to the dreamer, for the dreamer, about the dreamer.* This is probably the most important rule of all because it will save you from making major mistakes when interpreting dreams. When other people are in your dream, remember they are probably there to help you learn something about yourself, not to show you something about them. Of course, there are exceptions, but think of Paul's admonition before you decide that your dream is an exception to the rule: *"And having in a readiness to revenge all disobedience, when your obedience is fulfilled"* (2 Cor. 10:6).

The second rule: *You seldom know for sure that your interpretation is correct until you can apply it to a real-life situation.* This is what makes prophetic dreams so difficult to understand. Take the Book of Revelation, for example. Many people speculate what various prophetic Scriptures represent, but no one can be positive of his or her interpretation except for those texts that have already come to pass and have become history. The parts that are still prophecy remain a mystery. Likewise, as long as the stage hasn't been set in your real life for the play that you've seen in your dream, you'll speculate about it, too. (The primary exception to this rule is when God reveals the meaning.)

The dreamer's circumstances provide very important clues for interpreting dreams, because a dream may have a literal meaning. Without the proper application, it's impossible to know the correct interpretation. Here's a good example:

> A Christian lady dreamed that her teenage son was sick. When the doctor examined him, he said the lad needed more vitamin C. After her son became even worse, the mother returned him to the doctor. The doctor said, "I don't understand this. He just needs vitamin C, and it's real easy to get."

Because this dream could easily have a natural application, it would be unwise to attempt an interpretation without first asking the mother if her son was actually sick or not. If he was, by all means, she should get him some vitamin C! But if he wasn't (and in this case he wasn't), vitamin C wouldn't do him much good. It was simply a symbol for Christ. God was telling her that her boy, who had a problem with anger and rebellion, needed counseling.

Once you have determined the proper application for your dream, it's usually rather easy to interpret. Therefore, always try to discover what your dream applies to before trying to decide what it means. If you do that, you'll maintain a lot higher batting average than you would otherwise. How do you do that? Two additional rules will answer that question.

The third rule: *Most dreams are parables, and most objects that appear in dreams are symbols, including people.* Do not consider objects or people to be literal, unless it's obvious they are literal—and it usually is evident when they are.

The fourth rule relates to helping others interpret their dreams. When you get involved in dream interpretation and master a few fundamentals, your friends will soon find out and *presto*, you're an expert! When they see how good you are, invariably they'll start asking you for help. So to help you help them, here are a few guidelines that I've developed over the years.

This rule is very important: *It's always the dreamer's place to determine if the interpretation is right or wrong.* The best way to avoid breaking this rule is try *not* to interpret their dreams. Instead, ask them a few questions that will lead them to their own interpretations. Subsequently, they'll not only have more confidence in dreams and their meanings, but they'll also begin to understand how to interpret dreams for themselves. In fact, you can help yourself interpret your own dreams by asking yourself the same questions that you ask your friends. The order of these questions isn't critical, but it is logical:

1. What is the dream's subject? What is it about? What is the action? What are the people saying and doing? For instance, is there a storm coming? An opportunity? Remember, most dreams apply to the dreamer's present circumstances.

2. To what past or present circumstances could the dream be applicable? What situation in the dreamer's life could it address? What question has he or she recently asked? What problem is the dreamer facing? Is there internal conflict? Inhibitions? Insecurities? Anxieties? Are there decisions to be made? Directions to be obtained?

3. Who does the dream refer to (personal, church, family)? Who is in the dream? If there is a person in the dream other than the dreamer, what is his or her relationship to the dreamer, and what is the name, age, race, occupation, hobby, likes and dislikes of this person? If he or she is a stranger, who or what does this person remind the dreamer of?

4. Where is the setting located? In the dreamer's house? At the office? In a stranger's home?

5. When is the dream referring to (past, present, future)? Is someone of a different age in the dream than they presently are in reality? Is something from the past considered to be present?

6. Why was the dream given? What action is required? Repentance? Intercession? Is it a confirmation? Instruction? Warning?

7. What symbols are used? Besides the obvious, what emotions, thoughts, questions, or impressions did the dreamer experience while dreaming? To understand each individual symbol, ask the dreamer, "What does this symbol mean to *you*?" Use association. Ask what the object, shape, number, color, vehicle, insect, animal, place, occupation, person, or name reminds them of?

8. And last, to summarize your investigation, ask the dreamer these three questions: What do *you* think the dream means? Who do you think it applies to? Why do you think you had the dream? And be gracious. It's always the dreamer's place to judge if the interpretation is right. Never force your interpretation upon anyone. *"Therefore all things whatsoever ye would that men should do to you, do ye even so to them..."* (Matt. 7:12).

Seek God's Help

In addition to these questions, ask God to give you *His* understanding of the dream. Joseph said interpretations belong to God. Apply the questions just given. Because many dreams are direct personal communication from God, He will often use symbols that mean something specific to the dreamer; therefore, a given symbol may not mean the same to someone else. For this reason, proper interpretation often requires insight from the one who actually dreamed the dream. Before venturing any interpretation concerning a specific symbol, remember to always ask the dreamer the question: "What does this object, color, person, etc. mean to *you?*"

If using association does not provide any meaning to the dreamer—if it does not remind them of something or someone in particular—then use the universal meaning for the symbol to help determine what God is saying. Often the symbol's meaning may be obtained from the way it, or a similar symbol, is used in the Bible.

Even with all the information you've gathered, you still might not fully understand the dream. So, to arrive at the interpretation, dissect the dream into small parts, or thoughts, and insert comments after each part. The dream's "story" will unfold as you go.

Revealing the Secrets of a Dream

Here's an actual dream that a friend asked me to help her interpret. Both she and her husband received a couple of dreams prior to this that seemed to indicate that they needed healing from some past wounds. She asked God for confirmation and direction and, as a result, had the following dream. I've quoted the entire dream, including her comments. As you read it, you'll see how difficult it would be to interpret without first separating it into bitesize pieces. I've also included my comments in the interpretation:

The dreamer writes:

I think I understand the reason I'm facing backward (past?), and the back windows (seeing the past?)—but that's as far as I can decipher, so far...

I'm in the driver's seat of an old, full-size, pickup truck with a camper on the back. I'm parked in an old, dirt parking area on the peripherals of a restaurant, like an old "hamburger joint." (It's not a fancy restaurant.) There seem to be no other cars around this "outer area." I've volunteered to help two people, a husband and wife (I think), who need transportation for themselves and several cardboard boxes of their goods and possessions (not sure what those goods are). Their car has broken down, or something, and they're stuck... (I think they're like folks you sometimes see around here, coming from out of state trying to find work—everything packed in their old vehicle— just kind of indigent, desperate, and needy.) The main theme seems to be that I am turned backward in the driver's seat trying to uncover the backseat cab windows. It must be one of those trucks with a backseat in the cab.

The scene changes:

Now the needy couple is in the truck's backseat. The back windows are covered with a cloth curtain on the back-passenger side and some kind of canvas, like a window shade, on the driver's side. So, I'm on my knees faced backward, and I'm trying to pull the back passenger-side, cloth curtain out of the way so I can see while driving. I'm explaining all this to the couple in the backseat as I struggle to tie the curtain back and make it stay back out of the window.

I spot my husband outside the truck (by the back passenger window I'm struggling with) and ask him to come help me uncover the windows. I explain to him that it will be dangerous for me to drive this big truck with the big camper on the back if I can't see clearly. He then comes around the back of the truck to my side to help me. In the dream I'm thinking how dumb it is to have these window coverings for privacy there in the first place.

The next scene:

We're all four outside the truck. We haven't gone anywhere, and the couple's boxes are now being unloaded while I watch. There's also no camper on the back of the truck anymore. The boxes are all empty—just empty cardboard boxes heaped up! A young man comes running across the lot to unload these, for he says he wants the boxes. I look to see if I want to keep any of the empty boxes myself, before they're crushed and unusable, but none seem usable; just old used boxes, in varying colors, bent-up, etc. Then I wake up.

By reading the dream slowly and prayerfully, you can see just where to stop and insert the different thoughts that the symbols inspire within your heart. The dream reveals its mysterious secrets as you carefully examine and ponder each part of its message. It's like breaking and eating bread. You chew each bite thoroughly before swallowing.

I'm in the driver's seat of an old, full-size, pickup truck with a camper on the back.

Your truck is the work you're presently doing within yourself. You're the driver of your "old" truck (life). The camper on the back probably represents problems or troubles of your past that are covered (but not dealt with). It's the "load" you carry.

I'm parked in an old, dirt parking area on the peripherals of a restaurant, like an old "hamburger joint." (It's not a fancy restaurant.) There seem to be no other cars around this "outer area."

You're not going anywhere because God always stops us for "unloading" (healing). In addition, you're alone on the parking lot as this is not a "group" thing. God usually deals with each one of us personally and heals us privately.

I've volunteered to help two people, a husband and wife (I think), who need transportation for themselves and several cardboard boxes of their goods and possessions (not sure what those goods are). Their car has broken down, or something, and they're stuck... (I think they're like folks you sometimes see around here, coming from out of state trying to find work—everything packed in their old vehicle—just kind of indigent, desperate, and needy.)

Those two people represent you and your husband. You've "volunteered" through prayer to "aid" yourself and your husband. Everything packed in your old, broken-down vehicle indicates that you're desperate, despondent, poverty-stricken—in need of a Savior.

The main theme seems to be that I am turned backward in the driver's seat trying to uncover the backseat cab windows. It must be one of those trucks with a backseat in the cab.

Your observation about the reason for being turned backward in the seat is right on—you're trying to uncover your past.

Now the needy couple is in the truck's backseat. The back windows are covered with a cloth curtain on the back-passenger side, and some kind of canvas, like a window shade, on the driver's side. So, I'm on my knees faced backward, and I'm trying to pull the back passenger-side cloth curtain out of the way so I can see while driving. I'm explaining all this to the couple in the backseat as I struggle to tie the curtain back and make it stay back out of the window.

Remember, what you're trying to uncover are old memories so that you can replace the wounds and bruises with useful wisdom. Being on your knees represents prayer. The curtain is your weapon of defense (self-justification or denial, including self-denial) to deflect the pain. Fear and pain are both curtains. (You need to push them out of the way to deal with your memories.)

I spot my husband outside the truck (by the back passenger window I'm struggling with) and ask him to come help me uncover the windows. I explain to him that it will be dangerous for me to drive this big truck with the big camper on the back if I can't see clearly. He then comes around the back of the truck to my side to help me.

I think God is telling you that you should enlist your husband's help in this healing process. As you said before, God wants you to be healed and not get bogged down in the process. You no doubt will need his (or some counselor's) help.

In the dream I'm thinking how dumb it is to have these window coverings for privacy there in the first place.

Yes, they're very dumb. Defense mechanisms imprison us, enslave us, rob us, and deceive us into thinking that they're helping us!

We're all four outside the truck. We haven't gone anywhere, and the couple's boxes are now being unloaded while I watch. There's also no camper on the back of the truck anymore. The boxes are all empty—just empty cardboard boxes heaped up!

This is the good part. No more covering, hiding, lugging useless junk around as you go forward. You just have to unload the boxes. And remember, those boxes and the things in them are nothing but old memories with their associated pains, offenses, and so forth.

A young man comes running across the lot to unload these, for he says he wants the boxes.

May I introduce *Jesus?*

I look to see if I want to keep any of the empty boxes myself before they're crushed and unusable, but none seem usable; just old used boxes, in varying colors, bent-up, etc.

Give all those old memories to Him. You don't need to keep even one. Those we keep are the ones we secretly want revenge or recompense for. So let Him have them all; they're not worth the space they take up in your heart!

Sweet dreams!

CHAPTER 15

Questions, Anyone?

To complete our discussion on dreams and their meanings, following are ten questions I've been commonly asked, along with valuable and informative answers:

1. When I have a dream, how do I know that it's from God?

In most cases, you will not know until you have correctly interpreted it. Once it's interpreted, if the message it contains agrees with the righteous principles found in the Bible, it's more than likely from Him. The Bible says, *"All scripture* [and I might add, "every dream that's from God"]...*is profitable for doctrine, for reproof, for correction, for instruction in righteousness"* (2 Tim. 3:16). If a dream's interpretation does not meet this test, I discount it. The dream itself may use language or symbols that are not in the Word; however, the correct interpretation will always conform to God's Word if the dream is from Him.

If we use our personal experience or our cultural perspective when interpreting dreams, we are subject to error. If we use any criteria other than God's Word to determine a dream's source, we are building on an incorrect foundation. The only valid test to decide whether a dream's message is from God is to ask yourself the same question you ask when determining if a doctrine is from God: "Does it agree with God's Word?" We should learn to discern and judge both doctrines and dreams.

The problem I've encountered in America is that our society has taught us that our dreams are nonsense. Therefore, we simply ignore them because there's nothing in the average dream to indicate that it's from God. There's no discernible anointing accompanying it. It's "just a dream." Most "anointed" dreams are actually "night visions" and need little or no interpretation. For the great majority of people, saints and sinners alike, the only real way of knowing if a dream is valid is to apply its message to the situation or life that it addresses and then evaluate its value and purpose. As I mentioned above, the actual content of a dream is not a valid test. The Bible says that God chooses the foolish things to confound the wise, so many very foolish and silly dreams are actually sealed messages from God:

> *For God speaketh once, yea twice, yet man perceiveth it not. In a dream, in a vision of the night, when deep sleep falleth upon men, in slumberings upon the bed; then he openeth the ears of men, and sealeth their instruction* (Job 33:14-16).

There is no better example than seven skinny cows eating seven fat cows (see Gen. 41:4). Talk about a pizza dream! Dreams are a lot like your mail. Without unsealing each envelope and reading each letter, there's no way of knowing just what each piece contains.

Because your own spirit can give you a dream, and it uses the same symbolism that God uses, it is necessary to "unseal" each dream before accepting or rejecting it. Jeremiah 29:8 says:

> *For thus saith the Lord of hosts, the God of Israel; Let not your prophets and your diviners, that be in the midst of you, deceive you, neither hearken to your dreams which ye cause to be dreamed.*

This Scripture informs us that all dreams aren't from God. If you want or fear something badly enough, you may dream about it. On the other hand, praying Christians need not fear receiving dreams from satan. Jesus said, *"If a son shall ask bread of any of you that is a father, will he give him a stone? or if he ask a fish, will he for a fish give him a serpent?"* (Luke 11:11). When you ask God to communicate with you, He will not allow satan to answer for Him or He wouldn't be faithful to His own Word.

2. How can I know if I'm interpreting dreams the right way?

First, you should learn Jesus' method of interpreting parables and Daniel's method of interpreting dreams, as discussed earlier. Follow their example. Afterward, test your results. Your work with dreams should bring you into harmony with God and His purposes for your life. If it does that, you can bet that you're going about it in the right way.

3. If my children have dreams, can I assume that God is talking to them also?

Yes! You certainly can. Jesus said, *"I thank Thee, O Father, Lord of heaven and earth, because Thou hast hid these things from the wise and prudent, **and hast revealed them unto babes"*** (Matt. 11:25b).

It's wise to listen carefully when your children recite their dreams, because sometimes God uses them as His little messengers. You should treat their dreams like all others. Judge each dream's message by the Bible.

4. What does it mean when my child wakes up in the middle of the night crying from a bad dream?

There are several things that may cause "bad" dreams. If you and your husband have a disagreement in front of your children, you may frighten them and open their hearts to fear. If they've been traumatized at some point in their lives, bad dreams may reveal they need counseling. On the other hand, some dreams are "body dreams." They are caused by things like pain. If you or your child has a stomachache, headache, or some other physical ailment, your dreams may be caused by your body's discomfort. Each case has to be judged on its own merits. In extreme cases, dreams may actually warn you of approaching calamity. There is no one single thing that causes bad dreams.

5. Since I really can't be positive about an interpretation unless I can apply it to the person or circumstance that it's about, are there some clues or something in each dream that will help me determine the subject matter it addresses?

Usually there are clues in every dream that reveal the subject. The very first part or scene of a dream presents the setting. By closely examining this first part, you can usually discern the dream's subject. If the dream has more than one scene, the first scene usually sets the stage for the play that follows. Each successive scene pertains to the same subject and carries the plot forward until the message is complete.

On rare occasions, you may wake up in the middle of a dream and then go back to sleep and finish dreaming. If you do, pay close attention to the point when you woke up. If your dream is somewhat of a panoramic view involving your past, present, and future, the point in the dream when you woke up may indicate where you are in reality. In other words, the first part is your past and the second part is your present situation and possibly even your future. Remember, this isn't a hard and fast rule, because there could be other reasons your sleep was interrupted.

6. Is it normal to dream several dreams in one night?

Yes. It is not uncommon for some people to dream several dreams in one night, especially if God has a lot to say to them. On the other hand, if you dream several dreams, and you don't wake up between them, they are all actually one dream. What appears to be several different dreams is actually different scenes from the same dream. Usually they are successive, but occasionally they're different views of the same thing.

7. Is it normal to dream several dreams in a row on successive nights, then go for several days or even weeks and not have a single dream that can be remembered?

Yes, it is normal. Sometimes prayer or even a fast may break the silence, but the absence of dreams is not uncommon at all. God doesn't seem to speak to anyone all the time. When He does speak, He has something important to say. Sometimes His apparent silence may have something to do with our lack of obedience in acting upon what He has already shared with us. In other words, why give us more when we haven't used what we've already been given?

8. I've dreamed several times that I lost my purse and was looking for it. What does that mean?

Your personal *purse* or *wallet* can represent something you "treasure" because of the valuables that you keep in it. It may also represent "your heart." The two are closely related. Jesus said, *"For where your treasure is, there will your heart be also"* (Luke 12:34). Your *purse* may also stand for "your own identity."

9. What does it mean when one dreams about crows?

You'll find the answer to that question, and hundreds more like it in the nine-part symbol dictionary at the end of this book, which covers most of the things you dream about.

10. Is it possible to have the author come and conduct a seminar on interpreting dreams in our church?

Yes, your pastor can call me or write to me in order to schedule a program. You may want to give him or her a copy of this book. Your pastor will then be familiar with my approach to dream interpretation and have an idea of what to expect from the seminar.

PART
II

Key Word Dictionary
of Dream Symbols
With Scriptural Illustrations

Animals / Birds / Fish / Insects

Refer to Chapter 11 for more in-depth coverage of the symbolism of certain animals, birds, and fish.

ALLIGATOR (or Crocodile) – *Ancient:* (*Note:* Alligators are Old World animals.) Evil out of the past (through inheritance or personal sin); danger; destruction; evil spirit. (See BEAR.)

Canst thou draw out leviathan [a crocodile] *with an hook? or his tongue with a cord which thou lettest down?...None is so fierce that dare stir him up: who then is able to stand before me?* (Job 41:1,10)

And they that are left of you shall pine away in their iniquity in your enemies' lands; and also in the iniquities of their fathers shall they pine away with them. If they shall confess their iniquity, and the iniquity of their fathers, with their trespass which they trespassed against Me, and that also they have walked contrary unto Me; And that I also have walked contrary unto them, and have brought them into the land of their enemies; if then their uncircumcised hearts be humbled, and they then accept of the punishment of their iniquity: Then will I remember My covenant... with Abraham will I remember; and I will remember the land (Leviticus 26:39-42).

ANT – *Industrious:* Wise; diligent; prepare for the future; nuisance; stinging or angry words.

Go to the ant, thou sluggard; consider her ways, and be wise: Which having no guide, overseer, or ruler, provideth her meat in the summer, and gathereth her food in the harvest (Proverbs 6:6-8).

He that gathereth in summer [like the ant] *is a wise son: but he that sleepeth in harvest is a son that causeth shame* (Proverbs 10:5).

BAT – *Witchcraft:* (*Note:* A bat is a creature of the night.) Flighty; unstable; fear (as in "She's deathly afraid of bats").

And these are they which ye shall have in abomination among the fowls; they shall not be eaten, they are an abomination...the bat (Leviticus 11:13a,19b).

BEAR – *Destroyer:* Destruction; an evil curse (through inheritance or personal sin, including financial loss or hardship); economic loss (as in "a bear market"); danger; opposition; Russia. (See SNAKE.)

As if a man did flee from a lion, and a bear met him; or went into the house, and leaned his hand on the wall, and a serpent bit him (Amos 5:19).

And [Elisha] *went up from thence unto Bethel: and as he was going up by the way, there came forth little children out of the city, and mocked him...and he turned back, and looked on them, and cursed them in the name of the Lord. And there came forth two she bears out of the wood, and tare forty and two children of them* (2 Kings 2:23-24).

BEAVER – *Industrious:* Busy (as in "busy as a beaver"); diligent; clever; ingenious.

He becometh poor that dealeth with a slack hand: but the hand of the diligent maketh rich (Proverbs 10:4).

Through wisdom is an house builded; and by understanding it is established (Proverbs 24:3).

BEES – *Chastisement or Offense:* Stinging words; affliction; busybody; busy (as in "busy as a bee"); gossip. (See HORNETS.)

And the Amorites, which dwelt in that mountain, came out against you, and chased [chastised] *you, as bees do, and destroyed you...in Seir, even unto Hormah* (Deuteronomy 1:44).

They compassed me about like bees; they are quenched as the fire of thorns: for in the name of the Lord I will destroy them (Psalm 118:12).

And withal they learn to be idle, wandering [or buzzing] *about from house to house; and not only idle, but tattlers also and busybodies, speaking things which they ought not* (1 Timothy 5:13).

BIRD – *Spirit:* Holy Spirit; demon; humanity; message. **Flock of Black Birds** = *Gossip;* slander; bitter words. (See CROW/RAVEN, EAGLE, OWL, VULTURE, etc.)

And John bare record, saying, I saw the Spirit descending from heaven like a dove, and it abode upon Him (John 1:32).

Curse not the king, no not in thy thought; and curse not the rich in thy bedchamber: for a bird of the air shall carry the voice, and that which hath wings shall tell the matter (Ecclesiastes 10:20).

And he cried mightily with a strong voice, saying, Babylon the great is fallen, is fallen, and is become the habitation of devils, and the hold of every foul spirit, and a cage of every unclean and hateful bird (Revelation 18:2).

BUG – *Problem:* Broken (as in "that machine has a bug in it"); listening (spying) device (as in "the FBI has that place bugged"). (See GARDENING, Chapter 24.)

BULL – *Persecution:* Spiritual warfare; opposition; accusation; slander; threat; economic increase (as in "a bull market"); boastful; wrong (as in "he's full of bull"); falsehood (as in "that's a bunch of bull"). (See CALF.)

Many bulls have compassed me: strong bulls of Bashan have beset me round (Psalm 22:12).

BUTTERFLY – *Freedom:* Flighty (flitting about); fragile; temporary glory; nervous (as in "public speaking gives me butterflies"). **Cocoon** = *Metamorphosis;* transformation; change. **Caterpillar** = *Devourer;* potential.

And be not conformed to this world: but be ye transformed by the renewing of your mind... (Romans 12:2).

...and that which the cankerworm hath left hath the caterpillar eaten (Joel 1:4).

BUZZARD – See VULTURE.

CALF – *Increase:* Prosperity; idolatry; false worship; stubbornness; children of the Kingdom. **Cow or Heifer** = *A rebellious woman.*

The inhabitants of Samaria [mixed, incorrect worship] *shall fear because of the calves* [idolatry, i.e., materialism, as seen in the popular prosperity doctrine] *of Bethaven* [house of vanity; i.e., as opposed to Bethel, the house of God]: *for the people thereof shall mourn over it, and the priests thereof that rejoiced on it, for the glory thereof, because it is departed from it* [See Jer. 7:8-11] (Hosea 10:5).

But unto you that fear my name shall the Sun of righteousness arise with healing in His wings; and ye shall go forth, and grow up as calves of the stall (Malachi 4:2).

For Israel slideth back as a [stubborn] *backsliding heifer* (Hosea 4:16a).

And he received them [gold earrings] *at their hand, and fashioned it with a graving tool, after he had made it a molten calf* [idol, i.e., covetousness (See Col. 3:5)]: *and they said, These be thy gods, O Israel, which brought thee up out of the land of Egypt. ...And the Lord plagued the people, because they made the calf, which Aaron* [their priest, or preacher] *made* (Exodus 32:4,35).

CAMEL – *Endurance:* (because of their ability to go for long periods without water): Long journey; ungainly (not graceful).

And so, after he had patiently endured, he obtained the promise (Hebrews 6:15).

CAT – *Self-willed:* Not trainable (unteachable spirit); predator; unclean spirit; bewitching charm (witchcraft); stealthy; sneaky; crafty; deception; self-pity. **Personal Pet** = *Something precious.*

And, behold, there met him a woman with the attire of an harlot, and subtle of heart. (She is loud and stubborn; her feet abide not in her house: Now is she without, now in the streets [ally cat]*, and lieth in wait at every corner). ...With her much fair speech she caused him to yield, with the flattering of her lips* [purring] *she forced him* (Proverbs 7:10-12,21).

CHICKEN – *Fear:* Cowardliness. **Hen** = *Protection;* gossip; **Rooster** = *Boasting;* bragging; proud. **Chick** = *Defenseless;* innocent.

Then I said unto you, Dread not, neither be afraid of them (Deuteronomy 1:29).

O Jerusalem, Jerusalem, which killest the prophets, and stonest them that are sent unto thee; how often would I have gathered thy children together, as a hen doth gather her brood under her wings, and ye would not! (Luke 13:34)

And he said unto Him, Lord, I am ready to go with thee, both into prison, and to death. And he said, I tell thee, Peter, the cock [rooster] *shall not crow this day, before that thou shalt thrice deny that thou knowest Me.* [John 18:27 reads: *Peter then denied again: and immediately the cock crew* (reminding Peter of his empty boast)] (Luke 22:33-34).

CLAM – *Sealed:* Closed; silent (as in "he clammed up and quit talking").

But He [Jesus] *held His peace, and answered nothing. Again the high priest asked Him, and said unto Him, Art thou the Christ, the Son of the Blessed?* (Mark 14:61)

COW – See CALF.

CRAB – *Crabby:* Disgruntled; ill tempered; easily angered; complaining; critical.

Do all things without murmurings and disputings (Philippians 2:14).

CRAWFISH – *Retreat:* Coward. **With Raised Claws** = *Defensive;* cautious; renege on a promise (as in "He got cold feet and crawfished out of the deal").

And all the men of Israel, when they saw the man [Goliath], *fled from him, and were sore afraid* (1 Samuel 17:24).

CROCODILE – See ALLIGATOR.

CROW/RAVEN – *Confusion:* Outspoken person, usually operating under the influence of a spirit of envy or strife (which causes confusion and disorder); hateful; direct path (straight line, as in "as the crow flies"); God's minister of justice or provision.

For where envying and strife is, there is confusion and every evil work (James 3:16).

...the raven shall dwell in it: and he shall stretch out upon it the line of confusion, and the stones of emptiness (Isaiah 34:11).

Let them be ashamed and brought to confusion together that rejoice at mine hurt: let them be clothed with shame and dishonor that magnify themselves [and speak] *against me* (Psalm 35:26).

The eye that mocketh at his father, and despiseth to obey his mother, the ravens of the valley [depression; grief; confusion, etc.] *shall pick it out...* (Proverbs 30:17).

...I have commanded the ravens to feed thee there. ...And the ravens brought him bread and flesh in the morning, and bread and flesh in the evening... (1 Kings 17:4,6).

DEER – *Graceful:* Swift; sure-footed; agile; timid. **Buck** = *Regal;* rule. **Antlers** = *Power;* authority. (See HORNS, Chapter 24, and WILD GAME, Chapter 16.)

He maketh my feet like hinds' [doe's] *feet: and setteth me upon my high places* (2 Samuel 22:34).

DINOSAUR – *Extinct:* Evil or trouble from the past (through inherited sin); guilt of past sins (as fossils remind one of the past). See ALLIGATOR.

DOG – *Strife:* Contention; offense; unclean spirit. **Personal Pet** = *Something precious, or a friend* (as in "man's best friend"). **Dog Wagging Tail** = *Friendly;* acceptance. **Tucked Tail** = *Guilt;* shame; cowardly. **Biting Pet** = *Rewarding evil for good* (as in "biting the hand that feeds him"); betrayal; unthankful. **Barking Dog** = *Warning;* incessant nuisance; annoyance. **Dog Trailing Game** = *Persistent;* obsession. **Rabid Dog** = *Single-minded pursuit of evil;* contagious evil; persecution; great danger.

> *But if ye bite and devour one another, take heed that ye be not consumed one of another* (Galatians 5:15).

> *He that passeth by, and meddleth with strife belonging not to him, is like one that taketh a dog by the ears* (Proverbs 26:17).

> *And they have rewarded me evil for good, and hatred for my love* (Psalm 109:5).

> *For men* [who are dogs] *shall be lovers of their own selves, covetous, boasters, proud, blasphemers, disobedient to parents, unthankful, unholy, without natural affection, trucebreakers, false accusers, incontinent, fierce, despisers of those that are good, traitors, heady, highminded, lovers of pleasures more than lovers of God* (2 Timothy 3:2-4).

BULLDOG – *Unyielding:* Stubborn; tenacious; dangerous.

> *And it came to pass, when the judge was dead, that they returned, and corrupted themselves more than their fathers, in following other gods to serve them, and to bow down unto them; they ceased not from their own doings, nor from their stubborn way* (Judges 2:19).

WATCHDOG – *Watchman:* Elder; minister (good or bad); alert; beware.

> *His watchmen are blind: they are all ignorant, they are all dumb dogs, they cannot bark; sleeping, lying down, loving to slumber. Yea, they are greedy dogs which can never have enough, and they are shepherds that cannot understand...* (Isaiah 56:10-11).

> *That thy foot may be dipped in the blood of thine enemies, and the tongue of thy dogs in the same* (Psalm 68:23).

DONKEY – *Obnoxious:* Self-willed; stubborn; unyielding; tenacious. **Braying** = *Bragging.* (See MULE.)

> *A whip for the horse, a bridle for the ass, and a rod for the fool's back* (Proverbs 26:3).

And when the ass saw the angel of the Lord, she thrust herself unto the wall, and crushed Balaam's foot against the wall: and he smote her again (Numbers 22:25).

But [Balaam] *was rebuked for his iniquity: the dumb ass speaking with man's voice forbad the madness of the prophet* (2 Peter 2:16).

DOVE – *Peace:* the Holy Spirit; gentle. (See BIRD.)

Also he sent forth a dove from him, to see if the waters were abated from off the face of the ground; but the dove found no rest for the sole of her foot, and she returned unto him into the ark... And he stayed yet other seven days; and again he sent forth the dove out of the ark; and the dove came in to him in the evening; and, lo, in her mouth was an olive leaf plucked off: so Noah knew that the waters were abated from off the earth. And he stayed yet other seven days; and sent forth the dove; which returned not again unto him any more (Genesis 8:8-12).

And into whatsoever house ye enter, first say, Peace be to this house. And if the son of peace be there, your peace shall rest upon it: if not, it shall turn to you again (Luke 10:5-6).

Though ye have lien among the pots, yet shall ye be as the wings of a dove covered with silver, and her feathers with yellow gold (Psalm 68:13).

And the Holy Ghost descended in a bodily shape like a dove upon Him, and a voice came from heaven, which said, Thou art My beloved Son; in Thee I am well pleased (Luke 3:22).

DRAGON – *Demon:* Spiritual warfare; the nation of China.

And he laid hold on the dragon, that old serpent, which is the Devil, and Satan, and bound him a thousand years (Revelation 20:2).

And there was war in heaven: Michael and his angels fought against the dragon; and the dragon fought and his angels (Revelation 12:7).

EAGLE – *Leader:* Prophet (true or false); to see from above (as in "an eagle's eye view"); minister; fierce predator; sorcerer; United States of America.

Ye have seen what I did unto the Egyptians, and how I bare you on eagles' wings, and brought you unto myself [Hosea 12:13 reads: *And by a prophet the Lord brought Israel out of Egypt, and by a prophet was he preserved*] (Exodus 19:4).

Calling a ravenous bird from the east, the man that executeth my counsel from a far country... (Isaiah 46:11).

ELEPHANT – *Invincible or Thick-skinned:* Not easily offended; powerful; large. **Elephant Ears** = *Extra sensitive hearing.* **Baby Elephant** = *Potential for greatness* (the beginning of something large). **White Elephant** = *Unusable item;* unsalable; unwanted.

I can do all things through Christ which strengtheneth me [Compare Romans 8:37, *"Nay, in all these things we are more than conquerors through Him that loved us."*] (Philippians 4:13).

FISH – *Spirit or Soul:* Person (good or bad); a person's character or motive (as in "Something sure smells fishy about him"); Holy Spirit; unclean spirit. (See FISHING, Chapter 24.)

Again, the kingdom of heaven is like unto a net, that was cast into the sea, and gathered [fish, i.e., souls] *of every kind: which, when it was full, they drew to shore, and sat down, and gathered the good into vessels, but cast the bad away* (Matthew 13:47-48).

FLEA – *Insignificant:* Nuisance; irritant; elusive.

After whom is the king of Israel come out? after whom dost thou pursue? after a dead dog, after a flea (1 Samuel 24:14).

FLY – *Unclean:* Corruption; demon; curse; nuisance.

Dead flies cause the ointment of the apothecary to send forth a stinking savor: so doth a little folly him that is in reputation for wisdom and honor (Ecclesiastes 10:1).

And the Lord did so; and there came a grievous swarm of flies into the house of Pharaoh, and into his servants' houses, and into all the land of Egypt: the land was corrupted by reason of the swarm of flies (Exodus 8:24).

FOX – *Subtlety:* Deception; cunning; also, a con man; false prophet; wicked leader; hidden sin (as in "foxes have holes," i.e., they hide).

Take us the foxes, the little foxes [subtle deception of the enemy or secret sins], *that spoil the vines: for our vines have tender grapes* (Song of Solomon 2:15).

And he said unto them, Go ye, and tell that fox [Herod, the sly, wicked king], *Behold, I cast out devils...* (Luke 13:32).

O Israel, thy prophets are like the foxes in the deserts. They have seen vanity and lying divination, saying, The Lord saith: and the Lord hath not sent them: and they have made others to hope that they would confirm the word (Ezekiel 13:4,6).

FROG – *Spirit:* Demon; witchcraft; curse; evil words (as in "casting a spell"); puffed up.

He sent...frogs, which destroyed them (Psalm 78:45).

And I saw three unclean spirits like frogs come out of the mouth [released and expressed through words] *of the dragon, and out of the mouth of the beast, and out of the mouth of the false prophet* (Revelation 16:13).

GIRAFFE – *Exalted:* Regal; proud; haughty; snob (because of looking down on others).

Let nothing be done through strife or vainglory; but in lowliness of mind let each esteem other better than themselves (Philippians 2:3).

GOAT – *Sinner:* Unbelief; stubborn; unyielding; strife; argumentative, negative person; scapegoat (blamed for other's wrongdoing).

And He shall set the sheep on His right hand, but the goats [sinners] *on the left* (Matthew 25:33).

But the goat, on which the lot fell to be the scapegoat, shall be presented alive before the Lord, to make an atonement with him, and to let him go for a scapegoat [to be blamed or cursed for the wrongs of others] *into the wilderness* (Leviticus 16:10).

HAWK – *Predator:* Sorcerer; evil spirit; a person who is for war. **Falcon** = *Hunter;* minister. (See EAGLE.)

Also of your own selves shall men [eagles or hawks, i.e., predators] *arise, speaking perverse things, to draw away disciples after them* (Acts 20:30).

He was a mighty hunter before [in the face of, i.e., against] *the Lord: wherefore it is said, Even as Nimrod the mighty hunter* [predator] *before* [against] *the Lord* [i.e., one who hunts the souls of men to build his own kingdom] (Genesis 10:9).

HOG – See SWINE.

HORNET or Wasp – *Affliction:* Stinging, biting words; slander; strife; curse (because of sin); persecution; trouble; offense; demon spirits. (See BEES.)

Moreover the Lord thy God will send the hornet among them, until they that are left, and hide themselves from thee, be destroyed (Deuteronomy 7:20).

HORSE – *Time/Work:* Flesh (as in "the works of the flesh"); the work of God's Spirit through people; spiritual warfare; one week (or another specific period of time); age; strength. **Dead Horse** = *Dead Work;* an unalterable situation; admonition to stop wasting energy on a lost cause (as in "he's flogging a dead horse", i.e., to make him get up and go).

They were as fed horses in the morning: every one neighed after his neighbor's wife [their works were works of the flesh; compare Galatians 5:19, *Now the works of the flesh are manifest, which are these; Adultery, fornication, uncleanness, lasciviousness.*] (Jeremiah 5:8).

An horse is a vain thing for safety: neither shall he deliver any by his great strength (Psalm 33:17).

HORSE'S RIDER – *Nature of time or work:* Anxious; happy; confident.

Then she saddled an ass, and said to her servant [in anguish of spirit], *Drive, and go forward; slack not thy riding for me, except I bid thee* (2 Kings 4:24).

And I saw, and behold a white horse: and he that sat on him had a bow; and a crown was given unto him: and he went forth conquering, and to conquer (Revelation 6:2).

And I looked, and behold a pale horse: and his name that sat on him was Death, and Hell followed with him (Revelation 6:8a).

FRONT HALF OF HORSE – *First part of time or work:* Beginning; ready.

BACK HALF OF HORSE – *Last part of time or work:* End; also, an offensive or obnoxious person.

BLACK HORSE – *Famine:* Bad times; evil. (See BLACK, *Chapter 9 and 18.*)

And when he had opened the third seal, I heard the third beast say, Come and see. And I beheld, and lo a black horse; and he that sat on him had a pair of balances in his hand (Revelation 6:5).

Behold, the days come, saith the Lord God, that I will send a famine in the land, not a famine of bread, nor a thirst for water, but of hearing the words of the Lord (Amos 8:11).

RED HORSE – *Persecution:* Anger; danger; opposition. (See RED, Chapters 9 and 18.)

And there went out another horse that was red: and power was given to him that sat thereon to take peace from the earth, and that they should kill one another: and there was given unto him a great sword (Revelation 6:4).

They shall put you out of the synagogues: yea, the time cometh, that whosoever killeth you will think that he doeth God service (John 16:2).

KICKING/LIFTING HEEL – *Threatening:* Betrayal; rebellion; persecution.

I speak not of you all: I know whom I have chosen: but that the scripture may be fulfilled, he that eateth bread with Me hath lifted up his heel against Me (John 13:18).

QUARTER HORSE – *Strong:* Good times; fast; agility; success.

And I saw, and behold a white [or quarter] horse: and he that sat on him had a bow; and a crown was given unto him: and he went forth conquering, and to conquer (Revelation 6:2).

HOUND – See DOG.

KANGAROO – *To Jump:* Predisposition; prejudiced (as in "a kangaroo court," where the verdict is decided before the person is even tried); to jump to a conclusion; Australia.

He that answereth a matter before he heareth it, it is folly and shame unto him (Proverbs 18:13).

Then shalt thou inquire, and make search, and ask diligently; and, behold, if it be truth, and the thing certain, that such abomination is wrought among you [See Deut. 17:8-13] (Deuteronomy 13:14).

KITTENS or PUPPIES – *Gifts:* Precious; helpless; must be attended to.

Now there are diversities of gifts, but the same Spirit (1 Corinthians 12:4).

Neglect not the gift that is in thee, which was given thee by prophecy, with the laying on of the hands of the presbytery (1 Timothy 4:14).

LAMB – See SHEEP.

LEOPARD – *Powerful:* Powerful leader (good or evil); predator; permanent, unchanging evil person; danger. (See LION.)

...A leopard shall watch over their cities: every one that goeth out thence shall be torn in pieces: because their transgressions are many, and their backslidings are increased (Jeremiah 5:6).

Can the Ethiopian change his skin, or the leopard his spots? then may ye also do good, that are accustomed to do evil (Jeremiah 13:23).

LICE – *Conviction:* Shame; guilt; accusation; affliction. (See FINGER, Chapter 24.)

...Aaron stretched out his hand with his rod, and smote the dust of the earth, and it became lice in man, and in beast; all the dust of the land became lice throughout all the land of Egypt. ... Then the magicians said unto Pharaoh, This is the finger [accusation] *of God: and Pharaoh's heart was hardened* [refused the conviction of God's Spirit], *and he hearkened not unto them...* (Exodus 8:17,19).

This they said, tempting Him, that they might have to accuse Him. But Jesus stooped down, and with His finger wrote on the [dust of the] *ground, as though He heard them not. ...And they which heard it, being convicted* [accused] *by their own conscience, went out* [ashamed, as one afflicted and infected by lice] *one by one, beginning at the eldest, even unto the last: and Jesus was left alone, and the woman standing in the midst* (John 8:6,9).

LION – *Dominion:* Christ; king; regal; bold; power; satan; religious tradition; destroying spirit. (See LEOPARD.)

And one of the elders saith unto me, Weep not: behold, the Lion of the tribe of Judah [Christ], *the Root of David, hath prevailed to open the book, and to loose the seven seals thereof* (Revelation 5:5).

A lion which is strongest among beasts, and turneth not away for any (Proverbs 30:30).

The wicked flee when no man pursueth: but the righteous are bold as a lion (Proverbs 28:1).

Be sober, be vigilant; because your adversary the devil, as a roaring lion, walketh about, seeking whom he may devour (1 Peter 5:8).

Beware lest any man spoil you [devour you or your blessings] *through philosophy and vain deceit, after the* [religious] *tra-*

dition of men, after the rudiments of the world, and not after Christ (Colossians 2:8).

MAGGOT – *Corruption:* Filthiness of the flesh; evil.

But I am a worm [Hebrew: maggot], *and no man; a reproach of men, and despised of the people* (Psalm 22:6).

MICE – *Devourer:* Curse; plague; timid (as in "Are you a man or a mouse?").

Then said they, What shall be the trespass offering which we shall return to him? They answered, Five golden emerods, and five golden mice...for one plague was on you all, and on your lords (1 Samuel 6:4).

And I will rebuke the devourer for your sakes, and he shall not destroy the fruits of your ground... (Malachi 3:11).

For God hath not given us the spirit of fear [Greek: timidity]; *but of power, and of love, and of a sound mind* (2 Timothy 1:7).

MONKEY – *Foolishness or Clinging:* Mischief; foolishness; dishonesty (as in "monkey business"); addiction (a heroin addict is said to "have a monkey on his back").

Though thou shouldest bray a fool in a mortar among wheat with a pestle, yet will not his foolishness depart from him (Proverbs 27:22).

They have stricken me, shalt thou say, and I was not sick; they have beaten me, and I felt it not: when shall I awake? I will seek it [wine or any addictive substance] *yet again* (Proverbs 23:35).

MOTH – *Deterioration:* (*Note:* A moth is an insect of darkness.) Loss through deceit; secret or undetected trouble; corruption; chastisement.

Therefore will I be unto Ephraim as a moth, and to the house of Judah as rottenness (Hosea 5:12).

Lay not up for yourselves treasures upon earth, where moth and rust doth corrupt... (Matthew 6:19).

MULE – *Stubborn:* Self-willed; tenacious; strong; also, unbelief (See DONKEY.)

Be ye not as the horse, or as the mule, which have no understanding: whose mouth must be held in with bit and bridle... (Psalm 32:9).

But they refused to hearken, and pulled away the shoulder, and stopped their ears, that they should not hear (Zechariah 7:11).

OSTRICH – *Denial* (as in, "he has his head stuck in the sand"): Hardheartedness toward one's own children (as an ostrich steps on its own young).

Even the sea monsters draw out the breast, they give suck to their young ones: [but] *the daughter of my people is become cruel, like the ostriches in the wilderness* (Lamentations 4:3).

OWL – *Circumspect (looking around):* Wisdom (as in "a wise old owl"); also, demon (because it is a bird of the night); curse.

And in all things that I have said unto you be circumspect... (Exodus 23:13).

And thorns [curses] *shall come up in her palaces...and it shall be...a court for owls* (Isaiah 34:13).

OYSTER – See PEARL.

PARROT – *Mimic:* Copy; mock; repeat; divination.

And he [Elisha] *went up from thence unto Bethel: and as he was going up by the way, there came forth little children out of the city, and mocked him, and said unto him, Go up, thou bald head; go up, thou bald head* (2 Kings 2:23).

PENGUIN – *Specialized:* Graceful in its own element (water), but awkward on land; vigilant (must constantly watch for its natural enemy, sharks). (See SEA TURTLE.)

Let every man abide in the same calling wherein he was called (1 Corinthians 7:20).

Be sober, be vigilant; because your adversary the devil, as a roaring lion, walketh about, seeking whom he may devour (1 Peter 5:8).

PIG – See SWINE.

PUPPY – See KITTENS or PUPPIES.

PYTHON – *Divination:* Imitation of the Holy Spirit's voice; religious spirit; legalism; control. (*Note:* divination is often associated with witchcraft and sorcery.) (See SNAKE.)

And it came to pass, as we went to prayer, a certain damsel possessed with a spirit of divination [Greek: Python] *met us, which brought her masters much gain by soothsaying* (Acts 16:16).

RABBIT – *Increase:* Fast growth; multiplication (good or evil increase). (See WILD GAME.)

An inheritance may be gotten hastily at the beginning: but the end thereof shall not be blessed (Proverbs 20:21).

RACCOON – *Mischief:* Night raider; rascal; thief; bandit; deceitful; obsession with or excessive cleanliness.

For they sleep not, except they have done mischief... (Proverbs 4:16).

It is as sport to a fool to do mischief... (Proverbs 10:23).

RAT – *Unclean:* Wicked person; jerk; devourer; plague (curse because of sin); betrayer (as in "ratting on someone"). (See MICE.)

Whoso [is a rat and] *rewardeth evil for good, evil shall not depart from his house* (Proverbs 17:13).

The wicked plotteth against the just, and gnasheth upon him with his teeth (Psalm 37:12).

And if ye walk contrary unto me, and will not hearken unto me; I will bring seven times more plagues [such as bubonic plague, carried by rats] *upon you according to your sins* (Leviticus 26:21).

ROACHES – *Infestation:* Unclean spirits; uncleanness; hidden sin.

Having therefore these promises, dearly beloved, let us cleanse ourselves from all filthiness of the flesh and spirit... (2 Corinthians 7:1).

SCORPION – *Sin Nature:* Lust of the flesh; temptation; deception; accusation; destruction; danger.

Behold, I give unto you power to tread on serpents and scorpions [the sin nature of the flesh], *and over all the power of the enemy: and nothing shall by any means hurt you* (Luke 10:19).

The [scorpion's] *sting of death is sin; and the strength of sin is the law* (1 Corinthians 15:56).

But I see another law in my members, warring against the law of my mind, and bringing me into captivity to the law [or nature] *of sin* [the scorpion] *which is in my members* (Romans 7:23).

SEA TURTLE – *Specialized:* Graceful in its own element (water), but awkward on land; rare (threatened with extinction). **Out of Water** = *Out of its natural element.* (See PENGUIN.)

SHEEP – *Innocent:* Defenseless; gentleness; Saint(s); unsaved person(s).

But go rather to the lost sheep of the house of Israel (Matthew 10:6).

And David spake unto the Lord when he saw the angel that smote the people, and said, Lo, I have sinned, and I have done wickedly: but these sheep [innocent people], *what have they done?* (2 Samuel 24:17a)

And He shall set the sheep [innocent, saved people] *on His right hand, but the goats* [guilty, unsaved people] *on the left* (Matthew 25:33).

SKUNK – *Repulsive:* Offensive; something that should be "put out"; something that one is better off leaving alone; dishonest person.

Dead flies cause the ointment of the apothecary to send forth a stinking savor: so doth a little folly him that is in reputation for wisdom and honor (Ecclesiastes 10:1).

SLOTH – *Lazy:* Lethargic; lifeless; slow.

But if any provide not for his own, and specially for those of his own house, he hath denied the faith, and is worse than an infidel (1 Timothy 5:8).

He also that is slothful in his work is brother to him that is a great waster (Proverbs 18:9).

By much slothfulness the building decayeth; and through idleness of the hands the house droppeth through (Ecclesiastes 10:18).

SNAIL – *Slow:* Unclean, immoral person (leaves a trail of slime).

These also shall be unclean unto you...the lizard, and the snail, and the mole (Leviticus 11:29-30).

SNAKE – *Curse:* Demon; deception; threat; danger; hatred; slander; critical spirit; witchcraft. **Fangs** = *Evil intent;* danger. **Rattles** = *Words;* threats; warning; alarm. (See BEAR.)

And the Lord God said unto the serpent, because thou hast done this, thou art cursed above all cattle, and above every beast of the field... (Genesis 3:14).

As if a man did flee from a lion, and a bear met him; or went into the house, and leaned his hand on the wall, and a serpent bit him (Amos 5:19).

They have sharpened their tongues like a serpent [slander]; *adders' poison is under their lips* (Psalm 140:3).

At the last it [alcohol] *biteth like a serpent, and stingeth like an adder* (Proverbs 23:32).

...and that [the person] *which is crushed breaketh out into a viper* [becomes bitter, critical, etc.] (Isaiah 59:5).

SPIDER (WEB) – *Evil:* Sin; deception; false doctrine; temptation; tenacious. **Web** = *Snare;* lies (as in "What tangled webs we weave when we first practice to deceive"). (See SCORPION.)

There be four things which are little upon the earth, but they are exceeding wise: ...The spider taketh hold with her hands [works, see Rom. 6:16], *and is in kings' palaces* (Proverbs 30:24,28).

And I find more bitter than death the woman, whose heart is snares and nets, and her hands as bands [or webs]: *whoso pleaseth God shall escape from her; but the sinner shall be taken by her* (Ecclesiastes 7:26).

BLACK WIDOW – *Danger:* Great danger; deadly; evil; slander.

But the tongue can no man tame; it is an unruly evil, full of deadly poison (James 3:8).

STORK – *Expectant:* New birth; new baby; new experience; that which is forthcoming.

Yea, the stork in the heaven knoweth her appointed times...but My people know not the judgment of the Lord (Jeremiah 8:7).

SWINE – *Unclean:* Selfish; backslider; unbeliever; glutton; fornicator; hypocrite; idolater. **Boar** = *Persecutor;* hostile to virtue; vicious; vengeful; danger.

But it is happened unto them according to the true proverb, The dog is turned to his own vomit again; and the sow that was washed to her wallowing in the mire (2 Peter 2:22).

Give not that which is holy unto the dogs, neither cast ye your pearls before swine, lest they trample them under their feet, and turn again and rend you (Matthew 7:6).

The boar out of the wood [i.e., from among the people] *doth waste it, and the wild beast of the field doth devour it* (Psalm 80:13).

For men shall be lovers of their own selves, covetous, boasters, proud, blasphemers, disobedient to parents, unthankful, unholy, without natural affection, trucebreakers, false accusers, incontinent, fierce, despisers of those that are good [Greek: hostile to virtue] (2 Timothy 3:2-3).

TERMITES – *Corruption:* Hidden destruction; secret sin; deception; demon spirits. (See MOTH.)

If the foundations be destroyed, what can the righteous do? (Psalm 11:3)

Ye have sown much, and bring in little; ye eat, but ye have not enough; ye drink, but ye are not filled with drink; ye clothe you, but there is none warm; and he that earneth wages earneth wages to put it into a bag with holes [as termites eat the strength of the walls of a house, causing damage and loss] (Haggai 1:6).

TERRAPIN – *Slow:* Withdrawn; cautious; protected; safe.

Wherefore, my beloved brethren, let every man be swift to hear, slow to speak, slow to wrath (James 1:19).

TICK – *Hidden:* Hidden unclean spirit; oblivious to one's true self (as in practicing self-justification and self-righteousness); parasite; pest.

Or if a soul touch any unclean thing...or the carcass of unclean creeping things, and if it be hidden from him; he also shall be unclean, and guilty (Leviticus 5:2).

The heart is deceitful above all things, and desperately wicked: who can know it? (Jeremiah 17:9)

TIGER – *Danger:* Powerful minister (danger for the devil!); evil, dangerous person (good or evil). (See LEOPARD.)

He that committeth sin is of the devil; for the devil sinneth from the beginning. For this purpose the Son of God was manifested, that He might destroy the works of the devil (1 John 3:8).

TOAD – See FROG.

TURKEY – *Foolish:* Dumb; clumsy (in word or deed); thanksgiving.

For man also knoweth not his time...as the birds that are caught in the snare; so are the sons of men snared in an evil time, when it falleth suddenly upon them (Ecclesiastes 9:12).

TURTLE – See TERRAPIN.

VULTURE – *Scavenger:* Unclean; impure; an evil person; also, all seeing; waiting (in an evil sense, as a person waiting for parents to die so he/she may get their possessions).

But these are they [which are unclean,] *of which ye shall not eat: the eagle...and the vulture after his kind* (Deuteronomy 14:12-13).

The eye that mocketh at his father, and despiseth to obey his mother, the ravens of the valley shall pick it out, and the young eagles [or vultures] *shall eat it* (Proverbs 30:17).

WASP – See HORNET.

WEASEL – *Wicked:* Renege on a promise (as in "weasel out of a deal"); informant or tattletale (as in "that weasel squealed on me"); a Judas (betrayer); traitor; informant.

And Judas Iscariot, one of the twelve, went unto the chief priests, to betray Him unto them (Mark 14:10).

WILD GAME – *Work:* **Hunting or Eating Deer, Birds, etc. =** *Seeking or doing God's Word and work;* sorcery. (See FOOD/MILK, TEETH and subheadings, Chapter 24.)

The slothful man roasteth not that which he took in hunting [he does not meditate on and act upon the revelation knowledge he receives from his studies of the Word of God]: *but the substance of a diligent man is precious* (Proverbs 12:27).

WOLF – *Predator:* Devourer; false prophet; evil minister or governor; person seeking his own gain; womanizer; God's minister of justice. **Fangs** = *Evil motive;* danger.

Beware of false prophets, which come to you in sheep's clothing, but inwardly they are ravening wolves (Matthew 7:15).

For I know this, that after my departing shall grievous wolves enter in among you, not sparing the flock. Also of your own selves shall men arise, speaking perverse things, to draw away disciples after them (Acts 20:29-30).

WORM – See MAGGOT.

CHAPTER 17

Buildings / Rooms / Places

Refer to Chapter 10 for more in-depth explanation of various rooms.

AIRPORT – *Waiting:* Preparing; being made ready (for ministry, travel, change, etc.); also, the Church. (See Chapter 12.)

Which sometime were disobedient, when once the longsuffering of God waited in the days of Noah, while the ark was a preparing, wherein few, that is, eight souls were saved by water (1 Peter 3:20).

But if they had stood in My counsel [waited for God's training and preparation in them to be completed], *and had caused My people to hear My words, then they should have turned them from their evil way, and from the evil of their doings* (Jeremiah 23:22).

ATTIC – *Mind:* Thought; attitude (good or bad); learning; spiritual realm. **Dusty Relics From the Past** = *Memories.*

Peter went up upon the housetop to pray...he fell into a trance, and saw heaven opened, and a certain vessel descending unto him, as it had been a great sheet knit at the four corners, and let down to the earth (Acts 10:9b-11).

Brethren, I count not myself to have apprehended: but this one thing I do, forgetting those things which are behind, and reaching forth unto those things which are before (Philippians 3:13).

BALCONY – *Spiritual Realm:* Spiritual oversight; spiritual viewpoint; to oversee. (See UPSTAIRS.)

After this I looked, and, behold, a door was opened in heaven: and the first voice which I heard was as it were of a trumpet talking with me; which said, Come up hither, and I will shew thee things which must be hereafter (Revelation 4:1).

BANK – *Secure:* Dependable; safe; saved; certain (as in "you can bank on it"); reward reserved in Heaven; the Church.

Wherefore then gavest not thou my money [talents, spiritual gifts, etc.] *into the bank* [submitted one's gifts and abilities to those whom God has placed in spiritual authority], *that at my coming I might have required mine own with usury?* (Luke 19:23)

But lay up for yourselves treasures in heaven...where thieves do not break through nor steal (Matthew 6:20).

BAR – See TAVERN.

BARBERSHOP – *Church:* Place of removal of old covenants of sin, occult, or religion. **Haircut** = *Putting away tradition or bad habits;* repenting of bad attitudes. (See HAIR, BEARD, Chapter 24, and BEAUTY SHOP, *Chapter 17.*)

That he told her all his heart, and said unto her. There hath not come a razor upon mine head; for I have been a Nazarite unto God from my mother's womb: if I be shaven [break the covenant], *then my strength will go from me, and I shall become weak, and be like any other man* (Judges 16:17).

And be not conformed to this world: but be ye transformed by the renewing of your mind... (Romans 12:2).

BARN – *Storehouse:* Church; relating to the work of the ministry; provision; large work. (See HAY, Chapter 24.)

Let both grow together until the harvest: and in the time of harvest I will say to the reapers, Gather ye together first the tares [hypocrites], *and bind them in bundles to burn them: but gather the wheat* [righteous] *into my barn* (Matthew 13:30).

Where no oxen are, the crib [or barn] *is clean: but much increase is by the strength of the ox* [ministry] (Proverbs 14:4).

And he said, This will I do: I will pull down my barns, and build greater [mega-churches]; *and there will I bestow all my fruits and my goods* (Luke 12:18).

BASEMENT – *Soul:* Carnal nature; lust; discouragement or depression; refuge; retreat; hidden; forgotten; secret sin; put away or stored (as in "it's put away in the basement"). (See FOUNDATION.)

Then took they Jeremiah, and cast him into the dungeon...and they let down Jeremiah with cords. And in the dungeon there was no water, but mire: so Jeremiah sunk in the mire (Jeremiah 38:6).

BATHROOM – *Desire or Cleansing:* Prayer of repentance; confession of offenses or sins to another person; passion; strong lust.

Wash you, make you clean; put away the evil of your doings from before mine eyes; cease to do evil (Isaiah 1:16).

The beginning of strife [or sexual lust] *is as when one letteth out water: therefore leave off contention* [and lust], *before it be meddled with* (Proverbs 17:14).

...David arose from off his bed, and walked upon the roof of the king's house: and from the roof he saw a woman washing herself; and the woman was very beautiful to look upon. ...And David sent messengers, and took her; and she came in unto him, and he lay with her; for she was purified from her uncleanness... (2 Samuel 11:2,4).

BEAUTY SHOP – *Church:* Preparation; vanity; holiness. (See BARBERSHOP.)

The inhabitants of Samaria [mixed, incorrect worship] *shall fear because of the calves of Bethaven* [(a play on words): Bethaven = house of vanity; i.e., as opposed to Bethel, the house of God]: *for the people thereof shall mourn over it, and the priests thereof that rejoiced on it, for the glory thereof, because it is departed from it* (Hosea 10:5).

Favor is deceitful, and beauty is vain: but a woman that feareth the Lord, she shall be praised (Proverbs 31:30).

But if a woman have long hair, it is a glory to her: for her hair is given her for a covering (1 Corinthians 11:15).

Give unto the Lord the glory due unto His name; worship the Lord in the beauty of holiness (Psalm 29:2).

BEDROOM – *Rest:* Salvation; meditation; intimacy; privacy; peace; covenant (as in marriage), or an evil covenant (as in natural or spiritual adultery); self-made (harmful) conditions (as in "you made your bed, now sleep in it").

Stand in awe, and sin not: commune with your own heart upon your bed, and be still (Psalm 4:4).

If I ascend up into heaven, Thou art there: if I make my bed in hell, behold, Thou art there [See Isa. 28:18-20] (Psalm 139:8).

Marriage is honorable in all, and the bed [is to be kept] *undefiled: but whoremongers and adulterers God will judge* (Hebrews 13:4).

Ye adulterers and adulteresses, know ye not that the friendship of the world is enmity with God?... (James 4:4)

BUILDING FRAME (a house under construction) – See FOUNDATION.

BUS STATION – See AIRPORT.

CAFETERIA – *Service:* Church; people or work; teaching; ministry of helps.

For I was an hungered, and ye gave me meat: I was thirsty, and ye gave me drink: I was a stranger, and ye took me in (Matthew 25:35).

CAPITAL (National or State) – *Government:* Natural or spiritual government; abusive control; corruption.

And he said unto them, The kings of the Gentiles exercise lordship over them; and they that exercise authority upon them are called benefactors. But ye shall not be so: but he that is greatest among you, let him be as the younger; and he that is chief, as he that doth serve (Luke 22:25-26).

CASTLE – *Exalted Dwelling:* Noble dwelling; King's (Christ's) dwelling place; exalted; defended stronghold. (See FORT).

And David dwelt in the castle; therefore they called it the city of David (1 Chronicles 11:7).

A brother offended is harder to be won than a strong city: and their contentions are like the bars of a castle (Proverbs 18:19).

CHURCH BUILDING – *Church:* Congregation; may represent one's own Church. (See CHURCH SERVICE, Chapter 24.)

And I say also unto thee, That thou art Peter, and upon this rock I will build My church; and the gates of hell shall not prevail against it (Matthew 16:18).

CITY – *Characteristic:* That for which the city is known (for example: **Las Vegas** = *Gambling, prostitution, etc.*); the Church; a person's character.

Even as Sodom and Gomorrah...giving themselves over to fornication, and going after strange flesh, are set forth for an example, suffering the vengeance of eternal fire... [Compare Ezekiel 16:49-50: *"Behold, this was the iniquity of thy sister Sodom, pride, fullness of bread, and abundance of idleness was in her and in her daughters, neither did she strengthen the hand of the poor and needy. And they were haughty, and committed abomination* (homosexuality) *before me: therefore I took them away as I saw good."*] (Jude 7).

Save that the Holy Ghost witnesseth in every city [Church], *saying that bonds and afflictions abide me* (Acts 20:23).

He that hath no rule over his own spirit is like a city that is broken down, and without walls (Proverbs 25:28).

CONCRETE SLAB – See FOUNDATION.

COUNTRY – *Isolated:* Quiet; peaceful; restful; removed from the city. (A country, see NATION.)

And He said unto them, Come ye yourselves apart into a desert [or country] place, and rest a while: for there were many coming and going, and they had no leisure so much as to eat (Mark 6:31).

COURTHOUSE – *Judgment:* Trial; persecution; justice; legal matter; local government. (See JUDGE, LAWYER, Chapter 22, and MISCARRIAGE, Chapter 24.)

Judges and officers shalt thou make thee in all thy gates [places of judgment], which the Lord thy God giveth thee, throughout thy tribes: and they shall judge the people with just judgment [See Deuteronomy 17:6-13.] (Deuteronomy 16:18).

I have declared, and have saved, and I have shewed, when there was no strange god among you: therefore ye are my witnesses, saith the Lord, that I am God (Isaiah 43:12).

Shall the throne of iniquity [evil court] have fellowship with Thee, which frameth mischief by a law? (Psalm 94:20)

Dare any of you, having a matter against another, go to law before the unjust, and not before the saints? [See Matthew 18:15-19.] (1 Corinthians 6:1).

COTTON GIN – See FACTORY.

DEATH ROW – *Death Sentence:* Doomed; Cursed. (See DEATH, Chapter 24.)

But God came to Abimelech in a dream by night, and said to him, Behold, thou art but a dead man, for the woman which thou hast taken; for she is a man's wife (Genesis 20:3).

DEN – See LIVING ROOM.

DESERT – *Barren:* Unproductive; dry; spiritual wasteland; without hope; need for revival.

They wandered in the wilderness in a solitary way; they found no city to dwell in. Hungry and thirsty, their soul fainted in them (Psalm 107:4-5).

Then shall the lame man leap as an hart, and the tongue of the dumb sing: for in the wilderness shall waters break out, and streams in the desert (Isaiah 35:6).

FACTORY – *Work or Source:* Production; getting things done; the Kingdom of God; the Church; the "world"; worldly, apostate church; the motions of sin; fabrication (including lies, heresy, false worship). **Idle Factory** = *Not busy;* not reaching full potential; natural workplace (when applicable). (See MACHINES, Chapter 24.)

And He said unto them, How is it that ye sought Me? wist ye not that I must be about My Father's business? (Luke 2:49)

Not slothful in business; fervent in spirit; serving the Lord (Romans 12:11).

FARM – See FARMER, Chapter 22.

FORT – *Stronghold:* Well-defended position. **If dreamer is within the fort** = *Secure; safe;* protected; well-defended. **If without** = *Unsafe;* vulnerable. **Walls broken down** = *Need to build up or repair fortifications.* (See CASTLE.)

For the weapons of our warfare are not carnal, but mighty through God to the pulling down of strong holds; (2 Corinthians 10:4).

And he fortified the strong holds, and put captains in them, and store of victual, and of oil and wine. And in every several city he put shields and spears, and made them exceeding strong, having Judah and Benjamin on his side (2 Chronicles 11:11-12).

FOUNDATION – *Foundation* (as in "a concrete slab for a building under construction"): Established; stable; unstable (when shaky); not ready to proceed with construction (when incomplete); the Gospel; sound doctrine; church government; building program.

If the foundations be destroyed, what can the righteous do? (Psalm 11:3)

Lest haply, after he hath laid the foundation, and is not able to finish it, all that behold it begin to mock him (Luke 14:29).

According to the grace of God which is given unto me, as a wise masterbuilder, I have laid the foundation, and another buildeth thereon....For other foundation can no man lay than that is laid, which is Jesus Christ [See Hebrews 6:1-2.] (1 Corinthians 3:10-11).

And are built upon the foundation of the apostles and prophets, Jesus Christ Himself being the chief corner stone (Ephesians 2:20).

GROUND FLOOR – See LIVING ROOM.

HOSPITAL – *Care:* Church; place of healing; mercy; persons who are wounded or sick.

And Jesus answering said, A certain man went down from Jerusalem to Jericho, and fell among thieves, which...wounded him, and departed, leaving him half dead...But a certain Samaritan...had compassion on him, and went to him, and bound up his wounds, pouring in oil and wine...and brought him to an inn [or hospital], *and took care of him* (Luke 10:30,33-34).

For I am poor and needy, and my heart is wounded within me [Compare Psalm 147:3: *"He healeth the broken in heart, and bindeth up their wounds."*] (Psalm 109:22).

But He [Jesus] *was wounded for our transgressions, He was bruised for our iniquities: the chastisement of our peace was upon Him; and with His stripes we are healed* (Isaiah 53:5).

HOTEL – *Public place for rest or business:* Church (place for rest in Christ); public gathering; travel; business travel; temporary stop; rest.

And from thence, when the brethren heard of us, they came to meet us as far as Appii Forum, and The three taverns: whom when Paul saw, he thanked God, and took courage (Acts 28:15).

HOUSE – *Person or family:* Individual; Church. When naturally interpreted, it means a dwelling place. **Home** = *Heart* (as in "home is where the heart is"); identity; roots.

When the unclean spirit is gone out of a man, he walketh through dry places, seeking rest; and finding none, he saith, I will return unto my house [the person] *whence I came out* (Luke 11:24).

And they said, Believe on the Lord Jesus Christ, and thou shalt be saved, and thy house [family] (Acts 16:31).

For I have not dwelt in an house [made with hands] *since the day that I brought up Israel unto this day; but have gone from tent to tent, and from one tabernacle to another* [i.e., from one Church to another and from one person to another] (1 Chronicles 17:5).

NEW HOUSE – *New life (as in salvation):* Change; revival; new move (natural or spiritual). (See MOVING VAN, Chapter 23.)

Therefore if any man be in Christ, he is a new creature [or creation, i.e., new house]: *old things are passed away; behold, all things are become new* (2 Corinthians 5:17).

For we know that if our earthly house of this tabernacle [our body] were dissolved [by death], *we have a building of God, an house not made with hands, eternal in the heavens* (2 Corinthians 5:1).

OLD HOUSE – *Past:* Inheritance, e.g., one's Grandfather's or Grandmother's religion, ways, or temperament; established tradition. **An old house in good condition** = *God's ways;* righteousness; diligence. **In bad condition** = *Our sins or the sins of our forefathers.* Needing revival (when in need of repair or remodeling); untended (when unpainted or the property is grown over with weeds); neglect; unusable (when beyond repair); ruin. (See GRANDMOTHER, Chapter 22.)

Now the Lord had said unto Abram, Get thee out of thy country, and from thy kindred, and from thy father's house [natural and spiritual inheritance], *unto a land that I will shew thee* (Genesis 12:1).

Thus saith the Lord, Stand ye in the ways, and see, and ask for the old paths [or the old house of God], *where is the good way, and walk therein, and ye shall find rest for your souls...* (Jeremiah 6:16).

HOUSE TRAILER – *Temporary:* Place; situation; relationship.

Whereas ye know not what shall be on the morrow. For what is your life? It is even a vapor, that appeareth for a little time, and then vanisheth away (James 4:14).

HOUSE UNDER CONSTRUCTION – See FOUNDATION.

JAIL – See PRISON.

KITCHEN – *Heart:* Intent; motive; plans; passion; ambition; affliction (as in "If you can't take the heat, stay out of the kitchen"). (See OVEN and REFRIGERATOR, Chapter 24.)

For they have made ready their heart like an oven, whiles they lie in wait: their baker sleepeth all the night; in the morning it burneth as a flaming fire (Hosea 7:6).

For the word of God is quick, and powerful, and sharper than any twoedged sword, piercing even to the dividing asunder of soul and spirit, and of the joints and marrow, and is a discerner of the thoughts and intents of the heart [where things are cooked up, or planned] (Hebrews 4:12).

LIBRARY – *Knowledge:* Education; learning; research; wisdom; study; distraction (when noisy). (See BOOK and NOISE, Chapter 24.)

Wisdom is the principal thing; therefore get wisdom: and with all thy getting get understanding (Proverbs 4:7).

Ever learning, and never able to come to the knowledge of the truth (2 Timothy 3:7).

Study to shew thyself approved unto God, a workman that needeth not to be ashamed, rightly dividing the word of truth (2 Timothy 2:15).

LIVING ROOM – *Revealed:* Everyday or current affairs; that which is manifest; truth exposed; without hypocrisy. (See PORCH.)

And when they could not come nigh unto Him for the press, they uncovered the roof where He was [living room]: and when they had broken it up, they let down the bed wherein the sick of the palsy lay. When Jesus saw their faith, He said unto the sick of the palsy, Son, thy sins be forgiven thee (Mark 2:4-5).

MALL – *World:* Worldliness; ripe field for evangelism.

Love not the world, neither the things that are in the world. If any man love the world, the love of the Father is not in him (1 John 2:15).

Therefore disputed He in the synagogue with the Jews, and with the devout persons, and in the market daily with them that met with Him (Acts 17:17).

MOTEL – See HOTEL.

NATION (or Nationality) – *Characteristic:* That for which the people are known. Some examples are: **France** = *Romance.* **Germany** = *Industrious;* hardworking. **Israel (a Jew)** = *Shrewd business dealings* (as in "he jewed the price down"); *persecuted.* May represent the actual nation. (See CITY.)

Israel shall be a proverb and a byword among all people… (1 Kings 9:7).

OFFICE – *Place or position of authority:* Official; oversee; type of office indicates meaning, for example, if it is a governmental office, it refers to government (can be civil or spiritual).

…If a man desire the office of a bishop, he desires a good work (1 Timothy 3:1).

PARK – *Rest:* Peace; God's blessing; God's provision (as in "the Garden of Eden"); leisure; vagrancy.

And the Lord shall guide thee continually, and satisfy thy soul in drought, and make fat thy bones: and thou shalt be like a watered garden, and like a spring of water, whose waters fail not (Isaiah 58:11).

PORCH (FRONT) – *Public:* Open to everyone; exposed; revealed.

But he denied, saying, I know not, neither understand I what thou sayest. And he went out into the porch; and the cock crew [knew!] (Mark 14:68).

And by the hands of the apostles were many signs and wonders wrought among the people; (and they were all with one accord in Solomon's porch [public witness]) (Acts 5:12).

Let the priests, the ministers of the Lord, weep between the porch and the altar [public prayer and confession], *and let them say, Spare Thy people, O Lord...wherefore should they say among the people, Where is their God?* (Joel 2:17)

PRISON – *Bondage:* Rebellion; strong emotion (such as depression, fear, rebellion, hatred, etc.); addiction (alcoholic, dope, etc.). **Prisoners** = *Lost souls;* stubborn sinners; persecuted saints.

The Spirit of the Lord is upon me, because He hath anointed me to preach the gospel to the poor; He hath sent me to heal the brokenhearted, to preach deliverance to the captives, and recovering of sight to the blind, to set at liberty them that are bruised (Luke 4:18).

And deliver them who through fear of death were all their lifetime subject to bondage (Hebrews 2:15).

Having eyes full of adultery, and that cannot cease from sin... (2 Peter 2:14).

In meekness instructing those that oppose themselves; if God peradventure will give them repentance to the acknowledging of the truth; and that they may recover themselves out of the snare of the devil, who are taken captive by him [the devil] *at His* [God's] *will* (2 Timothy 2:25-26).

Then took they Jeremiah, and cast him into the dungeon...that was in the court of the prison...so Jeremiah sunk in the mire (Jeremiah 38:6).

Turn you to the strong hold, ye prisoners of hope... (Zechariah 9:12).

RESTAURANT (Café) – See CAFETERIA.

ROOF – *Covering:* Protection; mind; thought.

What I tell you in darkness, that speak ye in light: and what ye hear in the ear, that preach ye upon the housetops (Matthew 10:27).

Woe to the rebellious children, saith the Lord, that take counsel, but not of Me; and that cover with a covering, but not of My spirit... (Isaiah 30:1).

And it came to pass in an eveningtide, that David arose from off his bed, and walked upon the roof of the king's house: and from the roof he saw a woman washing herself; and the woman was very beautiful to look upon (2 Samuel 11:2).

SCHOOL – *Teaching or learning:* Church; people or work; teaching ministry; training.

But when divers were hardened, and believed not, but spake evil of that way before the multitude, he departed from them, and separated the disciples [Church], *disputing daily in the school of one Tyrannus* (Acts 19:9).

Then they went out to see what was done; and came to Jesus, and found the man, out of whom the devils were departed, sitting at the feet of Jesus [being counseled or taught], *clothed, and in his right mind...* (Luke 8:35).

TAVERN – *World:* Worldliness; irresponsible living; escape from grief or reality; fellowship.

Enter ye in at the strait gate: for wide is the gate, and broad is the way, that leadeth to destruction, and many there be which go in thereat (Matthew 7:13).

And take heed to yourselves, lest at any time your hearts be overcharged with surfeiting, and drunkenness, and cares of this life, and so that day come upon you unawares (Luke 21:34).

For they eat the bread of wickedness, and drink the wine of violence (Proverbs 4:17).

And be not drunk with wine, wherein is excess; but be filled with the Spirit (Ephesians 5:18).

Give strong drink unto him that is ready to perish, and wine unto those that be of heavy hearts (Proverbs 31:6).

TRAIN STATION – See AIRPORT.

UPSTAIRS (or UPPER ROOM) – *Spiritual:* Thought (godly or carnal); prayer; spiritual service. (See ATTIC.)

And when they were come in, they went up into an upper room, where abode both Peter, and James, and John...these all continued with one accord in prayer and supplication... (Acts 1:13-14).

...Paul preached unto them...and continued his speech until midnight. And there were many lights in the upper chamber, where they were gathered together (Acts 20:7-8).

YARD – See BACK and FRONT, Chapter 19.

ZOO – *Strange:* Commotion; confusion; chaos; disarray (as in "this place is a regular zoo!"); very busy place; noisy strife (like a zoo at feeding time); **Family visit** = *Quality time with the family.*

And they were all amazed, and they glorified God, and were filled with fear, saying, We have seen strange things to day (Luke 5:26).

For where envying and strife is, there is confusion and every evil work (James 3:16).

CHAPTER 18

Colors

Refer to Chapter 9 for a more in-depth coverage of many of the colors.

BLACK – *Lack:* Sin; ignorance; grief; mourning; gloomy; evil; ominous; famine; burned.

For at the window of my house I looked...and beheld...among the youths, a young man void of understanding... He went the way to [a harlot's] house, in the twilight, in the evening, in the black and dark night (Proverbs 7:6-9).

For the hurt of the daughter of my people am I hurt; I am black; astonishment hath taken hold on me. Is there no balm in Gilead; is there no physician there? why then is not the health of the daughter of my people recovered? (Jeremiah 8:21-22)

Our skin was black like an oven because of the terrible famine [lack of substance] (Lamentations 5:10).

I am black, but comely, O ye daughters of Jerusalem, as the tents of Kedar, as the curtains of Solomon (Song of Solomon 1:5).

His head is as the most fine gold, his locks are bushy, and black as a raven (Song of Solomon 5:11).

BLUE – *Spiritual:* Spiritual gift; divine revelation; heavenly visitation; depressed (as in "singing the blues"); a male infant. **Medium or**

Dark Blue = *God's Spirit or Word;* blessing; healing; good will. **Very Light Blue** = *Spirit of man;* evil spirit; corrupt.

And upon the table of shewbread they shall spread a cloth of blue, and put thereon the dishes, and the spoons.... And they shall take a cloth of blue, and cover the candlestick of the light, and his lamps...and all the oil vessels thereof, wherewith they minister unto it (Numbers 4:7,9).

Which were clothed with blue, captains and rulers, all of them desirable young men... (Ezekiel 23:6).

The blueness of a wound cleanseth away evil... (Proverbs 20:30).

And suddenly there was with the angel a multitude of the heavenly host praising God, and saying, Glory to God in the highest, and on earth peace, good will toward men (Luke 2:13-14).

BROWN (or Tan) – *Dead* (as dead grass is brown): repentant; born again; humble; without spirit.

For all flesh is as [green] *grass, and all the glory of man as the flower of grass. The grass withereth* [turns brown in death, i.e., repentance], *and the flower thereof falleth away* (1 Peter 1:24).

GRAY – *Not Defined:* Unclear (as in "the gray area between right and wrong"); vague, not specific; hazy; deceived; deception; hidden; crafty; false doctrine; grief. **Gray Hair** = *Wisdom, age, or weakness.*

The hoary [white or gray] *head is a crown of glory, if it be found in the way of righteousness* (Proverbs 16:31).

Strangers have devoured his strength, and he knoweth it not [deception]: *yea, gray hairs are here and there upon him, yet he knoweth not* (Hosea 7:9).

GOLD – See GOLD; Chapter 20.

GREEN – *Life:* Mortal; flesh; carnal; envy; inexperienced; immature; renewal. Evergreen = *Eternal life;* immortal. (See GRASS and TREE, Chapter 24.)

Every moving thing that liveth shall be meat for you; even as the green herb have I given you all things (Genesis 9:3).

For all flesh is as [green] *grass, and all the glory of man as the flower of grass. The grass withereth, and the flower thereof falleth away* (1 Peter 1:24).

I have seen the wicked in great power, and spreading himself like a green bay tree (Psalm 37:35).

For if they do these things in a green tree [mortal days of Christ's flesh], *what shall be done in the dry* [after His death, without His physical presence]? (Luke 23:31)

ORANGE – *Energy:* Great jeopardy; harm; danger. (A common color combination is orange and black together, which usually signifies evil or great danger). Bright or fire orange = Power; force; energy; energetic; danger.

But I say unto you, That whosoever is angry with his brother without a cause shall be in danger of the judgment...but whosoever shall say, Thou fool, shall be in danger of hell fire [fire is orange] (Matthew 5:22).

Can a man take fire in his bosom, and his clothes not be burned? (Proverbs 6:27)

PINK – *Flesh:* Sensual; sensuous (as in "hot pink bikini"); immoral. Moral (as in "a heart of flesh"); chaste. A female infant.

A new heart also will I give you, and a new spirit will I put within you: and I will take away the stony [hard] *heart out of your flesh, and I will give you an* [pink (chaste, virtuous)] *heart of flesh* [Compare 2 Corinthians 11:2: *"...I have espoused you to one husband, that I may present you as a chaste virgin to Christ."*] (Ezekiel 36:26).

PURPLE – *Royal:* Rule (good or evil); majestic; noble.

...And purple raiment that was on the kings of Midian... (Judges 8:26).

And they clothed him with purple, and platted a crown of thorns, and put it about his head (Mark 15:17).

RED – *Passion:* Emotion; anger; hatred; lust; sin; enthusiasm; zeal.

And there went out another horse that was red: and power was given to him that sat thereon to take peace from the earth, and that they should kill one another: and there was given unto him a great sword [See James 4:1.] (Revelation 6:4).

Come now, and let us reason together, saith the Lord: though your sins be as scarlet, they shall be as white as snow; though they be red like crimson, they shall be as wool (Isaiah 1:18).

SILVER – See SILVER, Chapter 20.

TAN – See BROWN.

TURQUOISE – *Spiritual Authority* (when used in Indian jewelry): (See INDIAN, Chapter 22.)

Write ye also for the Jews, as it liketh you, in the king's name, and seal it with the king's ring: for the writing which is written in the king's name, and sealed with the king's ring, may no man reverse (Esther 8:8).

WHITE – *Pure:* Without mixture; unblemished; spotless; righteousness; blameless; truth; innocence.

And to her was granted that she should be arrayed in fine linen, clean and white: for the fine linen is the righteousness of saints (Revelation 19:8).

The leprosy therefore of Naaman shall cleave unto thee...and he went out from his presence a leper as white as snow [cursed, completely covered, without mixture, i.e., without mercy] (2 Kings 5:27).

YELLOW – *Gift:* A gift (with feeling); gift from or of God; marriage; family; honor; deceitful gift; timidity; fear; cowardliness. Welcome home (as in "a yellow ribbon"). (See ROSE, Chapter 24.)

Though ye have lien among the pots, yet shall ye be as the wings of a dove [spiritual] covered with silver [knowledge], and her feathers with yellow gold [spirit of wisdom and the glory of God] (Psalm 68:13).

House and riches are the inheritance of fathers and a prudent wife is [a gift] *from the Lord* (Proverbs 19:14).

For God hath not given us the spirit of fear; but of power, and of love, and of a sound mind (2 Timothy 1:7).

Directions

Refer to Chapter 10 for more information on some of these directional terms.

BACK (as in **Back Yard** or **Back Door**) – *Past:* Previous event or experience (good or evil); that which is behind (in time—for example, your past sins or the sins of your forefathers); unaware; unsuspecting; hidden; memory. (See DOOR, Chapter 24.)

And Abraham...looked, and behold behind him a ram caught in a thicket by his horns: and Abraham...offered him up for a burnt offering in the stead of his son [Compare John 8:58: "Jesus said unto them, Verily, verily, I say unto you, Before (behind, i.e., before in time) *Abraham was, I am."] (Genesis 22:13).*

And he commanded them, saying, Behold, ye shall lie in wait against the city, even [hidden] behind the city... (Joshua. 8:4).

Brethren, I count not myself to have apprehended: but this one thing I do, forgetting those things which are behind [of the past], and reaching forth unto those things which are before (Philippians 3:13).

DOWN – *Beneath:* Humbled; demotion; worldly.

But God is the judge: He putteth down one, and setteth up another (Psalm 75:7).

The Lord looked down from heaven upon the children of men, to see if there were any that did understand, and seek God (Psalm 14:2).

EAST (Hebrew: "In front of you when facing the rising sun") – *Beginning:* Law of Moses (therefore, blessed or cursed); birth; first; anticipate; false religion (as in "Eastern religions").

And it came to pass, as they journeyed from the east [beginning, or from God's law, i.e., backsliding], *that they found a plain in the land of Shinar; and they dwelt there* (Genesis 11:2).

And, behold, seven ears, withered, thin, and blasted with the east wind [cursed by the law], *sprung up after them... And the seven thin and ill favored kine that came up after them are seven years: and the seven empty ears blasted* [cursed] *with the east wind shall be seven years of famine* (Genesis 41:23,27).

And Moses stretched forth his rod over the land of Egypt, and the Lord brought an east wind [curse of the law] *upon the land all that day, and all that night; and when it was morning, the east wind brought the locusts* [curse] (Exodus 10:13).

As far as the east [law] *is from the west* [grace], *so far hath He removed our transgressions from us* (Psalm 103:12).

FRONT (as in **Front Yard** or **Front Porch**) – *Future or Now:* In the presence of; a prophecy of future events (that which is to come); immediate; current.

The earth also was corrupt before [in the presence of] *God, and the earth was filled with violence* (Genesis 6:11).

Write the things which thou hast seen, and the things which [presently] *are* [before, or in front of you], *and the things which shall be hereafter* (Revelation 1:19).

NORTH (on your left hand when you are facing east) – Spiritual: Judgment; Heaven or heavenly; spiritual warfare (as in "taking your inheritance").

The north wind driveth away rain: so doth an angry countenance [spirit judging (reproving)] *a backbiting tongue* (Proverbs 25:23).

And the word of the Lord came unto me the second time, saying, What seest thou? And I said, I see a seething pot; and the face thereof is toward the north. Then the Lord said unto me, Out of the north an evil shall break forth upon all the inhabitants of the land (Jeremiah 1:13-14).

Ye have compassed this mountain long enough: turn you northward [toward your promised inheritance] (Deuteronomy 2:3).

LEFT – *Spiritual:* Weakness (of people); God's strength or ability demonstrated through people's weakness; rejection. **Left Turn** = *Spiritual change.*

And He said unto me, My grace is sufficient for thee: for My strength is made perfect in weakness....For when I am weak [as people's left hands may be weak when compared to their right], *then am I strong* (2 Corinthians 12:9a-10b).

Among all this people there were seven hundred chosen men lefthanded [spiritually empowered or gifted]; *every one could sling stones* [accurate words of knowledge] *at an hair breadth, and not miss* (Judges 20:16).

And Ehud came unto [the king]...*and Ehud said, I have a message from God unto thee...and Ehud put forth his left hand, and took the dagger from his right thigh, and thrust it into his belly* (Judges 3:20-21).

And He shall set the sheep on His right hand, but [reject] *the goats* [sinners] *on the left* (Matthew 25:33).

SOUTH (Hebrew: "On your right hand when facing east") – *Natural:* World; sin; temptation; trial; flesh; corruption; deception.

So Joshua smote all the country...of the south...he left none remaining, but utterly destroyed all that breathed [flesh], *as the Lord God of Israel commanded* (Joshua 10:40).

Out of the south [flesh or world] *cometh the whirlwind: and cold* [rejection, God's judgment for sin] *out of the north* (Job 37:9).

RIGHT – *Natural:* Authority; power; the strength of humanity (flesh), or the power of God revealed through flesh (i.e., Christ or the Church); accepted. **Right Turn** = *Natural change.*

And if thy right eye offend thee, pluck it out [the right eye symbolizes both of the natural eyes, for one can lust with either eye], *and cast it from thee...And if thy right hand offend thee, cut if off* [likewise, one can steal with either hand, therefore the right hand represents both natural hands], *and cast it from thee...* (Matthew 5:29-30).

And Joseph said unto his father, Not so, my father: for this is the firstborn; put thy right hand upon his head [acknowledging or transferring authority] (Genesis 48:18).

Thy right hand, O Lord, is become glorious in power: Thy right hand [Jesus, the natural expression of the invisible God who reveals that authority and power], *O Lord, hath dashed in pieces the enemy* (Exodus 15:6).

And He shall set the sheep [those accepted of God] *on His right hand, but* [reject] *the goats* [sinners] *on the left* (Matthew 25:33).

Who [Christ] *is gone into heaven, and is on the right hand* [position of authority] *of God; angels and authorities and powers being made subject unto Him* (1 Peter 3:22).

UP – *Above:* Help; advancement; promotion; difficulty (as in "it's all uphill from here"); salvation.

He sent from above, He took me, He drew me out of many waters (Psalm 18:16).

WEST (Hebrew: "the region of the evening [setting] sun") – *End:* (as in "the end of the day"): Grace; death; last; conformed.

And the Lord turned a mighty strong west wind [the doctrine of grace], *which took away the locusts* [curse], *and cast them into the Red sea; there remained not one locust in all the coasts of Egypt* (Exodus 10:19).

As far as the east [law] *is from the west* [grace], *so far hath He removed our transgressions from us* (Psalm 103:12).

And He said also to the people, When ye see a cloud [of glory] *rise out of the west* [grace of God], *straightway ye say, There cometh a shower* [revival]; *and so it is* (Luke 12:54).

Metals

Refer to Chapter 9 and Chapter 13 for more in-depth coverage of most of these metals.

BRASS – *Word:* Word of God or humanity; judgment; hypocrisy; self-justification; fake; human tradition.

And His feet [words] *like unto fine* [purified] *brass, as if they burned in a furnace; and His voice as the sound of many waters* (Revelation 1:15).

Though I speak with the tongues of men and of angels, and have not charity, I am become as sounding brass, or a tinkling cymbal (1 Corinthians 13:1).

Instead of which king Rehoboam made shields of brass [in place of gold], *and committed them to the hands of the chief of the guard, that kept the entrance of the king's house* (2 Chronicles 12:10).

Above all, taking the [gold] *shield of faith* [not the brass shield of self-justification], *wherewith ye shall be able to quench all the fiery darts of the wicked* (Ephesians 6:16).

Because I knew that thou art obstinate, and thy neck is an iron sinew [stubborn self-will], *and thy brow brass* [brazen, rude, etc.] (Isaiah 48:4).

GOLD – *Glory or wisdom:* Truth; something precious; righteousness; glory of God; self-glorification.

Then Asa brought out silver and gold out of the treasures of the house of the Lord... (2 Chronicles 16:2).

In whom are hid all the treasures of wisdom [gold] *and knowledge* [silver] (Colossians 2:3).

For if there come unto your assembly a man with a gold ring, in goodly apparel, and there come in also a poor man in vile raiment; and ye have respect to him that [glorifies himself with gold and] *weareth the gay clothing....Are ye not then partial in yourselves, and are become judges of evil thoughts?* (James 2:2-4)

IRON – *Strength:* Powerful; invincible; stronghold; stubborn.

And the fourth kingdom shall be strong as iron: forasmuch as iron breaketh in pieces and subdueth all things... (Daniel 2:40).

Because I knew that thou art obstinate [stubborn], *and thy neck is an iron sinew* [self-will], *and thy brow brass* (Isaiah 48:4).

Therefore shalt thou serve thine enemies which the Lord shall send against thee...and He shall put a yoke of iron [curse-bondage] *upon thy neck, until He have destroyed thee* (Deuteronomy 28:48).

LEAD – *Weight:* Wickedness; sin; burden (the cares of the world); judgment; fool or foolishness.

And he said, This is wickedness...and he cast the weight of lead upon the mouth thereof (Zechariah 5:8).

Thou didst blow with thy wind, the sea covered them: they sank as lead in the mighty waters (Exodus 15:10).

A stone [or lead] *is heavy, and the sand weighty; but a fool's wrath is heavier than them both* (Proverbs 27:3).

Wherefore seeing we also are compassed about with so great a cloud of witnesses, let us lay aside every weight, and the sin which doth so easily beset us, and let us run with patience the race that is set before us (Hebrews 12:1).

PLATINUM – *Elect:* Exalted; treasure; precious.

For where your treasure is, there will your heart be also (Matthew 6:21).

SILVER – *Knowledge:* **Knowledge of God** = *Redemption.* **Knowledge of the World** = *Idolatry;* spiritual adultery. **Silver Coins** = *Revelation knowledge.*

Yea, if thou criest after knowledge, and liftest up thy voice for understanding; if thou seekest her as silver, and searchest for her as for hid treasures [revelation knowledge] (Proverbs 2:3-4).

And this is life eternal [redemption], *that they might know Thee the only true God, and Jesus Christ, whom Thou hast sent* (John 17:3).

For a certain man named Demetrius, a silversmith, which made silver shrines for Diana, brought no small gain unto the crafts-men (Acts 19:24).

STEEL – See IRON.

TIN – *Dross:* Waste; worthless; cheap; also purification. (For TIN ROOF, see ROOF, Chapter 4.)

And I will turn my hand upon thee, and purely purge away thy dross [sin], *and take away all thy tin* (Isaiah 1:25).

Numbers

For very in-depth interpretations of numbers, see Chapters 4, 5, 6, 7, and 8.

ONE – *Beginning:* First—in time, rank, order, or importance; new.

In the beginning God created the heaven and the earth. ... And the evening and the morning were the first day (Genesis 1:1,5b).

And it came to pass in the six hundredth and first year, in the first month, the first day of the month, the waters were dried up from off the earth: and Noah removed the covering of the ark... (Genesis 8:13).

TWO – *Divide:* Judge; separate; discern; (by implication) witness.

And God said, Let there be a firmament in the midst of the waters, and let it divide the waters from the waters. ...And the evening and the morning were the second day (Genesis 1:6,8).

And the king said, Divide the living child in two, and give half to the one, and half to the other. And all Israel heard of the judgment which the king had judged...they saw that the wisdom of God was in him, to do judgment (1 Kings 3:25,28).

At the mouth of two witnesses, or three witnesses, shall he that is worthy of death be put to death; but at the mouth of one witness he shall not be put to death (Deuteronomy 17:6).

THREE – *Conform:* Obey; copy; imitate; likeness; tradition.

And God said...let the dry land appear: and it was so. ...And God said, Let the earth bring forth grass, the herb yielding seed, and the fruit tree yielding fruit after his kind, whose seed is in itself, upon the earth: and it was so. ...And the evening and the morning were the third day (Genesis 1:9,11,13).

For whom He did foreknow, He also did predestinate to be conformed to the image of His Son... (Romans 8:29).

FOUR – *Reign:* Rule (over the world); kingdom; dominion; dominance; creation (including things in Heaven and earth); world.

And God made two great lights; the greater light to rule the day, and the lesser light to rule the night: he made the stars also. And to rule over the day and over the night, and to divide the light from the darkness.... And the evening and the morning were the fourth day (Genesis 1:16,18-19).

FIVE – *Serve:* Works; service; bondage (including debt, sickness, phobias, etc.); taxes; prison; sin; motion.

And God said, Let the waters bring forth abundantly the moving creature that hath life, and fowl that may fly above the earth in the open firmament of heaven. ...And the evening and the morning were the fifth day (Genesis 1:20,23).

Let Pharaoh do this, and let him appoint officers over the land, and take up the fifth part of the land of Egypt in the seven plenteous years (Genesis 41:34).

And if a man will at all redeem ought of his tithes, he shall add thereto the fifth part thereof (Leviticus 27:31).

Jesus answered them, Verily, verily, I say unto you, Whosoever committeth sin is the servant of sin [Compare Romans 7:5: *For when we were in the flesh, the motions of sins...did work in our members to bring forth fruit unto death.*] (John 8:34).

SIX – *Image:* Humanity; flesh; carnal; idol; form.

And God said, Let us make man in Our image, after Our like-ness...And the evening and the morning were the sixth day (Genesis 1:26,31).

Here is wisdom. Let him that hath understanding count the number of the beast: for it is the number of a man; and his num-ber is Six hundred threescore and six (Revelation 13:18).

SEVEN – *Complete:* All; finished; rest.

Thus the heavens and the earth were finished, and all the host of them. And God blessed the seventh day, and sanctified it: because that in it he had rested from all His work which God created and made (Genesis 2:1,3).

EIGHT – *Put off* (as in putting off "the old man," i.e., the works of the flesh): Sanctify; manifest; reveal; die; death. By implication, new beginnings (the result of putting off the old life is a new life or beginning).

And he that is eight days old shall be circumcised among you, ev-ery man child in your generations... [Compare Colossians 2:11: *"In whom also ye are circumcised with the circumcision made without hands, in putting off the body of the sins of the flesh by the circumcision of Christ."*] (Genesis 17:12).

Now they began on the first day of the first month to sanctify, and on the eighth day of the month came they to the porch of the Lord: so they sanctified the house of the Lord in eight days (2 Chronicles 29:17).

...In the days of Noah, while the ark was a preparing, wherein few, that is, eight souls were saved by water. The like figure where-unto even baptism doth also now save us (not the putting away of the filth of the flesh [the baptism of repentance], *but the answer of a good conscience toward God* [i.e., the putting away of the guilt of sin (See Heb. 9:14)], *by the resurrection of Jesus Christ)* (1 Peter 3:20-21).

Lie not one to another, seeing that ye have put off the old man with his deeds (Colossians 3:9).

Knowing that shortly I must put off this my tabernacle [i.e., die], *even as our Lord Jesus Christ hath shwed me* (2 Peter 1:14).

NINE – *Harvest:* Fruit; fruitfulness; promises brought to fruition (fulfilled).

And Jesus answering said, Were there not ten cleansed? but where are the nine? [the fruit, or harvest, of thanksgiving. See Hebrews 13:15] (Luke 17:17).

And when Abram was ninety years old and nine, the Lord appeared to Abram, and said unto him, I am the Almighty God; walk before me, and be thou perfect. Then Abraham fell upon his face, and laughed, and said in his heart, Shall a child be born unto him that is an hundred years old? and shall Sarah, that is ninety years old, bear? (Genesis 17:1,17)

And the children of Israel again did evil in the sight of the Lord...And the Lord sold them into the hand of Jabin king of Canaan...And the children of Israel cried unto the Lord: for he had nine hundred chariots of iron; and twenty years he mightily oppressed the children of Israel [the fruit of their sin—God's harvest of judgment (See Hosea 6:10-11 and TWENTY)] (Judges 4:1-3).

TEN – **Measure** (for the purpose of accepting or rejecting that which is measured): Try or trial; test, or to be tested; temptation.

Fear none of those things which thou shalt suffer: behold, the devil shall cast some of you into prison, that ye may be tried; and ye shall have tribulation ten days... (Revelation 2:10).

...Thou art weighed in the balances [tried], *and art found wanting* [rejected] (Daniel 5:27).

NOTE: The meanings of the numbers from eleven through nineteen are antonyms of the numbers one through nine. (In other words, they are the reverse or the result of the application of the base numbers, one through nine.) For example, *three* means to "conform." The opposite of conforming, and the result of forced conformity, is rebellion. Therefore, *thirteen* means to "rebel." (See THREE and THIRTEEN.)

When a base number is multiplied by ten to obtain the meaning, couple the key word of the base number with the thought of acceptance or rejection. For example, the date, 5/5/50 means "service accepted" (or "rejected," as the case may be); *five* means to "serve," *ten* means "to measure for the purpose of accepting or rejecting"—therefore five times ten equals "service accepted/rejected." (See both the following example and the entry TWENTY.)

Then came Peter to him, and said, Lord, how oft shall my brother sin against me, and I forgive him? till seven times [completely]? *Jesus saith unto him, I say not unto thee, Until seven times: but, Until seventy times seven* [both completely forgive (seven) the offense and completely accept (seven times ten) the offender!] (Matthew 18:21-22).

ELEVEN – *End:* Finish; last; stop.

And when they came that were hired about the eleventh hour, they received every man a penny. Saying, These last have wrought but one hour, and thou hast made them equal unto us, which have borne the burden and heat of the day (Matthew 20:9,12).

TWELVE – *Joined:* United. By implication, govern; government; oversight. (Government is the means by which people are united into common purposes and goals.)

Then He called His twelve disciples together [joined or united them], *and gave them power and authority over all devils, and to cure diseases. And He sent them to preach the kingdom* [government] *of God, and to heal the sick* (Luke 9:1-2).

That ye may eat and drink at My table in My kingdom, and sit on thrones judging the twelve tribes of Israel (Luke 22:30).

Now I beseech you, brethren, by the name of our Lord Jesus Christ, that ye all speak the same thing, and that there be no divisions among you; but that ye be perfectly joined together in the same mind and in the same judgment [See Hebrews 13:17.] (1 Corinthians 1:10).

THIRTEEN – *Rebel:* Rebellion; revolution; rejection; change.

Twelve years they [by force] *served Chedorlaomer, and in the thirteenth year they rebelled* (Genesis 14:4).

FOURTEEN – *Double:* Duplicate; reproduce; recreate; disciple; servant; bond-slave *(employee)*.

And at that time Solomon held a feast...before the Lord our God, seven days and seven days, even fourteen days (1 Kings 8:65).

FIFTEEN – *Grace:* Free; liberty; salvation; save; sin covered; honor.

And I will add unto thy days fifteen years; and I will deliver thee and this city out of the hand of the king of Assyria... (2 Kings 20:6).

So I bought her [Gomer, Hosea's adulterous wife] *to me for fifteen pieces of silver...* (Hosea 3:2).

Fifteen cubits upward did the waters prevail; and the mountains were covered (Genesis 7:20).

SIXTEEN – *Spirit:* Free-spirited; without boundaries; without limitation; without law (and therefore without sin [See Romans 4:15.]); salvation.

Wherefore I pray you to take some meat: for this is for your health: for there shall not an hair fall from the head of any of you. ... And we were in all in the ship two hundred threescore and sixteen souls. And...they lightened the ship, and cast out the wheat into the sea. (Acts 27:34,37-38).

SEVENTEEN – *Incomplete:* Immature; undeveloped; unfinished; childish; naive; a babe in Christ.

These are the generations of Jacob. Joseph, being seventeen years old, was feeding the flock with his brethren; and the lad was with the sons of Bilhah (Genesis 37:2).

And I bought the field...and weighed him the money, even seventeen shekels of silver. For thus saith the Lord of hosts, the God of Israel; Houses and fields and vineyards shall be possessed again in this land (Jeremiah 32:9,15).

EIGHTEEN – *Put on:* Judgment; destruction; captivity; overcome; put on (the Spirit of) Christ.

And the anger of the Lord was hot against Israel, and He sold them into the hands of the Philistines...and that year they vexed and oppressed the children of Israel: eighteen years... (Judges 10:7-8).

Or those eighteen, upon whom the tower in Siloam fell, and slew them, think ye that they were sinners above all men that dwelt in Jerusalem? (Luke 13:4)

And, behold, there was a woman which had a spirit of infirmity eighteen years, and was bowed together, and could in no wise lift up herself. And ought not this woman, being a daughter of Abraham, whom Satan hath bound [put his bondage on, i.e., overcome], *lo, these eighteen years, be loosed from this bond on the sabbath day?* (Luke 13:11,16)

NINETEEN – *Barren:* Ashamed; repentant; selflessness; without self-righteousness.

And Joab returned from following Abner: and when he had gathered all the people together, there lacked of David's servants nineteen men and Asahel (2 Samuel 2:30).

What fruit had ye then in those things whereof ye are now ashamed? for the end of those things is death (Romans 6:21).

TWENTY – *Holy:* Tried and approved (or *unholy:* tried and found wanting). **Two** = *Separated.* **Ten** = *Measured.* (See TWO and TEN.)

And round about the throne were four and twenty seats: and upon the seats I saw four and twenty elders sitting [holy elders in authority], *clothed in white raiment; and they had on their heads crowns of gold* (Revelation 4:4).

HUNDRED – *Fullness:* Full measure; full recompense; full reward, etc.

Then Isaac sowed in that land, and received in the same year an hundredfold [full harvest]: *and the Lord blessed him* (Genesis 26:12).

But he shall receive an hundredfold [full recompense:] *now in this time, houses, and brethren, and sisters, and mothers, and children, and lands, with persecutions; and in the world to come eternal life* (Mark 10:30).

THOUSAND – *Maturity:* Full stature; mature service; mature judgment, etc.

And they commanded the people, saying, When ye see the ark of the covenant of the Lord your God...then ye shall remove from your place, and go after it. Yet there shall be a space between you and it, about two thousand cubits by measure [follow using mature judgment (Compare Ephesians 5:17: *"Wherefore be ye not unwise, but understanding what the will of the Lord is."*)]: *come not near unto it, that ye may know the way by which ye must go: for ye have not passed this way heretofore* (Joshua 3:3-4).

And Saul said to David, Thou art not able to go against this Philistine to fight with him: for thou art but a youth, and he a man of war [mature] *from his youth....And he was armed with a coat of mail; and the weight of the coat was five thousand* [mature service] *shekels of brass* (1 Samuel 17:33,5).

Till we all come in the unity of the faith, and of the knowledge of the Son of God, unto a perfect [mature] *man, unto the measure of the stature of the fullness of Christ* (Ephesians 4:13).

CHAPTER 22

People / Relatives / Trades

Refer to Chapter 13 for more information on certain people, relatives, and trades.

ACTOR – *Pretending:* Insincere; role-playing: idol (hero) worship; hypocrite.

And when thou prayest, thou shalt not be as the hypocrites are: for they love to pray standing in the synagogues and in the corners of the streets, that they may be seen of men. Verily I say unto you, They have their reward (Matthew 6:5).

ATTORNEY – *Advocate:* Christ; legal defense; accuser. (See LAWYER.)

Put me in remembrance: let us plead together: declare thou [state your case], *that thou mayest be justified* [or, acquitted] (Isaiah 43:26).

My little children, these things write I unto you, that ye sin not. And if any man sin, we have an advocate with the Father, Jesus Christ the righteous (1 John 2:1).

BABY – *New:* Beginning; new idea; new work (church); dependant; helpless; innocent; sin; natural baby.

And I, brethren, could not speak unto you as unto spiritual, but as unto carnal, even as unto babes in Christ (1 Corinthians 3:1).

As newborn babes, desire the sincere milk of the word, that ye may grow thereby (1 Peter 2:2).

Behold, I will do a new thing; now it shall spring forth [new birth]; *shall ye not know it? I will even make a way in the wilderness, and rivers in the desert* (Isaiah 43:19).

But every man is tempted, when he is drawn away of his own lust, and enticed. Then when lust hath conceived, it bringeth forth sin: and sin, when it is finished, bringeth forth death (James 1:14-15).

BAKER – *Instigator:* One who cooks up (and serves) ideas; originator; Christ; satan; minister; self. (See OVEN, Chapter 24.)

They are all adulterers, as an oven heated by the baker [inflamed by lust, tempted by satan], *who ceaseth from raising after he hath kneaded the dough, until it be leavened* (Hosea 7:4).

For they have made ready their heart like an oven, whiles they lie in wait: their baker [minister] *sleepeth all the night; in the morning it burneth as a flaming fire* (Hosea 7:6).

BRIDE (as participating in a marriage ceremony) – *Church:* Covenant (good or evil). **Groom** = *Christ;* natural marriage when naturally interpreted. (See MARRIAGE, Chapter 24.)

For as a young man marrieth a virgin, so shall thy sons marry thee: and as the bridegroom rejoiceth over the bride, so shall thy God rejoice over thee [the Church] (Isaiah 62:5).

For this cause shall a man leave his father and mother, and shall be joined unto his wife, and they two shall be one flesh. This is a great mystery: but I speak concerning Christ and the church (Ephesians 5:31-32).

Be ye not unequally yoked together with unbelievers: for what fellowship hath righteousness with unrighteousness? and what communion hath light with darkness? (2 Corinthians 6:14)

BROTHER – *Self:* Spiritual or natural brother; someone he reminds you of. (See FRIEND.)

But why dost thou judge thy brother? or why dost thou set at nought thy brother? (Romans 14:10a)

Therefore thou art inexcusable, O man, whosoever thou art that judgest: for wherein thou judgest another [your brother], *thou condemnest thyself; for thou that judgest doest the same things* (Romans 2:1).

Remember them that are in bonds, as bound with them; and them which suffer adversity, as being yourselves also in the body (Hebrews 13:3).

BROTHER-IN-LAW – *Partiality or adversary:* Fellow minister; someone he reminds you of (see FRIEND); problem relationship; partner; oneself; he may represent himself.

I charge thee before God, and the Lord Jesus Christ, and the elect angels, that thou observe these things without preferring one before another, doing nothing by partiality (1 Timothy 5:21).

And Esther [the king's wife] *said, The adversary and enemy is this wicked Haman...* [close friend of the king (as a wife's husband's brother is a friend of her husband, but not necessarily a friend to her)] (Esther 7:6).

CAPTAIN – *In charge:* Christ; overseer; elder.

For it became Him, for whom are all things, and by whom are all things, in bringing many sons unto glory, to make the captain of their salvation perfect through sufferings (Hebrews 2:10).

CARPENTER – *Builder:* Preacher; evangelist; laborer (good or evil); Christ.

Unto carpenters, and builders, and masons, and to buy timber and hewn stone to repair [edify] *the house* [of God] (2 Kings 22:6).

So the carpenter encouraged the goldsmith, and he that smootheth with the hammer him that smote the anvil...and he fastened it [the idol] *with nails, that it should not be moved* (Isaiah 41:7).

Is not this [Jesus] *the carpenter, the son of Mary...and they were offended at Him* (Mark 6:3).

CARTOON CHARACTER – *Person:* One who is like or is acting in the same way as the cartoon character. For example, **Goofy** = *Foolish:* dumb actions. **Mickey Mouse** = *Sensitive hearing* (because of his large ears): insignificant (as in "you mean that mickey mouse thing?"). (See SUPERMAN and PHANTOM.)

> *Then said all the trees* [people] *unto the bramble* [bad, unsuitable, corrupt person], *Come thou, and reign over us* (Judges 9:14).

CIRCUS PERFORMER – See CIRCUS and TRAPEZE ACT – Chapter 24 and CLOWN, below.

CLOWN – *Fool:* Foolish works of the flesh; the "old self"; childish; mischief. (See DRUNK.)

> *The heart of the wise is in the house of mourning; but the heart of fools* [clowns] *is in the house of mirth* (Ecclesiastes 7:4).

> *It is as sport to a fool to do mischief...* (Proverbs 10:23).

COOK – See BAKER.

DAUGHTER – See ONE'S CHILDREN.

DENTIST – *Physician:* Dreaded, fearful encounter; trial; Christ; minister of the Gospel.

> *Out of the same mouth proceedeth blessing and cursing. My brethren, these things ought not so to be* (James 3:10).

DETECTIVE – *Investigate:* Searching for answers; spy.

> *I will go down now, and see whether they have done altogether according to the cry of it, which is come unto Me; and if not, I will know* (Genesis 18:21).

DOCTOR – *Healer:* Authority; Christ; preacher; medical doctor.

> *When Jesus heard it, He saith unto them, They that are whole have no need of the physician, but they that are sick: I came not to call the righteous, but sinners to repentance* (Mark 2:17).

> *And had suffered many things of many physicians, and had spent all that she had, and was nothing bettered, but rather grew worse* (Mark 5:26).

And Asa in the thirty and ninth year of his reign was diseased in his feet, until his disease was exceeding great: yet in his disease he sought not to the Lord, but to the physicians [he would not repent, but died under the chastening hand of God (See 1 Corinthians 11:30-32).] (2 Chronicles 16:12).

Luke, the beloved physician, and Demas, greet you (Colossians 4:14).

DRIVER – *Control:* Self; Christ; pastor; teacher; satan; the emphasis may be on the nature of the driver (careless, careful, frantic, confident, selfish, rude, kind, etc.). **Passenger** = *Self:* Church member; family member. When a school bus driver represents a teacher, his passengers usually represent his students. (See FRIEND.)

And the watchman told, saying...and the driving is like the driving of Jehu the son of Nimshi; for he driveth furiously (2 Kings 9:20).

DRUG ADDICT – See ADDICTION, Chapter 24.

DRUNK – *Influenced:* Under a spell (i.e., under the influence of the Holy Spirit or a demonic spirit, such as witchcraft); controlled; addicted; fool; unchangeable; stubborn; rebellious; selfish; self-indulging; proud; conceited; arrogant; boastful.

And be not drunk with [natural] *wine, wherein is excess; but be filled with the Spirit* [new wine, see Acts 2:13-18] (Ephesians 5:18).

And take heed to yourselves, lest at any time your hearts be overcharged with surfeiting, and drunkenness, and cares of this life, and so that day come upon you unawares (Luke 21:34).

And they shall say unto the elders of his city, This our son is stubborn and rebellious, he will not obey our voice; he is a glutton, and a drunkard (Deuteronomy 21:20).

A wise man feareth, and departeth from evil: but the fool [or drunk] *rageth, and is confident* [arrogant and boastful] (Proverbs 14:16).

The way of a fool [or drunk] *is right in his own eyes: but he that hearkeneth unto counsel is wise* (Proverbs 12:15).

DWARF – *Small:* Made small by comparison (as in "David was dwarfed by the giant").

I am small and despised: yet do not I forget thy precepts (Psalm 119:141).

EMPLOYEE – *Servant:* **Fellow Employee** = *Self,* another employee (see FRIEND), or the actual employee when naturally interpreted.

Servants [or employees], *obey in all things your masters* [employers] *according to the flesh; not with eyeservice, as menpleasers; but in singleness of heart, fearing God* (Colossians 3:22).

EMPLOYER – *Authority:* Pastor; Christ; satan; someone he or she resembles, in position, action or character (see NAME, Chapter 24); actual employer when naturally interpreted.

Masters [or employers], *give unto your servants* [employees] *that which is just and equal; knowing that ye also have a Master in heaven* (Colossians 4:1).

FAMILY – *Relatives:* Spiritual family (Church) or natural family.

And the ark of God remained with the family of Obededom in his house three months. And the Lord blessed the house of Obededom, and all that he had (1 Chronicles 13:14).

Of whom the whole family [Church] *in heaven and earth is named* (Ephesians 3:15).

FARMER – *Laborer:* Preacher; pastor; Christ; minister. **Farm** = *Field of labor;* an area of ministry; the Kingdom of God; the Church. (See BARN, Chapter 17, and GARDENING, Chapter 24.)

The sower [farmer] *soweth the word* (Mark 4:14).

Now he that ministereth seed to the sower both minister bread for your food, and multiply your seed sown, and increase the fruits of your righteousness (2 Corinthians 9:10).

FATHER – *Authority:* God; author; originator; source; inheritance; tradition; custom; satan; natural father.

Have we not all one father? hath not one God created us?... (Malachi 2:10).

Honor thy father and mother; which is the first commandment with promise (Ephesians 6:2).

...I seek not yours, but you: for the children ought not to lay up for the parents, but the parents for the children (2 Corinthians 12:14).

And Adah bare Jabal: he was the father of such as dwell in tents, and of such as have cattle. And his brother's name was Jubal: he was the father of all such as handle the harp and organ (Genesis 4:20-21).

Ye are of your father the devil, and the lusts of your father ye will do. He was a murderer from the beginning, and abode not in the truth, because there is no truth in him. When he speaketh a lie, he speaketh of his own: for he is a liar, and the father [originator] *of it* (John 8:44).

FATHER-IN-LAW – *Law:* Authoritative relationship based upon law (as in "Moses' law or Church government"); legalism; problem (authoritative) relationship; he may represent himself.

And Moses' father in law said unto him, The thing that thou doest is not good (Exodus 18:17).

FIREMAN – *Helper:* Christ; pastor or minister; counselor; public servant.

God is our refuge and strength, a very present help in trouble (Psalm 46:1).

Call unto Me, and I will answer thee, and shew thee great and mighty things, which thou knowest not (Jeremiah 33:3).

FISHERMAN – See FISHING, Chapter 24.

FOREIGNER – *Alien:* Not of God; of the flesh; demonic; not of this world (therefore heavenly). (See NATION, Chapter 17.)

Our inheritance is turned to strangers [or foreigners], *our houses to aliens* (Lamentations 5:2).

As cold waters to a thirsty soul, so is good news from a far country [the Kingdom of Heaven] (Proverbs 25:25).

FRIEND – *Self:* The character or circumstance of one's friend reveals something about oneself. Sometimes one friend represents another (look for another with the same name, initials, color hair, job or trade, or one with similar traits, character, talents, personality, features, circumstances, etc. (See NAME, Chapter 24); actual friend when naturally interpreted.

And he [King Saul] *took Agag the king of the Amalekites alive* [thus symbolically sparing himself (his own flesh)], *and utterly destroyed all the people with the edge of the sword* (1 Samuel 15:8).

GAMBLER – *Risk Taker:* Taking chances; covetous; if dishonest, cheat; underhand dealing. (See CARDS, Chapter 24.)

If they say thus unto us, Tarry until we come to you; then we will stand still in our place, and will not go up unto them. But if they say thus, Come up unto us; then we will go up: for the Lord hath delivered them into our hand: and this shall be a sign unto us (1 Samuel 14:9-10).

GARDENER – See FARMER.

GENERAL – *Highest Authority:* Christ; apostle; (if evil) evil principality.

And God hath set some in the church, first apostles, secondarily prophets, thirdly teachers, after that miracles, then gifts of healings, helps, governments, diversities of tongues (1 Corinthians 12:28).

For we wrestle not against flesh and blood, but against principalities, against powers, against the rulers of the darkness of this world, against spiritual wickedness in high places (Ephesians 6:12).

GIANT – *Strongman:* Champion; stronghold; challenge; obstacle; trouble; spiritual warfare; one's own fleshly nature (to be overcome).

...The land, through which we have gone to search it, is a land that eateth up the inhabitants thereof; and all the people that we

saw in it are men of a great stature. And there we saw the giants, the sons of Anak...and we were in our own sight as grasshoppers, and so we were in their sight (Numbers 13:32-33).

GOVERNOR – *Rule:* Christ; person in charge (good or bad).

And if ye offer the blind for sacrifice [to God], *is it not evil? ... offer it now unto thy governor; will he be pleased with thee, or accept thy person? saith the Lord of hosts* (Malachi 1:8).

GRANDCHILD – *Heir:* Oneself; inherited blessing or iniquity; one's spiritual legacy; actual grandchild when naturally interpreted. (See GRANDMOTHER.)

When I call to remembrance the unfeigned faith that is in thee, which dwelt first in thy grandmother Lois, and thy mother Eunice; and I am persuaded that in thee also (2 Timothy 1:5).

Keeping mercy for thousands, forgiving iniquity and transgression and sin, and that will by no means clear the guilty; visiting the iniquity of the fathers upon the children, and upon the children's children, unto the third and to the fourth generation (Exodus 34:7).

So these nations feared the Lord, and served their graven images, both their children, and their children's children... (2 Kings 17:41).

GRANDMOTHER (or Grandfather) – *Past:* Spiritual inheritance (good or evil). (See ANTIQUES, Chapter 24, and HOUSE, Chapter 17.) Self-examination for inherited traits, faults, or sins.

When I call to remembrance the unfeigned faith that is in thee, which dwelt first in thy grandmother Lois, and thy mother Eunice; and I am persuaded that in thee also (2 Timothy 1:5).

A good man leaveth an inheritance to his children's children... (Proverbs 13:22).

And they that are left of you shall pine away in their iniquity in your enemies' lands; and also in the iniquities of their fathers shall they pine away with them. If they shall confess their iniquity, and the iniquity of their fathers.... Then will I remember

My covenant...with Abraham...and I will remember the land (Leviticus 26:39-40,42).

GROOM – See BRIDE, Chapter 22, and MARRIAGE, Chapter 24.

HARLOT – *Seduction:* The worldly church; adultery; fornication; temptation; snare; unclean person; stubborn. (See SEX, Chapter 24.)

And upon her forehead was a name written, MYSTERY [RE-LIGION], BABYLON THE GREAT, THE MOTHER OF HARLOTS AND ABOMINATIONS OF THE EARTH (Revelation 17:5).

And I find more bitter than death the woman, whose heart is snares and nets, and her hands as bands: whoso pleaseth God shall escape from her; but the sinner shall be taken by her (Ecclesiastes 7:26).

Therefore the showers have been withholden, and there hath been no latter rain; and thou hadst a whore's forehead, thou refusedst to be ashamed (Jeremiah 3:3).

HUSBAND – *Authority:* God or Christ; a divorcee's first husband sometimes represents "the world" (her bondage to sin before she was saved), natural husband; also satan.

Unto the woman He said...thy desire shall be to thy husband, and he shall rule over thee (Genesis 3:16).

For thy Maker is thine husband; the Lord of hosts is His name... The God of the whole earth shall He be called (Isaiah 54:5).

Surely as a wife treacherously departeth from her husband, so have ye dealt treacherously with Me, O house of Israel [or Church], *saith the Lord* (Jeremiah 3:20).

INDIAN – *First:* Flesh (as in "the old self"); firstborn; chief; fierce; savvy; native.

Lie not one to another, seeing that ye have put off the old man with his deeds (Colossians 3:9).

Reuben, thou art my firstborn, my might, and the beginning of my strength, the excellency of dignity, and the excellency of power [as Christ is the firstborn among many brethren] (Genesis 49:3).

Then pleased it the apostles and elders, with the whole church, to send chosen men of their own company to Antioch with Paul and Barnabas; namely, Judas surnamed Barsabas, and Silas, chief men among the brethren (Acts 15:22).

JUDGE – *Authority:* God; conscience. **Evil Judge** = *satan;* evil authority. (See COURTHOUSE, Chapter 17, and LAWYER, Chapter 22.)

But God is the judge: he putteth down one, and setteth up another (Psalm 75:7).

Grudge not one against another, brethren, lest ye be condemned: behold, the judge standeth before the door (James 5:9).

Shall the throne of iniquity [authority of satan, an evil judge] *have fellowship with thee, which frameth mischief by a law?* (Psalm 94:20)

For if we would judge ourselves [obey our conscience], *we should not be judged* (1 Corinthians 11:31).

LAWYER – *Advocate:* Christ; a legalistic minister. **Crooked Lawyer** = *The devil's advocate* (the accuser of the brethren). (See COURTHOUSE, Chapter 17, and JUDGE, Chapter 22.)

My little children, these things write I unto you, that ye sin not. And if any man sin, we have an advocate [Lawyer] *with the Father, Jesus Christ the righteous* (1 John 2:1).

And he said, Woe unto you also, ye lawyers! for ye lade men with burdens grievous to be borne, and ye yourselves touch not the burdens with one of your fingers (Luke 11:46).

And I heard a loud voice saying in heaven, Now is come salvation, and strength, and the kingdom of our God, and the power of His Christ: for the accuser [evil, crooked, lying advocate] *of our brethren is cast down, which accused them before our God day and night* (Revelation 12:10).

LESBIAN – See HOMOSEXUAL ACTS, Chapter 24.

MAN (Stranger) – *Angel, oneself, or demon:* God's messenger (angel); person with evil intent; danger. **Kind Stranger** = *Jesus;* a minister of mercy; helper (see FRIEND). **White-headed stranger** = *Wisdom.* (See NAME, Chapter 24.)

And when they were departed, behold, the angel [a strange man, or messenger] *of the Lord appeareth to Joseph in a dream, saying, Arise, and take the young child and his mother, and flee into Egypt...for Herod will seek the young child to destroy him* (Matthew 2:13).

Be not forgetful to entertain [also hear, or heed] *strangers: for thereby some have entertained angels unawares* (Hebrews 13:2).

But a certain Samaritan, as he journeyed, came where he was: and when he saw him, he had compassion on him (Luke 10:33).

MECHANIC – *Minister:* Christ; prophet; pastor; counselor; need for adjustment in theology, attitude, relationship, etc. **Mechanic's Tools** = *Word of God:* Gifts of the Spirit; wisdom and knowledge.

And I have filled him with the spirit of God, in wisdom, and in understanding, and in knowledge, and in all manner of workmanship [to manufacture and repair], *to devise cunning works, to work in gold* [to glorify God], *and in silver* [redemption through the knowledge of God], *and in brass* [the Word of God] (Exodus 31:3-4).

All scripture is given by inspiration of God, and is profitable for doctrine, for reproof, for correction, for instruction in righteousness (2 Timothy 3:16).

MIDGET – See DWARF.

MOTHER – *Source:* Church; spiritual or natural mother; love; kindness. **Mother-in-law** = *Legalistic church;* meddler; trouble; she may represent herself. (See FATHER-IN-LAW.)

And Adam called his wife's name Eve [Hebrew: life-giver]; *because she was the mother* [source] *of all living* (Genesis 3:20).

And of Zion [the Church] *it shall be said, This and that man was born* [again] *in her: and the highest himself shall establish her. The Lord shall count, when He writeth up the people, that this man was born* [again] *there* (Psalm 87:5-6).

OLD MAN (Unknown) – *Wisdom* **(especially if he is white-headed):** Carnal (as in "put off the old man"); weak; fool (as in "there's no fool like an old fool").

And Elihu...answered and said, I am young, and ye are very old; wherefore I was afraid, and durst not shew you mine opinion. I said, Days should speak, and multitude of years should teach wisdom (Job 32:6-7).

The hoary [white or gray] *head is a crown of glory, if it be found in the way of righteousness* (Proverbs 16:31).

Great men are not always wise: neither do the aged always understand judgment (Job 32:9).

ONE'S CHILDREN – *Oneself or themselves:* Character or behavior reveals something about oneself (or something about one's own child if the dream is to be naturally interpreted). Sometimes children gathered together from different families from one's own Church represent the Church members.

Behold, every one that useth proverbs shall use this proverb against thee, saying, As is the mother, so is her daughter [or, as is the daughter, so is her mother; as is the father, so is his son, etc.] (Ezekiel 16:44).

And I will give children to be their princes, and babes shall rule over them. As for My people, children are their oppressors, and women rule over them... (Isaiah 3:4,12).

PASSENGER – See DRIVER.

PASTOR – See PREACHER.

PASTOR'S WIFE – See PREACHER.

PHANTOM – *Spirit:* the Holy Spirit; something that has the appearance of reality, but is not real; imaginary.

PHYSICIAN – See DOCTOR and DENTIST.

PILOT – See DRIVER.

POLICE – *Authority:* Natural (civil) or spiritual authority (pastors, etc.), good or evil; protection; angels or demons; an enforcer of a curse of the law (because of transgression or an evil covenant).

Let every soul be subject unto the higher powers [police, etc]. For there is no power but of God: the powers that be are ordained of God. For he is the minister of God to thee for good. But if thou do that which is evil, be afraid; for he beareth not the sword in vain: for he is the minister of God, a revenger to execute wrath upon him that doeth evil (Romans 13:1,4).

And when they [persecute you and] *bring you unto the synagogues* [churches], *and unto magistrates* [civil courts], *and powers* [natural or spiritual], *take ye no thought how or what thing ye shall answer, or what ye shall say* (Luke 12:11).

Shall the throne of iniquity [authority of satan] *have fellowship with thee, which frameth mischief by a law?* (Psalm 94:20)

And of the angels He saith, Who maketh His angels spirits, and His ministers a flame of fire. Are they not all ministering spirits [as public servants, or police], *sent forth to minister for them who shall be heirs of salvation?* (Hebrews 1:7,14)

PREACHER – *Messenger:* God's representative; spiritual authority (good or evil, because he can also represent satan); deception. **Pastor's Wife** = *Church;* or she may represent herself.

And I will give you pastors [preachers and teachers] *according to Mine heart, which shall feed you with knowledge and understanding* (Jeremiah 3:15).

Woe be unto the pastors that destroy and scatter the sheep of My pasture! saith the Lord (Jeremiah 23:1).

For such are false apostles [preachers], *deceitful workers, transforming themselves into the apostles of Christ* (2 Corinthians 11:13).

PRESIDENT – See GOVERNOR.

REPAIRMAN – See MECHANIC.

SISTER – *Self:* Spiritual sister (sister in Christ); someone she reminds you of (see NAME, Chapter 24); the Church; she may represent herself.

For whosoever shall do the will of My Father which is in heaven [the Church], the same is My brother, and sister, and mother (Matthew 12:50).

SISTER-IN-LAW – Someone she reminds you of or she may represent her family, herself, or the dreamer when the dreamer is female (see FRIEND). Other possibilities are: **Brother's Wife** = *Brother.* **Husband's Sister** = *Church.* **Wife's Sister** = *Wife.* *(Note: In any case, if she is the wife of a minister, she may represent the Church.)*

Thou shalt not uncover the nakedness of thy brother's wife: it is thy brother's nakedness (Leviticus 18:16).

SOLDIER – *Warfare:* Spiritual warfare; angel (protection); demon (accuser or opponent); persecution. (See GUNS/BULLETS, Chapter 24.)

And there was war in heaven: Michael and his angels fought against the dragon; and the dragon fought and his angels...the accuser of our brethren is cast down, which accused them before our God day and night (Revelation 12:7,10).

Thou therefore endure hardness, as a good soldier of Jesus Christ. No man that warreth entangleth himself with the affairs of this life; that he may please Him who hath chosen him to be a soldier (2 Timothy 2:3-4).

The words of his mouth were smoother than butter, but war was in his heart: his words were softer than oil, yet were they drawn swords (Psalm 55:21).

SON – See ONE'S CHILDREN.

SUPERMAN – *God:*

Behold, I am the Lord, the God of all flesh: is there any thing too hard for Me? (Jeremiah 32:27)

THIEF – *Hidden:* Deceiver; deception; fraud; destruction; satan; evil intent; works of the flesh; unexpected loss. **The thief's victim**

= *One who is a victim of false doctrine* (as in truth lost through tradition or philosophy); loss of liberty, or even salvation; also temptation; unaware; secret; covert operation; God's judgment (curse) on the wicked.

The thief cometh not, but for to steal, and to kill, and to destroy... (John 10:10).

Beware lest any man [thief] *spoil* [rob] *you* [of the truth] *through philosophy and vain deceit, after the tradition of men, after the rudiments of the world, and not after Christ* (Colossians 2:8).

Whoso is partner with a thief hateth his own soul: he heareth cursing, and bewrayeth it not (Proverbs 29:24).

For yourselves know perfectly that the day of the Lord so cometh as a thief in the night. But ye, brethren, are not in darkness, that that day should overtake you as a thief (1 Thessalonians 5:2,4).

TRAPEZE ARTIST – See TRAPEZE ACT, Chapter 24.

WARRIOR – See SOLDIER.

WHORE – See HARLOT.

WIFE – *Covenant:* Joined; job; business; hobby; Church; dedicated involvement in any activity, such as a job, business, Church, etc.; help; her husband's own person; she may represent herself. (See MARRIAGE, Chapter 24.)

Which things are an allegory: for these [two wives of Abraham] *are the two covenants...* (Galatians 4:24).

For the husband is the head of the wife, even as Christ is the head of the church: and He is the savior of the body. This is a great mystery: but I speak concerning Christ and the church (Ephesians 5:23,32).

But he that is married [to his wife, job, business, hobby, etc.] *careth for the things that are of the world, how he may please his wife* [his own flesh] (1 Corinthians 7:33).

WITCH – *Witchcraft:* Control; evil influence; evil intent; seduction; non-submissive wife; rebellion; slander; gossip; worldly church; evil spirit.

For rebellion is as the sin of witchcraft... (1 Samuel 15:23).

But there was none like unto Ahab, which did sell himself to work wickedness in the sight of the Lord, whom [the witch] *Jezebel his wife stirred up* [or controlled] (1 Kings 21:25).

Notwithstanding I have a few things against thee, because thou sufferest that woman Jezebel, which calleth herself a prophetess, to teach and to seduce my servants to commit fornication, and to eat things sacrificed unto idols (Revelation 2:20).

WOMAN (Stranger) – *Spirit:* Seducing spirit; temptation; deception; witchcraft; God's messenger (angel); one's own self. (See HARLOT, Chapter 22, and NAME, Chapter 24.)

To deliver thee from the strange woman, even from the stranger which flattereth with her words (Proverbs 2:16).

It is like leaven, which a woman took and hid in three measures of meal, till the whole was leavened (Luke 13:21).

For a whore is a deep ditch; and a strange woman is a narrow pit (Proverbs 23:27).

Vehicles and Parts

Refer to Chapter 12 for more detailed coverage of certain vehicles.

AIRPLANE – *Person or Work:* Church (large airplane, such as a passenger plane); travel. **Small Airplane** = *A person or personal ministry;* oversight. **Flying or Soaring** = *Moved by the Spirit;* ministering in the gifts of the Spirit. **Flying Near Electrical Power Lines** = *Danger;* caution; need for much prayer. **Flying Too Low** = *Insufficient power (prayer) or preparation (training);* not following (being led by) the Spirit. **Airplane Crash** = *Failure;* Church split (the survivors are those remaining after the split.); personal disaster (i.e., a failed marriage, business venture, etc.). (See FALLING, Chapter 24; for PILOT see DRIVER, Chapter 22.)

And He rode upon a cherub, and did fly: yea, He did fly upon the wings of the wind (Psalm 18:10).

And when they were come up out of the water, the Spirit of the Lord caught away Philip, that the eunuch saw him no more... (Acts 8:39).

JET – Ministry or Minister: Powerful; fast. **Passenger Jet** = Church. **Fighter** = Individual person or ministry.

And a certain Jew named Apollos...an eloquent man, and mighty in the scriptures, came to Ephesus (Acts 18:24).

AMBULANCE – *Help:* Urgent need; emergency; salvation.

My help cometh from the Lord, which made heaven and earth (Psalm 121:2).

AUTOMOBILE – *Life:* Person; ministry. **New Car** = *New ministry or new way of life.* **Automobile Breakdown** = *Problem;* sickness; trouble; opposition; hindrance (to one's ministry, career, livelihood, etc.). **Limousine** = *Important;* pride. (See VAN or SUV.)

And he made him to ride in the second chariot [limousine] *which he had; and they cried before him, Bow the knee: and he made him ruler over all the land of Egypt* (Genesis 41:43).

And he said, Come with me, and see my zeal for the Lord. So they made him ride in his chariot (2 Kings 10:16).

Wherefore we would have come unto you, even I Paul, once and again; but Satan hindered us (1 Thessalonians 2:18).

CONVERTIBLE (with the top up) – *Covered:* The emphasis is on the covering of the auto owner or driver's life (i.e., spirit, attitude, covenant, etc.).

CONVERTIBLE (with the top down) – *Uncovered:* Everything revealed; open, nothing hidden; self-righteous or unsaved person; "Living in the fast lane"; not submitted to authority; pride; sin or evil exposed. (See MOTORCYCLE.)

And herein do I exercise myself, to have always a conscience void of offense toward God, and toward men (Acts 24:16).

And he drank of the wine, and was drunken; and he was uncovered within his tent (Genesis 9:21).

But every woman that prayeth or prophesieth with her head uncovered [not under or submitted to authority, including obedience to (the authority of) her conscience] *dishonoureth her head: for that is even all one as if she were shaven* (1 Corinthians 11:5).

Woe to the rebellious children, saith the Lord, that take counsel, but not of Me; and that cover with a covering, but not of My spirit, that they may add sin to sin (Isaiah 30:1).

AUTO JUNKYARD – *Ruined:* Waste; wrecked; lost souls; corruption. (See GARBAGE DUMP, Chapter 24.)

The wicked shall be turned into hell [the junkyard of wrecked lives], *and all the nations that forget God* (Psalm 9:17).

But he knoweth not that the dead are there; and that her [a harlot's] *guests are in the depths of hell* (Proverbs 9:18).

Therefore hell hath enlarged herself, and opened her mouth without measure: and their glory, and their multitude, and their pomp, and he that rejoiceth, shall descend into it (Isaiah 5:14).

AUTO WRECK – *Strife:* Contention; conflict; confrontation; calamity; offense; mistake or sin in ministry (as in "failure to maintain right-of-way"). (See BOAT.)

The chariots [automobiles, i.e., people] *shall rage in the streets, they shall jostle one against another in the broad ways* [worldly churches or paths of unrighteousness]: *they shall seem like torches, they shall run like the lightnings* (Nahum 2:4).

BATTERY – *Power:* Strength; prayer; motivation; weak; without spiritual power.

But ye, beloved, building [charging] *up yourselves on your most holy faith, praying in the Holy Ghost* (Jude 20).

BICYCLE – *Works:* Works of the flesh (i.e., not of faith); legalism; self-righteousness; working out life's difficulties (as in riding uphill or in sand or mud); messenger (as in "paper delivery young person"); **Bicycle Built for Two (or with child seat)** = *Family;* more than one person involved.

Christ is become of no effect unto you, whosoever of you are justified by the law [works]; *ye are fallen from grace* (Galatians 5:4).

Now the works of the flesh are manifest, which are these; Adultery, fornication, uncleanness, lasciviousness (Galatians 5:19).

BLIMP – *Weak:* Moved by every wind; wimp; controlled; powerless; aimless; puffed up.

That we henceforth be no more children, tossed to and fro, and carried about with every wind of doctrine, by the sleight of men, and cunning craftiness, whereby they lie in wait to deceive (Ephesians 4:14).

BOAT – *Support:* Life; person; recreation; spare time. **Large Ship** = *The Church.* **Small Boat** = *Personal ministry.* **Sailboat** = *Moved by the Spirit.* **Powerboat** = *Powerful ministry or fast progress.* **Battleship** = *Spiritual warfare;* rescue. **Shipwreck** = *Apostasy;* church split.

A window [revelation knowledge] *shalt thou make to the ark* [Church], *and in a cubit shalt thou finish it above; and the door* [Christ] *of the ark shalt thou set in the side thereof; with lower* [body], *second* [soul], *and third* [spirit] *stories shalt thou make it* (Genesis 6:16).

Now it came to pass on a certain day, that He went into a ship with His disciples: and He said unto them, Let us go over unto the other side of the lake. And they launched forth. But as they sailed He fell asleep: and there came down a storm of wind on the lake; and they were filled with water [despair], *and were in jeopardy* [see STORM] (Luke 8:22-23).

Holding faith, and a good conscience; which some having put away concerning faith have made shipwreck (1 Timothy 1:19).

BRAKES – *Stop:* Hindrance; resist; wait. **Brakes Fail** = *Overcome;* not able to discontinue a bad habit or change a tradition; no resistance to temptation.

Now when they had gone throughout Phrygia and the region of Galatia, and were forbidden of the Holy Ghost to preach the word in Asia, after they were come to Mysia, they assayed to go into Bithynia: but the Spirit suffered them not (Acts 16:6-7).

Having eyes full of adultery, and that cannot cease from sin... [brakes fail] (2 Peter 2:14).

BUS – *Ministry:* **School Bus** = *Teaching or youth ministry;* learning; working together. **Driver** = *Teacher;* pastor; Christ. **Passenger** = *Student.* **Passenger on Tour Bus** = *Sojourner;* Christian; sightseer. (See DRIVER, Chapter 22.)

And Elisha came again to Gilgal...and the sons of the prophets were sitting before him [as he taught them]: *and he said unto his servant, Set on the great pot, and seethe pottage for the sons of the prophets* (2 Kings 4:38).

And the things that thou hast heard of me among many witnesses, the same commit thou [teach] to faithful men, who shall be able to teach others also (2 Timothy 2:2).

By faith he sojourned in the land of promise, as in a strange country... (Hebrews 11:9).

CAR – See AUTOMOBILE.

FIRE TRUCK – *Emergency Assistance:* Quick response to an urgent need; help on its way.

FOUR WHEEL DRIVE VEHICLE – See TIRES and PICKUP TRUCK.

HELICOPTER – *Ministry:* Individual; the Church; versatile. **Hovering** = *No forward motion;* stationary; lack of progress.

Preach the word; be instant in season, out of season; reprove, rebuke, exhort... (2 Timothy 4:2).

MOTOR – *Power:* Motive; motivation; anointing.

How God anointed Jesus of Nazareth with the Holy Ghost and with power: who went about doing good, and healing all that were oppressed of the devil; for God was with Him (Acts 10:38).

MOTORCYCLE – *Individual:* Personal ministry; independence; rebellion; selfish; pride; swift progress.

But chiefly them that walk after the flesh in the lust of uncleanness, and despise government. Presumptuous are they, selfwilled, they are not afraid to speak evil of dignities (2 Peter 2:10).

For rebellion is as the sin of witchcraft, and stubbornness is as iniquity and idolatry... (1 Samuel 15:23).

MOVING VAN – *Change:* Geographical move (natural or spiritual, i.e., moving from one house or place to another, or moving from one church to another, including changing denominations); relocation.

Son of man...prepare thee stuff for removing, and remove by day in their sight; and thou shalt remove from thy place to another place in their sight... (Ezekiel 12:2-3).

PICKUP TRUCK – *Work:* Personal ministry or natural work. (See AUTOMOBILE.)

And they carried the ark of God in a new cart out of the house of Abinadab: and Uzza and Ahio drave the cart (1 Chronicles 13:7).

...And when he [Jacob] *saw the wagons which Joseph had sent to carry him, the spirit of Jacob their father revived* [revival] (Genesis 45:27).

For every man shall bear his own burden [drive his own truck, i.e., do his own work, natural or spiritual] (Galatians 6:5).

RAFT – *Adrift:* Without direction; aimless; powerless; makeshift.

And the rest, some on boards, and some on broken pieces of the ship. And so it came to pass, that they escaped all safe to land (Acts 27:44).

That we henceforth be no more children, tossed to and fro, and carried about with every wind [or current] *of doctrine...* (Ephesians 4:14).

REAR VIEW MIRROR – *Word:* **Driving Backward (using the rear view mirror)** = *Operating by the letter of the Word* (instead of by God's Spirit); legalism; looking back. (See MIRROR, Chapter 24.)

Who also hath made us able ministers of the new testament; not of the letter, but of the spirit: for the letter killeth, but the spirit giveth life (2 Corinthians 3:6).

But his [Lot's] *wife looked back from behind him* [regretting having to leave the things of this world], *and she became a pillar of salt* (Genesis 19:26).

ROLLER COASTER – *Unstable:* Emotional instability; unfaithfulness; wavering; manic-depressive; depression; trials; excitement.

Every valley shall be exalted, and every mountain and hill shall be made low: and the crooked shall be made straight, and the rough places plain [or smooth] (Isaiah 40:4).

But let him ask in faith, nothing wavering. For he that wavereth is like a wave of the sea driven with the wind and tossed. For let not that man think that he shall receive any thing of the Lord. A double minded man is unstable in all his ways (James 1:6-8).

ROWBOAT – See ROWING, Chapter 24.

SCHOOL BUS – See BUS.

SEAT BELT – *Security:* Safety; assurance. **Unfastened** = *Unsafe* (lack of prayer, commitment, attention to detail, etc.).

...Bind the sacrifice with cords [vows, commitment, etc.], *even unto the horns of the altar* (Psalm 118:27).

SHIP – See BOAT.

STATION WAGON – See VAN or SUV.

TANK – *Impenetrable:* Natural or spiritual warfare; comparable to chariots in Scripture.

And the children of Israel cried unto the Lord: for he had nine hundred chariots of iron; and twenty years he mightily oppressed the children of Israel (Judges 4:3).

TIRES – *Spirit:* Life (as in "where the rubber meets the road"); spiritual condition. **Four Wheel Drive** = *Full ministry;* full gospel foundation. **Deflated Tire** = *Discouragement;* dismay; hindrance; lack of prayer.

And took off their chariot wheels, that they drave them heavily [discouraged them]: *so that the Egyptians said, Let us flee from the face of Israel; for the Lord fighteth for them against the Egyptians* (Exodus 14:25).

Whithersoever the spirit was to go, they went, thither was their spirit to go; and the wheels were lifted up over against them:

for the spirit of the living creature was in the wheels (Ezekiel 1:20).

TRACTOR (FARM) – *Powerful Work:* Slow but powerful ministry; preaching (when plowing).

But ye shall receive power, after that the Holy Ghost is come upon you: and ye shall be witnesses unto Me...unto the uttermost part of the earth (Acts 1:8).

And with great power gave the apostles witness of the resurrection of the Lord Jesus: and great grace was upon them all (Acts 4:33).

TRACTOR TRAILER – *Large Burden:* Ministry; powerful and/ or large work (truck size is often in proportion to the burden or size of the work); the Church.

And they set the ark of God upon a new cart...and Uzzah and Ahio...drave the new cart (2 Samuel 6:3).

And believers were the more added to the Lord, multitudes [large work] *both of men and women* (Acts 5:14).

TRAIN – *Continuous:* Unceasing work; the Church; connected; fast. **Train Wreck = *Similar to* Airplane Crash.** (See AIRPLANE, Chapter 23, and RAILROAD TRACK, Chapter 24.)

And they continued steadfastly in the apostles' doctrine and fellowship, and in breaking of bread, and in prayers (Acts 2:42).

TRANSMISSION – *Change:* Steps; change of direction, change of purpose or intensity of ministry; transformation.

And be not conformed to this world: but be ye transformed by the renewing of your mind... (Romans 12:2).

TRUCK – See PICKUP TRUCK and TRACTOR TRAILER.

VAN or SUV – *Family:* Natural or church family; family ministry; fellowship.

For this cause I bow my knees unto the Father of our Lord Jesus Christ, Of whom the whole family in heaven and earth is named (Ephesians 3:14-15).

But if we walk in the light, as He is in the light, we have fellowship one with another, and the blood of Jesus Christ His Son cleanseth us from all sin (1 John 1:7).

WHEELS – See TIRES.

Miscellaneous

ABORTION – *Aborted Project:* Cutoff; failure. (See MISCARRIAGE.)

ACCIDENT – *Trouble:* (may be caused by) Not listening to instruction; inattention to detail; going too fast; careless operator; failure to maintain control. (See AUTO WRECK, Chapter 23.)

ACID – *Bitter:* Offense; carrying a grudge; hatred; sarcasm.

For I perceive that thou art in the gall of bitterness, and in the bond of iniquity (Acts 8:23).

Looking diligently lest any man fail of the grace of God; lest any root of bitterness [Greek: acridity, i.e., desire for revenge (carrying a grudge)] *springing up trouble you, and thereby many be defiled* (Hebrews 12:15).

ACORN – *Potential* (for greatness): Small, but significant.

And there came an angel of the Lord, and sat under an oak which was in Ophrah, that pertained unto Joash the Abiezrite: and his son Gideon threshed wheat by the winepress, to hide it from the Midianites. And the angel of the Lord appeared unto him, and said unto him, The Lord is with thee, thou mighty man of valor (Judges 6:11-12).

ADDICTION – *Bound:* Bondage; obsessed; demon possession. (See DRUGS.)

And deliver them who through fear of death were all their life-time subject to bondage (Hebrews 2:15).

ADULTERY – *Sin:* Idolatry; pornography. (See SEX.)

Ye [spiritual] adulterers and adulteresses, know ye not that the friendship of the world is enmity with God?... (James 4:4).

And I find more bitter than death the woman, whose heart is snares and nets, and her hands as bands: whoso pleaseth God shall escape from her; but the sinner shall be taken by her (Ecclesiastes 7:26).

Such is the way of an adulterous woman; she eateth, and wipeth her mouth, and saith, I have done no wickedness (Proverbs 30:20).

But I say unto you, That whosoever looketh on a woman to lust after her hath committed adultery with her already in his heart (Matthew 5:28).

AIR CONDITIONER – *Spiritual Conditioning:* Spiritual ministry (as in ministering in the gifts of the Spirit); cool off (cease from being angry); calm down (as in "he needs to chill out").

He therefore that ministereth to you the Spirit, and worketh miracles among you, doeth he it by the works of the law, or by the hearing of faith? (Galatians 3:5)

ALCOHOL – *Intoxicant:* Holy Spirit; addiction (bondage). (See DRUNK, Chapter 22).

And be not drunk with wine, wherein is excess; but be filled with the Spirit (Ephesians 5:18).

And take heed to yourselves, lest at any time your hearts be overcharged with surfeiting, and drunkenness, and cares of this life, and so that day come upon you unawares (Luke 21:34).

And wine that maketh glad the heart of man, and oil to make his face to shine, and bread which strengtheneth man's heart (Psalm 104:15).

ALTAR – *Sacrifice:* Service; offering; prayer; consecration; worship.

Unto the place of the altar, which he had made there at the first: and there Abram called on the name of the Lord (Genesis 13:4).

But I will sacrifice unto thee with the voice of thanksgiving; I will pay that that I have vowed. Salvation is of the Lord (Jonah 2:9).

ANGEL – *Messenger:* help; encouragement; deliverance.

The angel of the Lord encampeth round about them that fear Him, and delivereth them (Psalm 34:7).

For He shall give His angels charge over thee, to keep thee in all thy ways (Psalm 91:11).

ANKLES – *Faith:* **Weak Ankles** = *Weak faith;* unsupported; undependable. **Sprained Ankle** = *Unfaithfulness;* broken promise.

And when the man that had the line in his hand went forth eastward, he measured a thousand cubits, and he brought me through the waters; the waters were to the ankles [faith, the first step into the Spirit (See KNEES, HIPS, and RIVER).] (Ezekiel 47:3).

Confidence in an unfaithful man in time of trouble is like a broken tooth, and a foot out of joint (Proverbs 25:19).

ANTENNA – *Receiver:* Attentive; receptive; listening. **Broken Antenna** = *Unable to hear or understand;* not listening.

But they understood not this saying, and it was hid from them, that they perceived it not: and they feared to ask Him of that saying (Luke 9:45).

ANTIQUES – *Past:* Inherited from our forefathers (good or evil); memories. (See ATTIC, Chapter 17; GRANDMOTHER, Chapter 22; and ROCKING CHAIR, Chapter 24.)

Thus saith the Lord, Stand ye in the ways, and see, and ask for the old paths, where is the good way, and walk therein, and ye shall find rest for your souls... (Jeremiah 6:16).

ANTLERS – See HORNS.

APPLES – *Fruit:* Words; sin; temptation; appreciation (as in "giving a teacher an apple"); fruit of the Spirit.

A word fitly spoken is like apples of gold [words of wisdom] *in pictures of silver* (Proverbs 25:11).

And when the woman saw that the tree was good for food, and that it was pleasant to the eyes, and a tree to be desired to make one wise, she took of the fruit thereof, and did eat, and gave also unto her husband with her; and he did eat (Genesis 3:6).

Either make the tree good, and his fruit good; or else make the tree corrupt, and his fruit corrupt: for the tree is known by his fruit. O generation of vipers, how can ye, being evil, speak good things? for out of the abundance of the heart the mouth speaketh (Matthew 12:33-34).

But the fruit of the Spirit is love, joy, peace, longsuffering, gentleness, goodness, faith, meekness, temperance: against such there is no law (Galatians 5:22-23).

ARM – *Strength or Weakness:* Savior; deliverer; helper; aid; reaching out (showing mercy); striker.

Who hath believed our report? and to whom is the arm of the Lord revealed? (Isaiah 53:1)

With a strong hand, and with a stretched out arm [reaching out to those in need]: *for His mercy endureth for ever* (Psalm 136:12).

For a bishop must be blameless, as the steward of God...not soon angry...no striker... (Titus 1:7).

Thus saith the Lord; Cursed be the man that trusteth in man, and maketh flesh his arm, and whose heart departeth from the Lord (Jeremiah 17:5).

ARROWS – See BOW/ARROWS.

ASHES – *Memories* (That which has been reduced to ashes remains only in memory.): Repentance; ruin; destruction; burnout.

Your remembrances are like unto ashes... (Job 13:12).

Wherefore I abhor myself, and repent in dust and ashes [bringing sin to remembrance] (Job 42:6).

ATOM BOMB – *Power:* Holy Spirit outpouring (the atom bomb is both a sign of the last days and a parable of God's mighty power); miracle power; sudden destruction.

But ye shall receive power, after that the Holy Ghost is come upon you: and ye shall be witnesses unto me both in Jerusalem, and in all Judaea, and in Samaria, and unto the uttermost part of the earth (Acts 1:8).

And it shall come to pass in the last days, saith God, I will pour out of my Spirit upon all flesh...And I will shew wonders in heaven above, and signs in the earth beneath; blood, and fire, and vapor [pillar or column] *of smoke* [a description of the fireball and mushroom cloud of an atomic blast] (Acts 2:17-19).

For when they shall say, Peace and safety; then sudden destruction cometh upon them, as travail upon a woman with child; and they shall not escape (1 Thessalonians 5:3).

AUTUMN – *End:* Completion; change; repentance.

But we are all as an unclean thing, and all our righteousnesses are as filthy rags; and we all do fade as a leaf; and our iniquities, like the wind, have taken us away (Isaiah 64:6).

The harvest is past, the summer is ended, and we are not saved (Jeremiah 8:20).

AVALANCHE – *Sudden, Irresistible Force:* Sudden destruction; sudden, unplanned change; overwhelming situation; divine judgment (because it comes from above).

He, that being often reproved hardeneth his neck, shall suddenly be destroyed, and that without remedy (Proverbs 29:1).

AXE – *Word:* Gospel; preaching; exhorting others; rebuke; repentance.

And now also the axe [Word of God, i.e., command to repent] *is laid unto the root of the trees: therefore every tree which bringeth not forth good fruit is hewn down, and cast into the fire* (Matthew 3:10).

Iron sharpeneth iron; so a man sharpeneth the countenance of his friend [by exhorting or reproving him] (Proverbs 27:17).

If the iron [axe] *be blunt, and he do not whet the edge* [study God's Word to be able to use His wisdom and knowledge], *then must he put to more strength: but wisdom is profitable to direct* (Ecclesiastes 10:10).

BACK DOOR – See BACK, Chapter 19, and DOOR.

BADGE – *Authority:* Ordained; deputized (given authority); (See POLICE, Chapter 22.)

And He ordained twelve, that they should be with Him, and that He might send them forth to preach (Mark 3:14).

BAND AID – *Insufficient Aid:* Patching or covering something up instead of curing the real problem. **Person wearing numerous Band Aids** = *Hurt or wounded* (as in "you hurt my feelings").

Is there no balm in Gilead; is there no physician there? why then is not the health of the daughter of my people recovered? (Jeremiah 8:22)

BARRICADE – *Closed:* Obstacle; hindered; path blocked.

After they were come to Mysia, they assayed to go into Bithynia: but the Spirit suffered them not (Acts 16:7).

Wherefore we would have come unto you, even I Paul, once and again; but Satan hindered us (1 Thessalonians 2:18).

BASEBALL CARDS – Hero Worship: Esteem for another person (proper or improper).

And to esteem them very highly in love for their work's sake... (1 Thessalonians 5:13).

And there went out a champion out of the camp of the Philistines, named Goliath, of Gath, whose height was six cubits and a span (1 Samuel 17:4).

BASEBALL GAME – See PLAY.

BATHING – *Cleansing:* Sanctification; repentance; temptation. (See SOAP, WASHBASIN, and WASHCLOTH.)

Wash me thoroughly from mine iniquity, and cleanse me from my sin. For I acknowledge my transgressions: and my sin is ever before me (Psalm 51:2-3).

Husbands, love your wives, even as Christ also loved the church, and gave Himself for it; that He might sanctify and cleanse it with the washing of water by the word (Ephesians 5:25-26).

And it came to pass in an eveningtide, that David arose from off his bed, and walked upon the roof of the king's house: and from the roof he saw a woman washing herself; and the woman was very beautiful to look upon (2 Samuel 11:2).

BEARD – *Covering:* Humanity; relating to the heart. **Rough, Unshaven Face** = *Spiritual neglect or uncleanness;* coarse or harsh personality. (See HAIR.)

They shall not make baldness upon their head, neither shall they shave off the corner of their beard... [self-justification] (Leviticus 21:5).

BED – *Rest:* Salvation; meditation; intimacy; peace; covenant (as in marriage), or an evil covenant (as in natural or spiritual adultery); self-made (harmful) conditions (as in "You made your bed, now sleep in it!").

Stand in awe, and sin not: commune with your own heart upon your bed, and be still (Psalm 4:4).

If I ascend up into heaven, Thou art there: if I make my bed in hell, behold, Thou art there [See Isaiah 28:18-20.] (Psalm 139:8).

Marriage is honorable in all, and the bed [is to be kept] *undefiled: but whoremongers and adulterers God will judge* (Hebrews 13:4).

BELLS – *A Sign indicating: 1. Change* (as in "the times are changing"). *2. God's Presence* (as in "the manifestation of the Spirit...the gift of tongues"). *3. Vanity* (when used as jewelry); pride.

A golden bell [the gifts of the Spirit] *and a pomegranate* [the fruit of the Spirit], *a golden bell and a pomegranate, upon the hem of the robe* [of righteousness] *round about* (Exodus 28:34).

Though I speak with the tongues of men and of angels, and have not charity [love], *I am become as...a tinkling cymbal* [or bell] (1 Corinthians 13:1).

Wherefore tongues [spiritual bells] *are for a sign, not to them that believe, but to them that believe not...* (1 Corinthians 14:22).

Moreover the Lord saith, Because the daughters of Zion are haughty, and walk with stretched forth necks and wanton eyes, walking and mincing as they go, and making a tinkling with [bells on] *their feet* (Isaiah 3:16).

BELLY – *Spirit:* Desire; lust; heart; feelings; selfishness; self-worship; sickness.

He that believeth on Me, as the scripture hath said, out of his belly [spirit] *shall flow rivers of living water* (John 7:38).

The words of a talebearer are as wounds, and they go down into the innermost parts of the belly [spirit or heart] (Proverbs 26:22).

Whose end is destruction, whose God is their belly [their own spirit, or self], *and whose glory is in their shame, who mind earthly things* (Philippians 3:19).

BESTIALITY – *Inordinate Lust:* Unnatural, deviant sex acts (as in oral or anal sex); obscene. (See SEX.)

Neither shalt thou lie [have sex] *with any beast to defile thyself therewith: neither shall any woman stand before a beast to lie down thereto: it is confusion* (Leviticus 18:23).

For this is the will of God, even your sanctification, that ye should abstain from fornication: That every one of you should know how to possess his vessel [wife] *in sanctification and honor; Not in the lust of concupiscence* [strong, inordinate lust], *even as the Gentiles which know not God* (1 Thessalonians 4:3-5).

BIKINI – *Uncovered:* Carnal; seduction; temptation; insufficient covering.

Thy nakedness shall be uncovered, yea, thy shame shall be seen... (Isaiah 47:3).

BINGO – *Winner or Correct:* Sudden victory; correct answer, idea, or understanding.

Know ye not that they which run in a race [or compete in a game] *run all, but one receiveth the prize? So run, that ye may* obtain (1 Corinthians 9:24).

He saith unto them, But whom say ye that I am? And Simon Peter answered and said, Thou art the Christ, the Son of the living God (Matthew 16:15-16).

BINOCULARS – *Insight:* Understanding; prophetic vision; future event. **Not Focused (blurred)** = *Without understanding or insight.* (See TELESCOPE.)

Howbeit when He, the Spirit of truth, is come...He will shew you things to come (John 16:13).

And not as Moses, which put a vail over his face, that the children of Israel could not steadfastly look to the end of that which is abolished (2 Corinthians 3:13).

BLADDER – See URINATING.

BLANKET – *Covering:* Covenant; hidden; **Comforter** = *Holy Spirit.*

And your covenant with death shall be disannulled, and your agreement with hell shall not stand; when the overflowing scourge shall pass through, then ye shall be trodden down by it. For the bed is shorter than that a man can stretch himself on it: and the covering narrower than that he can wrap himself in it (Isaiah 28:18,20).

But the Comforter, which is the Holy Ghost, whom the Father will send in my name, he shall teach you all things, and bring all things to your remembrance, whatsoever I have said unto you (John 14:26).

BLEEDING – *Wounded:* Hurt, naturally or emotionally; spiritually dying; offended; in strife; gossip; unclean. (See HOSPITAL, Chapter 17, and BLOOD, Chapter 24.)

He healeth the broken in heart, and bindeth up their wounds (Psalm 147:3).

The words of a talebearer are as wounds... (Proverbs 18:8).

BLIND – *Without Understanding:* **Total blindness** = *Self-righteousness;* self-justification; hating one another; willful ignorance. **Tunnel vision** = *Narrow mindedness;* legalistic. **Cataracts or Dim-sightedness** = *Blinded by the deceitfulness of riches.*

Let them alone: they be blind leaders of the blind. And if the blind lead the blind, both shall fall into the ditch (Matthew 15:14).

Because thou sayest, I am rich, and increased with goods, and have need of nothing; and knowest not that thou art wretched, and miserable, and poor, and blind... [self-righteous, without understanding] (Revelation 3:17).

Thou blind [self-righteous] *Pharisee, cleanse first that which is within the cup and platter, that the outside of them may be clean also* (Matthew 23:26).

But he that lacketh these things is blind [self-righteous], *and cannot see afar off* [and is proud], *and hath forgotten that he was purged from his old sins* (2 Peter 1:9).

But he that hateth his brother is in darkness, and walketh in darkness, and knoweth not whither he goeth, because that darkness hath blinded his eyes (1 John 2:11).

BLOOD – *Life of the Flesh:* Covenant; murder; defiled; unclean; pollution; purging; testimony; witness; guilt.

For the life of the flesh is in the blood... (Leviticus 17:11).

Cursed be he that taketh reward to slay an innocent person... [such as a doctor in performing an abortion for pay] (Deuteronomy 27:25).

And shed innocent blood, even the blood of their sons and of their daughters [through abortion], *whom they sacrificed unto the idols of Canaan* [or convenience]: *and the land was polluted with blood* (Psalm 106:38).

And if a woman have an issue, and her issue in her flesh be blood, she shall be put apart seven days: and whosoever toucheth her shall be unclean until the even (Leviticus 15:19).

When I say unto the wicked, O wicked man, thou shalt surely die; if thou dost not speak to warn the wicked from his way, that wicked man shall die in his iniquity; but his blood will I require at thine hand (Ezekiel 33:8).

BLOOD TRANSFUSION – *Change:* Regeneration; salvation; deliverance; infusion of power from on high.

Not by works of righteousness which we have done, but according to His mercy He saved us, by the washing of regeneration, and renewing of the Holy Ghost (Titus 3:5).

And be not conformed to this world: but be ye transformed by the renewing of your mind, that ye may prove what is that good, and acceptable, and perfect, will of God (Romans 12:2).

BLUEPRINTS – *Plans:* Word of God (including personal prophecies); specific instructions.

Who serve unto the example and shadow of heavenly things, as Moses was admonished of God when he was about to make the tabernacle: for, See, saith He, that thou make all things according to the pattern shewed to thee in the mount (Hebrews 8:5).

BODY ODOR – *Uncleanness:* Bad attitude; filthiness of the flesh; rejected.

Having therefore these promises, dearly beloved, let us cleanse ourselves from all filthiness of the flesh and spirit, perfecting holiness in the fear of God [See James 4:8.] (2 Corinthians 7:1).

Wherefore lay apart all filthiness and superfluity of naughtiness... (James 1:21).

Dead flies cause the ointment of the apothecary to send forth a stinking savor: so doth a little folly him that is in reputation for wisdom and honor (Ecclesiastes 10:1).

BOLTS – See NUTS AND BOLTS.

BONES – *Spirit:* Condition of the heart; death; that which is eternal.

Woe unto you, scribes and Pharisees, hypocrites! for ye are like unto whited sepulchres, which indeed appear beautiful outward, but are within full of dead men's bones, and of all uncleanness (Matthew 23:27).

Then he said unto me, Son of man, these bones are the whole house of Israel: behold, they say, Our bones are dried, and our hope is lost: we are cut off for our parts (Ezekiel 37:11).

A merry heart doeth good like a medicine: but a broken spirit drieth the bones (Proverbs 17:22).

BOOK – *Record:* Knowledge; Word of God; hearts of people; witness; remembrance (good or evil); conscience; education; research; study. If the book's subject is revealed in the dream, research that subject (or read that book). (See LIBRARY, Chapter 17.)

And I saw the dead, small and great, stand before God; and the books were opened: and another book was opened, which is the book of life: and the dead were judged out of those things which were written in the books [their hearts], *according to their works* (Revelation 20:12).

Then they that feared the Lord spake often one to another: and the Lord hearkened, and heard it, and a book of remembrance was written before Him for them that feared the Lord, and that thought upon His name (Malachi 3:16).

Ye are our epistle written in our hearts, known and read of all men (2 Corinthians 3:2).

BOOTS – See SHOES/BOOTS.

BOW/ARROWS – *Words or Person:* Accusations; slander; gossip; prayer; deliverance. **Bow** = *Tongue;* Power. **Quiver** = *Heart.* **Arrows** = *Words.*

Who whet their tongue like a sword, and bend their bows to shoot their arrows, even bitter words (Psalm 64:3).

For, lo, the wicked bend their bow, they make ready their arrow upon the string, that they may privily [secretly] *shoot at the upright in heart* (Psalm 11:2).

A man that beareth false witness against his neighbor is a maul, and a sword, and a sharp arrow (Proverbs 25:18).

And he said, Open the window eastward. And he opened it. Then Elisha said, Shoot. And he shot. And he said, The arrow of the Lord's deliverance...for thou shalt smite the Syrians...till thou have consumed them (2 Kings 13:17).

And He [God] *hath made my mouth like a sharp sword; in the shadow of His hand hath He hid me, and made me a polished* [arrow] *shaft; in His quiver* [heart] *hath He hid me* (Isaiah 49:2).

BOWL – See POT/PAN/BOWL.

BOX – *Container:* Religious Tradition (as in "you can't keep God in a box"); legalistic doctrine. **A collection or pile of Cardboard Boxes** = *Memories* (each memory contains the emotions, regrets, joy, grief, sadness, etc. of the previous experience). **Disposing of old Boxes** = *Renouncing and forsaking the past.* **Gift wrapped Box** = *Special Gift;* spiritual gift.

Brethren, I count not myself to have apprehended: but this one thing I do, forgetting those things which are behind, and reaching forth unto those things which are before... (Philippians 3:13).

BOXING – *Striving:* Preaching; deliverance; trial; tribulation. (See WRESTLING.)

I have fought a good fight, I have finished my course, I have kept the faith (2 Timothy 4:7).

And every man that striveth for the mastery is temperate in all things. Now they do it to obtain a corruptible crown; but we an incorruptible. I therefore so run, not as uncertainly; so fight I, not as one that beateth the air [shadow boxing] (1 Corinthians 9:25-26).

BREAD – *Life or Word:* Doctrine; covenant; the Church; substance; provision (money, food, etc.).

But He answered and said, It is written, Man shall not live by bread alone, but by every word that proceedeth out of the mouth of God (Matthew 4:4).

And when Gideon was come, behold, there was a man that told a dream unto his fellow, and said, Behold, I dreamed a dream, and, lo, a cake of barley bread [common man's bread] *tumbled into the host of Midian, and came unto a tent, and smote it that it fell, and overturned it, that the tent lay along. And his fellow answered and said, This* [bread] *is nothing else save the sword* [Word of God in the hand] *of Gideon the Son of Joash, a man of Israel: for into his hand hath God delivered Midian, and all the host* (Judges 7:13-14).

I speak not of you all: I know whom I have chosen: but that the scripture may be fulfilled, He that eateth bread [made a covenant] *with Me hath lifted up his heel* [betrayal] *against Me* [See EATING] (John 13:18).

Neither did we eat any man's bread for nought; but wrought with labor and travail night and day, that we might not be chargeable to any of you (2 Thessalonians 3:8).

BREAD MOLD – *Unfit:* Tradition; without revelation; stale; defiled.

...and all the bread of their provision was dry and moldy [people under the law] (Joshua 9:5b).

Ye offer polluted [molded] *bread upon mine altar; and ye say, Wherein have we polluted thee? In that ye say, The table of the Lord is contemptible* (Malachi 1:7).

Therefore let us keep the feast, not with old leaven, neither with the leaven of malice and wickedness; but with the unleavened [or unmolded] *bread of sincerity and truth* (1 Corinthians 5:8).

Why do thy disciples transgress the tradition of the elders? for they wash not their hands when they eat bread. But He answered and said unto them, Why do ye also transgress the commandment of God by your tradition? ...*Thus have ye made the commandment* [bread] *of God of none effect* [useless, as molded bread] *by your tradition* (Matthew 15:2-3,6).

BRICKS – *Human-made stone* (unacceptable to God): Human effort; works of the flesh; incorruptible building material (will not rot, as wood does).

And if thou wilt make me an altar of stone, thou shalt not build it of hewn stone [or brick]: *for if thou lift up thy tool upon it, thou hast polluted it* (Exodus 20:25).

A people that provoketh me to anger continually to my face; that sacrificeth in gardens, and burneth incense upon altars of brick (Isaiah 65:3).

And they made their lives bitter with hard bondage, in morter, and in brick, and in all manner of service in the field: all their service, wherein they made them serve, was with rigour (Exodus 1:14).

BRIDGE – *Support or Way:* Faith; trial (of faith); joined.

And he rose up that night, and took his two wives, and his two wo-menservants, and his eleven sons, and passed over the ford [Hebrew: a crossing place] *Jabbok* (Genesis 32:22).

When thou passest through the waters, I will be with thee; and through the rivers, they shall not overflow thee... (Isaiah 43:2a).

There hath no temptation [trial] *taken you but such as is common to man: but God is faithful, who will not suffer you to be tempted above that ye are able; but will with the temptation also make a way* [bridge] *to escape, that ye may be able to bear it* (1 Corinthians 10:13).

BRIERS – *Snare:* Obstacle; hindrance; trial; wicked person; rejected; cursed. (For stickers or burrs, see THORNS.)

Upon the land of my people shall come up thorns and briers... (Isaiah 32:13).

The best of them is as a brier: the most upright is sharper than a thorn hedge... (Micah 7:4).

But that which beareth thorns and briers is rejected, and is nigh unto cursing; whose end is to be burned (Hebrews 6:8).

BROOM – *Cleaning or Witchcraft:* Clean house (put away sin). (See SWEEPING.)

And when He had made a scourge of small cords, He drove them all out of the temple, and the sheep, and the oxen; and poured out the changers' money, and overthrew the tables (John 2:15).

Thou shalt not suffer a witch to live (Exodus 22:18).

Now the works of the flesh are manifest, which are these...witch-craft [manipulation and control]... (Galatians 5:19-20).

BUBBLE GUM – *Childish:* Foolishness; immaturity.

The heart of him that hath understanding seeketh knowledge: but the mouth of fools feedeth on foolishness (Proverbs 15:14).

Foolishness is bound in the heart of a child; but the rod of correction shall drive it far from him (Proverbs 22:15).

BULLETS – See GUNS/BULLETS.

BUTTER – *Works:* Doing (or not doing) the Word or will of God. (See CHEESE for explanation); deceptive motives, words, or works; smooth talker; deceiver.

The words of his mouth were smoother than butter, but war was in his heart: his words were softer than oil, yet were they drawn swords (Psalm 55:21).

Surely the churning of milk bringeth forth butter...so the forcing of wrath bringeth forth strife (Proverbs 30:33).

Butter [knowledge gained through experience (See Hebrews 5:12-14.)] *and honey* [Holy Spirit] *shall he eat, that he may know to refuse the evil, and choose the good* (Isaiah 7:15).

CALENDAR – *Time:* Date; event; appointment. (See CLOCK, Chapter 24, for specific numbers see Chapter 21.)

Also, O Judah, he hath set [a date for] *an harvest* [of retribution] *for thee, when I returned the captivity of My people* (Hosea 6:11).

CAMERA – *Memory:* Bringing things to remembrance.

I will remember the works of the Lord: surely I will remember thy wonders of old (Psalm 77:11).

CAMPING OUT – *Temporary:* Abiding; recreation; rest; youth ministry. **Campfire** = *Fellowship.*

The angel of the Lord encamps round about them that fear Him, and delivers them (Psalm 34:7).

CANCER – *Offense:* Heresy; unforgiven offense; bitterness; **Cancer of the Tongue**: Scornful words; sarcasm; **Bladder Cancer**: Hate speech; bitter envy; **Breast Cancer:** May indicate stress or when applicable, bitterness from spouse's infidelity; when naturally interpreted, sometimes a terminal disease.

And their word will eat as doth a canker: of whom is Hymenaeus and Philetus (2 Timothy 2:17).

But if ye have bitter envying and strife in your hearts, glory not, and lie not against the truth (James 3:14).

CARDS – *Facts:* Honesty (as in "putting all your cards on the table"); truth; expose or reveal; dishonesty; underhanded dealing; cheating; wisdom (as in "knowing when to hold and when to fold").

...Provide things honest in the sight of all men (Romans 12:17).

CARNIVAL – *Worldly:* Festivity; party spirit; exhibitionism; divination; competition. (See ROLLER COASTER, Chapter 23.)

And take heed to yourselves, lest at any time your hearts be overcharged with surfeiting, and drunkenness, and cares of this life, and so that day come upon you unawares (Luke 21:34).

And it came to pass, as we went to prayer, a certain damsel possessed with a spirit of divination met us, which brought her masters much gain by soothsaying [fortune-telling] (Acts 16:16).

CD or CASSETTE TAPE – *Recording:* Memory; Listening to Recorded Music = *Reliving the past through memory;* worship.

And the second time the cock crew. And Peter called to mind the word that Jesus said unto him, Before the cock crow twice, thou shalt deny Me thrice. And when he thought thereon, he wept (Mark 14:72).

CELL PHONE – See TELEPHONE.

CHAIR – *Rest or Position:* Quietness; position of authority (as in "chair of a board meeting").

For thus saith the Lord God, the Holy One of Israel; In returning and rest shall ye be saved; in quietness and in confidence shall be your strength... (Isaiah 30:15).

And love the uppermost rooms at feasts, and the chief seats in the synagogues (Matthew 23:6).

CHECK (Bank) – *Faith* (the currency of the Kingdom of God): provision; trust. **Bad Check** = *Fraud;* deception; hypocrisy; lack of faith or prayer.

Now faith is the substance of things hoped for, the evidence of things not seen (Hebrews 11:1).

And He said unto them, Why are ye so fearful? how is it that ye have no faith [as in an overdrawn account]? (Mark 4:40)

And the apostles said unto the Lord, Increase our faith (Luke 17:5).

CHEESE – *Works:* Doing (or not doing) the Word or will of God. (See BUTTER.)

Jesus saith unto them, My meat [solid food] *is to do the will of Him that sent Me, and to finish His work* [i.e., butter and cheese is liquid milk (God's Word) made into solid food (God's work). Compare First Peter 2:2: *"As newborn babes, desire the sincere milk of the word, that ye may grow thereby"* (become mature doers of the Word)] (John 4:34).

Hast Thou not poured me out as milk, and curdled me like cheese? (Job 10:10)

CHESS – *Strategy:* Carefully plan your next move; deliberate, purposeful action; stalemate; depending upon the context, checkmate indicates personal defeat or defeated enemy.

And I will put enmity between thee and the woman, and between thy seed and her seed; it shall bruise thy head, and thou shalt bruise His heel (Genesis 3:15).

CHEWING – *Meditate* **(as in, "let me chew on that awhile"):** Receiving wisdom and understanding. **Chewing Bubble Gum** = *Childishness;* foolishness. **Chewing Tough Meat** = *Hard saying or difficult work.* (See EATING, FOOD/MILK, and TEETH.)

Meditate [chew] *upon these things; give thyself wholly to them; that thy profiting may appear to all* (1 Timothy 4:15).

My mouth shall speak of wisdom; and the meditation of my heart shall be of understanding (Psalm 49:3).

The thought [meditation or planning] *of foolishness is sin: and the scorner is an abomination to men* (Proverbs 24:9).

CHOKING – *Hindrance:* Stumbling over something (as in "too much to swallow"); hatred or anger (as in "I could choke him!"); unfruitful (as in "the weeds choked the tomatoes").

And the cares of this world, and the deceitfulness of riches, and the lusts of other things entering in, choke the word, and it becometh unfruitful (Mark 4:19).

CHRISTMAS (Christmas season, tree or gifts, including a Christmas Tree with gifts underneath) – *Gift:* Season of rejoicing; spiritual gifts; a surprise; good will; benevolence; commercialism. **Discarded Christmas Tree** = *Rejected;* thrown out; unchurched (gifted) person.

If ye then, being evil, know how to give good gifts unto your children: how much more shall your heavenly Father give the Holy Spirit to them that ask Him? (Luke 11:13)

Follow after charity, and desire spiritual gifts, but rather that ye may prophesy (1 Corinthians 14:1).

CHURCH SERVICE – *Worship:* True or false worship; tradition.

God is a Spirit: and they that worship Him must worship Him in spirit and in truth (John 4:24).

Howbeit in vain do they worship Me, teaching for doctrines the commandments of men (Mark 7:7).

CIGARETTES – See SMOKING.

CIRCUS – *Show:* Entertainment; a worldly, "seeker friendly" church service. (See ZOO, Chapter 17.)

And when thou prayest, thou shalt not be as the hypocrites are: for they love to pray standing in the synagogues and in the corners of the streets, that they may be seen of men. Verily I say unto you, They have their reward (Matthew 6:5).

CIVIL TRIAL – See COURTHOUSE, Chapter 17.

CLOCK – *Time:* Late; early; delay. **Grandfather Clock** = *Past* (for significant numbers see Chapter 21). (See CALENDAR.)

Redeeming the time, because the days are evil (Ephesians 5:16).

CLOSET – *Private:* Personal; prayer; secret sin (as in "skeletons in the closet"); something hidden.

But thou, when thou prayest, enter into thy closet, and when thou hast shut thy door, pray to thy Father which is in secret; and thy

Father which seeth in secret shall reward thee openly (Matthew 6:6).

For nothing [good or evil] *is secret, that shall not be made manifest; neither any thing hid, that shall not be known and come abroad* (Luke 8:17).

For there is nothing covered, that shall not be revealed; neither hid, that shall not be known (Luke 12:2).

CLOTHING – *Covering:* Righteousness; spirit (attitude). **Filthy Clothes** = *Unrighteousness;* self-righteousness; uncleanness. (See COAT and SKIRT.)

But put ye on the Lord Jesus Christ, and make not provision for the flesh, to fulfill the lusts thereof (Romans 13:14).

Let thy priests be clothed with righteousness... (Psalm 132:9).

For if there come unto your assembly a man with a gold ring [self-glorification], *in goodly apparel, and there come in also a poor man in vile raiment* (James 2:2).

But we are all as an unclean thing, and all our righteousnesses are as filthy rags (Isaiah 64:6).

As he clothed himself with cursing like as with his garment, so let it come into his bowels like water, and like oil into his bones (Psalm 109:18).

CLOUDS – *Change or Covering:* Trouble; distress; threatening; thoughts (of trouble); confusion; hidden; covered (see FOG). **White Clouds** = *Good change;* glory; revival.

That day is a day of wrath, a day of trouble and distress, a day of wasteness and desolation, a day of darkness and gloominess, a day of clouds and thick darkness (Zephaniah 1:15).

Ask ye of the Lord rain in the time of the latter rain; so the Lord shall make bright clouds, and give them showers of rain [revival], *to every one grass in the field* (Zechariah 10:1).

COAT – *Covering:* Anointing; authority; protection; grief; shame; confusion. **Shirt** = *Covering as pertaining to the heart: i.e., righteousness* *or sin.* **Without a Shirt (male or female)** = *Self-righteousness (self-jus-tification);* legalism; shame, temptation. (See CLOTHING.)

And he took the mantle of Elijah that fell from him, and smote the waters, and said, Where is the Lord God of Elijah? and when he also had smitten the waters, they parted hither and thither: and Elisha went over. And when the sons of the proph-ets which were to view at Jericho saw him, they said, The spirit [anointing, and therefore the authority] *of Elijah doth rest on Elisha...* (2 Kings 2:14-15).

Let mine adversaries be clothed with shame, and let them cover themselves with their own confusion, as with a mantle (Psalm 109:29).

As he loved cursing, so let it come unto him: as he delighted not in blessing, so let it be far from him. As he clothed himself with cursing like as with his garment, so let it come into his bowels like water, and like oil into his bones. Let it be unto him as the gar-ment which covereth him, and for a girdle wherewith he is girded continually (Psalm 109:17-19).

COFFEE – *Bitter or Stimulant:* Desire for revenge (bitter envy-ing); bitter memories; wake-up call; become sober.

But if ye have bitter envying and strife in your hearts, glory not, and lie not against the truth (James 3:14).

Wherefore he saith, Awake thou that sleepest, and arise from the dead, and Christ shall give thee light (Ephesians 5:14).

Young men likewise exhort to be sober minded (Titus 2:6).

COINS – *Revelation:* Finding silver coins indicates receiving biblical revelation; **Changing paper money into coins or need-ing change** = *Impending Change* (as in moving to a new location or changing churches, etc.). (See MONEY, Chapter 24 and SILVER, Chapter 20.)

And He said unto them, Unto you it is given to know the mystery of the kingdom of God: but unto them that are without, all these things are done in parables (Mark 4:11).

COMFORTER – See BLANKET.

COMPASS – See MAP.

CORD – See ROPE/CORD.

CORNET – See TRUMPET.

CORN FIELD – *Harvest Field:* Economy (prosperity, when ears are large and full; famine, when ears are shrunk and dried). (See GRAIN.)

> *The seven good cows are seven years; and the seven good ears* [of corn] *are seven years: the dream is one. And the seven thin and ill favored cows that came up after them are seven years; and the seven empty ears blasted with the east wind shall be seven years of famine* (Genesis 41:26-27).

> *Say not ye, There are yet four months, and then cometh harvest? behold, I say unto you, Lift up your eyes, and look on the fields; for they are white already to harvest* (John 4:35).

> *Also, O Judah, he hath set an harvest [of judgment] for thee, when I returned the captivity of my people* (Hosea 6:11).

CORNUCOPIA (Horn of Plenty) – *Abundance:* Abundance without measure or limitation; goodness without end; blessed.

> *And all these blessings shall come on thee, and overtake thee, if thou shalt hearken unto the voice of the Lord thy God. Blessed shall be the fruit of thy body, and the fruit of thy ground, and the fruit of thy cattle, the increase of thy kine, and the flocks of thy sheep. Blessed shall be thy basket and thy store* (Deuteronomy 28:2,4-5).

> *But the fruit of the Spirit is love, joy, peace, longsuffering, gentleness, goodness, faith, meekness, temperance: against such there is no law* (Galatians 5:22-23).

> *Now unto him that is able to do exceeding abundantly above all that we ask or think, according to the power that worketh in us* (Ephesians 3:20).

COUCH – *Rest:* At ease; unconcerned; lazy (as in "couch potato").

His soul shall dwell at ease; and his seed shall inherit the earth (Psalm 25:13).

That lie upon beds of ivory, and stretch themselves upon their couches, and eat the lambs out of the flock, and the calves out of the midst of the stall (Amos 6:4).

CROSSROADS – *Decision:* Confusion; choice; job change; career change; geographical move. **Right Turn** = *Natural change.* **Left Turn** = *Spiritual change.* (See RIGHT and LEFT, Chapter 19.)

And a certain ruler asked him, saying, Good Master, what shall I do to inherit eternal life? Now when Jesus heard these things, He said unto him, Yet lackest thou one thing: sell all that thou hast, and distribute unto the poor, and thou shalt have treasure in heaven: and come, follow Me [forsaking both riches and positions of authority]. *And when he heard this* [requirement to change, both naturally and spiritually], *he was very sorrowful: for he was very rich* (Luke 18:18,22-23).

CROWN – *Authority or Reward:* Rule; honor; glory; power; promotion.

And he brought forth the king's son, and put the crown upon him...and they made him king, and anointed him...and said, God save the king (2 Kings 11:12).

And when the chief Shepherd shall appear, ye shall receive a crown of glory [reward] *that fadeth not away* (1 Peter 5:4).

CRYING (as in **weeping**) – See TEARS.

CRYING OUT – See TELEPHONE.

CRYSTAL BALL – *Vision:* Future; divination; fortune telling; prediction.

Then the Lord said unto me, The prophets prophesy lies in My name: I sent them not, neither have I commanded them, neither spake unto them: they prophesy unto you a false vision and divination, and a thing of nought, and the deceit of their heart (Jeremiah 14:14).

And it came to pass, as we went to prayer, a certain damsel possessed with a spirit of divination met us, which brought her masters much gain by soothsaying [fortune telling] (Acts 16:16).

CURSING – See PROFANITY (Cursing).

CURTAIN – See VEIL.

DAM – *Blocked:* Restricted; holding back; reserve; hindrance; source of (or potential for) great power; a way over an obstacle (as a hunter crossing a stream on a beaver dam). (See BEAVER, Chapter 16, BRIDGE and WATER, Chapter 24.)

That the waters which came down from above stood and rose up upon an heap [were temporarily restricted or stopped from flowing] *very far from the city Adam...and those* [waters] *that came down toward the sea of the plain, even the salt sea, failed, and were cut off: and the people passed over right against Jericho* (Joshua 3:16).

DANCING – *Worship:* Idolatry; prophesying (true or false); joy; romance; seduction; lewdness. (See PLAY.)

And it came to pass, as soon as he came nigh unto the camp, that he saw the [golden] *calf, and the dancing* [idol worship]: *and Moses' anger waxed hot, and he cast the tables out of his hands, and brake them beneath the mount* [See 1 Corinthians 10:7] (Exodus 32:19).

Let them praise His name in the dance... (Psalm 149:3).

The joy of our heart is ceased; our dance is turned into mourning (Lamentations 5:15).

But when Herod's birthday was kept, the daughter of Herodias [belly] *danced before them, and pleased* [lustful] *Herod* (Matthew 14:6).

DARKNESS – See NIGHT.

DAY – *Light:* Knowledge; truth; manifest; good; evil revealed. (See LIGHT.)

And God saw the light, that it was good: and God divided the light from the darkness. And God called the light Day, and the darkness he called Night... (Genesis 1:4-5).

Every man's work shall be made manifest: for the day shall declare it... (1 Corinthians 3:13).

But all things that are reproved are made manifest by the light [of day]: *for whatsoever doth make manifest is light* (Ephesians 5:13).

DEATH – *Termination:* Repentance; loss; sorrow; failure; separation; the end of a relationship; physical death, when naturally interpreted.

Verily, verily, I say unto you, Except a corn of wheat fall into the ground and die, it abideth alone: but if it die, it bringeth forth much fruit (John 12:24).

I protest by your rejoicing which I have in Christ Jesus our Lord, I die daily (1 Corinthians 15:31).

Forasmuch then as the children are partakers of flesh and blood, he also himself likewise took part of the same; that through death he might destroy him that had the power of death, that is, the devil (Hebrews 2:14).

They are dead, they shall not live; they are deceased, they shall not rise: therefore hast thou visited and destroyed them, and made all their memory to perish (Isaiah 26:14).

DEED – See TITLE/DEED.

DEER HUNTING – See DEER, Chapter 16.

DEFECATION – See FECES.

DESK – *Work:* Position (such as supervisor, manager, pastor, etc.). **Desktop Cluttered** = *Disorganized;* taking on too much responsibility; behind on schedule.

...If a man desire the office of a bishop, he desires a good work (1 Timothy 3:1).

DIAMOND – *Hard:* Unchangeable; hardheaded; hard-hearted; eternal (as in "a diamond is forever"). Gift of the Spirit; something valuable or precious.

Behold, I have made thy face strong against their faces, and thy forehead strong against their foreheads. As an adamant [diamond], *harder than flint have I made thy forehead...* (Ezekiel 3:8-9).

Yea, they made their hearts as an adamant stone [diamond], *lest they should hear the law, and the words which the Lord of hosts hath sent in His spirit by the former prophets: therefore came a great wrath from the Lord of hosts* (Zechariah 7:12).

A gift is as a precious stone in the eyes of him that hath it: whithersoever it turneth, it prospereth (Proverbs 17:8).

DIRT – **Soiled:** Defiled by sin. **Digging up Dirt** = Looking for shameful or criminal activity in someone's life. **Good Soil** = Disciple.

But the wicked are like the troubled sea, when it cannot rest, whose waters cast up mire and dirt (Isaiah 57:20).

But he that received seed into the good ground is he that hears the word, and understands it; which also bears fruit... (Matthew 13:23).

DIRTY LAUNDRY – *Sin:* Need for repentance; shameful (hidden) deeds.

Wash you, make you clean; put away the evil of your doings from before mine eyes; cease to do evil (Isaiah 1:16).

DISH – See POT/PAN/BOWL.

DIPLOMA – *Finished:* Graduation; recognition of achievement; promotion.

DITCH – *Habit or Snare:* Religious tradition; addiction; lust; passion; sin.

Let them [religious leaders] *alone: they be blind leaders of the blind. And if the blind lead the blind, both shall fall into the ditch* (Matthew 15:14).

He made a pit, and digged it, and is fallen into the ditch which he made (Psalm 7:15).

For a whore is a deep ditch; and a strange woman is a narrow pit (Proverbs 23:27).

DIVORCE – *Permanent Separation:* End of something (including relationships).

What therefore God hath joined together, let not man put asunder (Mark 10:9).

DOMINOS – *Continuous:* Chain reaction (as with dominos, each causing the next one to fall).

And they shall fall one upon another... (Leviticus 26:37).

DOOR – *Entrance:* Christ; (new) opportunity; way; avenue; mouth.

Then said Jesus unto them again, Verily, verily, I say unto you, I am the door of the sheep (John 10:7).

Withal praying also for us, that God would open unto us a door of utterance, to speak the mystery of Christ... (Colossians 4:3).

Set a watch, O Lord, before my mouth; keep the door of my lips (Psalm 141:3).

DRAWER – *Storage:* Thoughts; memory; indicates one's life is disorganized when contents are untidy; cluttered thoughts.

For God is not the author of confusion [Greek: disorder], *but of peace, as in all churches of the saints* (1 Corinthians 14:33).

DREAMING (dreaming that you are dreaming) – *Message:* A message within a message; aspiration; vision. (See SLEEP.)

And they said unto him, We have dreamed a dream, and there is no interpreter of it. And Joseph said unto them, Do not interpretations belong to God?... (Genesis 40:8).

DRESS – See COAT.

DRINKING ALCOHOL – See DRUNK, Chapter 22.

DRINKING FOUNTAIN – See WATER FOUNTAIN.

DROUGHT – See RAIN.

DROWNING – *Overcome:* Self-pity; depression; grief; sorrow; temptation; backslid; excessive debt. (See FLOOD.)

But they that will be rich fall into temptation and a snare, and into many foolish and hurtful lusts, which drown men in destruction and perdition (1 Timothy 6:9).

To appoint unto them that mourn in Zion, to give unto them beauty for ashes, the oil [anointing] *of joy for mourning, the garment of praise for* [those who are drowning in] *the spirit of heaviness...* (Isaiah 61:3).

DRUGS – *Influence:* Spell; sorcery; witchcraft; control; religion (legalism); medicine; healing. (See WITCH, Chapter 22.)

For rebellion is as the sin of witchcraft... (1 Samuel 15:23).

O foolish Galatians, who hath bewitched you, that ye should not obey the truth... (Galatians 3:1).

A merry heart doeth good like a medicine... (Proverbs 17:22).

DRUNKENNESS – See DRUNK, Chapter 22.

DYNAMITE – *Power:* Miracle; potential; danger; destruction.

But when the multitudes saw it [the miracle of healing], *they marvelled, and glorified God, which had given such power unto men* (Matthew 9:8).

Behold, I give unto you power to tread on serpents and scorpions, and over all the power of the enemy... (Luke 10:19).

When I was daily with you in the temple, ye stretched forth no hands against Me: but this is your hour, and the power of darkness (Luke 22:53).

EARRINGS – *Hearing:* Desire to hear (gold earrings may indicate desire for man's honor and financial prosperity); idolatry; vanity.

For the time will come when they will not endure sound doctrine; but after their own lusts shall they heap to themselves teachers, having itching ears... (2 Timothy 4:3).

...the people gathered themselves together unto Aaron, and said unto him, Up, make us gods, which shall go before us...So all the people brake off the golden earrings which were in their ears, and brought them unto Aaron. And he received them at their hand, and fashioned it with a graving tool, after he had made it a molten calf: and they said, These be thy gods, O Israel, which brought thee up out of the land of Egypt (Exodus 32:1-4).

EARTHQUAKE – *Upheaval:* Change (by crisis), thus repentance; trial; God's judgment; disaster; trauma; shock.

And suddenly there was a great earthquake, so that the foundations of the prison were shaken... (Acts 16:26).

Thou shalt be [judged and therefore] *visited of the Lord of hosts with thunder, and with earthquake, and great noise, with storm and tempest, and the flame of devouring fire* (Isaiah 29:6).

Whose voice then shook the earth: but now he hath promised, saying, Yet once more I shake not the earth only, but also heaven. And this word, Yet once more, signifieth the removing of those things that are shaken, as of things that are made, that those things which cannot be shaken may remain (Hebrews 12:26-27).

EATING – *Partake:* Participate; experience; out-working; covenant; agreement; friendship; fellowship; devour; consume. (See CHEWING, FOOD/MILK, and TEETH.)

Jesus saith unto them, My meat is to do the will of Him that sent Me, and to finish His work (John 4:34).

Such is the way of an adulterous woman; she eateth, and wipeth her mouth, and saith, I have done no wickedness (Proverbs 30:20).

And I took the little book out of the angel's hand, and ate it up; and it [God's promises] *was in my mouth sweet as honey; and as soon as I had eaten* [experienced] *it, my belly was bitter* [working out our salvation is always with tribulation (See Acts 14:22; Philippians 2:12.)] (Revelation 10:10).

And the men took of their victuals [ate with them], *and asked not counsel at the mouth of the Lord. And Joshua…made a league* [covenant] *with them, to let them live…* (Joshua 9:14-15).

…He that eateth bread [declaring his friendship, or agreement] *with Me hath lifted up his heel against Me* (John 13:18).

ECHO – *Repetition:* Gossip; accusation; voice of many; mocking; mimic.

But they cried, saying, Crucify Him, crucify Him (Luke 23:21).

EGG – *Promise:* Promising new thought; plan; potential; revelation; fragile. **Rotten Egg** = *Bad Person* (as in "he's a bad egg"); a person who breaks promises; bad company; bad idea; uncertainty (as in "don't count your eggs before they hatch"); without promise.

Or if he shall ask an egg [that which has been promised], *will he offer him a scorpion?* (Luke 11:12)

Meditate upon these things [brood over them]; *give thyself wholly to them* [hatch them out and feed the hatchlings]; *that thy profiting may appear to all* (1 Timothy 4:15).

ELECTRICITY – *Power:* Holy Spirit or sorcery. **Power Lines** = *Spiritual power;* dangerous obstacle when flying (see AIRPLANE). **Electrical Outlet** = *Power source;* Holy Spirit. **Burned Power Outlet** = *Offense;* anger. **Power Cord Unplugged** = *No power;* lack of prayer; lack of authority. (See LIGHTNING.)

For the kingdom of God is not in word, but in power (1 Corinthians 4:20).

But ye shall receive power, after that the Holy Ghost is come upon you… (Acts 1:8).

Even him, whose coming is after the working of Satan with all power and signs and lying wonders (2 Thessalonians 2:9).

ELEVATOR – *Changing Position:* Going into the spiritual realm; elevated. **Going Down** = *Demotion or trial;* backsliding. (For significant floor numbers, see Chapter 21).

> *After this I looked, and, behold, a door was opened in heaven: and the first voice which I heard...said, Come up hither, and I will shew thee things which must be hereafter* (Revelation 4:1).

> *The wise shall inherit glory: but shame shall be the promotion of fools* (Proverbs 3:35).

ENVELOPE – **Sealed***:* Important message from God (must be unsealed, or interpreted); personal instructions; prophecy.

> *For God speaks once, yea twice, yet man perceives it not. In a dream, in a vision of the night, when deep sleep falls upon men, in slumberings upon the bed; Then He opens the ears of men, and seals their instruction* (Job 33:14-16).

EXPLOSION – *Sudden:* Sudden expansion or increase (as in "that church has had explosive growth since the new pastor arrived"); swift change; destruction. (See VOLCANO.)

> *I have declared the former things from the beginning; and they went forth out of My mouth, and I shewed them; I did them suddenly, and they came to pass* (Isaiah 48:3).

EYES – *Desire (Good or Evil):* Covetousness; passion; lust; revelation; understanding; the window to the soul (thus revealing what is in the heart). **Winking** = *Deceitfulness or cunning;* hiding true desire. **Eyes Tightly Closed** = *Unbelief;* willful ignorance.

> *The light of the body is the eye: therefore when thine eye is single, thy whole body also is full of light; but when thine eye is evil, thy body also is full of darkness* (Luke 11:34).

> *Wilt thou set thine eyes* [desire] *upon that which is not? for riches certainly make themselves wings; they fly away as an eagle toward heaven* (Proverbs 23:5).

> *Hell and destruction are never full; so the eyes* [passions] *of man are never satisfied* (Proverbs 27:20).

> *I will set no wicked thing before mine eyes...* (Psalm 101:3).

The eyes of your understanding being enlightened... (Ephesians 1:18).

He [the deceitful man] *winketh with his eyes, he speaketh with his feet, he teacheth with his fingers* (Proverbs 6:13).

And the times of this ignorance [idolatry] *God winked at; but now commandeth all men every where to repent* (Acts 17:30).

They have not known nor understood: for He hath shut their eyes, that they cannot see; and their hearts, that they cannot understand (Isaiah 44:18).

FACE – *Heart:* Sad; glad; mad; bad; etc.; the same as another person (when one looks into the mirror of another person's heart, he see his own heart's reflection (See Proverbs 27:19 below); before or against another person (as in "get out of my face!"); the actual person's face.

As in water face answereth to face, so the heart of man to [the heart of] *man* [See Romans 2:1.] (Proverbs 27:19).

He was a mighty hunter before [Hebrew: in the face of, i.e., against] *the Lord: wherefore it is said, Even as Nimrod the mighty hunter before the Lord* (Genesis 10:9).

FAIR – See CARNIVAL.

FALL – See AUTUMN.

FALLING – *Unsupported:* Loss of support (financial, moral, public, etc.); trial; succumb; backsliding.

He that trusteth in his riches shall fall: but the righteous shall flourish as a branch (Proverbs 11:28).

My brethren, count it all joy when ye fall into divers temptations (James 1:2).

Pride goeth before destruction, and an haughty spirit before a fall (Proverbs 16:18).

The mouth of strange women is a deep pit: he that is abhorred of the Lord shall fall therein (Proverbs 22:14).

FEATHERS – *Covering:* Spirit. **Wet Feathers** = *Offense* (as in "madder than a wet hen"); protection; weightless. (See WINGS.)

He shall cover thee with His feathers, and under His wings shalt thou trust: His truth shall be thy shield and buckler (Psalm 91:4).

FECES – *Unclean:* Offensive; impure; need for repentance.

Having therefore these promises, dearly beloved, let us cleanse ourselves from all filthiness of the flesh and spirit, perfecting holiness in the fear of God (2 Corinthians 7:1).

FEET – *Walk:* Way; thoughts (meditation); words; offense; stubborn (when unmovable); rebellion (when kicking); heart; sin. **Lame Feet** = *Unbelief or error;* doubt. **Diseased Feet** = *Offense* (toward God or people). **Barefoot** = *Without preparation;* Without understanding; without protection; without salvation; novice (as in "tenderfoot"); easily offended (as in tender feet). (See SHOES, SOCKS, and ANKLE.)

And your feet [heart mind and soul] *shod with the preparation of the gospel of peace* (Ephesians 6:15).

And make straight paths for your feet, lest that which is lame be turned out of the way; but let it rather be healed. Looking diligently lest any man fail of the grace of God; lest any root of bitterness springing up trouble you, and thereby many be defiled (Hebrews 12:13,15).

[Unwise] *Confidence in an unfaithful man in time of trouble is like a...foot out of joint* [unfaithful, cannot be trusted, it will not support your weight] (Proverbs 25:19).

And he said, Who art Thou, Lord? And the Lord said, I am Jesus whom thou [hast rebelled against and therefore] *persecutest: it is hard for thee to kick against the pricks* (Acts 9:5).

Then Asa was wroth with the seer, and put him in a prison house; for he was in a rage with him because of this thing. And Asa oppressed some of the people the same time. And Asa...was diseased in his feet, until his disease was exceeding great: yet in his disease he sought not to the Lord, but to the physicians [his heart was wrong but he would not repent] (2 Chronicles 16:10,12).

FENCE – *Boundaries:* Barrier; obstacles; religious traditions; doctrines; inhibitions.

And the Lord said, Behold, the people is one, and they have all one language; and this they begin to do: and now nothing will be restrained [Hebrew: fenced] *from them, which they have imagined to do* (Genesis 11:6).

And I will make thee unto this people a fenced brasen wall: and they shall fight against thee, but they shall not prevail against thee: for I am with thee to save thee and to deliver thee, saith the Lord (Jeremiah 15:20).

FIELD – *World:* God's work; harvest; opportunity; mixed multitude.

The field is the world; the good seed are the children of the kingdom; but the tares are the children of the wicked one (Matthew 13:38).

Say not ye, There are yet four months, and then cometh harvest? behold, I say unto you, Lift up your eyes, and look on the fields; for they are white already to harvest (John 4:35).

For Demas hath forsaken me, having loved this present world... (2 Timothy 4:10).

FINDING ITEMS – See LOST and FOUND.

FINGER – *Feeling:* Sensitivity; discerning; conviction; works. **Pointing Finger** = *Accusation;* direction (as in "he went that way"); instruction.

And He gave unto Moses, when He had made an end of communing with him upon mount Sinai, two tables of testimony, tables of stone, written with the finger [Spirit] *of God* (Exodus 31:18).

But if I with the finger [conviction of the Spirit] *of God cast out devils, no doubt the kingdom of God is come upon you* [See LICE.] (Luke 11:20).

Then shalt thou call, and the Lord shall answer; thou shalt cry, and He shall say, Here I am. If thou take away from the midst of thee the yoke, the putting forth of the finger [pointing an accusing finger at others], *and speaking vanity* (Isaiah 58:9).

Their land also is full of idols; they worship the work of their own hands, that which their own fingers have made (Isaiah 2:8).

He winketh with his eyes, he speaketh with his feet, he teacheth with his fingers [works or the example of his own life] (Proverbs 6:13).

FIRE/HEAT – *Passion:* Power; God's Word or Spirit; revival; anger; envy; jealousy; strife; desire; lust; zeal; trial; affliction; gossip. **Fireplace** = *Heart.* (See OVEN.)

Is not My word like as a fire? saith the Lord; and like a hammer that breaketh the rock [stony heart] *in pieces?* (Jeremiah 23:29)

Wherefore thus saith the Lord God of hosts, Because ye speak this word, behold, I will make My words in thy mouth fire, and this people wood, and it shall devour them (Jeremiah 5:14).

I indeed baptize you with water unto repentance: but He that cometh after me is mightier than I, whose shoes I am not worthy to bear: He shall baptize you with the Holy Ghost, and with fire [power and purification] (Matthew 3:11).

Even so the tongue is a little member, and boasteth great things. Behold, how great a matter a little fire kindleth! And the tongue is a fire, a world of iniquity: so is the tongue among our members, that it defileth the whole body, and setteth on fire the course of nature; and it is set on fire of hell (James 3:5-6).

But if they cannot contain, let them marry: for it is better to marry than to burn (1 Corinthians 7:9).

How long, Lord? wilt thou be angry for ever? shall Thy jealousy burn like fire? (Psalm 79:5)

How long, Lord? wilt thou hide thyself for ever? shall thy wrath burn like fire? (Psalm 89:46)

Where no wood is, there the fire goeth out: so where there is no talebearer, the strife ceaseth (Proverbs 26:20).

If fire [gossip or slander] *break out, and catch in thorns* [becomes a hindrance or curse to one's neighbor], *so that the stacks of corn, or the standing corn, or the field, be consumed therewith; he that kindled the fire* [started the gossip or slander] *shall surely make restitution* (Exodus 22:6).

FIREWOOD – See WOOD.

FISHING – *Hope:* Witnessing; evangelizing; preaching; discouragement (without hope); asking questions (as in "he's fishing for answers").

And He saith unto them, Follow Me, and I will make you fishers of men (Matthew 4:19).

Or saith He it altogether for our sakes? For our sakes, no doubt, this is written: that he that ploweth [or fishes (preaches)] *should plow in hope; and that he that thresheth in hope should be partaker of his hope* (1 Corinthians 9:10).

Simon Peter saith unto them, I go a fishing. They say unto him, We also go with thee. They went forth, and entered into a ship immediately; and that night they caught nothing [discouragement, hopelessness] (John 21:3).

FIST – See HANDS.

FLAG – *Identity* (as in a ship's flag): Patriotism; victory or conquest (as in the Marines raising the flag on Iwo Jima).

And the children of Israel shall pitch their tents, every man by his own camp, and every man by his own standard [flag], *throughout their hosts* (Numbers 1:52).

FLASHLIGHT – See LIGHT.

FLOOD – *Overwhelm:* Temptation; sin; judgment; depression; overcome. (See DROWN.)

...When the enemy shall come in like a flood, the Spirit of the Lord shall lift up a standard against him (Isaiah 59:19).

When thou passest through the waters, I will be with thee; and through the rivers, they shall not overflow thee... (Isaiah 43:2).

Because ye have said, We have made a covenant with death, and with hell are we at agreement; when the overflowing scourge shall pass through, it shall not come unto us: for we have made lies our refuge...the hail shall sweep away the refuge of lies, and the waters shall overflow the hiding place (Isaiah 28:15,17).

FLOWERS – *Glory:* Temporary; gift; romance. **Lily** = *Death;* funeral; mourning. **Bud** = *Potential;* **Bud unfolding** = *Good growth;* time of fulfillment at hand; glory revealed; **Dead or dried flowers** = *Withdrawn or dried up affections;* without passion; needs watering (prayer); untended. (See ROSE.)

For all flesh is as grass, and all the glory of man as the flower of grass. The grass withereth, and the flower thereof falleth away (1 Peter 1:24).

I am the rose of Sharon, and the lily of the valleys [sorrows and death] (Song of Solomon 2:1).

FLYING – See AIRPLANE.

FOG – *Confusion or Temporary:* Clouded issues or thoughts; obscurity; uncertainty.

If I be wicked, woe unto me; and if I be righteous, yet will I not lift up my head. I am full of confusion; therefore see Thou mine affliction (Job 10:15).

O Ephraim, what shall I do unto thee? O Judah, what shall I do unto thee? for your goodness is as a morning cloud [fog], *and as the early dew it goes away* [is temporary] (Hosea 6:4).

Whereas ye know not what shall be on the morrow. For what is your life? It is even a vapor [fog], *that appears for a little time, and then vanishes away* (James 4:14).

FOOD/MILK – *Work:* **Milk** = *Word of God;* foundational truth; teaching. **Solid Food** = *Work of God.* **Fat** = *Excess;* abundance. (See EATING and MUSHROOMS.)

As newborn babes, desire [to receive] *the sincere milk of the word, that ye may grow thereby* (1 Peter 2:2).

Jesus saith unto them, My meat is to do the will of Him that sent Me, and to finish His work (John 4:34).

For when for the time ye ought to be teachers [workers], *ye have need that one teach you again which be the first principles of the oracles of God; and are become such as have need of milk, and not of strong meat. For every one that useth milk* [is being taught and] *is unskillful in the word of righteousness: for he is a babe* (Hebrews 5:12-13).

The first of the firstfruits of thy land [newborn Christians] *thou shalt bring into the house of the Lord thy God. Thou shalt not seethe* [indoctrinate] *a kid* [babe in Christ] *in his mother's* [Church's] *milk* [doctrine, i.e., laws and traditions] (Exodus 23:19).

...All the fat is the Lord's (Leviticus 3:16).

...burn the fat for a sweet savor unto the Lord (Leviticus 17:6b).

FOOT – See FEET.

FOOTBALL GAME – *Teamwork:* Competition; unsportsman-like conduct. **Stepping out of bounds** = *Disqualified;* conduct out of order. (See PLAY.)

And if a man also strive for masteries, yet is he not crowned, except he strive lawfully (2 Timothy 2:5).

FOREIGN MADE (something made oversees, such as a dress, car, or gun) – *Alien:* Not of God; of the flesh; demonic. Not of this world (therefore heavenly). (See NATION, Chapter 17, and FOREIGNER, Chapter 22.)

Our inheritance is turned to strangers [or foreigners], *our houses to aliens* (Lamentations 5:2).

That at that time ye were without Christ, being aliens from the commonwealth of Israel... Now therefore ye are no more strangers and foreigners, but fellow citizens... (Ephesians 2:12,19).

Quenched the violence of fire, escaped the edge of the sword, out of weakness were made strong, waxed valiant in fight, turned to flight the armies of the aliens [or foreigners] (Hebrews 11:34).

Jesus answered, My kingdom is not of this world: if My kingdom were of this world, then would My servants fight... (John 18:36).

FOREST – *Foreboding:* Fearful place. **Lost in the Forest** = *Confusion;* without direction. (See TREE.)

Thou makest darkness, and it is night: wherein all the beasts of the forest do creep forth (Psalm 104:20).

They wandered in the wilderness in a solitary way; they found no city to dwell in. Hungry and thirsty, their soul fainted in them (Psalm 107:4-5).

FRUIT – See APPLES.

FUNERAL – *Death:* Loss of someone or something; grieving over one's loss; closure; bringing things to an end. (See GRAVE.)

And he said, While the child was yet alive, I fasted and wept: for I said, Who can tell whether God will be gracious to me, that the child may live? But now he is dead, wherefore should I fast? can I bring him back again? I shall go to him, but he shall not return to me (2 Samuel 12:22-23).

FURNACE – *Heat Source:* Heart; vengeance; wrath; zeal; anger. (See OVEN.)

My heart was hot within me, while I was musing the fire burned: then spake I with my tongue (Psalm 39:3).

And he looked toward Sodom and Gomorrah...and, lo, the smoke of the country went up as the smoke of a furnace [God's judgment manifest] (Genesis 19:28).

GAMES – See BINGO, CARDS, DOMINOES, and PLAY.

GARBAGE (DUMP) – *Rejected:* Filth; hell; evil; vile; corruption.

And if thine eye offend thee, pluck it out: it is better for thee to enter into the kingdom of God with one eye, than having two eyes to be cast into hell [Greek: valley of (the son of) Hinnom; gehenna fire, i.e., the garbage dump of Jerusalem, used (figuratively) as a name for the place (or state) of everlasting punishment] *fire: Where their worm dieth not, and the fire is not quenched* (Mark 9:47-48).

But I keep under my body, and bring it into subjection: lest that by any means, when I have preached to others, I myself should be a castaway (1 Corinthians 9:27).

GARDENING – *Working:* Church; ministry (such as a counseling ministry); pleasant pastime. **Garden** = *Church;* field of labor. **Vegetables** = *Fruit of one's labor; Garden Pests = Weights and sins that devour one's fruit.* (See WEEDS and FLOWERS.)

...And Abel was a keeper of sheep, but Cain was a tiller of the ground. And in process of time it came to pass, that Cain brought of the fruit of the ground an offering unto the Lord (Genesis 4:2-3).

And the Lord shall guide thee continually, and satisfy thy soul in drought, and make fat thy bones: and thou shalt be like a watered garden, and like a spring of water, whose waters fail not (Isaiah 58:11).

Yet I had planted thee a noble vine, wholly a right seed: how then art thou turned into the degenerate plant of a strange vine unto me? (Jeremiah 2:21)

Neglect not the gift that is in thee, which was given thee by prophecy, with the laying on of the hands of the presbytery. Meditate upon these things; give thyself wholly to them; that thy profiting may appear to all (1 Timothy 4:14-15).

GAS FUMES – *Deception:* Deceiving spirit; evil motive; envy; false accusations; slander; danger; poisonous doctrine.

Be not a witness against thy neighbor without cause; and deceive not with thy lips (Proverbs 24:28).

And Jesus answered and said unto them, Take heed that no man deceive you (Matthew 24:4).

But if ye have bitter envying and strife in your hearts, glory not, and lie not against the truth. This wisdom descendeth not from above, but [ascends from envy and] *is earthly, sensual, devilish* (James 3:14-15).

GASOLINE – *Fuel:* Prayer; inflammatory gossip; contention; strife; danger.

But ye, beloved, building up [refueling] *yourselves on your most holy faith, praying in the Holy Ghost* (Jude 20).

Where no wood [fuel] *is, there the fire goeth out: so where there is no talebearer, the strife ceaseth. As coals are to burning coals, and wood* [or gasoline] *to fire; so is a contentious man to kindle strife* (Proverbs 26:20-21).

GHOST – *Spirit:* Haunt; problem from one's past; torment; unjustified fear. (See PHANTOM, Chapter 21.)

And when the disciples saw Him walking on the sea, they were troubled, saying, It is a spirit [ghost]; *and they cried out for fear* (Matthew 14:26).

GLOVES – *Covering:* Protection; safe; careful (as in "handle with kid gloves"). **White Gloves** = *Clean;* inspection. **Black or Dirty Gloves** = *Evil works.* (See BLACK, WHITE, Chapter 18, and HANDS, Chapter 24.)

Who shall ascend into the hill of the Lord? or who shall stand in His holy place? He that hath clean hands, and a pure heart; who hath not lifted up his soul unto vanity, nor sworn deceitfully (Psalm 24:3-4).

GLUE – *Adhere:* Unity; cleave together; tenacious.

Who, when he came, and had seen the grace of God, was glad, and exhorted them all, that with purpose of heart they would cleave [Greek: glue] *unto the Lord* (Acts 11:23).

GOLF – See PLAY.

GRADUATION – See DIPLOMA.

GRAIN – *Seed:* Word of God; harvest. The condition of the grain (including wheat, rye, oats, corn, etc.) may indicate (future) condition of the economy, as in Genesis 41:22-23,27 below.

Now the parable is this: The seed is the word of God (Luke 8:11).

And I saw in my dream, and, behold, seven ears [or heads of grain] *came up in one stalk, full and good: And, behold, seven ears, withered, thin, and blasted with the east wind, sprung up after them… and the seven empty ears blasted with the east wind shall be seven years of famine* (Genesis 41:22-23,27).

GRAPES – *Fruit:* The Spirit of promise (Holy Spirit); fruit of the Spirit; promise of wrath. **Pomegranate** = *The Word of God* (because of the seeds).

Ye shall know them by their fruits. Do men gather grapes of thorns…? (Matthew 7:16)

And they came unto the brook of Eshcol, and cut down from thence a branch with one cluster of grapes [the promise of the Holy Spirit (see Eph. 1:13)], *and they bare it between two upon a staff; and they brought of the pomegranates, and of the figs* (Numbers 13:23).

But the fruit of the Spirit is love, joy, peace, longsuffering, gentleness, goodness, faith, meekness, temperance: against such there is no law (Galatians 5:22-23).

GRASS – *Flesh:* Self (as "in the flesh"); the Word of God.

For all flesh is as grass… (1 Peter 1:24).

Ask ye of the Lord rain in the time of the latter rain; so the Lord shall make bright clouds, and give them showers of rain, to every one grass [the revelation of Christ] *in the field* (Zechariah 10:1).

DRIED GRASS – *Death:* Repentance; spiritual drought. (See BROWN, Chapter 18.)

The fourteenth day of the second month at even they shall keep it [the passover], *and eat it with unleavened bread* [sincerity and truth] *and bitter herbs* [a repentant heart] (Numbers 9:11).

My heart is smitten, and withered like grass; so that I forget to eat my bread (Psalm 102:4).

The grass withereth, the flower fadeth: because the spirit of the Lord bloweth upon it [bringing conviction and repentance]: *surely the people is grass. The grass withereth, the flower* [human glory] *fadeth: but the word of our God shall stand for ever* (Isaiah 40:7-8).

MOWED GRASS – *Chastisement:* Sickness; financial need or distress; emotional and mental depression or anguish. **Mowing Grass** = *Repentance* (as in "crucifying the flesh"); preaching against sin. (See HAY.)

Thus hath the Lord God shewed unto me; and, behold, He formed grasshoppers in the beginning of the shooting up of the latter growth; and, lo, it was the latter growth after the king's mowings. And it came to pass, that when they had made an end of eating the grass of the land, then I said, O Lord God, forgive, I beseech Thee: by whom shall Jacob arise? for he is small (Amos 7:1-2).

For this cause many are weak and sickly among you, and many sleep [mowed down]. *For if we would judge ourselves, we should not be judged. But when we are judged, we are chastened of the Lord, that we should not be condemned with the world* (1 Corinthians 11:30-32).

GRAVE – *Buried:* End of all flesh; hidden; forgotten; terminal.

They spend their days in wealth, and in a moment go down to the grave (Job 21:13).

And as it is appointed unto men once to die, but after this the judgment (Hebrews 9:27).

Free among the dead, like the slain that lie in the grave, whom Thou rememberest no more: and they are cut off from Thy hand (Psalm 88:5).

GRAVEL PIT – *Source:* The Word of God; abundant supply.

A land wherein thou shalt eat bread without scarceness, thou shalt not lack any thing in it; a land whose stones [words] *are iron* [strength], *and out of whose hills thou mayest dig brass* [the Word of God] (Deuteronomy 8:9).

Study [dig] *to shew thyself approved unto God, a workman that needeth not to be ashamed, rightly dividing the word of truth* (2 Timothy 2:15).

GRAVEL ROAD – See HIGHWAY.

GRAVEYARD (or Grave) – *Hidden:* Out of the past; curse; evil inheritance; hypocrisy; death; demon. (See GRANDMOTHER, Chapter 22.)

Woe unto you, scribes and Pharisees, hypocrites! for ye are like unto whited sepulchres, which indeed appear beautiful outward, but are within full of dead men's bones, and of all uncleanness (Matthew 23:27).

Woe unto you, scribes and Pharisees, hypocrites! for ye are as graves which appear not, and the men that walk over them are not aware of them (Luke 11:44).

GUM – *Sticky:* Grudge; offense (hard to forgive, as gum is hard to remove when it is stuck to the bottom of one's shoe). **Chewing gum** = *Contemplating;* meditating (as in, "let me chew on that awhile"); idling away one's time; annoyance (when one is "popping" gum). **Chewing bubble gum** = *Childishness;* foolishness. (See BUBBLE GUM.)

And when ye stand praying, forgive, if ye have ought against any: that your Father also which is in heaven may forgive you your trespasses. But if ye do not forgive, neither will your Father which is in heaven forgive your trespasses (Mark 11:25-26).

GUNS/BULLETS – *Words:* Accusations; slander; gossip; power. **Broken or Inoperative Gun** = *Without authority or ability;* without power; hindered. (See BOW/ARROWS.)

That they may shoot in secret at the perfect: suddenly do they shoot at him, and fear not (Psalm 64:4).

When a strong man armed keepeth his palace, his goods are in peace: but when a stronger than he shall come upon him, and overcome him, he taketh from him all his armor wherein he trusted, and divideth his spoils (Luke 11:21-22).

Then certain of the vagabond Jews, exorcists, took upon them [selves, i.e., not authorized by God] *to call over them which had evil spirits the name of the Lord Jesus, saying, We adjure you by Jesus whom Paul preacheth. ...And the evil spirit answered and said, Jesus I know, and Paul I know; but who are ye? And the man in whom the evil spirit was leaped on them, and overcame them, and prevailed against them, so that they fled out of that house naked and wounded* (Acts 19:13-16).

.22 CALIBER – Weak or Ineffective Weapon: Without power; lack of prayer and fasting.

I know thy works: behold, I have set before thee an open door, and no man can shut it: for thou hast a little strength [or power], *and hast kept My word, and hast not denied My name* (Revelation 3:8).

.357 CALIBER (or other High-Powered Pistol or Rifle) – *Powerful*: Spiritual power through acceptable service; covenant; effective; the power of evil working through agreement (acquiescence) or conquest (our defeat).

For the weapons of our warfare are not carnal, but mighty through God to the pulling down of strong holds (2 Corinthians 10:4).

...Of whom a man is overcome, of the same is he brought in bondage [See Romans 6:16.] (2 Peter 2:19).

HAIL – *Judgment:* Punishment; destruction; bombardment.

Judgment also will I lay to the line, and righteousness to the plummet: and the hail shall sweep away the refuge of lies... (Isaiah 28:17).

I smote you with blasting and with mildew and with hail in all the labors of your hands; yet ye turned not to Me, saith the Lord (Haggai 2:17).

HAIR – *Covering:* Covenant; humanity; the old (sinful) nature; doctrine; tradition. **Long-Haired Man** = *Defiance;* rebellion. **Woman With Long Hair** = *Glorified.* **Shaving** = *Putting away the filthiness or nature of the flesh.* **Haircut** = *Removing or breaking covenants or religious traditions.* **Hair Growing Back Out** = *Restoring the covenant (or tradition).* (See BARBERSHOP, Chapter 17.)

> *But if a woman have long hair, it is a glory to her: for her hair is given her for a covering* (1 Corinthians 11:15).

> *That he told her all his heart, and said unto her. There hath not come a razor upon mine head; for I have been a Nazarite unto God from my mother's womb: if I be shaven* [break the covenant], *then my strength will go from me, and I shall become weak, and be like any other man* (Judges 16:17).

> *And thus shalt thou do unto them, to cleanse them…let them shave all their flesh* [removing the old nature] *and so make themselves clean* (Numbers 8:7).

HALL – *Passageway:* Way. **Long Hallway** = *Passage of Time.* **Dark Hallway** = *Ominous Time;* trouble; sickness.

> *Thus saith the Lord, Stand ye in the ways, and see, and ask for the old paths, where is the good way, and walk therein, and ye shall find rest for your souls. But they said, We will not walk therein* (Jeremiah 6:16).

HAMMER – *Force:* Word of God; preaching; evil words; destruction. **Tack Hammer** = *Tactful;* weak. (See NAILS.)

> *Is not My word like as a fire? saith the Lord; and like a hammer that breaketh the rock* [stony heart] *in pieces?* (Jeremiah 23:29)

> *A man that beareth false witness against his neighbor is a maul* [hammer], *and a sword, and a sharp arrow* (Proverbs 25:18).

HANDS – *Works:* Deeds (good or evil); labor; service; idolatry; spiritual warfare. **Raised Hands** = *Worship;* surrender. **Clinched Fist** = *Fighting or anger.* **Two People Shaking Hands** = *Covenant;* agreement. **Hands Trembling** = *Weakness or fear.* **Hands Outstretched, Palms Up** = *Helplessness.* **Hands Covering Face (or Face in One's**

Hands) = *Grief;* guilt; shame; laughter. (Other self-explanatory uses of hands include: waving good-by; begging; prayer (clasped together); calling someone to "come" or to "follow.")

> *I will therefore that men pray every where, lifting up holy hands, without wrath and doubting* (1 Timothy 2:8).

> *For thou shalt eat the labor of thine hands* (Psalm 128:2).

> *Give them according to their deeds, and according to the wickedness of their endeavors: give them after the work of their hands...* (Psalm 28:4).

> *Every wise woman buildeth her house: but the foolish plucketh it down with her hands* (Proverbs 14:1).

> *Their idols are silver and gold, the work of men's hands* (Psalm 115:4).

> *Be not thou one of them that strike* [shake] *hands, or of them that are sureties for debts* (Proverbs 22:26).

> *Yea, thou shalt go forth from him* [into captivity], *and thine hands upon thine head: for the Lord hath rejected thy confidences, and thou shalt not prosper in them* (Jeremiah 2:37).

HAT – *Covering:* Protection; thought; attitude; activities (as in "wearing many different hats").

> *For He put on righteousness as a breastplate, and an helmet* [the hope] *of salvation upon His head...* (Isaiah 59:17).

HAY – *To Bundle:* Prepare (as in "make hay while the sun shines"); gather people together (as a church) in the name of the Lord but with wrong (selfish) motives; carnality. (See GRASS.)

> *Now if any man build upon this foundation gold, silver, precious stones, wood, hay, stubble; every man's work shall be made manifest...and the fire shall try every man's work of what sort it is* (1 Corinthians 3:12-13).

> *For all flesh is as grass...* (1 Peter 1:24).

HEAD – *Authority:* God; Christ; government; husband; pastor; employer; power.

But I would have you know, that the head of every man is Christ; and the head of the woman is the man; and the head of Christ is God (1 Corinthians 11:3).

Therefore David ran, and stood upon the Philistine, and took his sword...and slew him, and cut off his head therewith. And when the Philistines saw their champion was dead [their power and authority was broken], *they fled* (1 Samuel 17:51).

The hoary [white] *head is a crown of glory, if it be found in the way of righteousness* (Proverbs 16:31).

The ancient and honorable, he is the head... (Isaiah 9:15).

HEAT – See FIRE/HEAT.

HEDGE – *Protection:* Shield; barrier; hidden. (See FENCE and WALL.)

Hast not Thou made an hedge about him, and about his house, and about all that he hath on every side? Thou hast blessed the work of his hands, and his substance is increased in the land (Job 1:10).

HIGHWAY – *Way:* the Christian faith; truth; way of life (as in "life in the fast lane"); Christ; a person (as in "he knows the way, follow him"); way of error. **Under Construction** = *In Preparation;* change; hindrance. **Crossroads** = *Decision;* change of direction. **Long Highway** = *Time.* (See CROSSROADS, PATH, SIGN, and AUTO WRECK, Chapter 23.)

And an highway shall be there, and a way, and it shall be called The way of holiness; the unclean shall not pass over it; but it shall be for those: the wayfaring men, though fools, shall not err therein (Isaiah 35:8).

Enter ye in at the strait gate: for wide is the gate, and broad is the [high]*way, that leadeth to destruction, and many there be which go in thereat: because strait is the gate, and narrow is the* [high]*way, which leadeth unto life, and few there be that find it* (Matthew 7:13-14).

Jesus saith unto him, I am the way... (John 14:6a).

The chariots [or automobiles] *shall rage in the streets, they shall jostle one against another* [causing offense] *in the broad ways* [highways that lead to destruction, i.e., worldly churches, false doctrine or sin]: *they shall seem like torches, they shall run like the lightnings* (Nahum 2:4).

DEAD-END ROAD or STREET – *Change Directions:* Stop; repent; certain failure; no advancement possible (as in "that's a dead-end job"); a point at which you must review the way you are going or what you are doing and make the necessary changes in direction.

Now therefore thus saith the Lord of hosts; Consider your ways. Ye have sown much, and bring in little; ye eat, but ye have not enough; ye drink, but ye are not filled with drink; ye clothe you, but there is none warm; and he that earneth wages earneth wages to put it into a bag with holes. Thus saith the Lord of hosts; Consider your ways (Haggai 1:5-7).

GRAVEL ROAD – *Way:* God's Word and way (unless it is muddy, dusty, etc.).

Thus saith the Lord, Stand ye in the ways, and see, and ask for the old paths, where is the good way, and walk therein, and ye shall find rest for your souls... (Jeremiah 6:16).

MUDDY ROAD – *Flesh:* Man's way; lust; passion; temptation; offense; strife; sin; need for caution; impassable; difficulty caused by the weakness of the flesh. **Mud** = *Flesh, in its weakness;* **Ruts** = *Habits or addictions of the flesh;* traditions of man. (See DITCH.)

I sink in deep mire [mud], *where there is no standing...* (Psalm 69:2).

But the wicked are like the troubled sea, when it cannot rest, whose waters cast up mire [mud] *and dirt* (Isaiah 57:20).

Watch and pray, that ye enter not into temptation: the spirit indeed is willing, but the flesh is weak (Matthew 26:41).

HIPS (LOINS) – *Mind:* Truth; joint (as in a relationship "out of joint," i.e., offense between brethren); reproduction.

Wherefore gird up the loins of your mind, be sober... (1 Peter 1:13).

Stand therefore, having your loins girt about with truth... (Ephesians 6:14).

...the waters were to the knees. Again he measured a thousand, and brought me through; the waters were to the loins (Ezekiel 47:4).

For he was yet in the loins of his father, when Melchizedek met him (Hebrews 7:10).

HOMOSEXUAL ACTS – *Against Nature:* Rebellion; disobedience (i.e., wives not obeying their husbands [witch], husbands not bearing their responsibility of headship properly [wimp]); Also signifies *Abuse of Authority* (leaders using authority for personal gain and fame); fornication when naturally interpreted. (See SEX.)

For this cause God gave them up unto vile affections: for even their women did change the natural use into that which is against nature [or against the way God made all things in the beginning].... *And even as they did not like to retain God in their knowledge, God gave them over to a reprobate mind, to do those things which are not convenient; being filled with all unrighteousness, fornication...disobedient to parents* [or husbands] (Romans 1:26-30).

Thou art thy mother's daughter, that lotheth [rebelled against] *her husband and her children; and thou art the sister of thy sisters, which loathed their husbands and their children....Behold, this was the iniquity of thy sister Sodom, pride, fullness of bread, and abundance of idleness was in her and in her daughters, neither did she strengthen the hand of the poor and needy. And they were haughty, and committed abomination before Me...* (Ezekiel 16:45,49-50).

Let every soul be subject unto the higher powers. For there is no power but of God: the powers that be are ordained of God [and therefore God given authority should not be misused] (Romans 13:1).

Thou shalt not lie with mankind, as with womankind: it is abom-ination (Leviticus 18:22).

HONEY – *Strength:* Power; Holy Spirit anointing and enlighten-ment; wisdom; knowledge; pleasant experience.

And he said unto them, Out of the eater came forth meat, and out of the strong [Christ] *came forth sweetness...* [honey, i.e., strength (See Romans 5:6.)] (Judges 14:14).

A wise man is strong; yea, a man of knowledge increaseth strength (Proverbs 24:5).

Then said Jonathan, My father hath troubled the land: see, I pray you, how mine eyes have been enlightened, because I tasted a little of this honey (1 Samuel 14:29).

The full soul loatheth an honeycomb; but to the hungry soul every bitter thing is sweet (Proverbs 27:7).

HORNS – *Authority:* Power; ability; kings; anointing (anointing oil was carried in a horn).

All the horns [authority and ability] *of the wicked also will I cut off; but the horns of the righteous shall be exalted* (Psalm 75:10).

God is the Lord, which hath shewed us light: bind the sacrifice with cords [vows], *even unto the horns* [power and authority, i.e., unto Christ (see 1 Cor. 1:24)] *of the altar* (Psalm 118:27).

Because ye have thrust with side and with shoulder, and pushed all the diseased with your horns, till ye have scattered them abroad [misuse of authority] (Ezekiel 34:21).

And the ten horns which thou sawest are ten kings... (Revelation 17:12).

HOUSECOAT (Robe) – *Idleness:* Unprepared; lazy; resting; at ease.

By much slothfulness the building decays; and through idleness of the hands the house drops through (Ecclesiastes 10:18).

And ye yourselves like unto men that wait for their lord, when he will return from the wedding; that when he comes and knocks, they may open unto him immediately (Luke 12:36).

HUNTING – See WILD GAME, Chapter 16.

ICE – See SNOW/ICE.

INCENSE – *Prayer:* Worship; idolatry.

And the smoke of the incense, which came with the prayers of the saints, ascended up before God out of the angel's hand (Revelation 8:4).

INCEST – *Inordinate affection:* Improper relationship; impure desires (improper emotional attraction toward another Christian instead of the proper and normal brother/sister affection, as addressed in First Timothy 5:2 below).

Rebuke not an elder, but intreat him as a father; and the younger men as brethren; The elder women as mothers; the younger as sisters, with all purity (1 Timothy 5:1-2).

INSURANCE – *Faith:* Protection; prepared; safe; covered; confidence; future provision for one's family.

The God of my rock; in Him will I trust: He is my shield, and the horn of my salvation, my high tower, and my refuge, my savior; Thou savest me from violence (2 Samuel 22:3).

INTERSECTION – See HIGHWAY.

IRONING – *Correction:* Change; sanctification; exhortation; instruction in righteousness; God's discipline; repentance; working out problem relationships; reconciliation (as in "ironing out differences"); pressure (from trials).

That He might present it to himself a glorious church, not having spot, or wrinkle, or any such thing; but that it should be holy and without blemish (Ephesians 5:27).

JAM – *Sticky situation:* Trouble (as in "he's in a jam"); tight place.

I was not in safety, neither had I rest, neither was I quiet; yet trouble came (Job 3:26).

JELLY – *Unstable:* Shaky; fearful; trembling.

I am poured out like water, and all my bones are out of joint: my heart is like wax; it is melted in the midst of my bowels (Psalm 22:14).

JEWELRY – *Treasure:* Desire; precious; God's gifts; idolatry; self-glorification; pride. **Jewel** = *Precious person;* gifted person; truth. (See SILVER, GOLD, Chapter 20, DIAMOND and RING, Chapter 24.)

For the time will come when they will not endure sound doctrine; but after their own lusts shall they heap to themselves teachers, having itching ears [desire for doctrines that justify or please the lust of the flesh. (Compare Matthew 6:21: *"For where your treasure is, there will your heart be also."*)] (2 Timothy 4:3).

A gift is as a precious stone in the eyes of him that hath it: whithersoever it turneth, it prospereth. (Proverbs 17:8).

For if there come unto your assembly a man with a gold ring [self-glorification], *in goodly apparel...* (James 2:2).

As a jewel of gold in a swine's snout, so is a fair woman which is without discretion (Proverbs 11:22).

JOGGING – See RUNNING.

JOKER – *Mocker:* Foolish person. (See CLOWN, *Chapter 22.*)

Fools make a mock at sin: but among the righteous there is favor (Proverbs 14:9).

JUDO – See MARTIAL ARTS.

KARATE – See MARTIAL ARTS.

KEY – *Knowledge:* Authority; wisdom; understanding; ability; important or indispensable (as in "the key person"); Christ.

Woe unto you, lawyers! for ye have taken away the key of knowledge... (Luke 11:52).

All things were made by Him; and without Him was not any thing made that was made (John 1:3).

And I have filled him with the spirit of God, in wisdom, and in understanding, and in knowledge, and in all manner of workmanship (Exodus 31:3).

KICKING – See FEET.

KILL – *Hatred:* Murder. Killing Someone = *Speaking evil of another* (with malicious intent); doing harm to another with word or deed. Being Killed = *Hated;* being spoken against (if dreamer experiences great fear while dreaming of being killed, the dream may reveal the need for deliverance from a spirit of fear).

Whosoever hateth his brother is a murderer: and ye know that no murderer hath eternal life abiding in him (1 John 3:15).

For we ourselves also were sometimes foolish, disobedient, deceived, serving divers lusts and pleasures, living in malice and envy, hateful, and hating one another (Titus 3:3).

For God hath not given us the spirit of fear; but of power, and of love, and of a sound mind (2 Timothy 1:7).

KISS – *Agreement:* Covenant; enticement; betrayal; covenant breaker; deception; seduction; friend. (See SEX.)

Kiss the Son, lest He be angry, and ye perish from the way, when His wrath is kindled but a little... (Psalm 2:12).

Faithful are the wounds of a friend, but the kisses of an enemy are deceitful (Proverbs 27:6).

But Jesus said unto him, Judas, betrayest thou the Son of man with a kiss? (Luke 22:48)

And Joab said to Amasa, Art thou in health, my brother? And Joab took Amasa by the beard with the right hand to kiss him. But Amasa took no heed to the sword that was in Joab's hand: so he smote him therewith in the fifth rib...and he died... (2 Samuel 20:9-10).

And, behold, there met him a woman with the attire of an harlot, and subtle of heart. So she caught him, and kissed him...He goeth after her straightway, as an ox goeth to the slaughter, or as a fool to the correction of the stocks...and knoweth not that it is for his life. Her house is the way to hell, going down to the chambers of death (Proverbs 7:10,13,22-23,27).

KNEES – *Submission:* Obey; worship; serve; stubborn; unyielding. (See ANKLES, HIPS.)

But what saith the answer of God unto him? I have reserved to myself seven thousand men, who have not bowed the knee to the image of Baal (Romans 11:4).

For it is written, As I live, saith the Lord, every knee shall bow to Me, and every tongue shall confess to God (Romans 14:11).

Again he measured a thousand, and brought me through the waters; the waters were to the knees... [submission to God's Spirit] (Ezekiel 47:4a).

KNIVES – *Words:* Revelation; truth; sharp or angry rebuke; accusations; gossip. **Pocket Knife** = *Personal revelation of practical use or value.* (See SWORD.)

Thy tongue deviseth mischiefs; like a sharp razor, working deceitfully (Psalm 52:2).

This witness is true. Wherefore rebuke them sharply [cut them off], *that they may be sound in the faith* (Titus 1:13).

LADDER – *Ascend or Descend:* Enable; way of escape; way of entrance; struggle (if hard to climb); steps upward (as in "the necessary steps for a promotion"). **Fireman's Ladder** = *Rescue;* help. (See STAIRS.)

And he dreamed, and behold a ladder set up on the earth, and the top of it reached to heaven: and behold the angels of God ascending and descending on it. And, behold, the Lord stood above it, and said...the land whereon thou liest, to thee will I give it, and to thy seed (Genesis 28:12-13).

And no man hath ascended [climbed] *up to heaven, but He that came down from heaven, even the Son of man which is in heaven* (John 3:13).

LAWNMOWER – See GRASS.

LEAVEN – *Spirit (Good or Evil):* Attitude; sin; false doctrine; hypocrisy; self-justification; self-righteousness; self-importance; anger; pride; zeal.

Therefore let us keep the feast, not with old leaven, neither with the leaven of malice and wickedness; but with the unleavened bread of sincerity and truth (1 Corinthians 5:8).

And He charged them, saying, Take heed, beware of the leaven of the Pharisees [hypocrisy (see Luke 12:1) and self-righteousness (see Matt. 16:6,12], *and of the leaven of Herod* [pride and the abuse of authority (see Matt. 2:13;14:6-9)] (Mark 8:15).

Your glorying [pride, boasting, self-importance] *is not good. Know ye not that a little leaven leaveneth the whole lump?* (1 Corinthians 5:6)

LEAVES – *Words:* First manifestation of faith; testimony; words without corresponding works; self-justification (covering oneself with self-justifying words to hide shame, as Adam did); temporary.

We having the same spirit of faith, according as it is written, I believed, and therefore have I spoken; we also believe, and therefore speak (2 Corinthians 4:13).

And seeing a fig tree [symbolizing Israel under the Law of Moses] *afar off having leaves, He came, if haply He might find any thing thereon: and when He came to it, He found nothing but leaves* [words without corresponding works]; *for the time of figs was not yet. And Jesus answered and said unto it, No man eat fruit of thee hereafter for ever. And His disciples heard it* (Mark 11:13-14).

And the eyes of them both were opened, and they knew that they were naked; and they sewed fig leaves together, and made themselves aprons (Genesis 3:7).

But we are all as an unclean thing...and we all do fade as a leaf; and our iniquities, like the wind, have taken us away (Isaiah 64:6).

LEGS – *Support:* Spirit; strength. **Female Legs** = *Seduction* (see THIGH; for **Shaving Legs**, see HAIR).

He delighteth not in the strength of the horse: he taketh not plea-sure in the legs [strength] *of a man* (Psalm 147:10).

The legs of the lame are not equal: so is a parable in the mouth of fools [i.e., does not support or relate to his doctrine] (Proverbs 26:7).

The spirit of a man will sustain [or support] *his infirmity; but a wounded* [or broken] *spirit who can bear?* (Proverbs 18:14)

LEMON – *Sour:* Bad deal (as in "that car we bought is a lemon"); crabby.

They gave Him vinegar to drink mingled with gall: and when He had tasted thereof, He would not drink (Matthew 27:34).

For I perceive that thou art in the gall of bitterness, and in the bond of iniquity (Acts 8:23).

LETTER – See ENVELOPE.

LIGHT – *Manifest:* Revealed; exposed. **Lights Turned Off** = *Without understanding or manifestation.* **Flashlight** = *Personal knowl-edge or understanding;* guidance. **Dim Light** = *Without full knowledge or understanding.*

But all things that are reproved are made manifest by the light: for whatsoever doth make manifest is light (Ephesians 5:13).

But he that doeth truth cometh to the light, that his deeds may be made manifest, that they are wrought in God (John 3:21).

And there were many lights in the upper chamber, where they were gathered together [openly, not in secret] (Acts 20:8).

Thy word is a lamp unto my feet, and a light unto my path (Psalm 119:105).

LIGHTNING – *Power:* Instant miracle; judgment; destruction; knowledge. (See THUNDER and ELECTRICITY.)

And the seventy returned again with joy, saying, Lord, even the devils are subject unto us through Thy name. And He said unto them, [when you cast them out] *I beheld Satan as lightning fall from heaven* [i.e., by God's miraculous power] (Luke 10:17-18).

Cast forth lightning, and scatter them: shoot out Thine arrows, and destroy them (Psalm 144:6).

LIPS – *Words:* Seduction; speech. (See KISS and PEN/ PENCIL.)

With her much fair speech she caused him to yield, with the flattering of her lips she forced [persuaded or seduced] *him* (Proverbs 7:21).

In the multitude of words there wanteth not sin: but he that refraineth his lips is wise (Proverbs 10:19).

LOST AND FOUND – *Lose/Gain:* **Lost** = *Truth lost through tradition;* gift lost through neglect; soul lost through sin. **Found** = *Revelations or gifts received from God.* **Finding Silver Coins or Knives** = *Receiving revelation knowledge.* (See SILVER, Chapter 20, and KNIVES, Chapter 24.)

Beware lest any man spoil you [cause you to lose the truth] *through philosophy and vain deceit, after the tradition of men, after the rudiments of the world, and not after Christ* (Colossians 2:8).

When they were filled, he said unto his disciples, Gather up the fragments that remain, that nothing be lost (John 6:12).

Thy words were found, and I did eat [partake of them, i.e., obey] *them; and thy word was unto me the joy and rejoicing of mine heart...* (Jeremiah 15:16).

LUMBER – See WOOD.

MACHINES – *Work or Motion:* Idle words; productivity. (See FACTORY, Chapter 17.)

Lo, this only have I found, that God hath made man upright; but they have sought out many inventions (Ecclesiastes 7:29).

But I say unto you, That every idle word that men shall speak, they shall give account thereof in the day of judgment (Matthew 12:36).

For when we were in the flesh, the motions of sins [like a motor running], *which were by the law, did work in our members to bring forth fruit unto death* (Romans 7:5).

MAP – *Directions:* Word of God; correction; advice.

For the commandment is a lamp; and the law is light; and reproofs of instruction are the way [or map] *of life* (Proverbs 6:23).

MARRIAGE – *Covenant:* The Church as the Bride of Christ; agreement; joined. **Sexual Intimacy** = *One in agreement.* **Interruption of Intimacy** = *Interference or trouble in the marriage or covenant relationship.* (See SEX.) Natural marriage when naturally interpreted.

For this cause shall a man leave his father and mother, and shall be joined unto his wife, and they two shall be one flesh. This is a great mystery: but I speak concerning Christ and the church (Ephesians 5:31-32).

Shall we then hearken unto you to do all this great evil, to transgress against our God in marrying strange wives? [of making covenants with those who are not in agreement with God (see Exod. 23:32; 2 Cor. 6:14)] (Nehemiah 13:27).

And to the angel of the church in Pergamos [Greek: much marriage, i.e., covenants of sin, therefore much worldliness] *write...* (Revelation 2:12).

MARTIAL ARTS (Karate and Judo) – *Spiritual Warfare:* Deliverance ministry; self-defense.

For we wrestle not against flesh and blood, but against principalities, against powers, against the rulers of the darkness of this world, against spiritual wickedness in high places (Ephesians 6:12).

MEDICINE – See DRUGS.

MICROPHONE – *Voice:* Authority; ministry; influence.

What I tell you in darkness, that speak ye in light: and what ye hear in the ear, that preach ye upon the housetops (Matthew 10:27).

MICROSCOPE – *Examine:* Close examination; self-examination; discern (as in discerning of spirits).

But let a man examine himself, and so let him eat of that bread, and drink of that cup (1 Corinthians 11:28).

MICROWAVE OVEN – *Instant:* Quick work; sudden; impatience; convenience.

For He will finish the work, and cut it short in righteousness: because a short work will the Lord make upon the earth (Romans 9:28).

MILK – See FOOD/MILK.

MINISTERING – *Ministering:* Including preaching, praying for the sick, working miracles, teaching a class or teaching children, etc., is God showing the dreamer his or her calling, or confirming his or her calling; dreaming of ministering overseas confirms a call to the mission field. Another common interpretation is the message being preached by the dreamer is a message from God, either to deliver, or a personal message from God directly to the dreamer.

And a vision appeared to Paul in the night; There stood a man of Macedonia, and prayed him, saying, Come over into Macedonia, and help us (Acts 16:9).

MIRROR – *God's Word or One's Heart:* Looking at oneself; looking back; memory; past; vanity; Moses' law. (See REAR VIEW MIRROR, Chapter 23.)

For now we see through a glass [Moses' Law, which is as a mirror], *darkly* [in dark sayings, or parables]; *but then face to face: now I know in part; but then shall I know even as also I am known* (1 Corinthians 13:12).

As in water [or a mirror] *face answereth to face, so the heart of man to man* [Compare Romans 2:1: *"Therefore thou art inexcusable, O man, whosoever thou art that judgest: for wherein thou judgest another, thou condemnest thyself; for thou that judgest doest the same things."*] (Proverbs 27:19).

MISCARRIAGE – *Abort:* Failure; loss; repentance; unjust judgment (as in "miscarriage of justice").

Give them, O Lord: what wilt thou give? give them a miscarrying womb and dry breasts (Hosea 9:14).

Then when lust hath conceived, it bringeth forth sin: and sin, when it is finished, bringeth forth death [unless repentance (miscarriage) stops the process. Compare Psalm 7:14: *"Behold, he travaileth with iniquity, and hath conceived mischief, and brought forth falsehood."*] (James 1:15).

Therefore the law is slacked, and judgment doth never go forth: for the wicked doth compass about the righteous; therefore wrong judgment proceedeth (Habakkuk 1:4).

MISSILE – See ROCKET.

MONEY – *Power:* Provision; wealth; natural talents and skills; spiritual riches (i.e., faith, wisdom, spiritual gifts, etc.); power; authority; the strength of people (as opposed to trusting in God); covetousness.

But thou shalt remember the Lord thy God: for it is He that giveth thee power to get wealth... (Deuteronomy 8:18).

Are we not counted of him strangers? for he hath sold us, and hath quite devoured also our money [wealth, health, etc.] (Genesis 31:15).

Wherefore then gavest not thou my money [talents, spiritual gifts, etc.] *into the bank* [submitted to those God has placed in authority], *that at my coming I might have required mine own with usury?* (Luke 19:23)

For the love of money is the root of all evil: which while some coveted after, they have erred from the faith, and pierced themselves through with many sorrows (1 Timothy 6:10).

The inhabitants of Samaria shall fear because of the calves of Bethaven [Hebrew: House of Vanity; i.e., as opposed to Bethel, the house of God]: *for the people thereof shall mourn over it* [because of the economic depression brought on the land because the sin of covetousness], *and the priests thereof that rejoiced on it, for the glory thereof, because it is departed from it* [See Jeremiah 7:8-11] (Hosea 10:5).

For wisdom is a defense, and money is a [person's] *defense: but the excellency of knowledge is, that wisdom giveth life to them that have it* (Ecclesiastes 7:12).

If therefore ye have not been faithful in the unrighteous mammon, who will commit to your trust the true riches? (Luke 16:11)

MOON – *Church* **(true or apostate):** To rule; to manifest the works of darkness; occult; false worship. **Moon as Blood** = *Persecution.* (See SUN.)

And God made two great lights; the greater light to rule the day [**Sun** = Christ], *and the lesser light to rule the night* [**Moon** = Church]: *He made the stars also* (Genesis 1:16).

Blessed be the God and Father of our Lord Jesus Christ, who hath blessed us with all spiritual blessings in heavenly places [as the Moon is in the heavens] *in Christ* (Ephesians 1:3).

And for the precious fruits brought forth by the sun [see 1 Cor. 3:6], *and for the precious things* [salvation] *put forth by the moon* [Church] (Deuteronomy 33:14).

Moreover the light of the moon [Church] *shall be as the light of the sun* [Christ], *and the light of the sun* [Christ] *shall be sevenfold* [complete, nothing hidden], *as the light of seven days, in the day that the Lord bindeth up the breach of His people, and healeth the stroke of their wound* (Isaiah 30:26).

But in those days, after that tribulation, the sun shall be darkened, and the moon [Church] *shall not give her light* [darkness, as in John 9:4b: "The night cometh, when no man can work"] (Mark 13:24).

The sun shall be turned into darkness, and the moon into blood [Church persecuted], *before that great and notable day of the Lord come* (Acts 2:20).

And he put down the idolatrous priests...that burned incense unto Baal, to the sun, and to the moon...and to all the host of heaven (2 Kings 23:5).

MOUNTAIN – *Exalted:* Obstacle; difficulty; challenge; kingdom (nation).

Now therefore give me this mountain, whereof the Lord spake in that day; for thou heardest in that day how the Anakims [giants] *were there, and that the cities were great and fenced...* (Joshua 14:12).

And the heaven departed as a scroll when it is rolled together; and every mountain [nation] *and island* [independent country] *were moved out of their places* [shift of the balance of power, economic, military, political, etc.] (Revelation 6:14).

MOVIE – See PICTURE.

MOVING (as in changing churches, jobs, houses, etc.) – *Change:* (See HOUSE, subheading NEW HOUSE, Chapter 17.)

Therefore, thou son of man, prepare thee stuff for removing, and remove by day in their sight; and thou shalt remove from thy place to another place in their sight... (Ezekiel 12:3).

MUD (Muddy Road, Path, or River) – See HIGHWAY, DITCH, and RIVER.

MURDER – See KILL.

MUSHROOM – *Quick:* Sudden growth; sudden or unexpected appearance; fragile; deadly poison.

Then said the Lord, Thou hast had pity on the gourd, for the which thou hast not labored, neither madest it grow; which came up in a night [like a mushroom], *and perished in a night* (Jonah 4:10).

I have declared the former things from the beginning; and they went forth out of my mouth, and I shewed them; I did them suddenly, and they came to pass (Isaiah 48:3).

MUSIC – *Worship:* Of God; of idols (Idolatry); activity or action that proceeds from the heart. **Playing Instruments** = *Prophesying;* ministering in the gifts of the Spirit; worshiping. (See TRUMPET.)

And, lo, thou art unto them as a very lovely song of one that hath a pleasant voice, and can play well on an instrument: for they hear thy words, but they do them not (Ezekiel 33:32).

That at what time ye hear the sound of the cornet, flute, harp, sackbut, psaltery, dulcimer, and all kinds of music, ye fall down and worship the golden image that Nebuchadnezzar the king hath set up (Daniel 3:5).

NAILS – *Words:* Word of God or man; wisdom; vows; covenant; fasten; steadfast; permanent; unmovable; unchangeable; secure (as in "they stole everything that wasn't nailed down"). (See HAMMER.)

The words of the wise are as goads, and as nails fastened by the masters of assemblies, which are given from one shepherd (Ecclesiastes 12:11).

So the carpenter encouraged the goldsmith, and he that smootheth with the hammer him that smote the anvil, saying, It [the idol] *is ready for the soldering: and he fastened it with nails* [words (doctrines, vows or covenant promises)], *that it should not be moved* (Isaiah 41:7).

NAME – *Identity:* Authority; reputation; the name's meaning (for example, *Jill* means "youthful"); a person whose name rhymes with the name in the dream; a person with the same initials; a different person with the same name or similar personality, nature, character, or reputation; the actual person in the dream. (See FRIEND, Chapter 22.)

Then said God, Call his name Lo-ammi [Hebrew: Not My people]: *for ye are not My people, and I will not be your God* (Hosea 1:9).

And they said, Go to, let us build us a city and a tower, whose top may reach unto heaven; and let us make us a name [reputation], *lest we be scattered abroad upon the face of the whole earth* (Genesis 11:4).

NAPKIN – *Covering:* Hiding something; need to wipe away stains (repent).

Such is the way of an adulterous woman; she eats, and wipes her mouth, and saith, I have done no wickedness (Proverbs 30:20).

NECK – *Will:* Self-willed; stubborn; unbelief; authority; rule.

But they obeyed not, neither inclined their ear, but made their neck stiff, that they might not hear, nor receive instruction (Jeremiah 17:23).

And Pharaoh took off his ring from his hand, and put it upon Joseph's hand...and put a gold chain about his neck (Genesis 41:42).

NEWSPAPER – *Announcement:* Important event; public exposure; news; prophecy; gossip.

For nothing is secret, that shall not be made manifest; neither any thing hid, that shall not be known and come abroad (Luke 8:17).

NIGHT – *Darkness:* Ignorance; hidden; unknown course of action; sin; power of evil; stealth (as in "they crept in under cover of darkness").

Then Jesus said unto them, Yet a little while is the light with you. Walk while ye have the light, lest darkness come upon you: for he that walketh in darkness knoweth not whither he goeth (John 12:35).

But if a man walk in the night, he stumbleth [sins], *because there is no light in him* (John 11:10).

When I was daily with you in the temple, ye stretched forth no hands against Me: but this is your hour, and the power of darkness (Luke 22:53).

For they that sleep sleep in the night; and they that be drunken are drunken in the night (1 Thessalonians 5:7).

NOISE – *Annoyance:* Interference (like static interferes with proper radio reception). **Loud Noise** = *Alarm;* sudden fright.

And when Joshua heard the noise of the people as they shouted, he said unto Moses, There is a noise of war in the camp (Exodus 32:17).

It is better to dwell in the wilderness, than with a contentious and an angry woman (Proverbs 21:19).

NOSE – *Busybody or Discern:* Nosy (as in "sticking your nose into other people's business"); meddling; strife; smell (discern). **Nosebleed** = *Strife;* trouble.

But let none of you suffer as a murderer, or as a thief, or as an evildoer, or as a busybody in other men's matters [being nosy] (1 Peter 4:15).

Surely…the wringing of the nose bringeth forth blood: so the forcing of wrath bringeth forth strife (Proverbs 30:33).

They have ears, but they hear not: noses have they, but they smell not (Psalm 115:6).

NUCLEAR BOMB – See ATOM BOMB.

NUDITY – *Uncovered or Flesh:* In (or of) the flesh; self-justification and self-righteousness (not under grace, see Galatians 5:4); impure; ashamed; stubborn; temptation; lust; using sex to control others (which is witchcraft); exhibitionism; innocence (as in "a nude baby or child"); open (i.e., revealed); truth; honest; nature; vulnerable.

Because thou sayest, I am rich, and increased with goods, and have need of nothing; and knowest not that thou art wretched, and miserable, and poor, and blind, and naked (Revelation 3:17).

Behold, I come as a thief. Blessed is he that watcheth, and keepeth his garments, lest he walk naked, and they see his shame (Revelation 16:15).

Therefore the showers have been withholden, and there hath been no latter rain; and thou hadst a whore's forehead [stubborn], *thou refusedst to be ashamed* (Jeremiah 3:3).

And he stripped off his clothes also, and prophesied before Samuel in like manner, and lay down naked all that day and all that night... (1 Samuel 19:24).

And they were both naked, the man and his wife, and were not ashamed (Genesis 2:25).

NUTS AND BOLTS – *Essential:* Bottom line (as in "getting down to the real nuts and bolts of an issue"); indispensable; wisdom; to fasten. **Lock Washer** = *Secure;* unmovable; unyielding.

Wisdom is the principal [essential] *thing; therefore get wisdom: and with all thy getting get understanding* (Proverbs 4:7).

OAK TREE – *Strength:* Pillar of strength; elder; unmoveable; shelter; shaded. (See ACORN.)

Yet destroyed I the Amorite before them, whose height was like the height of the cedars, and he was strong as the oaks; yet I destroyed his fruit from above, and his roots from beneath (Amos 2:9).

OIL – *Anointing:* **Clear Oil** = *Holy Spirit anointing;* healing. **Dirty Oil** = *Unclean spirit;* hate; lust; seduction; deception; slick (slippery); danger of slipping.

Is any sick among you? Let him call for the elders of the church; and let them pray over him, anointing him with oil in the name of the Lord (James 5:14).

But the wise took oil [the Holy Spirit] *in their vessels with their lamps* (Matthew 25:4).

The words of his mouth were smoother than butter, but war was in his heart: his words were softer than oil, yet were they drawn swords (Psalm 55:21).

For the lips of a strange woman drop as an honeycomb, and her mouth is smoother than oil (Proverbs 5:3).

ORCHARD – *Fruit:* Fruitful (if well-tended and productive); need for repentance and sanctification if in need of pruning or weeding; Church. (See FARMER, Chapter 22 and WEEDS, Chapter 24.)

Ye shall know them by their fruits. Do men gather grapes of thorns, or figs of thistles? Even so every good tree bringeth forth good fruit; but a corrupt tree bringeth forth evil fruit (Matthew 7:16-17).

Every branch in Me that beareth not fruit He taketh away: and every branch that beareth fruit, He purgeth it, that it may bring forth more fruit (John 15:2).

For we are laborers together with God: ye are God's husbandry [Greek: farm or orchard], *ye are God's building* (1 Corinthians 3:9).

OVEN – *Heart:* Heat of passion; one's imagination "cooking up" good or evil; meditation; judgment. (See BAKER, Chapter 22; KITCHEN, Chapter 17; FURNACE and FIRE/HEAT, Chapter 24.)

For they have made ready their heart like an oven, whiles they lie in wait: their baker sleepeth all the night; in the morning it burneth as a flaming fire [consumed with passion] (Hosea 7:6).

Thou shalt make them as a fiery oven in the time of thine anger: the Lord shall swallow them up in His wrath, and the fire shall devour them [make them as a burned cake] (Psalm 21:9).

But if they cannot contain, let them marry: for it is better to marry than to burn [with lust] (1 Corinthians 7:9).

PAINTING – *Covering:* Regenerate; remodel; renovate; teaching; love. **House Painter's Brush** = *Ministry or minister.* **Painting** = *Preaching;* covering up (hiding) sin. **Paint** = *Doctrine;* truth or deception. **Artist's Painting** = *Words;* illustrative message; eloquent; humorous; articulate. (See Chapter 18 for COLORS.)

And above all things have fervent charity among yourselves: for charity [is the paint which] *shall cover the multitude of sins* (1 Peter 4:8).

Woe unto you, scribes and Pharisees, hypocrites! for ye are like unto whited [painted] *sepulchres, which indeed appear beautiful outward, but are within full of dead men's bones, and of all uncleanness* (Matthew 23:27).

Not by works of righteousness which we have done, but according to His mercy He saved us, by the washing of regeneration, and renewing of the Holy Ghost (Titus 3:5).

And a certain Jew named Apollos, born at Alexandria, an eloquent man [like a skillful artist], *and mighty in the scriptures, came to Ephesus* (Acts 18:24).

PANT – *Desire*: Diligent pursuit; work; tired.

As the deer pants after the water brooks, so pants my soul after thee, O God (Psalm 42:1).

PANTS (clothing) – *Work*: Different pants indicate different activities, depending upon whether they are casual (jeans), work uniform, dress slacks, etc.

But what went ye out for to see? A man clothed in soft raiment? Behold, they which are gorgeously appareled, and live delicately, are in kings' courts (Luke 7:25).

PAPER – *Write*: Record; instructions to write a book or song; take note.

Thus speaketh the Lord God of Israel, saying, Write thee all the words that I have spoken unto thee in a book (Jeremiah 30:2).

PARACHUTING – *Leave*: Bail out; escape; flee; saved. **Parachute** = *God's promises;* salvation; faith.

But when they persecute you in this city, flee ye into another... (Matthew 10:23).

PATH – *Way*: Life; private walk with God; Gospel; salvation; error; misjudgment. (See HIGHWAY.)

Thus saith the Lord, Stand ye in the ways, and see, and ask for the old paths, where is the good way, and walk therein, and ye shall find rest for your souls... (Jeremiah 6:16).

Wherefore I was grieved with that generation, and said, They do always err in their heart; and they have not known My ways (Hebrews 3:10).

PEANUT – *Insignificant:* (as in "he works for peanuts"); odd (as in "that guy's a nut").

PEARL – *Treasure:* Truth; precious; favorite person; vanity.

Who, when he had found one pearl of great price, went and sold all that he had, and bought it (Matthew 13:46).

Give not that which is holy unto the dogs, neither cast ye your pearls before swine, lest they trample them under their feet, and turn again and rend you (Matthew 7:6).

In like manner also, that women adorn themselves in modest apparel, with shamefacedness and sobriety; not with braided hair, or gold, or pearls, or costly array (1 Timothy 2:9).

PEN/PENCIL – *Tongue:* Indelible words; covenant; agreement; contract; vow; publish; record; permanent; unforgettable; gossip.

My heart is inditing a good matter...my tongue is the pen of a ready writer (Psalm 45:1).

For thou writest bitter things against me, and makest me to possess the iniquities of my youth (Job 13:26).

How do ye say, We are wise, and the law of the Lord is with us? Lo, certainly in vain made he it; the pen [word] *of the scribes is in vain* [See Jeremiah 17:1.] (Jeremiah 8:8).

PERFUME – *Influence:* Seduction; enticement; temptation; persuasion; deception; Holy Spirit.

...I discerned among the youths, a young man void of understanding...And, behold, there met him a woman with the attire of an harlot, and subtle of heart...So she caught him, and kissed him, and with an impudent face said unto him...I have perfumed my bed with myrrh, aloes, and cinnamon. Come, let us take our fill of love until the morning... (Proverbs 7:7,10,13,17-18).

Dead flies cause the ointment of the apothecary to send forth a stinking savor: so doth a little folly him that is in reputation for wisdom and honor (Ecclesiastes 10:1).

PERSPIRATION – See SWEAT.

PICTURE – *Memory:* Conscience; past experience; circumstance; imagination; a message within itself (as in "a picture is worth a thousand words"). Picture Taken With an Important Person = *Honor;* promotion. Unusual Picture Frame = *Attitude* (as in "a peculiar frame of mind"); Old or Antique Frame = *Time or age* (as in "memories from the past").

Then ye shall drive out all the inhabitants of the land from before you, and destroy all their pictures [pornography, etc.], *and destroy all their molten images, and quite pluck down all their high places* [See Isaiah 2:11-12,16.] (Numbers 33:52).

How much more shall the blood of Christ...purge your conscience [both conscious and unconscious memories with the associated guilt] *from dead works to serve the living God?* (Hebrews 9:14)

PIE – *Whole:* Business endeavors (as in "having a finger in a lot of pies"); part of the action (as in "I'd like a piece of that pie, myself"). For **Fruit Pie**, see APPLES. Also see PUMPKIN.

And one of the company said unto Him, Master, speak to my brother, that he divide the inheritance with me (Luke 12:13).

PILLS – See DRUGS.

PING PONG GAME – *Reciprocal exchange:* verbal discourse; indecisive (bouncing back and forth between two opinions or decisions; unstable. (See YO YO.)

A double minded man is unstable in all his ways (James 1:8).

PIPE – See SMOKING.

PISTOL – See GUNS/BULLETS.

PLATE – See POT/PAN/BOWL.

PLAY – *Worship:* Idolatry; covetousness; true worship; spiritual warfare; striving; competition. (See MUSIC, DANCING.)

Neither be ye idolaters, as were some of them; as it is written, The people sat down to eat and drink, and rose up to play [See Exodus 32:19.] (1 Corinthians 10:7).

Mortify therefore your members which are upon the earth; fornication, uncleanness, inordinate affection, evil concupiscence, and covetousness, which is idolatry (Colossians 3:5).

Know ye not that they which run in a race [or play a competitive game] *run all, but one receiveth the prize? So run* [or strive, fight, etc.] *that ye may obtain* (1 Corinthians 9:24).

POMEGRANATE – See GRAPES.

POND – See SWIMMING POOL.

POSTAGE STAMP – *Seal:* Authority; authorization; small or seemingly insignificant, but powerful.

...the writing which is written in the king's name, and sealed with the king's ring, may no man reverse (Esther 8:8).

Labor not for the meat which perisheth, but for that meat which endureth unto everlasting life, which the Son of man shall give unto you: for Him hath God the Father sealed [given authority] (John 6:27).

POT/PAN/BOWL – *Vessel:* Doctrine; tradition; a determination or resolve; form of the truth; a person.

An instructor of the foolish, a teacher of babes, which hast the form [container] *of knowledge and of the truth in the law* (Romans 2:20).

And thou shalt make the dishes thereof, and spoons [precepts] *thereof, and covers* [spirit] *thereof, and bowls* [doctrines] *thereof, to cover* [the people] *withal: of pure gold* [God's wisdom] *shalt thou make them* [See Isaiah 28:9-10 and GOLD, Chapter 20.] (Exodus 25:29).

And the word of the Lord came unto me the second time, saying, What seest thou? And I said, I see a seething pot [angry determination]; *and the face thereof is toward the north* [judgment] (Jeremiah 1:13).

And I will stretch over Jerusalem the line of Samaria, and the plummet of the house of Ahab: and I will wipe Jerusalem as a man wipeth a dish, wiping it, and turning it upside down (2 Kings 21:13).

For this is the will of God, even your sanctification, that ye should abstain from fornication: That every one of you should know how to possess his vessel [body or wife] *in sanctification and honor; Not in the lust of concupiscence, even as the Gentiles which know not God* (1 Thessalonians 4:3-5).

PRAYING FOR THE SICK – See MINISTERING.

PREACHING – See MINISTERING.

PREGNANCY – *In Process:* Sin or righteousness in process; desire; anticipation; expectancy. Labor Pains = *Trials.* (See BABY.)

Shall I bring to the birth, and not cause to bring forth? saith the Lord: shall I cause to bring forth, and shut the womb? saith thy God (Isaiah 66:9).

Then when lust hath conceived, it bringeth forth sin: and sin, when it is finished, bringeth forth death. [Compare Psalm 7:14: "Behold, he travaileth with iniquity, and hath conceived mischief, and brought forth falsehood."] (James 1:15).

For nation shall rise against nation, and kingdom against kingdom: and there shall be earthquakes in divers places, and there shall be famines and troubles: these are the beginnings of sorrows [Greek: throes of childbirth] (Mark 13:8).

PROFANITY (cursing) – *A Curse:* (sometimes self-inflicted); Uncontrolled anger; hatred. (See BEAR, Chapter 16.)

As he loved cursing, so let it come unto him: as he delighted not in blessing, so let it be far from him. As he clothed himself with cursing like as with his garment, so let it come into his bowels like water, and like oil into his bones (Psalm 109:17-18).

As the bird by wandering, as the swallow by flying, so the curse causeless shall not come (Proverbs 26:2).

Let all bitterness, and wrath, and anger, and clamor, and evil speaking, be put away from you, with all malice (Ephesians 4:31).

PUMPKIN – *Witchcraft:* Deception; snare; witch; trick (as in "Halloween trick-or-treat").

For they intended evil against Thee; they imagined a mischievous device, which they are not able to perform (Psalm 21:11).

PURSE (or Wallet) – *Treasure:* Heart; personal identity; precious; valuable; when empty, spiritually bankrupt. (See BANK, Chapter 17.)

For where your treasure is [purse, wallet, bank account, or precious possessions], *there will your heart be also* (Matthew 6:21).

A good man out of the good treasure of the heart bringeth forth good things: and an evil man out of the evil treasure bringeth forth evil things (Matthew 12:35).

This he said, not that he cared for the poor; but because he was a thief, and had the bag [purse], *and bare what was put therein* (John 12:6).

RADIO (SOUND) – *Unceasing:* Continuous; unrelenting; contentious; unbelieving; tradition; news; the Gospel being broadcast.

A foolish woman is clamorous [talking continually]: *she is simple, and knoweth nothing* (Proverbs 9:13).

A continual dropping in a very rainy day and a contentious woman are alike (Proverbs 27:15).

RADIO TOWER – *Broadcast:* Truth or error: Gospel; witness.

And this gospel of the kingdom shall be preached [broadcast] *in all the world for a witness unto all nations; and then shall the end come* (Matthew 24:14).

RAGS – *Useless:* Poor; humble; self-righteousness. (See CLOTHING and WASHCLOTH.)

But we are all as an unclean thing, and all our righteousness are as filthy rags; and we all do fade as a leaf; and our iniquities, like the wind, have taken us away (Isaiah 64:6).

RAILROAD TRACK– *Tradition:* Unchanging; habit; stubborn; Gospel; caution (as in "stop, look, and listen"); danger. (See TRAIN, Chapter 23.)

And He said unto them, Full well ye reject the commandment of God, that ye may keep your own tradition. Making the word of God of none effect through your tradition... (Mark 7:9,13).

Beware lest any man spoil you through philosophy and vain deceit, after the tradition of men, after the rudiments of the world, and not after Christ (Colossians 2:8).

Therefore, brethren, stand fast, and hold the traditions [stay on the established track] *which ye have been taught.... Now we command you, brethren, in the name of our Lord Jesus Christ, that ye withdraw yourselves from every brother that walketh disorderly, and not after the tradition which he received of us* (2 Thessalonians 2:15; 3:6).

RAIN – *Life:* Revival; Holy Spirit; Word of God; depression; trial; disappointment (as in "raining on someone's parade"). **Drought** = *Blessings withheld* (because of sin); without God's presence.

Ask ye of the Lord rain in the time of the latter rain; so the Lord shall make bright clouds, and give them showers of rain, to every one grass in the field (Zechariah 10:1).

For as the rain cometh down, and the snow from heaven, and returneth not thither, but watereth the earth, and maketh it bring forth and bud, that it may give seed to the sower, and bread to the eater: So shall My word be that goeth forth out of My mouth: it shall not return unto Me void, but it shall accomplish that which I please... (Isaiah 55:10-11).

And the rain descended, and the floods came, and the winds blew, and beat upon that house [of the unwise man]; *and it fell: and great was the fall of it* (Matthew 7:27).

Therefore the showers have been withholden, and there hath been no latter rain; and thou hadst a whore's forehead, thou refusedst to be ashamed (Jeremiah 3:3).

RAINBOW – *Covenant:* Promise; good; protection.

I do set My bow in the cloud, and it shall be for a token of a covenant between Me and the earth (Genesis 9:13).

RAPE – *Violating Another's Will:* Violation; abuse of authority; hate; desire for revenge; murder. (See SEX.)

And she answered him, Nay, my brother, do not force me...do not thou this folly. Howbeit he would not hearken unto her voice: but, being stronger than she, forced her, and lay with her. Then Amnon hated her exceedingly; so that the hatred wherewith he hated her was greater than the love wherewith he had loved her. And Amnon said unto her, Arise, be gone (2 Samuel 13:12,14-15).

But if a man find a betrothed damsel in the field, and the man force her, and lie with her: then the man only that lay with her shall die: But unto the damsel thou shalt do nothing; there is in the damsel no sin worthy of death: for as when a man riseth against his neighbor, and slayeth him [murder], *even so is this matter* (Deuteronomy 22:25-26).

RAPTURE – *Revival* **(Personal or concerning the Church):** Spiritual awakening; warning of unpreparedness if left behind!

After two days will He revive us: in the third day He will raise us up, and we shall live in His sight (Hosea 6:2).

O Lord, I have heard Thy speech, and was afraid: O Lord, revive Thy work in the midst of the years, in the midst of the years make known; in wrath remember mercy (Habakkuk 3:2).

RED LIGHT – See SIGN.

REED – *Weak:* A spiritually weak person; opposition that comes through the weakness of the flesh; affliction (when used as a whip).

Now, behold, thou trustest upon the staff of this bruised reed, even upon Egypt, on which if a man lean, it will go into his hand, and pierce it: so is Pharaoh king of Egypt unto all that trust on him (2 Kings 18:21).

Watch and pray, that ye enter not into temptation: the spirit indeed is willing, but the flesh is weak (Matthew 26:41).

REFRIGERATOR – *Heart:* Motive; attitude; thoughts. **Stored Food** = *Memories stored in the heart;* **Spoiled Food** = *Harboring a grudge;* unclean thoughts or desires.

A good man out of the good treasure of the heart bringeth forth good things: and an evil man out of the evil treasure bringeth forth evil things (Matthew 12:35).

For from within, out of the heart of men, proceed evil thoughts, adulteries, fornications, murders, thefts, covetousness, wickedness, deceit, lasciviousness, an evil eye, blasphemy, pride, foolishness (Mark 7:21-22).

RIFLE – See GUNS/BULLETS.

RING – *Covenant:* Authority (as in "a signet ring"); eternity (unending); prestige. **Wedding Ring** = *Covenant.* **Engagement Ring** = *Promise.* **Rings Worn as Jewelry** = *Self-glorification.* (See GOLD, Chapter 20, and JEWELRY, Chapter 24.)

...the writing which is written in the king's name, and sealed with the king's ring, may no man reverse (Esther 8:8).

For if there come unto your assembly a man with a gold ring [self-glorification], *in goodly apparel...* (James 2:2).

RIVER – *Spirit or Life:* Spirit of God; spirit of man; righteousness; judgment. **Long River** = *Time.* **Steady Flowing Current** = *Passage of Time.* **Rapids** = *Danger;* tossed about. **Deep or Wide** = *Difficulty;* obstacle; impassable; incomprehensible. **Muddy River** = *Spirit of the World;* religious traditions of people; sin; wickedness. (See WATER, SWIMMING, and BRIDGE.)

He that believeth on Me, as the scripture hath said, out of his belly shall flow rivers of living water. (But this spake He of the Spirit, which they that believe on Him should receive...) (John 7:38-39).

Afterward he measured a thousand [mature]; *and it was a river that I could not pass over* [see Eph. 3:8]: *for the waters were risen, waters to swim in, a river that could not be passed over* (Ezekiel 47:5).

But let judgment run down as waters, and righteousness as a mighty stream (Amos 5:24).

The king's heart is in the hand of the Lord, as the rivers of water: He turneth it whithersoever He will (Proverbs 21:1).

When thou passest through the waters, I will be with thee; and through the rivers, they shall not overflow thee... (Isaiah 43:2).

DRY RIVER BED – *Barren:* Religion (as compared to true worship); tradition; backslidden condition; repentant (as when Israel obeyed and crossed the Jordan on dry ground after their forefathers refused to go in and possess the land).

A drought is upon her waters [wells, lakes, and rivers]; *and they shall be dried up: for it is the land of graven images, and they are mad upon their idols* (Jeremiah 50:38).

ROAD – *Way:* **Long Road** = *Time.* See HIGHWAY.

ROBBERY – See THIEF, Chapter 22.

ROCKET – *Power:* Powerful ministry; swift progress; swift destruction; sudden, unexpected attack; war.

But God shall shoot at them with an arrow [or rocket]: *suddenly shall they be wounded* (Psalm 64:7).

Therefore shall his calamity come suddenly; suddenly shall he be broken without remedy (Proverbs 6:15).

He, that being often reproved hardeneth his neck, shall suddenly be destroyed, and that without remedy (Proverbs 29:1).

ROCKING CHAIR – *Old:* Past; memories; meditation; rest; retirement.

Thus saith the Lord, Stand ye in the ways, and see, and ask for [or remember] *the old paths, where is the good way, and walk therein, and ye shall find rest for your souls...* (Jeremiah 6:16).

ROLLER SKATES (or Roller Blades) – *Speed:* Fast; swift advancement or progress; skillful.

For He will finish the work, and cut it short in righteousness: because a short [quick] *work will the Lord make upon the earth* (Romans 9:28).

ROOF – *Covering:* Oversight; government or covenant (good or evil); Holy Spirit. **Rooftop** = *Revealed;* manifest.

Woe to the rebellious children, saith the Lord, that take counsel, but not of Me; and that cover with a covering, but not of My spirit, that they may add sin to sin (Isaiah 30:1).

What I tell you in darkness, that speak ye in light: and what ye hear in the ear, that preach ye upon the housetops (Matthew 10:27).

ROOT – *Attitude:* Hidden sin (Some common roots [wrong attitudes or values] include the following: love of money, bitterness [desire for revenge], low self-esteem, fearfulness, selfishness, an independent spirit [rebelliousness], etc.); conviction; steadfastness; pure motive; cause; reason; source; stable; unmovable.

And now also the axe is laid unto the root of the trees [God's commandment to repent]... (Matthew 3:10).

For the love of money is the root of all evil: which while some coveted after, they have erred from the faith... (1 Timothy 6:10).

Looking diligently lest any man fail of the grace of God; lest any root of bitterness springing up trouble you, and thereby many be defiled [Compare James 3:14: *"But if ye have bitter envying and strife in your hearts, glory not, and lie not against the truth."*] (Hebrews 12:15).

For if the firstfruit be holy, the lump is also holy: and if the root be holy, so are the branches [and fruit] (Romans 11:16).

ROPE/CORD – *Bondage:* Sin; covenant; vow; hindrances; rescue; salvation.

His own iniquities shall take the wicked himself, and he shall be holden with the cords of his sins (Proverbs 5:22).

...Bind the sacrifice with cords, even unto the horns of the altar (Psalm 118:27).

So Ebed-melech…took thence old cast clouts and old rotten rags, and let them down by cords into the dungeon to [save] *Jeremiah* (Jeremiah 38:11).

ROSE – *Romance:* Love; courtship. **Red Rose** = *Passion.* **Yellow Rose Garden** = *Marriage counseling.*

I am the rose of Sharon, and the lily of the valleys (Song of Solomon 2:1).

ROUND (SHAPE) – *Spiritual:* Grace; mercy; compassion; forgiveness; approximate (as in "rounding off your taxes to the nearest dollar"). (See SQUARE.)

Ye shall not round the corners of your heads, neither shalt thou mark the corners of thy beard [to round the corners is self-justification and hypocrisy, rather than judging oneself rightly] (Leviticus 19:27).

And when ye reap the harvest of your land, thou shalt not wholly reap the corners of thy field…neither shalt thou gather every grape of thy vineyard; thou shalt leave them for the poor and stranger [by rounding the corners of the fields (leaving the produce in the corners) and not completely gleaning the fields, they showed grace and mercy to the poor]… (Leviticus 19:9-10).

ROWING – *Work:* Working out life's problems (personal or ministry); earnest prayer; spiritual labor. (See BICYCLE, Chapter 23.)

And He saw them toiling in rowing; for the wind was contrary unto them… (Mark 6:48).

Because for the work of Christ he was nigh unto death, not regarding his life, to supply your lack of service toward me (Philippians 2:30).

RUB BOARD – *Rough:* Hard correction; not diplomatic; cleansing; weariness (as in "The wash woman is worn out").

The man, who is the Lord of the land, spake roughly to us… (Genesis 42:30a).

Wash you, make you clean; put away the evil of your doings from before Mine eyes; cease to do evil (Isaiah 1:16).

RUG – *Covering:* Covenant; Holy Spirit; deception or covering things up (as in "sweeping things under the rug").

For there is nothing hid [swept under the rug], *which shall not be manifested; neither was any thing kept secret, but that it should come abroad* (Mark 4:22).

But have renounced the hidden things of dishonesty, not walking in craftiness, nor handling the word of God deceitfully; but by manifestation of the truth commending ourselves to every man's conscience in the sight of God (2 Corinthians 4:2).

RUNNING – *Striving:* Working out one's salvation; faith; haste; trial.

Know ye not that they which run in a race run all, but one receiveth the prize? So run, that ye may obtain (1 Corinthians 9:24).

If thou hast run with the footmen, and they have wearied thee, then how canst thou contend with horses?... (Jeremiah 12:5a)

RUTS – See DITCH.

SALT – *Seasoning or Preservative:* Covenant; acceptable; memorial; rejected. (See SEA.)

Salt is good: but if the salt have lost his saltiness, wherewith will ye season it? Have salt in yourselves, and have peace one with another (Mark 9:50).

Ought ye not to know that the Lord God of Israel gave the kingdom over Israel to David for ever, even to him and to his sons by a covenant of salt? (2 Chronicles 13:5).

But his wife looked back from behind him, and she became a pillar of salt (Genesis 19:26).

But the miry places thereof and the marshes thereof shall not be healed; they shall be given to salt (Ezekiel 47:11).

SAND – *Flesh:* Improper foundation; weakness; weariness; drudgery; hindrance; childish (as in a child's sandbox); unclean (as in a cat's sandbox). (See SEACOAST.)

And every one that heareth these sayings of mine, and doeth them not, shall be likened unto a foolish man, which built his house upon the sand: And the rain descended, and the floods came, and the winds blew, and beat upon that house; and it fell: and great was the fall of it (Matthew 7:26-27).

A stone is heavy, and the sand weighty; but a fool's wrath is heavier than them both (Proverbs 27:3).

Wherefore seeing we also are compassed about with so great a cloud of witnesses, let us lay aside every weight, and the sin which doth so easily beset us, and let us run with patience the race that is set before us (Hebrews 12:1).

SAW HORSE (Carpenter's) – See SCAFFOLDING.

SCAFFOLDING – *Support*: Temporary support; under con-struction.

SEA – *Humanity:* (*Note:* Sea [salt] water is undrinkable.) People; nations; Gentiles; barrier. Salt Water = *Spirit of the world;* unclean; source of evil. Undertow = *Undercurrent;* discontent; murmuring (see Matthew 20:11).

Then thou shalt see, and flow together, and thine heart shall fear, and be enlarged; because the abundance of the sea [Gentiles] *shall be converted unto thee, the forces of the Gentiles shall come unto thee* (Isaiah 60:5).

The Lord said, I will bring again from Bashan [Hebrew: shame or sleep], *I will bring My people again from the depths of the sea* [worldliness] (Psalm 68:22).

Doth a fountain send forth at the same place sweet water and bitter? [poison, or sea water] *Can the fig tree, my brethren, bear olive berries? either a vine, figs? so can no fountain both yield salt* [sea] *water and fresh* (James 3:11-12).

SEACOAST – *Boundary:* Heart or soul (which contains and limits the spirits of people); flesh; limitations; weights. (See SAND.)

Fear ye not Me? saith the Lord: will ye not tremble at My presence, which have placed the sand [seed of Abraham, i.e., the Church] *for the bound of the sea* [people of the world (see SEA)] *by a perpetual decree, that it cannot pass it...* (Jeremiah 5:22).

O thou sword of the Lord, how long will it be ere thou be quiet? put up thyself into thy scabbard, rest, and be still. How can it be quiet, seeing the Lord hath given it a charge against Ashkelon [Hebrew: the fire of infamy, i.e., evil passion], *and against the sea shore* [flesh]? *there hath He appointed it* (Jeremiah 47:6-7).

SEED – *Word:* Word of God; saints; faith; words of people (revealing the heart); Christ; fullness of iniquity (as in "weeds gone to seed"). (See WEEDS.)

Now the parable is this: The seed is the word of God (Luke 8:11).

The field is the world; the good seed are the children of the kingdom; but the tares are the children of the wicked one (Matthew 13:38).

And the Lord said, If ye had faith as a grain of mustard seed, ye might say unto this sycamine tree, Be thou plucked up by the root, and be thou planted in the sea; and it should obey you (Luke 17:6).

A good man out of the good treasure of his heart bringeth forth that which is good; and an evil man out of the evil treasure of his heart bringeth forth that which is evil: for of the abundance of the heart his mouth speaketh [produces good or bad seed, revealing his heart] (Luke 6:45).

SELF-RISING FLOUR – See LEAVEN.

SEWAGE – *Corruption:* Filthiness of the flesh; sin; evil; corrupt authority; abuse of authority.

When the Lord shall have washed away the filth of the daughters of Zion...by the spirit of judgment, and by the spirit of burning (Isaiah 4:4).

And thou shalt have a paddle upon thy weapon; and it shall be, when thou wilt ease thyself abroad, thou shalt dig therewith, and shalt turn back [remember and acknowledge] *and cover* [confess your sins] *that which cometh from thee: For the Lord thy God walketh in the midst of thy camp, to deliver thee, and to give up thine enemies before thee; therefore shall thy camp be holy: that He see no unclean thing in thee, and turn away from thee* (Deuteronomy 23:13-14).

For he that soweth to his flesh shall of the flesh reap corruption... (Galatians 6:8).

SEWING – *Joining:* Union; reunion; counseling; reconciliation. **Sewing Notions** = *Inclination* (as in "I've got a notion to join the army"); idea.

And it came to pass...that the soul of Jonathan was knit [tied or sewed] *with the soul of David, and Jonathan loved him as his own soul* (1 Samuel 18:1).

SEX – *Agreement:* Covenant; unity; taken advantage of, or "used"; abuse of authority; when naturally interpreted it means love or fornication. **Masturbation** = *Self-gratification;* inordinate self-love; selfishness. **Genitals** = *Secret;* private matter; shame. (Concerning sex outside of marriage, see HOMOSEXUAL ACTS, KISS, HARLOT, Chapter 22, ADULTERY, BESTIALITY and RAPE; also see R- and X-RATED DREAMS, Chapter 17; for sex in marriage, see MARRIAGE).

Know ye not that your bodies are the members of Christ? shall I then take the members of Christ, and make them the members of an harlot? God forbid. What? know ye not that he which is joined to an harlot is one body? for two, saith he, shall be one flesh (1 Corinthians 6:15-16).

But if they cannot contain, let them marry: for it is better to marry than to burn [with lust] (1 Corinthians 7:9).

And if a man entice a maid that is not betrothed, and lie with her, he shall surely endow her to be his wife (Exodus 22:16).

Will ye steal, murder, and commit adultery, and swear falsely, and burn incense unto Baal, and walk after other gods whom ye know not; and come and stand before Me in this house, which is called by My name, and say, We are delivered to do all these abominations? (Jeremiah 7:9-10)

Therefore the Lord will smite with a scab the crown of the head of the daughters of Zion, and the Lord will discover [reveal] *their secret parts* [genitals, i.e., hidden sin] (Isaiah 3:17).

SHAVING – See HAIR.

SHIRT – See COAT.

SHOES/BOOTS – *Words:* Gospel; covenant; preparation. New Shoes = *New ministry or way of life.* House Slippers = *Self-examination.* Loafers = *Casual;* at ease; unconcern; hypocrisy; loafing. Combat or Heavy Boots = *Spiritual warfare.* Steel-Toed Boots = *Protection.* (See FEET.)

And your feet shod with the preparation of the gospel of peace (Ephesians 6:15).

Now this was the manner in former time in Israel concerning redeeming and concerning changing, for to confirm all things; a man plucked off his shoe, and gave it to his neighbor [as we would say, "I give you my word"]: *and this was a testimony in Israel* (Ruth 4:7).

This I say then, Walk in the Spirit, and ye shall not fulfill the lust of the flesh (Galatians 5:16).

SHOULDER – *Support:* Bearer (as in "burden bearer"); government; authority; responsibility; stubborn (see NECK). **Broad Shoulders** = *Strength;* consolation. **Drooped Shoulders** = *Tired;* overburdened; discouraged; hopelessness. **Bare Female Shoulders** = *Seduction;* temptation; witchcraft.

I removed his shoulder from the burden: his hands were delivered from the pots (Psalm 81:6).

For unto us a Child is born, unto us a Son is given: and the government shall be upon His shoulder (Isaiah 9:6).

But they refused to hearken, and pulled away the shoulder, and stopped their ears, that they should not hear (Zechariah 7:11).

SHOVEL – *Tongue:* Prayer; confession; gossip; slander; dig; search; inquire.

And he said, Thus saith the Lord, Make this valley full of ditches [pray]. *For thus saith the Lord, Ye shall not see wind, neither shall ye see rain; yet that valley shall be filled with water...* (2 Kings 3:16-17).

And thou shalt have a paddle [shovel blade] *upon thy weapon; and it shall be, when thou wilt ease thyself abroad, thou shalt dig therewith* [confess], *and shalt turn back* [repent] *and cover that* [uncleanness of the flesh, i.e., sin] *which cometh from thee* (Deuteronomy 23:13).

An ungodly man diggeth up evil: and in his lips there is as a burning fire (Proverbs 16:27).

Whoso diggeth a pit [with words or deeds] *shall fall therein: and he that rolleth a stone, it will return upon him* (Proverbs 26:27).

SHOWER – See BATHING.

SIDEWALK – See PATH.

SIGN – Directions: **Stop Sign** = Stop. **Yield** = Yield. **Detour** = Change of direction. **Intersection** = Decision or change. **Keep off the Grass** = Give no person offense.

I have also spoken by the prophets, and I have multiplied visions, and used similitudes [visible signs], *by the ministry of the prophets* (Hosea 12:10).

Give none offense, neither to the Jews, nor to the Gentiles, nor to the church of God: [Compare First Peter 1:24: *"For all flesh is as grass..."*] (1 Corinthians 10:32).

SKATEBOARD – *Balance:* Skillful maneuvering; skillful ministry; risky; fast. (See ROLLER SKATES.)

As for these four children, God gave them knowledge and skill in all learning and wisdom: and Daniel had understanding in all visions and dreams (Daniel 1:17).

SKIING (Water or Snow Skiing) – *Faith:* Supported by God's power through faith; fast progress.

So when they had rowed about five and twenty or thirty furlongs, they see Jesus walking on the sea, and drawing nigh unto the ship: and they were afraid. ...Then they willingly received Him into the ship: and immediately the ship was at the land whither they went (John 6:19-21).

And He said, Come. And when Peter was come down out of the ship, he walked on the water, to go to Jesus. But when he saw the wind boisterous, he [lost his faith and] *was afraid; and beginning to sink, he cried, saying, Lord, save me. And immediately Jesus stretched forth His hand, and caught him, and said unto him, O thou of little faith, wherefore didst thou doubt?* (Matthew 14:29-31)

SKIRT – *Covering:* Grace. **Lack of a Skirt** = *Uncovered;* shame because of sin; hypocrisy. (See CLOTHING.)

Also in thy skirts [that which is covered, or hidden] *is found the blood of the souls of the poor innocents: I have not found it by secret search, but upon all these* (Jeremiah 2:34).

Therefore will I discover thy skirts upon thy face [as when the wind blows a woman's skirt over her head], *that thy shame may appear* [be revealed] (Jeremiah 13:26).

SLEEP – *Unconscious:* Unaware (hidden or covered); ignorant; danger; death; rest; laziness. **Oversleep** = *Late;* to miss an appointment.

For the Lord hath poured out upon you the spirit of deep sleep, and hath closed your eyes: the prophets and your rulers, the seers hath He covered (Isaiah 29:10).

And that, knowing the time, that now it is high time to awake out of sleep: for now is our salvation nearer than when we believed (Romans 13:11).

It is vain for you to rise up early, to sit up late, to eat the bread of sorrows: for so He giveth His beloved sleep (Psalm 127:2).

Love not sleep, lest thou come to poverty; open thine eyes, and thou shalt be satisfied with bread (Proverbs 20:13).

SMILE – *Friendly:* Kindness; benevolent; good will; without offense; seduction. (See KISS, LIPS, and TEETH.)

A man that hath friends must shew himself friendly [smile]: *and there is a friend that sticketh closer than a brother* (Proverbs 18:24).

SMOKE – *Manifest Presence:* Evidence (as in "where there's smoke, there's fire"); to manifest (as smoke manifests a fire); glory of God; prayer; lying or boasting (as in "blowing smoke"); offense; temporary; cover-up (as in "a smoke screen"). (See SMOKING.)

And one cried unto another, and said, Holy, holy, holy, is the Lord of hosts: the whole earth is full of His glory...and the house was filled with smoke (Isaiah 6:3-4).

And the smoke of the incense, which came with the prayers of the saints, ascended up before God out of the angel's hand (Revelation 8:4).

And when he looked on him, he was afraid, and said, What is it, Lord? And He said unto him, Thy prayers and thine alms are come up [as incense] *for a memorial before God* (Acts 10:4).

As vinegar to the teeth, and as smoke to the eyes, so is the sluggard to them that send him (Proverbs 10:26).

And he looked toward Sodom and Gomorrah...and, lo, the smoke of the country went up as the smoke of a furnace [God's judgment manifest] (Genesis 19:28).

SMOKING – *Pride:* **Smoking Cigarettes** = *Pride or bitterness;* bitter memories; offense; unforgiving; envy; jealousy; self-righteousness. **Smoking a Cigar** = *Haughty;* arrogant. **Smoking a Pipe** = *Intellectual pride.* **Smoking Furnace** = *Offense;* anger; trouble.

Which say, Stand by thyself, come not near to me; for I am holier than thou. These are a smoke in my nose [as another person's cigarette smoke offends a non-smoker], *a fire that burneth all the day* (Isaiah 65:5).

Proud and haughty scorner is his name, who dealeth in proud wrath (Proverbs 21:24).

...we know that we all have knowledge. Knowledge puffeth up, but charity edifieth (1 Corinthians 8:1).

And it come to pass, when he heareth the words of this curse, that he bless [justify, or approve of] *himself in his heart, saying, I shall have peace, though I walk in the imagination of mine heart, to add drunkenness to thirst: The Lord will not spare him, but then the anger of the Lord and His jealousy shall smoke against that man* (Deuteronomy 29:19-20).

SNOW/ICE – *Word:* **Snow** = *Pure;* grace; covered; unrevealed; unfulfilled. **Dirty Snow** = *Impure.* **Snowdrift** = *Barrier;* hindrance; opposition; snare. **Ice** = *Hard Saying;* hard words; slippery; dangerous (as in "skating on thin ice"). (See HAIL.)

For as the rain cometh down, and the snow from heaven, and re-turneth not thither, but watereth the earth, and maketh it bring forth and bud, that it may give seed to the sower, and bread to the eater: So shall My word be that goeth forth out of My mouth... (Isaiah 55:10-11).

Shall vain words have an end? or what emboldeneth thee that thou answerest? I also could speak as ye do: if your soul were in my soul's stead, I could heap up words against you... [as a snowdrift] (Job 16:3-4).

Many therefore of His disciples, when they had heard this, said, This is an hard saying; who can hear it? (John 6:60)

But as for me, my feet were almost gone; my steps had well nigh slipped (Psalm 73:2).

SNOWSHOES – *Faith:* Walking in the Spirit; supported by faith in the Word of God. (**Snow** = *Word.* **Snowshoes** = *Faith.*) (See SNOW and SKIING.)

...when Peter was come down out of the ship, he walked on the water, to go to Jesus (Matthew 14:29).

For we walk by faith, not by sight (2 Corinthians 5:7).

SOAP – *Cleansing:* Conviction; forgiveness; prayer; repentance.

For though thou wash thee with nitre [strong soap], *and take thee much soap, yet thine iniquity is marked before Me, saith the Lord God* (Jeremiah 2:22).

Wash you, make you clean; put away the evil of your doings from before mine eyes; cease to do evil (Isaiah 1:16).

SOCKS – *Covering* **(same as an undergarment): Socks Without Shoes** = *Without full preparation.* **White Socks** = *Pure heart.* **Black or Dirty Socks** = *Impure heart.* (See WHITE, BLACK, Chapter 18. See also FEET, SHOES, Chapter 24.)

And your feet shod with the preparation of the gospel of peace [both word (shoes) and spirit (socks)] (Ephesians 6:15).

This I say then, Walk in the Spirit [white socks], *and ye shall not fulfill the lust of the flesh* (Galatians 5:16).

He that hath clean hands, and a pure heart [white socks]; *who hath not lifted up his soul unto vanity, nor sworn deceitfully* [black or dirty socks] (Psalm 24:4).

SPRING – *(New) Beginning:* Revival; fresh start; renewal; regeneration; salvation; refreshing.

For, lo, the winter is past, the rain is over and gone; the flowers appear on the earth; the time of the singing of birds is come, and the voice of the turtle is heard in our land (Song of Solomon 2:11-12).

Behold, I will do a new thing; now it shall spring forth; shall ye not know it? I will even make a way in the wilderness, and rivers in the desert (Isaiah 43:19).

Repent ye therefore, and be converted, that your sins may be blotted out, when the times of refreshing shall come from the presence of the Lord (Acts 3:19).

SQUARE (Shape) – *Legalistic:* Religious or religion (speaking the truth without love); no mercy; hard or harsh; of the world. (See ROUND.)

And when ye reap the harvest of your land, thou shalt not wholly reap the corners of thy field [making them square], *neither shalt thou gather the gleanings of thy harvest* [thus showing mercy to the needy] (Leviticus 19:9).

STAIRS – *Steps* (as in a process, sometimes including the concept of time): Promotion; ambition (self-promotion); procedure. **Stairs Going Down** = *Demotion;* backslide; failure. **Guardrail** = *Safety;* precaution; warning to be careful. (See LADDER.)

Neither shalt thou go up by steps unto Mine altar [self-promotion or politics], *that thy nakedness be not discovered thereon* (Exodus 20:26).

Then they hasted, and took every man his garment, and put it under him on the top of the stairs, and blew with trumpets, saying, Jehu is king (2 Kings 9:13).

When thou buildest a new house, then thou shalt make a battlement [wall or guardrail] *for thy roof* [or stairway], *that thou bring not blood upon thine house, if any man fall from thence* (Deuteronomy 22:8).

STAR – *Person:* Christian; apostle; saint; preacher; minister; leader or role model (good and bad, as a hero or movie star).

That in blessing I will bless thee, and in multiplying I will multiply thy seed as the stars of the heaven...and thy seed shall possess the gate of his enemies (Genesis 22:17).

And he [Joseph] *dreamed yet another dream, and told it his brethren, and said...Behold the sun and the moon and the eleven stars made obeisance to me. ...and his father rebuked him, and said unto him...Shall I and thy mother and thy brethren indeed come to bow down ourselves to thee to the earth?* (Genesis 37:9-10)

And they that be wise shall shine as the brightness of the firmament; and they that turn many to righteousness as the stars for ever and ever (Daniel 12:3).

And his tail [the false prophet (see Isa. 9:15)] *drew the third part of the stars of heaven* [Christians (see Dan. 11:33-35)], *and did cast them to the earth: and the dragon stood before the woman which was ready to be delivered, for to devour her child as soon as it was born* (Revelation 12:4).

Raging waves of the sea, foaming out their own shame; wandering stars, to whom is reserved the blackness of darkness for ever (Jude 13).

STEPS – See STAIRS.

STONE – *Witness:* Word; testimony; person; precept; accusations; persecution (as in false witness).

And Joshua said unto all the people, Behold, this stone shall be a witness unto us; for it hath heard all the words of the Lord which he spake unto us... (Joshua 24:27).

A man also or woman that hath a familiar spirit, or that is a wizard, shall surely be put to death: they shall stone them with stones [public witness or accusation]... (Leviticus 20:27).

Ye also, as lively stones [witnesses (see Acts 1:8)], *are built up a spiritual house...* (1 Peter 2:5).

STOP SIGN – See SIGN.

STORM – *Disturbance:* Change; spiritual warfare; judgment; sudden calamity or destruction; trial; persecution; opposition; witchcraft; outpouring (revival). White Tornado = *God's power;* revival. Dark Tornado = *Destruction;* great danger. Tornado sighted, but dreamer unharmed = *God's protection in day of calamity.* (See CLOUDS, THUNDER, and WIND.)

For thou hast been a strength to the poor, a strength to the needy in his distress, a refuge from the storm, a shadow from the heat, when the blast of the terrible ones is as a storm against the wall [an attack against the defenses of the righteousness] (Isaiah 25:4).

For when they shall say, Peace and safety; then sudden destruction cometh upon them, as travail upon a woman with child; and they shall not escape (1 Thessalonians 5:3).

...The Lord hath His way in the whirlwind and in the storm, and the clouds are the dust of His feet (Nahum 1:3).

Only with thine eyes shalt thou behold and see the reward of the wicked. Because thou hast made the Lord, which is my refuge, even the most High, thy habitation; There shall no evil befall thee, neither shall any plague come nigh thy dwelling (Psalm 91:8-10).

STOVE – See FURNACE and OVEN.

STREET – See HIGHWAY.

STUMBLE – *Fail:* Sin; backslide; mistake; become deceived; to be overcome; obstacle; ignorance.

But if a man walk in the night, he stumbleth [sins], *because there is no light in him* (John 11:10).

The bows of the mighty men are broken, and they that stumbled [failed through weakness] *are girded with strength* (1 Samuel 2:4).

When the wicked, even mine enemies and my foes, came upon me to eat up my flesh, they stumbled and fell [into their own snare] (Psalm 27:2).

STUMP – See TREE STUMP.

SUGAR – See HONEY.

SUICIDE – *Self-Destruction:* Self-hatred; grief; remorse; foolish action.

Be not righteous over much; neither make thyself over wise: why shouldest thou destroy thyself? (Ecclesiastes 7:16)

And he [Judas] *cast down the pieces of silver in the temple* [in remorse], *and departed, and went and hanged himself* (Matthew 27:5).

SUITCASE – *Personal:* Heart; travel; move; temporary (as in "living out of a suitcase").

Therefore, thou son of man, prepare thee stuff for removing [i.e., pack your bags], *and remove by day in their sight; and thou shalt remove from thy place to another place...* (Ezekiel 12:3).

For every man shall bear his own burden [personal responsibility] (Galatians 6:5).

SUMMER – *Harvest:* Harvest time; opportunity (as in "make hay while the sun shines"); trial; heat of affliction. (See SUN.)

For day and night Thy hand was heavy upon me: my moisture is turned into the drought of summer (Psalm 32:4).

He that gathereth in summer is a wise son: but he that sleepeth in harvest is a son that causeth shame (Proverbs 10:5).

SUN – *Heat:* God; light; goodness; affliction; persecution; trial; god of this world (arousing the heat of passion).

For the Lord God is a sun and shield... (Psalm 84:11).

But unto you that fear My name shall the Sun of righteousness arise with healing in His wings... (Malachi 4:2).

But when the sun was up, it was scorched; and because it had no root, it withered away. And have no root in themselves, and so endure but for a time: afterward, when affliction or persecution ariseth for the word's sake, immediately they are offended (Mark 4:6,17).

SWEAT – *Effort:* Hard work; works of the flesh.

In the sweat of thy face shalt thou eat bread, till thou return unto the ground; for out of it wast thou taken: for dust thou art, and unto dust shalt thou return (Genesis 3:19).

They [the Priests] *shall have linen bonnets upon their heads, and shall have linen breeches upon their loins; they shall not gird themselves with any thing that causes sweat* [thus revealing that we cannot come into God's presence through our own efforts] (Ezekiel 44:18).

And being in an agony He [Jesus] *prayed more earnestly: and His sweat was as it were great drops of blood falling down to the ground* (Luke 22:44).

SWEEPING – *Cleaning:* Repentance; change (as in "a sweeping change"); removing obstacles; rebuking evil doers. (See BROOM.)

Judgment also will I lay to the line, and righteousness to the plummet: and the hail shall sweep away the refuge of lies... (Isaiah 28:17).

Let all bitterness, and wrath, and anger, and clamor, and evil speaking, be put away from you, with all malice (Ephesians 4:31).

Having therefore these promises, dearly beloved, let us cleanse ourselves from all filthiness of the flesh and spirit, perfecting holiness in the fear of God (2 Corinthians 7:1).

For behold this selfsame thing, that ye sorrowed after a godly sort [repented], *what carefulness it wrought in you, yea, what clearing of yourselves, yea, what indignation, yea, what fear, yea, what vehement desire, yea, what zeal, yea, what revenge! In all things ye have approved yourselves to be clear* [or clean] *in this matter* (2 Corinthians 7:11).

Them that sin rebuke before all, that others also may fear (1 Timothy 5:20).

SWIMMING – *Spiritual* (as in spiritual acts or activity): Serving God; worshiping; operating the gifts of the Spirit; prophesying. (See RIVER, WATER, and DROWN.)

Afterward he measured a thousand; and it was a river [of God's Spirit] *that I could not pass over for the waters were risen, waters to swim in, a river that could not be passed over* (Ezekiel 47:5).

Unto me, who am less than the least of all saints, is this grace given, that I should preach among the Gentiles the unsearchable riches [the deep things of God that cannot be passed over] *of Christ* (Ephesians 3:8).

SWIMMING POOL – *Spiritual Place or Condition:* Church; home; family; God's blessings. **Dirty or Dry Pool or Pond** = *Corrupt or destitute spiritual condition;* backslidden.

I will open rivers in high places, and fountains in the midst of the valleys: I will make the wilderness a pool of water, and the dry land springs of water (Isaiah 41:18).

A drought is upon her waters [swimming pools, lakes and rivers]; *and they shall be dried up: for it is the land of graven images, and they are mad upon their idols* (Jeremiah 50:38).

As for thee also, by the blood of thy covenant I have sent forth thy prisoners out of the pit wherein is no water (Zechariah 9:11).

SWING (PORCH) – *Peaceful:* Rest; quietness; romance; fellowship. **Swinging High (Park Swing)** = *Danger;* immorality; infidelity.

...In returning and rest shall ye be saved; in quietness and in confidence shall be your strength... (Isaiah 30:15).

SWORD – *Words:* Word of God; critical words; evil intent; threat; strife; war; persecution. (See KNIVES.)

And take the helmet of salvation, and the sword of the Spirit, which is the word of God (Ephesians 6:17).

Who whet [sharpen] *their tongue like a sword, and bend their bows to shoot their arrows, even bitter words* (Psalm 64:3).

There is that speaketh like the piercing of a sword: but the tongue of the wise is health (Proverbs 12:18).

And there went out another horse that was red: and power [authority] *was given to him that sat thereon to take peace from the earth, and that they should kill one another: and there was given unto him a great sword* [of persecution] (Revelation 6:4).

TABLE – *Communion:* Agreement; covenant; conference; provision. **Under the Table** = *Deceitful dealings;* hidden motives; evil intent.

But I say, that the things which the Gentiles sacrifice, they sacrifice to devils, and not to God: and I would not that ye should have fellowship [communion] *with devils. Ye cannot drink the cup of the Lord, and the cup of devils: ye cannot be partakers of the Lord's table, and of the table of devils* (1 Corinthians 10:20-21).

And both these kings' hearts shall be to do mischief, and they shall speak lies at one [conference] *table; but it shall not prosper...* (Daniel 11:27).

Yea, they spake against God; they said, Can God furnish a table in the wilderness? (Psalm 78:19)

TAIL – *Last in time, rank, or importance:* That which follows; afterward; least. **Wagging Tail** = *Friendly.* **Tucked Tail** = *Guilt;* shame; cowardly. (See DOG, Chapter 16.)

The ancient and honorable, he is the head; and the prophet that teacheth lies, he is the tail (Isaiah 9:15).

And the Lord shall make thee the head, and not the tail; and thou shalt be above only, and thou shalt not be beneath... (Deuteronomy 28:13).

He shall lend to thee, and thou shalt not lend to him: he shall be the head, and thou shalt be the tail (Deuteronomy 28:44).

TAR – *Covering:* Repair; patch; bitterness; offense; hatred; grudge.

And when she could not longer hide him [Moses], *she took for him an ark of bulrushes, and daubed it with slime and with pitch* [tar], *and put the child therein; and she laid it in the flags by the river's brink* (Exodus 2:3).

For it is the day of the Lord's vengeance, and the year of recompenses for the controversy of Zion. And the streams thereof shall be turned into pitch [tar]...*and the land thereof shall become burning pitch* (Isaiah 34:8-9).

TASTING – *Experience:* Discern; try; test; judge. (See TEETH and CHEWING.)

...Cannot my taste discern perverse things? (Job 6:30)

O taste and see that the Lord is good... (Psalm 34:8).

But we see Jesus, who was made...for the suffering of death...that He by the grace of God should taste [experience] *death for every man* (Hebrews 2:9).

TEA (Iced Tea) – *Refreshing:* Grace; good news; salvation; time of refreshing; (as in "tea time"); revival.

As cold waters [or iced tea] *to a thirsty soul, so is good news* [the Gospel] *from a far country* [Heaven] (Proverbs 25:25).

To whom he said, This is the rest wherewith ye may cause the weary to rest; and this is the refreshing: yet they would not hear (Isaiah 28:12).

Repent ye therefore, and be converted, that your sins may be blotted out, when the times of refreshing shall come from the presence of the Lord (Acts 3:19).

TEACHING – See MINISTERING.

TEARS – *Grief:* Sorrow; anguish; repentance; prayer; judgment.

And straightway the father of the child cried out, and said with tears [heartfelt repentance], *Lord, I believe; help thou mine unbelief* (Mark 9:24).

This poor man cried, and the Lord heard him, and saved him out of all his troubles (Psalm 34:6).

TEETH – *Wisdom* **(especially wisdom teeth):** Experience; work out (as in "work out your own salvation"). **Brushing Teeth** = *Cleaning one's thoughts or words;* meditation. **Animal Teeth, (lion's, wolf's, etc.)** = *Danger.* (See FOOD/MILK, CHEWING. See also WOLF, Chapter 16.)

For when for the time ye ought to be teachers, ye have need that one teach you again which be the first principles of the oracles of God; and are become such as have need of milk, and not of strong meat. For every one that useth milk is unskillful in the word of righteousness: for he is a babe [has baby teeth]. *But strong meat belongeth to them that are of full age* [with adult teeth], *even those who by reason of use have their senses exercised to discern both good and evil* [wisdom] (Hebrews 5:12-14).

And I will take away his blood out of his mouth, and his abominations from between his teeth...and no oppressor shall pass through them any more... (Zechariah 9:7-8).

Wherewithal shall a young man cleanse his way? by taking heed thereto according to Thy word (Psalm 119:9).

BABY TEETH – *Immaturity:* Without experience; without wisdom or knowledge; innocent.

For before the child shall know to refuse the evil, and choose the good [replace baby teeth with adult teeth], *the land that thou abhorrest shall be forsaken of both her kings* [See Hebrews 12–14.] (Isaiah 7:16).

FALSE TEETH – *False or Replacement:* Wisdom or knowledge gained through experience or previous failures; logical reasoning (e.g., philosophy replacing truth); tradition; error.

And not only so, but we glory in tribulations [working out our salvation] *also: knowing that tribulation worketh patience; and patience, experience* [thus ignorance is replaced by wisdom]; *and experience, hope* (Romans 5:3-4).

Beware lest any man spoil you [replace the truth] *through* [or with] *philosophy and vain deceit, after the tradition of men, after the rudiments of the world, and not after Christ* (Colossians 2:8).

O Timothy, keep that which is committed to thy trust, avoiding profane and vain babblings, and oppositions of science falsely so called [replacing truth with the falsehoods of deceived, "learned" people] (1 Timothy 6:20).

TOOTHACHE – *Trial:* Trouble. **Broken Tooth** = *Bad experience;* problem; gaining wisdom (learning obedience) through suffering (**Tooth** = *Wisdom;* **ache** = *Suffering*). **Broken** = *Potential pain* (when or if pressure is applied); unfaithful; undependable friend or person; no faith; unbelief.

[Unwise] *Confidence in an unfaithful man in time of trouble is like a broken tooth, and a foot out of joint* (Proverbs 25:19).

Though He were a Son, yet learned He obedience by the things which He suffered (Hebrews 5:8).

What mean ye, that ye use this proverb concerning the land of Israel, saying, The fathers have eaten sour grapes, and the children's teeth are set on edge? (Ezekiel 18:2)

TELEPHONE – *Communication:* Prayer; message from God; counsel; gossip; enemy's voice. **Phone Inoperative or Busy** = *Prayer hindered.*

...whosoever shall call on the name of the Lord shall be saved (Acts 2:21).

...the same Lord over all is rich unto all that call upon Him (Romans 10:12).

Behold, the Lord's hand is not shortened, that it cannot save; neither His ear heavy, that it cannot hear: But...your sins have hid His face from you, that He will not hear (Isaiah 59:1-2).

Regard not them that have familiar spirits, neither seek [call upon or enquire] *after wizards, to be defiled by them...* (Leviticus 19:31).

TELESCOPE – *Future:* Prophetic vision of the future; at a distance; far away in time. (See BINOCULAR.)

After this I looked, and, behold, a door was opened in heaven: and the first voice...said, Come up hither, and I will shew thee things which must be hereafter (Revelation 4:1).

TELEVISION – *Vision:* Message; prophecy; preaching; news; evil influence; wickedness.

He hath said, which heard the words of God, and knew the knowledge of the most High, which saw the vision of the Almighty, falling into a trance, but having his eyes open (Numbers 24:16).

Then was the secret revealed unto Daniel in a night vision... (Daniel 2:19).

And they carried the ark [gospel] *of God in a new cart* [television evangelism] *out of the house of Abinadab* [Hebrew: father of generosity, i.e., liberal giving]: *and Uzza* [Hebrew: strength of humanity, i.e., money] *and Ahio* [Hebrew: brotherly, i.e., agreement of people] *drave the cart. And when they came unto the threshing floor of Chidon, Uzza put forth his hand to hold the ark; for the oxen* [ministers] *stumbled* [sinned]. *And the anger of the Lord was kindled against Uzza* [commerce, money, the source of people's strength], *and He smote him* [bringing economic depression], *because he put his hand to the ark: and there he died before God* (1 Chronicles 13:7,9-10).

Who knowing the judgment of God, that they which commit such things are worthy of death, not only do the same, but have pleasure in [watching] *them that do them* (Romans 1:32).

THIGH – *Flesh:* The natural self; works of the flesh; lust; seduction. (See LEGS.)

And as he passed over Penuel the sun rose upon him, and he halted upon his thigh [i.e., the power of the flesh was broken as a result of his encounter with God]. *Therefore the children of Israel eat not of the sinew which shrank, which is upon the hollow of the thigh, unto this day* [we are not to partake of the life of the flesh]... (Genesis 32:31-32).

Then the priest shall charge the woman with an oath of cursing... The Lord make thee a curse and an oath among thy people, when the Lord doth make thy thigh [flesh] *to rot* [i.e., sickness], *and thy belly* [spirit] *to swell* [i.e., puffed up in pride, haughty, angry, etc.] (Numbers 5:21).

...Uncover thy locks, make bare the leg, uncover the thigh [reveal the hidden works of the flesh]... (Isaiah 47:2).

THORNS – *Hindrance:* Gossip; evil circumstance; persecution; cares of this life; curse; defense (as in "a hedge of thorns"). **Stickers or Cockleburs** = *Irritant;* irritated (as in "a burr under his saddle"); minor afflictions.

But that which beareth thorns and briers is rejected, and is nigh unto cursing; whose end is to be burned (Hebrews 6:8).

If fire break out [rumor or gossip], *and catch in thorns* [becomes a curse to the one slandered], *so that the stacks of corn, or the standing corn, or the field, be consumed therewith; he that kindled the fire shall surely make restitution* (Exodus 22:6).

He also that received seed among the thorns is he that heareth the word; and the care of this world, and the deceitfulness of riches [and pleasures of this life (see Luke 8:14)], *choke the word, and he becometh unfruitful* (Matthew 13:22).

THUNDER – *Change or Without Understanding* (of what the Spirit is saying or of the signs of the times): Dispensational change (i.e., a change in the way God deals with His people); a warning of impending judgment or trouble. (See STORM and TRUMPET.)

[Jesus said,] *Father, glorify Thy name. Then came there a voice from heaven, saying, I have both glorified it, and will glorify it again. The people therefore, that stood by, and heard it, said that it thundered: others said, An angel spake to Him* (John 12:28-29).

The Lord also thundered in the heavens, and the Highest gave His voice; hail stones and coals of fire (Psalm 18:13).

TITLE/DEED – *Ownership:* Authorization; possession.

And the field, and the cave that is therein, were made sure [deeded] *unto Abraham for a possession of a buryingplace by the sons of Heth* (Genesis 23:20).

TNT – See DYNAMITE.

TONGUE – See BOW/ARROWS, PEN/PENCIL, and SHOVEL.

TORNADO – See STORM.

TOWEL – *Service:* Covering; surrender (as in "he's throwing in the towel").

He rose from supper, and laid aside His garments; and took a towel, and girded Himself. After that He poured water into a basin, and began to wash the disciples' feet, and to wipe them with the towel wherewith He was girded (John 13:4-5).

TRAPEZE ACT – *Supernatural Ministry:* Ministering in the gifts of the Spirit; complete trust (as the trapeze artist has to completely trust the "catcher"); risk taker. (See CIRCUS.)

TREE(S) – *Person or Covering:* Leader; shelter; false worship; evil influence. **Oak Tree** = *Strong shelter.* **Willow Tree** = *Sorrow.* **Evergreen Tree** = *Eternal life.* (See GREEN; LEAVES; for **Christmas Tree**, see CHRISTMAS.)

I have seen the wicked in great power, and spreading himself like a green bay tree (Psalm 37:35).

But I am like a green olive tree in the house of God... (Psalm 52:8).

The righteous shall flourish like the palm tree: he shall grow like a cedar [evergreen] *in Lebanon.* (Psalm 92:12).

And they set them up images and groves in every high hill, and under every green tree (2 Kings 17:10).

By the rivers of Babylon, there we sat down, yea, we wept, when we remembered Zion. We hanged our harps upon the willows in the midst thereof (Psalm 137:1-2).

And all the trees [people] *of the field* [world] *shall know that I the Lord have brought down the high tree* [haughty person], *have exalted the low tree* [humble person], *have dried up the green tree* [carnal person], *and have made the dry tree* [repented person, dead with Christ] *to flourish...* [prosper] (Ezekiel 17:24).

TREE STUMP – *Stubborn:* Unbelief; roots; tenacious; obstacle; unmovable; hope or promise of restoration; regeneration; Christ.

For there is hope of a tree, if it be cut down, that it will sprout again, and that the tender branch thereof will not cease. Though the root thereof wax old in the earth, and the stock thereof die in the ground; yet through the scent of water it will bud, and bring forth boughs like a plant (Job 14:7-9).

TRIP – See STUMBLE.

TROPHY – *Memorial:* Evidence of victory; award; competition; victory in spiritual warfare.

And the king of Israel answered and said, Tell him, Let not him that girdeth on his harness [sword] *boast himself as he that putteth it off* [as though he already had the victor's cup] (1 Kings 20:11).

And as David returned from the slaughter of the Philistine, Abner took him, and brought him before Saul with the head of the Philistine in his hand (1 Samuel 17:57).

TRUMPET – *Voice:* Announcement; preaching; prophesying; warning; call to assemble; worship; tongues; the Rapture. **Sounding Reveille** = *Beginning;* wake up; call to assemble. **Playing Taps** = *End;* finished.

Cry aloud, spare not, lift up thy voice like a trumpet [preach and prophesy], *and shew My people their transgression, and the house of Jacob their sins* (Isaiah 58:1).

For if the [voice of the] *trumpet give an uncertain sound* [a message in tongues without interpretation], *who shall prepare himself to the battle?* (1 Corinthians 14:8)

In a moment, in the twinkling of an eye, at the last trump: for the trumpet shall sound, and the dead shall be raised incorruptible, and we shall be changed (1 Corinthians 15:52).

Blow the trumpet in Zion, sanctify a fast, call a solemn assembly (Joel 2:15).

Wherefore he saith, Awake thou that sleepest, and arise from the dead, and Christ shall give thee light (Ephesians 5:14).

TSUNAMI – *Irresistible Force:* Overwhelm; disaster; destruction; calamity; judgment.

Judgment also will I lay to the line, and righteousness to the plummet: and the hail shall sweep away the refuge of lies, and the waters shall overflow the hiding place. And your covenant with death shall be disannulled, and your agreement with hell shall not stand; when the overflowing scourge shall pass through, then ye shall be trodden down by it (Isaiah 28:17-18).

TUNNEL – *Passage:* Transition; way of escape; troubling experience; trial; hope (as in "light at the end of the tunnel").

There hath no temptation taken you but such as is common to man: but God is faithful, who will not suffer you to be tempted above that ye are able; but will with the temptation also make a way to escape, that ye may be able to bear it (1 Corinthians 10:13).

UNDERTOW – See SEA.

URINATING – *Desire:* Full Bladder = *Pressure;* compelling urge; temptation (as in sexual lust or strife). Bladder Infection or Cancer = *Offense;* enmity; spirit. Urinating Blood = *Hatred;* desire for revenge (as in "he's out for blood!"); anger. (See CANCER.)

> *The beginning of strife is as when one letteth out water: therefore leave off contention* [or lust], *before it be meddled with* (Proverbs 17:14).

> *So and more also do God unto the enemies of David, if I leave of all that pertain to him by the morning light any that pisseth against the wall* (1 Samuel 25:22).

VACUUM CLEANER – See BROOM.

VEGETABLES – See GARDEN.

VEIL or VAIL – *Concealment:* Hidden; concealed (or revealed if veil or curtains are removed); covering; deception; without understanding; law; flesh.

> *Then opened He* [the veil or curtains of] *their understanding, that they might understand the scriptures* (Luke 24:45).

> *And not as Moses, which put a vail over his face, that the children of Israel could not steadfastly look to the end of that which is abolished: But their minds were blinded: for until this day remaineth the same vail untaken away in the reading of the old testament; which vail is done away in Christ* [see Mark 15:37-38]. *But even unto this day, when Moses is read, the vail is upon their heart. Nevertheless when it* [the nation of Israel] *shall turn to the Lord, the vail* [concealment] *shall be taken away* (2 Corinthians 3:13-16).

> *And Jesus cried with a loud voice, and gave up the ghost* [His flesh or "veil" having been pierced (torn)]. *And the veil of the temple was rent in twain from the top to the bottom* (Mark 15:37-38).

VINE – *Source or People:* Christ; person; family; city; nation; flesh; entanglement; snare.

I [Christ] *am the vine* [source], *ye are the branches: He that abideth in Me, and I in him, the same bringeth forth much fruit...* (John 15:5).

Yet I had planted thee a noble vine [nation or people], *wholly a right seed: how then art thou turned into the degenerate plant of a strange vine unto me?* (Jeremiah 2:21)

And the vine said unto them, Should I leave my wine, which cheereth God and man, and go to be promoted over the trees? (Judges 9:13)

VOLCANO – *Eruption:* Sudden violent reaction to pressure; emotionally unstable (as in sudden anger); trouble erupting; God's judgment.

For a fire is kindled in mine anger, and shall burn unto the lowest hell, and shall consume the earth with her increase, and set on fire the foundations of the mountains (Deuteronomy 32:22).

Upon the wicked He shall rain snares, fire and brimstone, and an horrible tempest: this shall be the portion of their cup (Psalm 11:6).

WALKING – *Progress:* Living in (being led by) the Spirit; living in sin. **Difficult Walking** = *Trials;* opposition.

This I say then, Walk in the Spirit, and ye shall not fulfill the lust of the flesh. ...If we live in the Spirit, let us also walk in the Spirit. (Galatians 5:16,25).

This I say therefore, and testify in the Lord, that ye henceforth walk not as other Gentiles walk, in the vanity of their mind (Ephesians 4:17).

WALL – *Barrier:* Obstacle; defense; limitation; unbelief. (See FENCE and HEDGE.)

...By my God have I leaped over a wall [obstacle] (2 Samuel 22:30).

They were a wall unto us both by night and day, all the while we were with them keeping the sheep (1 Samuel 25:16).

He shall recount his worthies: they shall stumble in their walk; they shall make haste to the wall thereof, and the defense shall be prepared (Nahum 2:5).

The rich man's wealth is his strong city, and as an high wall in his own conceit [he cannot be reached with the Gospel because of the barrier of his pride] (Proverbs 18:11).

WALLET – See PURSE.

WASHBASIN – *Prayer:* Repentance; petition (to God); self-justification (as when Pilate washed his hands at Christ's trial (see Matthew 27:24). (See BATHROOM, Chapter 17.)

Wash you, make you clean; put away the evil of your doings from before Mine eyes; cease to do evil (Isaiah 1:16).

O Jerusalem, wash thine heart from wickedness, that thou mayest be saved. How long shall thy vain thoughts lodge within thee? (Jeremiah 4:14)

WASHCLOTH – *Truth:* Doctrine; understanding. **Dirty Cloth** = *False Doctrine;* insincere apology; error. (See SOAP.)

Purge me with hyssop [a branch used as a brush in cleansing], *and I shall be clean: wash me, and I shall be whiter than snow* (Psalm 51:7).

Now ye are clean through the word [truth] *which I have spoken unto you* (John 15:3).

Who can bring a clean thing out of an unclean [dirty washcloth]? *not one* (Job 14:4).

WATER – *Spirit:* Word, and therefore the Spirit of God, the spirits of people, or the spirit of the enemy; unstable. **Stagnant, Muddy, or Polluted Water** = *Human doctrines and ways;* iniquity; haughty spirit; unkind. **Troubled Water** = *Trouble;* worry; sorrow; healing. **Water Leaking Through the Ceiling** = *Trial;* distress; depression; destruction. (See SWIMMING, FLOOD, and RIVER.)

The words of a man's mouth are as deep waters, and the wellspring of wisdom as a flowing brook (Proverbs 18:4).

That He might sanctify and cleanse it with the washing of water by the word (Ephesians 5:26).

Behold, the days come, saith the Lord God, that I will send a famine in the land, not a famine of bread, nor a thirst for water, but of hearing the words of the Lord (Amos 8:11).

Unstable as water, thou shalt not excel... (Genesis 49:4).

But the wicked are like the troubled sea, when it cannot rest, whose waters cast up mire and dirt (Isaiah 57:20).

What man is like Job, who drinketh up scorning like water? (Job 34:7)

WATER FOUNTAIN – *Spirit:* Words; spirits of people; Holy Spirit; salvation; source.

Doth a fountain send forth at the same place sweet water and bitter? Can the fig tree, my brethren, bear olive berries? either a vine, figs? so can no fountain both yield salt water and fresh (James 3:11-12).

...I am Alpha and Omega, the beginning and the end. I will give unto him that is athirst of the fountain of the water of life freely (Revelation 21:6).

For My people have committed two evils; they have forsaken Me the fountain of living waters, and hewed them out cisterns, broken cisterns [human doctrines], *that can hold no water* (Jeremiah 2:13).

WATERMELON – *Fruit:* Refreshing; picnic. **Seeds** = *Words.* **Water** = *Spirit.* **Sweet** = *Strength.* **Green** = *Life.* **Red** = *Passion;* the fruit of good or evil works; the pleasures of sin. (See GARDENING.)

We remember the fish, which we did eat in Egypt [the world, i.e., sin] *freely; the cucumbers, and the melons, and the leeks, and the onions, and the garlic* ["the spice of (sinful) life"] (Numbers 11:5).

Therefore shall they eat of the fruit of their own [backsliding] *way...* (Proverbs 1:31).

Say ye to the righteous, that it shall be well with him: for they shall eat the fruit of their doings (Isaiah 3:10).

Death and life are in the power of the tongue: and they that love it [righteousness] *shall eat the fruit thereof* (Proverbs 18:21).

WATER WELL – *Source:* Heart; spirits of people; the Holy Spirit.

Keep thy heart [well] *with all diligence; for out of it are the issues of life* (Proverbs 4:23).

These [deceivers] *are wells without water...to whom the mist of darkness is reserved for ever* (2 Peter 2:17).

Jesus answered and said unto her, If thou knewest the gift of God, and who it is that saith to thee, Give Me to drink; thou wouldest have asked of Him, and He would have given thee living water. Jesus answered and said unto her, Whosoever drinketh of this water shall thirst again: But whosoever drinketh of the water that I shall give him shall never thirst; but the water that I shall give him shall be in him a well of water springing up into everlasting life (John 4:10,13-14).

WEDDING – See MARRIAGE.

WEEDS – *Unkept:* Works of the flesh; sin; neglect; laziness; worry; the fullness of iniquity (if they are gone to seed). (See SEED.)

And the Lord God took the man, and put him into the garden of Eden to dress it and to keep it (Genesis 2:15).

I went by the field of the slothful, and by the vineyard of the man void of understanding; and, lo, it was all grown over with thorns, and nettles had covered the face thereof, and the stone wall thereof was broken down (Proverbs 24:30-31).

The waters compassed me about, even to the soul: the depth closed me round about, the weeds [fears, worries] *were wrapped about my head* (Jonah 2:5).

But in the fourth generation they shall come hither again: for the iniquity [weeds, i.e., works of the flesh] *of the Amorites is not yet full* [mature, i.e., gone to seed, therefore only capable of reproducing itself] (Genesis 15:16).

WESTERN – *Frontier* (as in "the wild west," or a western movie, etc.): Pioneering spirit; spiritual warfare; boldness; challenge.

When thou comest nigh unto a city to fight against it, then proclaim [the Gospel of] *peace unto it* (Deuteronomy 20:10).

Yet there shall be a space between you and it, about two thousand cubits by measure [i.e., use mature judgment]: *come not near unto it, that ye may know the way by which ye must go: for ye have not passed this way heretofore* (Joshua 3:4).

WHEAT FIELD – See CORN FIELD and GRAIN.

WIND – *Spirit or Doctrine* (**Therefore, wind can mean "The spirit of a doctrine"**): Holy Spirit; demonic or strong opposition (as in "a strong wind"); idle words. (See STORM.)

That we henceforth be no more children, tossed to and fro, and carried about with every wind of doctrine... (Ephesians 4:14).

The wind bloweth where it listeth, and thou hearest the sound thereof, but canst not tell whence it cometh, and whither it goeth: so is every one that is born of the Spirit (John 3:8).

And suddenly there came a sound from heaven as of a rushing mighty wind, and it filled all the house where they were sitting. And they were all filled with the Holy Ghost, and began to speak with other tongues, as the Spirit gave them utterance (Acts 2:2,4).

How long wilt thou speak these things? and how long shall the words of thy mouth be like a strong wind? (Job 8:2)

And the Lord said unto Satan, Behold, all that he [Job] *hath is in thy power...And, behold, there came a great* [or strong] *wind from the wilderness, and smote the four corners of the house, and it fell upon the young men, and they are dead...* (Job 1:12,19).

WINDOW – *Revealed:* Truth; prophecy; revelation; understanding; avenue of blessing; exposed; an unguarded opening for a thief to enter.

And it came to pass...that Abimelech king of the Philistines looked out at a window, and saw, and, behold, Isaac was sporting with Rebekah [and he realized she was] *his wife* (Genesis 26:8).

And that Lord answered the man of God, and said, Now, behold, if the Lord should make windows in heaven, might such a thing [blessing] *be? And he said, Behold, thou shalt see it with thine eyes, but shalt not eat thereof* (2 Kings 7:19).

They shall run to and fro in the city; they shall run upon the wall, they shall climb up upon the houses; they shall enter in at the windows like a thief (Joel 2:9).

WINE (or Strong Drink) – *Intoxicant:* Strong emotion (such as joy, anger, hate, or sorrow); Spirit (of God or spirits of people); revelation; truth; witchcraft; delusion; mocker. **Drinking Wine With Someone** = *Spiritual fellowship;* communion.

And be not drunk with [natural] *wine, wherein is excess; but be filled with the* [new wine of the] *Spirit* (Ephesians 5:18).

And no man putteth new wine [revelation] *into old bottles* [tradition, wrong or obsolete doctrine]; *else the new wine will burst the bottles, and be spilled, and the bottles shall perish. But new wine* [truth] *must be put into new bottles* [doctrines]; *and both are preserved* (Luke 5:37-38).

Give strong drink [the knowledge of God] *unto him that is ready to perish, and wine* [the Spirit of joy] *unto those that be of heavy hearts* [See Isaiah 61:3.] (Proverbs 31:6).

Others mocking said, These men are full of new wine. For these are not drunken, as ye suppose...But this is that which was spoken by the prophet Joel; And it shall come to pass in the last days, saith God, I will pour out of My Spirit upon all flesh: and your sons and your daughters shall prophesy, and your young men shall see visions, and your old men shall dream dreams (Acts 2:13,15-17).

For they eat the bread of wickedness, and drink the wine [spirit] *of violence* (Proverbs 4:17).

For their vine is of the vine of Sodom, and of the fields of Gomor-rah: their grapes are grapes of gall, their clusters [and therefore their wines] *are bitter* (Deuteronomy 32:32).

Wine is a mocker, strong drink is raging: and whosoever is deceived thereby is not wise (Proverbs 20:1).

The cup of blessing which we bless, is it not the communion of the blood of Christ? The bread which we break, is it not the communion of the body of Christ? (1 Corinthians 10:16)

WINGS – *Spirit:* Minister (prophet); Holy Spirit; shelter; demon. (See BIRD.)

Ye have seen what I did unto the Egyptians, and how I bare you on eagles' wings, and brought you unto Myself. [Compare Hosea 12:13: *"And by a prophet the Lord brought Israel out of Egypt, and by a prophet was he preserved."*] (Exodus 19:4).

He shall cover thee with His feathers [Spirit], *and under His wings shalt thou trust: His truth shall be thy shield and buckler* (Psalm 91:4).

But they that wait upon the Lord shall renew their strength; they shall mount up with wings as eagles; they shall run, and not be weary; and they shall walk, and not faint (Isaiah 40:31).

But unto you that fear My name shall the Sun of righteousness arise with healing in His wings [Spirit]; *and ye shall go forth, and grow up as calves of the stall* (Malachi 4:2).

WINTER – *Barren:* Death; dormant; waiting; cold (unfriendly). (See SNOW.)

The harvest is past, the summer is ended [and winter has come], *and we are not saved* (Jeremiah 8:20).

For ye shall be as an oak whose leaf fadeth, and as a garden that hath no water (Isaiah 1:30).

WOOD – *Life:* Temporary; flesh; humanity; carnal reasoning; lust; eternal (as in "a house made of cedars"); spiritual building material. (See TREE(S).)

Wherefore thus saith the Lord God of hosts, Because ye speak this word, behold, I will make My words in thy mouth fire, and this people wood, and it shall devour them (Jeremiah 5:14).

Where no wood is, there the fire goeth out: so where there is no talebearer [works of the flesh] *the strife ceaseth. As coals are to burning coals, and wood to fire; so is a contentious man to kindle strife* (Proverbs 26:20-21).

Now if any man build upon this foundation gold [wisdom], *silver* [knowledge], *precious stones* [the witness of God's Spirit], *wood* [carnal reasoning], *hay* [dead works], *stubble* [tradition] (1 Corinthians 3:12).

WRESTLING – *Striving:* Deliverance; resistance; persistence; trial; tribulation; controlling spirit (person) attempting to gain control. (See BOXING.)

And Jacob was left alone; and there wrestled a man [an angel] *with him until the breaking of the day. And he said, Let me go, for the day breaketh. And he said, I will not let thee go, except thou bless me. ...And He said, Thy name shall be called no more Jacob, but Israel: for as a prince hast thou power with God and with men, and hast prevailed* (Genesis 32:24,26,28).

For we wrestle not against flesh and blood, but against principalities, against powers, against the rulers of the darkness of this world, against spiritual wickedness in high places (Ephesians 6:12).

And the servant of the Lord must not strive [with people]; *but be gentle unto all men, apt to teach, patient* (2 Timothy 2:24).

YO YO – *Vacillating:* Unstable; indecisive; repeatedly changing one's mind.

And Elijah came unto all the people, and said, How long halt ye between two opinions? if the Lord be God, follow Him: but if Baal, then follow him. And the people answered him not a word (1 Kings 18:21).

A double minded man is unstable in all his ways. (James 1:8).

ZIPPER – *Closed or open:* Admonition to silence (as in "better zip up your lip"); revealed; **Unzipped Fly** = *Fornication;* exhibitionism; embarrassing exposure.

For this is the will of God, even your sanctification, that ye should abstain from fornication (1 Thessalonians 4:3).

About Ira L. Milligan

Ira Milligan and his wife, Judy, founded Servant Ministries Inc. in 1986. They have served God since 1962. They travel internationally, presenting such seminars as: Dreams and Their Interpretation; Counseling and Inner Healing; Spiritual Warfare; and Prophets and Personal Prophecy.

Ira has taught classes on counseling as a guest lecturer at Oral Roberts University. Ira and Judy have four children and eleven grandchildren. They currently reside in Tioga, Louisiana.

Other Books by Ira Milligan

EUROCLYDON
The Anatomy of a Scorpion
Rightly Dividing the Word

In the right hands, This Book will Change Lives!

Most of the people who need this message will not be looking for this book. To change their lives, you need to put a copy of this book in their hands.

> *But others (seeds) fell into good ground, and brought forth fruit, some a hundred-fold, some sixty-fold, some thirty-fold* (Matthew 13:8).

Our ministry is constantly seeking methods to find the good ground, the people who need this anointed message to change their lives. Will you help us reach these people?

> *Remember this—a farmer who plants only a few seeds will get a small crop. But the one who plants generously will get a generous crop* (2 Corinthians 9:6).

EXTEND THIS MINISTRY BY SOWING
3 BOOKS, 5 BOOKS, 10 BOOKS, OR MORE TODAY,
AND BECOME A LIFE CHANGER!

Thank you,

Don Nori Sr., Founder
Destiny Image
Since 1982

Made in the USA
Monee, IL
14 July 2024

61788064R00223